PRACTICAL SOLUTIONS

to Practically Every Problem

**The Early Childhood
Teacher's Manual**

Revised Edition

Steffen Saifer

 Redleaf Press
St. Paul, Minnesota
www.redleafpress.org

© 2003 Steffen Saifer
Cover photograph by Nita Winter.
Photographs © Susie Fitzhugh.

Published by: Redleaf Press
            450 N. Syndicate, Suite 5
            St. Paul, MN 55104

Visit us online at www.redleafpress.org

Library of Congress Cataloging-in-Publication Data

Saifer, Steffen, 1951–
  Practical solutions to practically every problem : the early childhood
teacher's manual / Steffen Saifer.— Rev. ed.
      p. cm.
  Includes bibliographical references and index.
  ISBN 1-929610-31-9 (pbk.)
  1. Education, Preschool—United States—Handbooks, manuals, etc. 2.
Preschool teaching—United States—Handbooks, manuals, etc. 3.
Preschool teachers—United States—Handbooks, manuals, etc. I. Title.
LB1140.2.S235 2003
372.21—dc21

                                                        2003000522

This revised version is dedicated to Lilia, Jonah, Laurentiu, Felicia, and to early childhood teachers everywhere, who work so hard, care so much, and still get so little in return.

Contents

Introduction ————————————

"It is only because of problems that we grow mentally and spiritually."
                                        M. Scott Peck

What Is Teaching?

Teaching is a complex combination of art, science, and craft. It is not any of these alone. On top of that, it is very influenced by politics, in which none of these aspects of teaching is typically an important consideration. Public policy directly affects education, even in the classroom, and is rarely responsive to the real needs of teachers, children, and families. The decision to keep programs for children birth to five underfunded—even compared to the meagerly funded K–12 system—is one example. As a nation, we spend on young children about one-hundredth of what we spend on older children. All this is to say that teachers are under a great deal of external pressure beyond their control in addition to taking on the difficult and never-ending task of being good teachers.

What makes teaching an *art* is that every teacher and every teaching and learning situation is unique, and it can always be done better—it's never perfect. When done well it is a thing of beauty that touches everyone involved in different ways. What makes teaching a *science* is that we know from research that some strategies are more effective than others, that all good teachers share some common elements (for one, they individualize), that some parts of the teaching and learning process are more important than others, and that certain methods will led to certain outcomes. As a science it is slowly evolving as the techniques for studying education improve. It is difficult to study teaching as a science because we can't isolate it in a laboratory or break it down into small pieces without losing its essence. What makes it a *craft* is that particular skills that can be honed with practice, such as effective behavior management, are necessary. One must have some mastery of the art, science, and craft of teaching to do it well.

What Is Good Teaching?

Many teachers of young children have been given the wrong message (or have misinterpreted the message) about the role of the teacher in relation to the child. They set up a dichotomy that puts child-centered practice on one side and teacher-directed practices on the other. They associate child-centered as good and teacher-directed as bad. Although there is some truth to this, it can lead teachers to be too detached and not interact enough or effectively with children. Good teaching requires high teacher *involvement* with many deep and meaningful interactions with children. Good teaching means teaching children according to their needs, interests, culture, and learning styles, and being very responsive to them. This necessitates knowing the children well and changing the way you teach to fit each child and particular group of children. Sometimes it means that you will need to be quite "directive" in the course of your work, which is more than acceptable, if it is done within a child-centered context. This child-centered context is created when, for most of the day, children spend their time engaged in solving the problems they are most interested in solving and pursuing interests (with educational value) they are most interested in pursuing. The role of the teacher is to help them solve those problems and pursue those interests at a higher, wider, and deeper level than they can do on their own. The educational term for this is "scaffolding," which is derived from the theories of Lev Vygotsky, a Russian psychologist (see resources on p. 213 for more information).

Here is an example of what this looks like in action. Several years ago, while the children were engaged in a variety of free choice activities, I sat next to Rami (a recently turned five-year-old), working with playdough. Of course, "free choice" is a misleading term as the children may choose from a limited number of carefully selected activities that contain a well-planned set of high-quality materials! Rami asked me if I would make a dinosaur for him with the playdough. I said, "I will *help* you make a dinosaur. Let's go look for some pictures of dinosaurs." We didn't find any, but we did find a large book with many wonderful photographs of cats, and he quickly agreed that we could make a cat instead. We looked at the pictures and talked about the shapes: a kind of round head, oval body, and so on. We set the book in front of us, open to a set of photographs of cats sitting upright, and I started to talk him through making the various parts with the playdough, never touching it myself. His attention span was remarkably long, his concentration beyond his years, and his cat was quite realistic. However, the playdough began to droop and the parts didn't stay together very well. This prompted me to purchase some clay, which is better for making representational objects. Playdough is a *process*-oriented material, clay is a *product*-oriented material, but classrooms need both, especially for children like Rami who was ready, able, and desired to make something representational.

While engaging with children in this way, good teachers focus as much on understanding (deep knowledge) as on developing children's simple knowledge (such as the names for things) and their skills. All three are important. Many children reach kindergarten being able to count by rote, but not understanding the relationships among numbers or between numbers and things. *Number sense* is the term used to describe this understanding of numbers while *counting* is the term for a simple knowledge of numbers and a particular basic skill. Good teachers engage children in further developing their simple knowledge and skills—counting higher, as well as helping them understand, for example, that "three" is the name we give to the set of objects consisting of 1+1+1. Since this is done in a child-centered context, had I been a better teacher, I might have said to Rami, "How many pieces of playdough did you use to make the cat, so you will know how many pieces you will need if you want to make one tomorrow," and then helped him to do this, if necessary.

From the above example, you can see that there is much to learn about teaching math as well as teaching all other content areas—the sciences, literacy, social skills, and so forth. In addition, the knowledge base for effectively teaching the content areas keeps growing and changing. Part of the job of being a teacher is to spend time improving your skills and knowledge about teaching the content areas through books, classes, articles, workshops, observing children, being coached or mentored, and watching other teachers. It's hard not to feel overwhelmed by this, but just take one area at a time and slowly increase your knowledge and abilities. Take a problem-solving approach and view yourself as a learner as much as a teacher. This creates a sense of the classroom as a learning community, another characteristic of classrooms with good teachers.

Sometimes learning and growing as a teacher is a bit painful (or at least uncomfortable). This is particularly true when you become aware of a "problem you didn't know you had." Everyone, even the best, most experienced teachers, currently has such problems because the fields of education and child development keep changing. You may only become aware that you

have a problem when you receive feedback from a colleague or supervisor, or attend a class or workshop, or read a book. As our understanding of children's development deepens, practices that seem fine one year can become outmoded or inadequate the next year. For example, using "time-out" or a reward system to control behavior, were at one time "state of the art." We now know that, although these strategies can be very effective, they are not the best ways to improve behavior because they do not help children learn new behaviors or gain self-control. Other examples of "problems you didn't know you had," come from the knowledge we gain from exemplary early childhood programs, such as the programs in Reggio Emilia, Italy, and from recent neuroscience research about brain development. In both cases, the new information tells us that children need to be challenged, our curricula needs to be deliberate and rigorous, partnerships with families and the community are critical, and positive emotions enhance learning and development while stress impedes them.

How to Use This Book

The purpose of this book is to help make your job easier and to help you be more efficient and effective. This book will empower you to do what you know is necessary and right so your classroom is a fabulous place for children (and for you and your coworkers) to be nurtured, to learn, and to grow.

This revised edition includes some new concerns, such as using computers with young children, working with English-language learners, and helping children cope with traumas and tragedies, as well as additional ideas for solving problems discussed in the previous edition. The resources have been updated. One of the biggest changes to our lives since the last edition is the presence of personal computers and the Internet, placing thousands more resources at our fingertips. Technology brings its own set of problems, such as unreliability—here today and gone tomorrow—and difficulty sorting to find something of value. The Web sites added to the resource lists have been screened for quality and are active at the time this book is being revised. Although some have a great deal of advertising and annoying graphics, all have helpful information. Undoubtedly, some of the Web sites will have moved or been deleted by the time the book is published and many more will be gone within a few years of publication.

Know and follow the policies and procedures your program has in place. If some of those policies and procedures limit your ability to help the children and their families thrive, work toward amending them in a helpful and positive way. Use this book as a resource and be open and clear with your supervisor and coworkers about what you want to change and why.

Also know your state's child care licensing requirements. If you work in a facility licensed by your state, you must abide by those regulations. If they are more stringent than the recommendations in this book, the state's requirements must take precedence. Even if you work in a program that is not required to follow the state's regulations, you will still benefit from the helpful safety and health procedures.

This book approaches issues from the perspective of problems, but it also offers positive solutions. You will never eliminate all the problems in early childhood education. Instead, I hope to help you manage them so, while working with young children and families, your experiences will be positive. When things are going well, no job on earth is more fun, more rewarding, and more important to society than teaching and caring for young children.

Carefully read the "Preventing Problems" section in each chapter. As you know, prevention is much easier than solving problems or coping with crises. If you didn't already believe in prevention, you would most likely be working with older children or in another field.

I have tried to make this book helpful to all early childhood educators. Although it focuses primarily on teachers of children between three and six years old, the book also offers numerous suggestions for working with younger children. Many of these ideas also work well with slightly older children. I make few distinctions between publicly funded and private programs, full-day and half-day programs, public schools and Head Start, or Montessori and developmental programs. In reality, excellent programs for young children have many more similarities than differences, and the differences are exciting. They are ones of style and emphasis, which make for the diversity we need in education. Likewise, all good teachers essentially do the same things, but with different styles, areas of strength, and talents. This book helps you solve problems while encouraging you to assert your own style.

I wrote this book for both experienced and new teachers, for teachers with formal educations, and for teachers without. I assumed that all readers would be intelligent, capable, quick learners, and people who care deeply. For the new or not formally trained teacher I have strived to be clear, concise, and free of jargon. All teachers will find many new and useful ideas in this book. By eliminating a great deal of theory, anecdotes, examples, and detailed explanations, I have tried to provide quick access to solutions. I have focused on the basic, most vital advice and information, which is based on current and revered theories. You can learn more about these theories through the resources listed at the end of most chapters.

Solving problems is hard. Rarely does one quick, easy answer suffice. Many times the cause of a problem is complex and multifaceted, or completely mysterious. Often problems are not what they appear to be on the surface. While I was in graduate school, an instructor told me a story about a four-year-old girl with whom she worked, who had temper tantrums at seemingly random times. However, after close observation the instructor discovered that the child threw these fits every time she had to do a difficult fine-motor task, such as pouring juice from a pitcher or putting together a ten-piece puzzle. Rather than face the embarrassment of failing, she chose to create a distraction. After an outside observer saw this connection, the child's teacher was able to assist her with fine-motor tasks in ways that called little attention to her problem. The teacher gradually offered less and less help as the child matured and her skills improved.

Choose the problems you most like to solve, because you never get rid of problems. Sometimes they become deeper, more interesting problems to solve. If you would rather balance a budget than help a child solve a conflict with another child, you should consider an administrative job rather than teaching.

I have been in meetings with well-known engineers who are in awe when I say I can help a parent or teacher deal with an angry three-year-old who bites. They quickly agree that this is much harder than rocket science. Unfortunately, at the present time our society puts a greater value on solving rocket problems than children's problems and pays the experts accordingly. Perhaps human nature prefers the esoteric to the mundane, even if the mundane will have a greater impact on the quality of life for everyone.

It is entirely possible to give too much attention to a problem and thereby make it worse. I worked with a three-year-old boy who pulled hair and pinched when the least bit frustrated. When discussing these behaviors with his mother, I said, "Well let's not worry too much about it. When his language skills improve (and they were a little slow) he will be less frustrated and he won't be aggressive anymore." I was not at all sure this would be true, but I was quite sure that it would be a good thing to not overreact to the behaviors. I was not even sure that his language skills would improve soon. I got very lucky, however, and his language skills did improve fairly quickly (as with most children between three and four) and his aggressive behaviors did stop. For some problems, patience is a great strategy. With lucky timing, you can make yourself look good by suggesting solutions when the problem has nearly run its course!

Sometimes implementing a practice or solution is impossible because of limitations of staff, funds, time, or other reasons. Knowing the best ways to fully solve the problem is still helpful. Then try partial or limited solutions because they are more realistic. You may be able to implement a fuller and deeper response to the problem at a later point. This book offers a variety of solutions for that very reason.

Place many "tools" in your strategies "toolbox" so you can draw from it when solving problems. Problems are most easily solved when you use the right tool. The more tools (or strategies) you have, the more effective you are likely to be in solving problems. If one tool does not work you can pull another from your toolbox. Sometimes it takes several tools to deal with one problem and still another when things are beginning to improve. For example, at first you may have to assist a child with verbal and gentle physical guidance to move from one activity to another—a very directive strategy akin to using a large tool. However, after a few weeks, you may be able to just

use a verbal reminder—a much less directive strategy akin to a much smaller tool.

The more severe the problem, the more complex, time-consuming, and difficult is the solution. In most cases you will have to use many approaches and be persistent and very patient. However, I firmly believe that every problem has a solution.

I mention classroom rules throughout the book. To get the most out of classroom rules, develop them with the children, explain the purpose of them clearly, make as few as possible, enforce them consistently, state them positively (such as, "Walk inside the classroom" rather than "Don't run"), make them visual by posting a picture of the rule, follow them yourself, and include fun rules (such as, "Run around a lot and yell loudly when you are outside," or, "Always ask for a hug when you need one").

One book cannot address all possible problems, and many good solutions are undoubtedly missing in this book. I hope the suggestions included here will serve to stimulate your own ideas. Write to me in care of the publisher and let me know what you have come up with, what worked well, what didn't, and what is missing. Any future editions of this book will include and acknowledge the best ideas sent by contributors.

Keep this book handy in your classroom and use it often. Wear it out. One of my favorite children's books is *Miss Rumphius*. In this book, Miss Rumphius learns that the purpose of life is to leave the world a more beautiful place than it was when she came into it. This is a noble value by which to live and to impart to children. Each day do something with or for your children that will make the world a little more beautiful. And have fun while you do it.

Steffen Saifer

The 20 Most Important Principles for Successful Preschool Teaching

1. Enjoy yourself! If you have fun, the children will have fun. Use humor generously.

2. Create an environment with specific learning centers, many soft places, and child-size furnishings. Make this environment cheerful but not overly stimulating, clean but not overly tidy.

3. Base all your actions on a clear, easily stated philosophy of early childhood education. For example, "Young children learn and grow best when they are touching and interacting with real things and have caring people around them."

4. Set your schedule so that the children spend most of their time in active learning of their own choosing. Provide opportunities to learn through playing games, using building toys, exploring objects from nature, acting out roles, reading books, and using art materials.

5. Observe the children at play to determine what problems they are interested in solving and what things they want to do. Help them do whatever it is they want to do at a higher level than they can do on their own. Provide indirect assistance—as much as necessary but the least amount possible. This assistance can be as unobtrusive as verbal encouragement ("That was almost it; try again.") or as direct as physically possible showing the children how or giving them the specific words to use.

6. Teach skills or give information individually or in very small groups, through active, playful, and meaningful activities. Don't break down activities into isolated skills. For example, develop cutting skills by having the children cut out nametags to tape to their cubbies rather than by having them cut predrawn lines on a sheet of paper.

7. Match your curriculum to the needs and interests of the children. Note that the type of activities you use and their length will be different for a group of children who have short attention spans, lots of anger, many emotional needs, and little interest in academics, than for a group of children who have longer attention spans, higher self-esteem, and a great deal of interest in academics.

8. Teach the children specific skills for getting along with others, solving conflicts, and acting cooperatively.

9. Give the children many chances to make decisions, be leaders, make real choices, and be responsible. Set as your goal that the children will be eager and interested in learning on their own in a class that almost runs itself. Encourage the children to be in control of themselves rather than to be controlled by you. For example, place a kitchen timer where the children can easily use it to set up a turn-taking system for themselves.

10. Tell the children often and enthusiastically what they are doing well and how they are competent. Be specific.

11. Teach the children correct behavior and give meaningful consequences, if needed, for continued misbehaviors. Avoid using rewards and punishment. Set as your goal that the children will get self-satisfaction from their own achievements and actions.

12. Give the children many opportunities to interact with each other and you in positive ways. Language is key. The difference between high- and low-quality early childhood classrooms is the amount of talking and the quality of that talking. In high-quality classrooms there are extended discussions, mutual questioning, sharing of insights and feelings, needs expressed, concerns responded to, books read and discussed, songs sung, and more.

13. Treat all children equitably but not identically. Recognize and meet individual needs and strengths.

14. Plan, critique, plan. Prepare your activities and environment thoroughly and carefully in advance. Review what worked and what didn't. Based on your review, plan again.

15. Know your children and their families well. Do everything you can to communicate with and receive information from parents. To establish rapport, increase your understanding of the child, and build trust. Do home visits with willing families. Invite families to your home.

16. Share ideas and problems with other professionals in the field. Ask a respected colleague or supervisor to observe you teaching and give you feedback. Using the insights you gain will benefit your classroom.

17. Take responsibility for your own growth and support the growth of other staff members. Don't wait to be sent to a class to learn a new skill or to solve a problem.

18. Know your limitations. Ask for help when you need it from someone who can advise you or get information from a book or magazine.

19. Use new ideas from reading, workshops, and training sessions to make changes in your classroom.

20. Accept responsibility for the quality of your program. Avoid excuses such as, "There isn't enough money," or, "There's not enough time." Rather than create problems or complain about them, help solve them.

Part I

Daily Dilemmas

1. The Daily Schedule: An Active and Purposeful Program

The key to a successful daily schedule is alternating long, active periods with short, quiet periods and alternating short, teacher-led activities with long, child-initiated activities. Young children are naturally active and learn best by exploring and discovering for themselves. Imposing long periods of quiet, sedentary activities on children will result in rebellious behaviors and will reduce vital learning opportunities.

The following samples will give you ideas for developing a workable schedule for your classroom. Make changes to fit your particular program's goals, equipment, meal schedule, space constraints, and the needs of your particular children.

Many half-day programs run less than four hours. Depending on whether you eliminate one or both meals, make adjustments to the following schedule. Keep about the same length of time for free choice and the outdoor/gym part of the schedule. Shorten other parts of the schedule if necessary.

Half-Day Toddler Program

8:30–8:45	Limited Free Choice (table toys, puzzles, playdough, and so on)
8:45–8:50	Circle Time
8:50–9:00	Hand Washing and Toileting
9:00–9:20	Breakfast
9:20–10:25	Free Choice (includes teacher-prepared art and individual attention)
10:25–10:35	Cleanup
10:35–10:40	Story
10:40–11:40	Outdoor/Gym (includes creative movement/dance)
11:40–11:45	Book Browse
11:45–11:50	Music
11:50–12:00	Hand Washing and Toileting
12:00–12:20	Lunch
12:20–12:25	Toothbrushing
12:25–12:30	Closing Circle and Dismissal

Full-Day Toddler Program

7:00–8:35	Free Choice (with some teacher-prepared activities and individual attention)
8:35–8:45	Cleanup
8:45–8:50	Circle Time
8:50–9:00	Hand Washing and Toileting
9:00–9:20	Breakfast
9:20–10:25	Outdoor/Gym (includes creative movement/dance)
10:25–10:35	Story
10:35–11:40	Free Choice (includes teacher-prepared art and individual attention)
11:40–11:45	Music
11:45–11:50	Book Browse
11:50–12:00	Hand Washing and Toileting
12:00–12:20	Lunch
12:20–12:25	Toothbrushing
12:25–12:30	Story
12:30–2:30	Naptime
2:30–2:50	Snack
2:50–4:00	Free Choice (includes teacher-prepared activities and individual attention)
4:00–4:05	Creative Drama or Story
4:05–5:30	Outdoor/Gym (includes creative movement/dance)
5:30–5:35	Music/Rhythm
5:35–6:00	Art and Limited Free Choice

Half-Day Preschool Program

8:30–8:45	Limited Free Choice (table toys, puzzles, playdough, and so on)
8:45–9:00	Circle Time
9:00–9:05	Hand Washing and Toileting
9:05–9:25	Breakfast
9:25–10:25	Free Choice (includes individual attention, teacher-prepared art, and hands-on math activities). Breakfast is available to eat when individual children wish.
10:25–10:35	Cleanup
10:35–10:45	Story Time
10:45–11:00	Small Group
11:00–11:45	Outdoor/Gym (includes creative movement/dance)
11:45–11:50	Silent Reading
11:50–11:55	Hand Washing and Toileting
11:55–12:15	Lunch
12:15–12:20	Toothbrushing
12:20–12:30	Music and Dismissal

Full-Day Preschool Program

7:00–8:35	Free Choice (includes individual attention, teacher-prepared art, and hands-on math activities)
8:35–8:45	Cleanup
8:45–9:00	Circle Time
9:00–9:05	Hand Washing and Toileting
9:05–9:25	Breakfast
9:25–10:15	Outdoor/Gym (includes creative movement/dance)
10:15–10:25	Story
10:25–10:40	Small Group
10:40–11:40	Free Choice (includes teacher-prepared activities and individual attention)
11:40–11:50	Cleanup
11:50–12:00	Music/Movement/Rhythm
12:00–12:05	Hand Washing and Toileting
12:05–12:25	Lunch
12:25–12:30	Toothbrushing
12:30–12:40	Silent Reading
12:40–2:10	Naptime
2:10–3:30	Free Choice (includes teacher-prepared activities and individual attention). Snack is available to eat when individual children wish.
3:30–3:40	Story
3:40–5:00	Outdoor/Gym (includes creative movement/dance)
5:00–5:15	Creative Drama
5:15–6:00	Art and Limited Free Choice

Resources

Web Sites

Classroom Schedule Samples. users.stargate.net/~cokids. Click on Teacher Pages, then on Classroom Schedule Samples.

Videos

NAEYC
1509 16th Street, N.W.
Washington, D.C. 20036-1426
www.naeyc.org
Daily Dilemmas: Coping with Challenges, 28 min.

2. Starting the Day Off Right

The tone of the day for you and the children is often set in the first few minutes of the day. Children arrive at the center in many different moods and with very different early morning experiences. By respecting those differences and accommodating them whenever possible, the children will have a much better chance for a successful day.

Preventing Problems

● Greet each child and parent individually as they enter. Look them in the eye and use their names.

● If you and the child feel comfortable, make physical contact with her by hugging or by touching the child on the arm or shoulder. This lets the child know that her presence is acknowledged and important.

● Children who have intense emotional needs, in particular, should be given attention and care as soon as they arrive. They usually come with their "tanks on empty" and you must fill those tanks with positive attention or they may seek the attention they need through inappropriate behavior.

● Arrange for children (and adults) to wash their hands soon after arriving. Invite parents who bring their children to school to help guide their child's hand washing. This will help stop the spread of germs from home and greatly control disease in your program. Make it a fun, interactive experience and a positive ritual.

● If children enter in a large group all at once, have them choose one of a variety of activities. If breakfast or a circle time comes early in the schedule, you may want to keep the children's choices limited to activities that can be cleaned up quickly. Use this time to greet each child individually, as described above.

● Set free choice time early in your schedule. Note that children get anxious and restless waiting for the period of time they like the best. Being surrounded by enticing materials, activities, and friends, and not being able to interact with them is difficult for young children. They may refuse to comply, act silly, or misbehave. Scheduling free choice early in the day for at least forty-five minutes will prevent behavior problems from occurring.

● Time your first meal or snack to make it work for your own group of children. Experiment with the timing so that as many children as possible are getting the food when they are hungry, but not when they are too hungry. If they are eating the food quickly and voraciously, are irritable, or do not listen well before the meal, then you are scheduling the meal too late. If many children pick at their food and are sleepy during the meal, then the meal is coming too soon. Kitchen staff can usually be more flexible with breakfast. If necessary, make it yourself with the children. Hungry or overfed children will be difficult children.

Dealing with Existing Problems

Children Who Have a Hard Time Separating from Their Parents

● Encourage parents to spend five or ten relaxed minutes when dropping off and picking up their children. Invite parents to chat with staff and play with their children during this time. This helps ease the transition for the children. However, encourage parents to leave quickly and smoothly once they have given their child a good-bye kiss. Both rushing in and out and lingering too long can add to the anxiety of separation.

● If the child is still anxious when the parent needs to leave, hold the child's hand or put your arm around her shoulders and say: "I'm glad you're here. Now it's time for parents to go to work and children to go to school. You'll see Mom again when she comes to pick you up. Let's go see what there is to do today." Lead the child away as you both wave good-bye.

● As a way to ease the transition, let the child bring in something comforting from home, such as a favorite stuffed animal. Or give the child something to hold that symbolizes the parent. This may be a picture of her parent(s) or an item from Mom's purse or Dad's pocket. Something like an extra house key works well because the child knows the parent must return to get it, which may be the cause of the separation fear.

Children Who Are Very Fussy at the Start of the Day

You may have children in your class who are highly active, lethargic, very grouchy, or defiant in the morning, but who improve as the day progresses. Parents may know the cause, or the problem may be due to one or more of the following reasons:

Allergies. A child who is sensitive to particular fabrics may be grouchy in the morning because of sleeping on synthetic bedding. If this type of allergy runs in the child's family, she is probably affected also. Using only cotton and other natural fibers for bedding and clothing should relieve the symptoms. Food allergies can also cause behavior problems. Many children are allergic to typical breakfast foods, such as milk, eggs, and wheat. Suggest to parents that they eliminate one category of food at a time to determine if the removal of this food improves the way their child feels. This is best done with the guidance of an understanding doctor. (See "Active and Distracted" on pp. 135–137 for more information.)

Lack of Food. Some children may arrive at school having had little or no dinner the previous night and little or no breakfast that morning. Securing food is your first priority, if the parents cannot. Teaching young children means meeting all their basic needs. Children who are hungry will learn little. In one public school, a kindergarten teacher was able to give a midmorning snack to the children from funds for children with special needs. Because the children made the snack themselves, it became a learning experience.

Lack of Sleep. Ask the child which TV show she watched the previous night to determine the time the child went to bed. Discuss with parents the importance of an early, consistent bedtime. Provide parents with easy to read, brief information about bedtime routines and strategies. Such information, and other parenting help, is available from the Web sites listed at the end of this chapter (p. 11). Make a cot available for any tired child to take a short nap at any time during the class.

Chaos: Too Much Going On at Once

Parents want to talk to you, several children are demanding your attention, the director needs you, your assistant has a question, and two children are chasing each other through the room. This probably sounds familiar, because all teachers have had mornings like this.

● Remember that children must always come first. Adults can wait. Greet and talk with parents each day, but if you are concerned about the children's behavior or well-being, ask an assistant to help the children or excuse yourself from the adult conversation.

● Keep a clipboard or note pad on a bulletin board posted near the door for parents, visitors, or other staff to write messages to you.

● To reduce attention-getting behaviors, greet children warmly and individually when they enter, as described earlier in this chapter. Make sure the children can get settled into the first routine of the day without much help. If the children cannot read their names, tape a picture of them in their cubbies. Have children help each other in the morning. "Ask three before you ask me" is a great classroom rule. The "three" refers to three other children. This will also foster independence and communication between children.

● Assign each adult, including yourself, some tasks to do each morning before the children arrive. Keep the written task-list posted. To provide variety and the opportunity to learn new skills, swap the set of tasks once a month. Make the task cards reusable by laminating them or covering with clear, self-stick plastic. The lists, prepared ahead of time, might look like this:

Adult # 1

a) Mix paints and set up easel.
b) Take out trikes and wagons.
c) Set out the following gross-motor equipment:

Equipment: large ball, frisbee, bat and ball
Located: classroom closet near front door
Place it: bench next to porch

Equipment: plastic climber
Located: storage shed behind building
Place it: grassy area in center of field

Adult # 2

a) Take chairs down from tables.
b) Wipe off tables.
c) Set out the following activities on tables:

Activity: Cherry Picker board game
Located: red storage shelf
Place it: round table

Activity: five puzzles
Located: puzzle rack on wood shelves
Place it: rectangular table by window

Resources

Chvojicek, R., N. Larson., and M. Henthorne. 2001. *Transition magician for families: Helping parents and children with everyday routines.* St. Paul: Redleaf Press.

Larson, N., M. Henthorne, and B. Plum. 1997. *Transition magician: Strategies for guiding young children in early childhood programs.* St. Paul: Redleaf Press.

Larson, N., M. Henthorne, and R. Chvojicek. 2001. *Transition magician 2: More strategies for guiding young children in early childhood programs.* St. Paul: Redleaf Press.

Web Sites

Easing Separation Anxiety (National Network for Child Care) www.nncc.org. Click on Search, then enter "separation anxiety" in the search box.

Specific bedtime issues:

Mr. Rogers' Neighborhood Parents' Page: Making the Transition to Bedtime pbskids.org/rogers/parents

iVillage Family Topics: Sleep www.ivillage.com/topics/family. Scroll down and click on Sleep.

General parenting:

Mr. Rogers' Neighborhood Parent Pages pbskids.org/rogers/parents

What You Need to Know About . . . Parenting and Family home.about.com/parenting

iVillage Family Topics www.ivillage.com/topics/family

Parenthood.com www.parenthoodweb.com

Parent News www.parentnews.com

National Parent Information Network www.npin.org

3. Circle Time: Meeting Individual Needs in a Group

Circle time, also called group time, refers to any time that a group of children are sitting together for an activity involving everyone. Typically this might include reading a story, sharing events from the weekend, playing rhythm instruments, or singing songs.

Preventing Problems

● Keep your circle time short! Most groups of toddlers have a maximum attention span of five to ten minutes. For most groups of preschoolers the maximum is ten to fifteen minutes. Start the year with the circle time lasting a few minutes and gradually increase the time throughout the year.

● Several short circle times with part of the group is better than a long one with the whole group. These can take place during the course of the day or simultaneously, if enough staff is available. Short circle times with small groups allow you to give more individual attention, increase children's chances for participation, and have fewer distractions for children.

● As a guideline to help children sit appropriately, give each one a rug-sample square. They can usually be purchased cheaply from carpet stores. As an alternative, you can laminate pieces of paper with children's names or a picture on them. Gluing a Velcro fastener

(the loop side) to the back can help make them stay in place on a carpeted surface. This provides individual spaces so children will not conflict with each other. Some groups of children, particularly older preschoolers, attend better when sitting on chairs placed around the circle.

● Hold circle activities away from toy shelves and other attractive places in the room. Make the circle big enough to seat all the children comfortably.

● Establish one or two simple circle time rules and remind children of them at the start of the circle. They might be the following:

▶ "Keep your hands next to your own body."

▶ "Talk only when no one else is talking."

● Avoid using circle time for teaching specific skills. Circle time is most successful when you use it for singing together, playing movement games (such as "Hokey Pokey"), listening to stories, participating in active group games that involve handling things or moving, watching films, planning activities for the day, making classroom rules, or assigning "jobs" for the day.

● Plan circle activities that are not too difficult nor too easy to follow, and are highly interesting to your particular group. Prepare well. Know your material well enough that you can stray from your plans, answer unexpected questions, and easily get back on track.

- Start off your circle time with an active but not boisterous game that requires the children to focus and attend, but not sit still and quiet. You might use the game "Follow the Rhythm." With everyone sitting around the circle, tap out a simple rhythm and then invite the children to repeat it. Make the rhythm a little harder each time you tap. Give some children a chance to lead the game. After playing for a minute or two, begin your circle activity. This type of activity will draw children to the circle who have not yet made the transition.

- If your planned activity does not hold the children's interest, have alternative activities to use or move on to the next activity.

- Place another adult (teacher, assistant, or volunteer) behind the children in the circle. There she or he can see the whole group and move quickly to an area where children are having a hard time. Sometimes just sitting behind them or gently touching their backs will settle them.

- If possible, involve all adults in the group activity. An assistant or volunteer who is doing other things within sight or sound of the circle will be distracting. Adults who participate can act as role models for the children.

- Occasionally provide an alternative to sitting in a circle. For example, have the children sit in two rows across from each other, facing each other. Do a variety of activities during which one partner interacts with the other verbally and physically.

Dealing with Existing Problems

Hitting, Arguing, or Talking with Each Other

Boredom during circle time is the most common cause of hitting, arguing, or talking with others. Follow the suggestions in "Preventing Problems" to make the circle time short and stimulating.

- Keep the children who "set each other off" away from each other in the circle. If necessary, assign seats.

- Focus your attention and encouragement on the children who are behaving well. Say things like the following, "Thank you, Sam, for looking right at me. It lets me know you're listening well."

- Give minimal attention to misbehavior.

- Remind the children of the circle time rules you have established.

- Begin your activity without waiting for everyone to join or be entirely quiet. Start with a louder voice to get the children's attention and quickly tone down your voice when the talking or moving has stopped.

- At the start of your activity, remind the children that they will have an opportunity to talk right after you have finished.

- During group games, give children opportunities to be the "teacher" and decide what the group should do. For example, a child can decide which body part everyone should shake during "Hokey Pokey."

- Use a nonverbal cue to get the children's attention, such as placing your thumb and index finger in the shape of an *L* and putting it by your ear (American Sign Language for *listen*). Use this cue to remind children that this is a time to listen. Quickly go back to your activity.

- Whenever possible, give children opportunities to talk and move in appropriate ways. Involve them actively during the circle. For example, invite the children to take turns holding the book being read. For well-known stories, leave off the ends of some sentences for the children to finish. Ask questions occasionally to give children opportunities to talk.

Can't Sit Still

- For a variety of reasons, some children cannot sit still for more than a few seconds. For these children, provide an alternative quiet activity, such as doing puzzles or drawing at a nearby table, where they will not distract the circle. This is not a punishment or a reward, but a recognition of the different needs of the children. If they were able to exercise control, they would. If other children want to do this additional activity also, explain that the children are choosing another activity because sitting quietly is difficult for them at this time, although they will get better at it. Tell the children who can sit still that they are able to sit and listen well and that you appreciate their participation in circle.

- For some active children, sitting on an adult's lap during circle will provide the soothing stimulation to keep them calm.

- Let the children who cannot sit still start the circle with the others, but when they are close to reaching their limit, give them a choice of alternative quiet activities or listening a little longer. Note that the time they are able to stay in the circle should gradually increase if you are also working on the root cause of the problem. (See "Helping Children with Challenging Behaviors," pp. 123–126, for more information.)

- If a child is still disruptive to the group, even after given the opportunity to do another activity, another adult (who is not leading the circle) should calmly guide him to a place where the child can be involved in a solitary activity but cannot be seen or heard. The adult should keep an eye on the child but give as little attention as possible, as the goal of disruptive behavior is usually to get attention. Tell the child that he can return to the activity or the circle when he is ready to work quietly. Give the child lots of encouragement when he does return and is quiet for a few seconds. Say something like the following: "I can tell that you're really listening because you're quiet. That's very polite because now everyone can hear."

Interruptions Directed to the Teacher

- Ignore the first interruption (unless the child needs to use the bathroom or has some other emergency). If the child interrupts again, he will likely keep interrupting until you will have to respond. Act on the second interruption. (Usually it will be a request like "Tie my shoe" or "Can I get a drink of water?" Or the child may ask a question about the activity.) Tell the child that you are very interested in what he has to say but that he must wait until the end of circle time. If the child interrupts again, signal by nodding your head to another adult to help the child with his needs. Go back to the activity quickly.

- Keep a mental note of the nature of the distraction. At a later time, talk with the child about what he may be able to do differently the next time so as not to interrupt.

- Some interruptions are great learning opportunities. They should be allowed, and you should follow through on them. For example, if a child complains that another child hit him, use the conflict resolution strategies discussed on p. 123. All the children will be interested and will learn from the experience.

Bored Children during "Show and Tell"

- Limit the number of children who share during "Show and Tell" by assigning some to share only on Monday, others on Tuesday, and so on. Consider doing "Show and Tell" in small groups, as this will keep the time appropriately short.

- Involve all the children in this activity by making sure the child who is talking speaks to the other children, not just to you. Encourage the other children to ask questions of the child who is sharing. Place yourself behind the child to facilitate this.

- Have children share family experiences, a picture they made, or what they did earlier in the day at school. Sharing themselves rather than things, helps children who have no item to share; develops the children's ability to review; and makes for more personal, meaningful sharing.

For additional ideas on getting children to circle and to the next activity after circle, read "Transitions: Structuring Unplanned Time" on pp. 123–124.

Resources

Briggs, P., T. Pilot, and J. Bagby. 2000. *Early childhood activities for creative educators.* Clifton Park, N.Y.: Delmar Learning.

Charner, K., ed. 1996. *The giant encyclopedia of circle time and group activities for children 3 to 6: Over 600 favorite circle time activities created by teachers for teachers.* Beltsville, Md.: Gryphon House.

Kriete, R. 1999. *The morning meeting book.* Greenfield, Mass.: Northeast Foundation for Children.

Spangler, C. B. 1997. The sharing circle: A child-centered curriculum. *Young Children* 52 (5): 74–78.

Web Sites

Circle Time Activities—Ideas submitted by teachers users.stargate.net/~cokids. Click on Teacher Pages, then on Circle Time Activities.

Circle Time Group Activities. daycare.about.com. Enter "circle time" in the search box.

Circle Time. Numerous resources. Education World. www.education-world.com/early_childhood. Click on Circle Time on the sidebar.

Videos

Educational Productions
900 SW Gemini Drive
Beaverton, OR 97008
www.edpro.com
Super Groups. Series includes three videos:
    Come Join In, 30 min.
    Give Yourself a Hand, 34 min.
    Once Upon a Time, 33 min.

4. Successful Small Group Learning

If you are not already doing so, schedule a time during the day for fifteen to twenty minutes of small group learning. Plan to have at least three small groups of children in three areas of the room (or at three tables) working on activities at the same time. If you have enough staff, plan on each group doing a different activity with an adult. Rotate the groups to a different activity each day, so by the third day, every child will have done all three activities. For the remaining two days of the week, repeat the more popular activities, introduce new activities, or do a combination of both. For the activities, include art or craft projects, dictating or writing stories, simple science activities, lotto games, simple board games, manipulating objects to learn counting and math, memory games, role-playing, solving social conflicts, and cooking projects. By doing this, you individualize more than you can in a large group. You can provide direct information, answer questions, encourage problem solving, and give more feedback to individual children. Also, you can provide more challenging activities than children can do on their own during free choice. Finally, with these small groups you are able to observe children better. You can more readily determine how they think, act, and feel and what their strengths and weaknesses are. You can "scaffold" their learning as described on p. 1 and you can then plan and adjust future activities accordingly.

Preventing Problems

● To get children to their places easily, name each group. Place a picture of that name on the table or the area where the children are to go. For example, the six children who are in the Tiger group will go to the table with the picture of the tiger placed in the center. Similarly, the children in the Bear group and those in the Elephant group will go to their tables. Give each child a picture tag that corresponds to her group. Attach this tag to the child's clothing. Within a few weeks, each child should know her group.

● Prepare all your materials and written instructions for the other adults ahead of time. Discuss the activities with the adults beforehand so your expectations are clear. Tell them why the children are doing the activity and what you want the children to gain from it.

● Develop activities that allow the children to handle real objects and that do not consist of children using only pencil and paper or adults demonstrating something or lecturing.

● Divide children into mixed groups. Include within each group some slow learners and some quick learners, some compliant children as well as difficult children. This allows children to learn from each other and to help each other.

● Individualize when you see the need. If a child is having difficulty, ask her to do only part of the activity, give extra help in accomplishing it, or offer a different way of doing it.

● Individualize according to abilities, but stretch them and challenge them a bit. For example, if your activity is making playdough, invite the child with poor small-motor coordination to pour liquids from the measuring cup into a large bowl. Encourage the child with good small-motor coordination to pour and measure a tablespoon of oil. Invite the child with reading skills to read the recipe for the group. Encourage the child with poor counting skills to count along with another child the number of tablespoons of salt needed. Plan for this before the activity.

● Make sure activities are meaningful to children and have an emotional connection for them. For example, teach the math concept of *half* in the context of sharing cookies during a snack.

● The focus of the activities should be on understanding, as much as on learning skills or information. See "Approach to Teaching" in the introduction for ways to do this.

Dealing with Existing Problems
Not Enough Staff

● Small group time requires a capable adult for each group. If only two are available, you can have two groups with the third involved in an activity they can do well on their own, with some occasional checking. In any case, include no more than six children in a small group.

● As an alternative to this or if you are the only adult, extend your free choice time and involve five or six children in a small group activity while the others are in free choice. When the first group is done, choose a different group of children to do the same activity, until all the children have participated. Unless you are doing a long project that will take several days to complete, select a different small group activity each day. The drawbacks to this system are that pulling children away from free choice activities is difficult, the continuity of their play is broken, and you cannot be actively involved in free choice while working with small groups.

● To minimize the drawbacks, allow children to save whatever they have constructed during free choice time by making themselves a "Do Not Touch" sign or placing their project in a special "saving" place. They can then pick up where they left off and not worry about others ruining their work. Also make free choice long enough so that children have time to play after they are done with small group, and you can have time to be with children during free choice.

Bored or Resistant Children

If your children clearly indicate that they would rather be doing something else, try some of these ideas:

● Plan activities that involve the children actively in movement or in handling real objects. Provide many chances for each child to talk and to do.

● Use more activities that are creative, that allow children to express themselves, and that do not require one correct answer. Using sets of three wood scraps and glue to build various sculptures is more satisfying than circling the picture of three balloons on a ditto sheet. Yet the same information—the concept of *three*—can be taught in both activities.

● Shorten each small group activity so that children have to sit for only a few minutes.

● Schedule very physical activities—such as outdoor play, gym play, or movement games—before and after your small group time.

● Lead a short stretching game (such as "Shake Your Sillies Out" or "Head, Shoulders, Knees, and Toes") just before small group time and/or between each small group activity.

Resources

Charner, K., ed. 1998. *The giant encyclopedia of science activities.* Beltsville, Md.: Gryphon House.

Charner, K., and C. Barnes, eds. 2000. *The giant encyclopedia of arts and crafts activities.* Beltsville, Md.: Gryphon House.

Davalos, S. R. 1999. *Making sense of art: Sensory-based art activities for young children, 3–5.* Shawnee Mission, Kans.: Autism Asperger Publishing.

Kohl, M. F. 1993. *ScienceArts: Discovering science through art experiences.* Bellingham, Wash.: Bright Ring Publishing.

————. 1994. *Preschool art: It's the process not the product.* Beltsville, Md.: Gryphon House.

————. 2000. *The big messy (but easy to clean up) art book.* Beltsville, Md.: Gryphon House.

Moomaw, S., and B. Hieronymus. 1995. *More than counting: Whole math activities for preschool and kindergarten.* St. Paul: Redleaf Press.

————. 1999. *More than painting: Exploring the wonders of art in preschool and kindergarten.* St. Paul: Redleaf Press.

————. 1999. *Much more than painting: Exploring the wonders of art in preschool and kindergarten.* St. Paul: Redleaf Press.

Timpl, R. 1997. *100 small group activities 3.* Ypsilanti, Mich.: High/Scope Press.

Web Sites

Activity ideas in art, math, science, and more
atozteacherstuff.com. Click on Lesson Plans, then on Preschool under Grade Level.

Lesson plans for various areas
www.lessonplanspage.com

Activity ideas listed alphabetically
www.theideabox.com. Click on Activities on the side bar.

Early Childhood Education on Line (ECEOL-L) Web Site
www.ume.maine.edu/ECEOL-L. Click on Curriculum and Environments.

Art Activities

Incredible Art Department
www.princetonol.com/groups/iad. Click on Lessons, then on Early Childhood.

About Daycare
daycare.about.com. Enter "art activities" in the search box.

The Chalkboard
patricia_f.tripod.com. Click on Assorted Art Activities on the side bar.

Early Childhood.com
www.earlychildhood.com. Click on Arts and Crafts on the side bar.

Kinder Art
www.kinderart.com

LessonPlansPage.com
www.lessonplanspage.com/ArtK1.htm

Math Activities

Early Childhood Educators' and Family Web Corner
users.stargate.net/~cokids. Click on Teacher Pages, then on Curriculum, then scroll down to Math section.

LessonPlansPage.com
www.lessonplanspage.com/MathK1.htm

Science

LessonPlansPage.com
www.lessonplanspage.com/ScienceK1.htm

Early Childhood Educators' and Family Web Corner
users.stargate.net/~cokids. Click on Teacher Pages, then
on Curriculum, then scroll down to Math section.

LessonPlansPage.com
www.lessonplanspage.com/ScienceK1.htm

Videos

High/Scope
Dept. 10
600 N. River Street
Ypsilanti, MI 48198
www.highscope.org
Small Group Time Video Series:
  Counting with Bears, 17 min.
  Plan-Do-Review with Found Materials, 25 min.
  Working with Staplers, 12 min.
  Representing with Sticks and Balls, 14 min.
  Exploring with Paint and Corks, 12 min.

5. Free Choice: Making Learning Fun

This part of the schedule is sometimes called work time, free play, choice time, and other names. Since young children learn best within complex play—that is set up, guided, and mediated by skilled teachers—free choice time provides great opportunities for learning. Free choice is the time children love the most. They get to decide what they want to do, how to do it, and for how long. The value of free choice depends on the quality of materials and equipment you have. It also depends on your ability to help children do what they choose at a higher level than they could do by themselves, to solve problems effectively, and to learn new skills. This all can happen when you listen and observe carefully and respond with suggestions, new materials, and questions.

Preventing Problems

● Schedule the first free choice time early in the day and for at least forty-five minutes.

● Rotate equipment. Keep some in storage and then bring out this equipment after several months. When you do this, put some other equipment away to reduce the boredom caused when children use the same toys every day.

● Change the dramatic play area fairly often. Have the children help you set up a post office for about three weeks, then a restaurant for several weeks, then a campground, and so on. Other ideas can come from common activities, the workplaces of the children's families, and popular places in the community. Have the children come up with other ideas. If space is available, have a permanent "house" area but change the materials and supplies on a regular basis.

● Set out a variety of activities to choose from, such as art materials, paint and easels, board games, puzzles, water play, and clay.

● Involve yourself with your children's play and move around the room. Don't control the play or tell them what to do. Ask questions. Add supplies and equipment to expand and deepen their play.

● Use free choice time to interact with some children one to one. Offer special time with the teacher as one of the choices.

● Establish a system where children place name cards at the area they choose to use. This will help them plan and think ahead. You can limit the number of children in each area by having a set number of hooks to place their name cards on.

● Set up long-term projects for children to pursue playfully and help guide them when necessary. Project ideas can come from children's interests. Invite them to help decide the subject of the projects. They might include designing and building a school bus, creating a large "sculpture" of a dinosaur, creating a model of the school or the neighborhood, or developing an elaborate hospital area. To help them learn through play, ask questions about what they need and how they can obtain or make it; read information about the subject of their projects; and help them use tools and skills to measure, count, write, diagram, graph, and negotiate. (See "The Project Approach" in "Selecting and Using a Curriculum," on p. 41, for further information.)

Dealing with Existing Problems

The Child Who Spends Most of His Time in One Area

This is not necessarily a problem. A child who is less than three years old or who is a slow learner needs to spend time using materials over and over. This is particularly true early in the year when equipment and games are new to the child. You should be concerned later in the year, with children older than three, and if persistent. It is an important educational goal that children experience a wide variety of activities.

● Add some variety to the child's play. Introduce new materials or suggest different ways to play with the same materials. Bring materials from another area of the room to that area. For example, bring paper and pens into the block area and suggest that the child draw a picture of her block structure.

● Entice the child into other areas by providing challenging and fun art projects, cooking projects, water or sand play, or woodworking or a new dramatic play center.

● If a child uses an area too often, close it to all children for one or two days per week. This will give the child a chance to try new areas.

● If enticements do not work and closing the area brings shrieks of protest, consider that the child is getting something from playing in that area that is vitally important to him emotionally or physically. Back down. Be patient. Let the child continue using that area for another few weeks before trying again to promote a change.

The Child Who Spends Very Little Time in Any One Area

Free choice can be overstimulating to some children. They are so excited by all the activities and choices that they can't settle down. So, you see them move quickly from area to area.

● Cut down on the number of choices offered if this does not adversely affect your program too much. Gradually add more choices, one at a time. Start the year off with a limited number of choices and then add more as the year progresses.

● For the child who is overstimulated, create a small, quiet area that is blocked off from most of the room, although make sure that you can easily see into the area. Typically this is a library corner. But if you have enough room, create another private place, containing a small table with one or two chairs. Encourage the child to play with building toys or other games in this area, perhaps with one friend. Stay with the child for a short time to help him focus on the activity. Ask questions, talk about what the child is doing, or do the activity yourself at the same time.

● Use a refrigerator box to make a private space for one child. Encourage the child to use this space when she feels overstimulated.

● Make freestanding cardboard dividers (one-and-a-half feet high) that can be placed on the sides and in front of the child while he works at the table on a project. This will cut down on the visual distractions around him.

● Another reason a child may not stay in any area of the room very long is that the activities there are not challenging. Provide different levels of complexity for different activities and within an activity. For example, make available a wide variety of art supplies and collage materials so that a child can create a simple or very detailed project according to his interest and ability. Provide math games that can be played at a variety of different levels.

● Before free choice time, ask the child to tell you what he will do and in which areas he will play. Encourage the child to stick to his plans. This will help the child who flits from one area to another to become organized. As most preschool children are developing self-organizing skills, doing this with all your children is a good idea.

Too Noisy, Too Boisterous

If fights break out and the noise level rises to an intolerable level, try some of the following ideas.

● Establish a classroom rule that only quiet voices can be used inside the classroom. Demonstrate what a quiet voice sounds like. Remind the children of the rule just before free choice. Let them know that they will be able to use loud voices when they are outside.

● Provide more activities with more challenges to keep the children's interest high.

● Put number limits on the noisiest areas, at least temporarily.

● Encourage children who are playing appropriately by saying something like the following: "Thank you for using a quiet voice. It helps make the room a pleasant place for everyone to work."

• Provide enough supplies to prevent arguments over toys. Purchase duplicates of popular toys, especially for toddlers.

• Provide supplies and activities that are fun and of high interest to the children—not too easy and not too difficult.

• If a particular child is responsible for the high noise level, remind her of the "quiet voice rule." Tell her that if the incident happens again, she will have to choose a quiet activity to do by herself. Follow through on the consequence if necessary. If this happens, tell her she can return to play anywhere when she feels ready. Every five to ten minutes, tell her she is playing well: "When you play well we can all hear each other, no one gets a headache, and everyone stays safe. Thank you."

• If there are two children who tend to "get each other going" when they play together, guide them into separate activities at the start of free choice. During play, catch them just before things start escalating and provide more structure and direction to their play. Tell them that they will not be able to play together if voices get too loud or the activity gets too wild. Follow through, if necessary. When they are playing well together, let them know: "You can play quietly and safely. Thank you for taking care of yourselves."

Too Messy

• Children may misuse the blocks, table games, the dramatic play area, or other areas, so materials are left in a mess or are damaged. If this happens, remind children of rules like the following:

   ▶ "Take blocks from the shelf as you need them to build."

   ▶ "Put items back in their place when you are finished using them."

   ▶ "Pick up anything from the floor that belongs on a table or shelf."

   ▶ "Use all materials so that they don't break or hurt anyone."

• Remind the children of these rules before they use the area and make sure each item has a specific place that is clearly labeled for the children. Lead children back to an area they have left messy and have them straighten it up before moving on to another activity.

• Observe the children's play carefully. If it starts to get out of control, which will lead to misuse of materials, help them by suggesting a different direction for the play, adding new materials, taking a role in the play, or redirecting them to different activities.

• Briefly demonstrate and discuss the various ways different materials can be used appropriately. Ask the children for ideas and help them determine if their ideas make safe and constructive use of the materials. (This is especially important to do when a new dramatic play area is set up.)

Resources

Berk, L. 1994. Research in Review. Vygotsky's theory: The importance of make-believe play. *Young Children* 50 (1): 30–39.

Casey, M. B., and M. Lippman. 1991. Learning to plan through play. *Young Children* 46 (4): 52–58.

Christie, J., and F. Wardle. 1992. How much time is needed for play? *Young Children* 47 (3): 28–32.

Crosser, S. 1994. Making the most of water play. *Young Children* 49 (5): 28–32.

Ford, S. 1993. The facilitator's role in children's play. *Young Children* 48 (6): 66–69.

Greenberg, P. 1992. Creating creative play opportunities. *Young Children* 47 (5): 51.

Nourot, P., and J. Van Hoorn. 1991. Research in review: Symbolic play in preschool and primary settings. *Young Children* 46 (6): 40–50.

Roskos, K., and J. Christie. 2002. Knowing in the doing: Observing literacy learning in play. *Young Children* 57 (2): 46–54.

Ward, C. 1996. Adult intervention: Appropriate strategies for enriching the quality of children's play. *Young Children* 51 (3): 20–25.

Web Sites

Back to Basics: Play in Early Childhood by Jill Englebright Fox www.earlychildhood.com/Articles/index.cfm. Click on Child Development, then scroll down to and click on article title.

Dramatic Play: A Daily Requirement for Children by Linda G. Miller, Ed.D. www.earlychildhood.com/Articles/index.cfm. Click on Child Development, then scroll down to and click on article title.

Free-Choice Time for Children Teaches Life Skills by Evelyn Peterson www.earlychildhood.com/Articles/index.cfm. Click on Child Development, then scroll down to and click on article title.

The Hummingbird Syndrome: Children Who Flit About during Play Time by Sandra Crosser www.earlychildhood.com/Articles/index.cfm. Click on Child Development, then scroll down and click on the article title.

Play as Curriculum by Francis Wardle, Ph.D. www.gymboreeplayuk.com. Click on Articles on Play and Music on the side bar, then on the article title.

Videos

Educational Productions
900 SW Gemini Drive
Beaverton, OR 97008
www.edpro.com
Hand in Hand: Supporting Children with Play Problems.
Series includes seven videos:
  When a Child Doesn't Play, 40 min.
  The Child Who Wanders, 30 min.
  The Child Who Dabbles, 30 min.
  The Child Who Appears Anxious, 30 min.
  The Child Who Appears Aloof, 30 min.
  The Child Who Is Ignored, 30 min.
  The Child Who Is Rejected, 39 min.
Play Power. Series includes two videos:
  Child's Play, 30 min.
  Time Together, 30 min.
NAEYC
1509 16th Street, N.W.
Washington, DC 20036-1426
www.naeyc.org
Dramatic Play: More than Playing House, 28 min.
Play—The Seed of Learning, 30 min.

6. Mealtimes Can Be Pleasant

Mealtimes are opportunities to teach children healthy eating habits, a positive attitude toward food, and pleasant manners. It can be a time for quiet reflection and conversation. However, some children use mealtimes to engage you in a power struggle or to assert themselves in a negative way. Some children have already developed very poor eating habits. The ideas in this chapter will help you make mealtimes relaxing and enjoyable for all.

Preventing Problems

● Arrange tables for eating so they are not close together. This will help keep the noise level down. To avoid the need for you or the children to get up and down often, set the tables so that all food, utensils, and supplies are close at hand.

● Sit in small groups of no more than five children per adult, if possible. This allows for calm conversation during the meal. Extra adults can be recruited from office staff, kitchen staff, drivers, parents, and senior volunteers, among others.

● Avoid making children wait at the table to start eating, or wait for others to finish at the end of the meal. This causes boredom, which leads to acting out. If they must sit for a short time, lead the children in a song, finger play, or simple riddle game to engage their interest.

● If everyone can begin the meal together without waiting, start with a short ritual, such as a grace (if you work in a religious-affiliated program); a poem about friendship; a song of thanks; or a "secular grace," such as "Thank you, Earth. Thank you, Sun. We won't forget what you have done" or "I like the moon. I like the trees. I like the food the earth brings me." This sets a quiet, contemplative tone to start the meal and gets all the children settled down and focused.

● To teach responsibility and manners, promote language skills, and reduce behavior problems, actively involve children during mealtimes. Before the meal, assign children to jobs such as "Waiters" (set the tables) and "Custodians" (wipe the tables, sweep the floor). Unless you are not permitted to do so for health reasons, serve food family-style in bowls for children to pass around and serve themselves. When finished, allow all the children to clear their own places, scrape their plates, throw away paper trash, and put dirty silverware in a container.

● To prevent children from licking serving spoons during family-style service, put bright red tape or another marker that can be felt as well as seen on the handle of the spoon. Remind children at the start of the meal that red-taped spoons are for serving and passing only. Explain to them that keeping the spoons away from their mouths keeps them clean and that using clean spoons helps everyone get fewer colds. Note that the greater the difference in size, look, and shape of the serving spoons from their own spoons, the easier it will be for the children to remember not to lick them.

● Because you are an important role model for good eating habits and manners, eat with the children and eat what they do. Provide choices of healthy foods whenever possible, or at least one alternative for the main protein dish at each meal. Often just providing this simple choice satisfies children's need for control regarding food. Similarly, when children can assemble their meals, they tend to eat it better than if it is presented fully prepared because it provides some control. For example, children can put together the ingredients for their own tacos, rather than being given ready-made ones.

• Offer food to children but do not force it on them. "Please take one bite of each item to be polite" is a good rule. If a sweet dessert is served, offer it to those children who have eaten all of the protein on their plates and at least one bite of everything else. This is not a reward but a way to make sure that children eat more than just dessert. A child who refuses to take even one bite should be allowed to refuse. With no pressure or tension the child will likely come around to eating. A relaxed attitude about food is conducive to good eating habits for everyone.

• Engage the children in low-key conversation during meals. Ask them about their families and about activities they did at home and school earlier in the day, discuss the food being eaten and where it came from, and share some things about yourself. This will set a calm tone, which is important for good digestion.

• Do frequent cooking projects with the children. To increase their knowledge and appreciation of the food they eat, serve the food you cooked with meals.

• Avoid using food for art projects. Pudding paintings and vegetable prints teach children that playing with and wasting food is okay. You will find that using food as art makes reinforcing proper eating habits during meals difficult. Finger paint and sponges work just as well as food for art projects.

• Visit the cook in the kitchen often. Ask her or him to demonstrate and explain to the children how to make some of their favorite dishes. Invite the cook to eat with your class so that he or she can see how the children respond to the food. Help the children send "thank-you" cards for especially good meals. This creates a positive attitude about the food served and the person cooking it.

Dealing with Existing Problems

The Overzealous Eater

This child grabs the food from the table, takes too much, eats very fast, or stuffs too much food in her mouth. The child may have to do this at home to get her share of food, she may be very hungry, or this may be how she has learned to eat.

• To start with, develop a clear system of serving the same amount of food to each child—one spoonful of vegetables, one slice of pizza, two ladles of soup, and so on. If leftovers remain for seconds, divide them up in equal portions for each child. If everyone does not want seconds, give thirds to the children who want them. Before each meal, remind the overzealous eater of your system for equal sharing of food. After a few weeks of this routine, scarcity should not be an issue for any child.

• Expect and, if necessary, teach children to have a few simple manners. This also helps keep mealtimes calm. For example, children from about three years of age should be expected to say, "Please pass the crackers" (and not reach across the table) and "Thank you." They also should be expected or taught to eat correctly with utensils, sit properly, and eat reasonably neatly and quietly.

• Sit next to the overzealous eater so you can help her slow down. Because she probably does the behavior out of habit, you will need to stop the child, show her how to chew slowly, talk her through the meal, and model good eating habits for several weeks. Tell the child that chewing food well is important. Explain to the child that chewing helps her body take in all the food's goodness and makes her grow tall and strong. Assure her that you will make sure that she will get enough food.

The Sloppy Eater

The child who is a sloppy eater is usually a child with some coordination difficulties or problems organizing herself. This child probably also has trouble with puzzles, writes or draws messily, and is a disheveled dresser. Getting slippery food from the plate to the mouth is not an easy task for any preschooler, but it is an exasperating one for the child with poor small-motor control.

• Help the child organize herself before she starts to eat. Help her place her glass where it won't be easily knocked over by a stray elbow or unruly arm. Make sure she has pulled her chair close to the table and is sitting straight. Help her put her plate directly in front of and near to her body. Sticky putty (typically used for securing posters to walls) can be used to help hold a plate or bowl to the table, making it less likely to move or tip over.

• Provide the child with a spoon for most foods since they allow more control than forks. A fork and a spoon together may provide even more control since the child can push the food onto her fork with the spoon. Because plates with high edges prevent food from easily falling off, use them if possible.

• Help the child who is a sloppy eater to fill her glass and soup bowl less than halfway and then provide additional servings when she is done. Point out that smaller amounts are easier to handle, and if spills do occur, there is less waste, less to clean, and less frustration.

• Do not focus too much attention on the problem, as this may humiliate the child and make it worse. Accept the child as having physical difficulties. Provide her with many nonthreatening, playful opportunities to improve her small-motor skills through activities such as cutting with scissors, doing simple puzzles, building with Lego building blocks or unit blocks, and painting at an easel.

The Picky Eater

• To begin with, provide the picky eater with small servings. Note that several small servings can feel less intimidating than one large serving of food.

• During meals, talk about how difficult and scary it can be to try new foods or foods that do not look good to children. Praise children who try new foods for their courage.

• Do not force any child to eat. Set a pleasant and relaxing tone, model good eating habits, give children control wherever possible (serving themselves, starting, and finishing when they are ready), and follow the other suggestions in "Preventing Problems." Allow the child who is a picky eater the time and autonomy to develop better eating habits without pressure.

• As you know, some children have acute taste buds and are very sensitive to foods. Other children have allergies to certain foods and are lucky enough that their bodies tell them not to eat those foods. These children may gag or vomit if forced to eat certain foods. If offered only the offending foods, they will go hungry for long periods rather than eat. Allow parents to provide meals from home, if they are able, with the condition that the meals will meet the nutritional requirements of the program. Allowing one child to eat potato chips and cake while insisting all others eat nutritious food is hypocritical. If the child has a note from a doctor stating that she is on a special diet, provide alternative foods.

Unappealing Food

Some children are picky eaters for good reason. They know, as well as adults do, that the food is not good. Child care centers and schools have a reputation for serving substandard food, and in many cases the reputation is warranted. Understandably, food is a big budget item. Much money can be saved by serving low-quality foods, and good cooks are hard to find at the wages most early childhood programs can afford to pay. But good food is a key aspect of a quality early childhood program. A great curriculum is severely marred when laced with bad food. A hungry child will be difficult to manage. She will have a hard time sitting still and concentrating and may become aggressive. Serving high-quality food makes an important statement about your respect for and care of children. This will not go unnoticed by parents. When children are enthusiastic about the food, problems at mealtimes are reduced.

• Educate the powers-that-be in your program about the importance of good food. Explain why the amount expended on good food is money well spent. Invite the director or principal to eat with the children often so she can see the impact of the food on the children. Ask to have a nutritionist consult with the program to improve the menu. This specialist can often provide ways of improving the food without adding much or any cost. To educate yourself about the issues, read about nutrition and cooking for children. Ask your director, cook, or nutritionist if you can suggest different meals or snacks.

Wasted Food

• If many children leave a great deal of food on their plates, which then gets scraped into the trash, serve much smaller portions. If the children serve themselves, set clear limits on the amounts they can take to start with. Explain that they can have additional portions if they wish.

• Give feedback to the cook about how much food is actually consumed. The cook may be able to prepare much less and save the program a great deal of money, which can then be used for equipment, supplies, or salaries.

• Follow the suggestions provided previously in this chapter on food not being eaten because it is unappealing or because the atmosphere during meals is not calm.

Losing Silverware in the Trash

This is a surprisingly common problem in preschool programs. Giving children the responsibility of clearing their own places is an excellent idea, but it is unrealistic to expect them to do this perfectly every time. The consequence in this case is the expense of losing silverware.

● A simple solution is to assign a child the job of "Environmentalist." Have this child stand by the trash and watch for any silverware that may accidentally get put in. Most children enjoy this job because it makes them feel important, and they do it well. In programs where organic trash is separated from litter, the "Environmentalist" can watch for correct separation of trash as well.

Too Much Noise

● To aid in eating slowly, enjoying the food, and digesting it well, make mealtimes calm and relatively quiet. Before the meal starts, remind children to use quiet, pleasant voices during the meal and not to talk while eating. If the noise level rises too high, shut off the main lights. (Dim lights are easily associated with hushed tones for young children.) In a very quiet voice, explain why you have turned down the lights.

● Use one signal consistently to get children to stop and be quiet. For example, you might use a special bell or the flashing of the lights. Or, you might raise your hand or place the thumb and forefinger of your right hand to make an *L*, and put it next to your ear. This is American Sign Language for *listen* and makes a good cue for quiet. It is instructive at the same time.

● To demonstrate acceptable behavior, converse with the children in quiet, pleasant tones. Have an adult strategically placed at each table to assist the children. Separate children who tend to be loud and boisterous when near each other.

Resources

American Academy of Pediatrics, American Public Health Association, and National Resource Center for Health and Safety in Child Care. 2002. *Caring for our children—National health and safety standards: Guidelines for out-of-home child care programs*, 2d ed. Elk Grove Village, Ill.: American Academy of Pediatrics.

Bickert, G., and L. Britt. 1995. *Food to grow and learn on: Recipes, literature, and learning activities for young children*. New York: Incentives Publications.

Birch, L., S. Johnson, and J. Fisher. 1995. Research in review: Children's eating: The development of food-acceptance patterns. *Young Children* 50 (2): 71–78.

Cosgrove, M. 1991. Cooking in the classroom: The doorway to nutrition. *Young Children* 46 (3): 43–46.

Endres, J. B., and R. E. Rockwell. 1993. *Food, nutrition, and the young child*, 4th ed. New York: Pearson Higher Education.

Katzen, K., and A. L. Henderson. 1994. *Pretend soup and other real recipes: A cookbook for preschoolers and up*. Berkeley, Calif.: Tricycle Press.

Weith, B., and T. Harms. 1981. *Cook and learn: Pictorial single portion recipes: A child's cookbook*. Menlo Park, Calif.: Addison-Wesley.

Web Sites

Getting Picky Eaters to Pick Less and Eat More by Mollie Aby-Valestrino www.earlychildhood.com/Articles/index.cfm. Click on Child Care, then scroll down and click on the article title.

Tips for Feeding Young Children www.cahe.nmsu.edu/pubs. Enter "feeding young children" in the search box.

Eating Habits and Mealtimes from the Field Guide to Parenting by Shelley Butler and Deb Kratz family.go.com. Enter "eating habits" in search box.

Nutrition. Many articles. National Network for Childcare www.nncc.org. Click on Articles and Resources, then on Nutrition.

Food and Young Children by Arlene Fulton and Janice Hermann www.agweb.okstate.edu/pearl. Click on Family and Consumer Information on the side bar, then on Health, Food, and Nutrition, then scroll down to article title.

7. Transitions: Structuring Unplanned Times

Transitions are those periods of time when the children are moving from one activity to the next. Because waiting, with no directions from the teacher, is difficult for young children, transitions can be a problem. Even a few minutes seems like a long time to children. The usual result is that children will wander, run around, or do things they are not supposed to do. Dealing with those behaviors further delays the next activity. Even if you experience no behavior problems, having short, smooth transitions means that more time will be spent in meaningful activities.

Preventing Problems

● Develop a consistent daily schedule with as few transitions as possible built into it. Plan in advance what each adult will do during transition times.

● Tell the children when a transition is about to occur and explain exactly what they are to do: "When you go inside the classroom, hang up your coat and then sit on the rug for a story."

● Structure staff time and duties so that as children move from one activity to another, something engaging is already happening at the next place.

● Have materials ready for the next activity so the transition will be short.

● Begin the next activity as soon as even one child is ready. The other children will be attracted by what is going on and will join quickly.

● Keep a list handy of favorite finger plays, short songs, and simple activities to use during transitions. Activities that involve using their hands, like finger plays or songs that include simple American Sign Language signs are great because they allow the children to be active and to use their hands in positive ways. Because the following simple games require no materials, consider using them for transition.

▶ Describe what a child is wearing and have the children guess whom you are describing.

▶ Have one child mime an action (playing the piano, sweeping, making a pizza) and the other children guess.

▶ Name a list of objects and have the children guess what category they belong to (such as bracelets, necklaces, and earrings are jewelry). After leading the activity once or twice, give the children opportunities to be the leader.

● During longer choice times, help children clean up after themselves as they engage in activities and before moving on to another activity. This "clean as you go" system helps eliminate long, tedious clean-up periods after the choice time is over.

Dealing with Existing Problems

Transition from Eating

● As children finish, have them clear their places and move immediately to the next activity, if possible. Avoid making everyone wait until all are finished eating. If the next activity is not quite ready, let them get paper and some pens to draw or let them browse through books while waiting.* Provide a place where unfinished pictures can be stored to work on later.

● If more than a few minutes will pass before the next activity begins, provide children with table toys so picking up will not take very long.

● If there is more than one teacher, one should begin the next activity while another helps the children who are still eating. If appropriate, invite the children to set up the next activity.

● To eliminate several transitions, consider having a snack or a meal take place during free choice time. Put the food out and let children eat when they are hungry (over a limited time period) with adult supervision. Make sure that every child washes her hands before eating and helps clean up after eating.

Transition to Outdoor Time

● Dismiss children from the previous activity a few at a time. This can be done by dismissing children by kinds of shoes, colors of shirts, or first letters of their names, and so on. If coats are needed, invite the children to help one another put them on, zipper, and button before asking for help from an adult.

---

* Book browsing should be more than a short transition activity. At least once a day provide a period when the children have plenty of time to look through books and/or when adults read to small groups or individuals on laps.

- If at all possible, avoid lining up. This produces only boredom and tension, which lead to pushing and hitting. Ideally, one teacher will go outside with the first children who are ready, and the others will follow when they are ready. Another teacher or adult can bring out the children who move a little slower.

- If there is only one teacher, involve the children in a song while helping to get them ready. A teacher on her own can also bring out all the children when they are close to being done with coats if it is not too cold. Zipping and helping with mittens and hats can be done outside so the children can begin to play as they are ready.

- To avoid a rush for coveted pieces of play equipment, arrange a schedule ahead of time. Write a list of all children who want to use a piece of equipment so names are visible and can be crossed off. Rotate who gets the toy first from day to day. Use a kitchen timer to time the length of turns.

Transition from Outdoors or from Free Choice

- Give a five-minute warning before the children have to finish playing. Use a clock for a visual cue for them to gauge five minutes. Say something like the following: "The long hand is on the five; when it reaches the six, it will be time to stop." Or, use a kitchen timer. Give the warning or have a child give the warning quietly and calmly to each small group of children or individual children as they are playing. Note that this is usually more effective than shouting to the whole group.

- When the five-minute period ends, have a child tell the others that it is time to put equipment away, ring a bell, or flash lights to focus the children's attention. Following these procedures makes the children feel like this transition is an aspect of the daily schedule, not an arbitrary directive from you. This results in less disappointment at having to end play. Also, you maintain your proper authority as the teacher by guiding the children to follow the daily schedule without being overly controlling.

Cleanup

- Label all shelves with names and pictures of materials for quick cleanups that require little adult assistance. Provide child-size mops, brooms, dustpans, sponges, and other clean-up materials where children can get them and put them back easily. Teach them how to use these materials.

- To make the work fun, make a game out of cleanup. Pretend that everyone is a robot or a clean-up monster from space. Or, encourage the children to be the quietest clean-up crew in the world. Singing songs while picking up can also be an effective way to engage children in the activity.

- Give generous encouragement to the children who are conscientious about cleaning up: "Thank you for working so hard to make our room pleasant for everyone."

Transition from Nap

- Let children get up off their cots or mats when they awaken. Guide them to quiet activities (playdough, puzzles, and so on), while you are getting others up and helping them with shoes.

- Move gradually and quietly from naptime into another activity. Cuddle with the children and talk with them. Ask them about their dreams. Turn on lights a few at a time if possible. If children are able to carry their own cots or mats, have them bring them to where they are stacked. (For transition to nap, see "Peaceful Naptimes" on pp. 29–31.)

Transition to Going Home

- Many programs end the day in free choice time or outdoor play, and parents pick up children during this time. This makes for a smooth transition and makes chatting with parents a little easier. Encourage children to put away what they have been using, before going home. Enlist parent support in cleanup.

- If children leave as a group, invite them to end the day by looking at books, listening to music, or drawing pictures. Dismiss them a few at a time when the bus is ready or when parents arrive. As they leave, encourage children to get their papers and art work to take home from cubbies or from a teacher.

- End the day by giving a hug or a handshake to each child as the child leaves to get on the bus, or in the family car. Say something to each child using his name, such as: "Good-bye, Carlos. Have fun with your Grandma this weekend and I will see you on Monday, in two days."

- Allow time to talk with parents about the day's events and to share any concerns or comments you or they may have.

Resources

Chvojicek, R., N. Larson, and M. Henthorne. 2001. *Transition magician for families: Helping parents and children with everyday routines.* St. Paul: Redleaf Press.

Larson, N., M. Henthorne, and B. Plum. 1997. *Transition magician: Strategies for guiding young children in early childhood programs.* St. Paul: Redleaf Press.

Larson, N., M. Henthorne., and R. Chvojicek. 2001. *Transition magician 2: More strategies for guiding young children in early childhood programs.* St. Paul: Redleaf Press.

Web Sites

Songs and Fingerplays for Terrific Transitions. About Daycare. daycare.about.com. Enter "transitions" in the search box.

Terrific Transition Ideas. About Daycare. daycare.about.com. Enter "transition" in the search box.

Terrific Transitions for the Preschool Classroom by Penny E. Warner www.earlychildhood.com/Articles/index.cfm. Click on Curriculum, then scroll down and click on article title.

Transition Time Tricks by Jean R. Feldman, Ph.D. www.earlychildhood.com/Articles/index.cfm. Click on Curriculum, then scroll down and click on article title.

8. Art: Mess without Stress

A mess during art time may mean that children are working hard and having fun. Too much mess, however, results in valuable time being wasted while cleaning up, ruined equipment, soiled clothes (that make parents unhappy), and frustration. The following suggestions will help you keep messes to a minimum, while promoting creativity.

Preventing Problems

● Establish a policy that clothes children wear to school can get messy. Children may still wear good clothes occasionally (often because they insist on it), but at least parents have been forewarned and are aware that clothes may become soiled.

● Keep a bottle or a stick of prewash stain remover handy to use on clothes (yours and the children's) in case of spills.

● Have a classroom rule that children will clean up their own messes and put away any materials that will not be used by others before moving on to another activity.

● Before the start of a project, give a few clear, specific directions for using materials. Include a visual reminder. For example, if you want fingerpaint limited to four tablespoons to avoid too much paint flowing, say so. Demonstrate putting four tablespoons of paint on the paper and put up a picture sign with four tablespoons drawn on it.

● Gather together all the materials you will need for an art project. Make the task easier by using a cart on wheels to hold and transport the materials.

● Do art activities in small groups while most of the children are outside, in another room, or engaged in other activities during free choice. To avoid a big clean-up job at the end, help the children clean up some of the mess after each small group.

● Keep art project items (cotton balls, buttons, paper scraps of the same texture and color) in separate, labeled containers. Do this to avoid the mess created by children rummaging through large boxes filled with a variety of collage materials, and to encourage a more thoughtful approach by giving the children clearer choices.

● Lay newspaper down across the whole table and tape the edges. Roll up the whole mess at the end of the project.

● Lay plastic or newspaper down on the floor beneath your easel or below the table where art work will be done.

● To catch drippy paint and spills quickly, place the art table and easels close to a sink. Add a small amount of liquid soap to paint. The quality of the paint will not change, and removing spots from clothes will be easier.

● Consider making "abstract art," which results from messy art projects, part of the aesthetic of your classroom. Note that an old table used only for art will look attractive with drips and spatters of colorful paint left on it. This allows children to be free from worrying about being neat and from spending time cleaning.

● Keep a trash can next to the art area. Both children and adults are more likely to use it.

● Provide a small-size broom and a large dustpan. Many children enjoy sweeping, especially when two can do the activity together—one sweeps while the other holds the dustpan.

● Keep a basin of soapy water with sponges and some towels nearby. Children can help themselves and clean up on their own. Use large auto or boat sponges because they make cleanup quick and easy. You can purchase these sponges cheaply from janitorial supply companies.

● Have at least one apron or smock for each child in the room. Although you may never use that many, there will be an extra if one gets too soiled or torn. Old adult-size shirts with short sleeves or with long sleeves cut off halfway make excellent smocks and can cost nothing if donated.

● Put Con-Tact paper over easels so that paint will wipe off easily.

● If the sink is far from the art area, keep a plastic basin of soapy water and a towel or a stack of damp towels nearby so that children can rinse their hands.

Dealing with Existing Problems
Drippy Paint

● Mix powdered tempera with nontoxic liquid corn-starch to keep it thick. This causes less dripping and makes painting more satisfying to children by giving them more control over the paint.

● Give children specific directions, individually at the easel, on wiping both sides of the brush on the edge of the container before painting with it. Many reminders may be needed.

Paint Spills and Waste

● Paint containers that are short and wide are less likely to tip over. Use frozen juice containers that you have cut down, half-pint milk cartons, and commer-cially produced plastic no-spill containers.

● Use paint brushes with short handles (about six inches). This gives children more control over the brush and eliminates the problem of the brush flipping out of the container or tipping it over. To eliminate the danger of one poking a child in the eye, consider cutting off and smoothing the ends of brush handles if they are pointy.

● To avoid wasting paint due to drying up, pour unused paint back into a storage jar or cover the individual containers at the end of each day. Wash brushes thoroughly each day to make them last.

Gluing

White glue squeezed from a bottle is often a cause of conflict between teachers and children. Teachers admonish children to "just use a little," and children feel frustrated because either nothing comes out or too much does. Too often there are not enough bottles for each child to have one, the tops glue shut, and children become too involved in the fun of pouring, squeezing, and smearing. Pouring, squeezing, and smearing are very important physical needs that young children have, but they can be better and more cheaply met through water or sand play.

● As an alternative to the squeeze bottle, put a small amount of glue in a cup for each child and provide an ice-cream stick, small brush, or plastic eyedropper (with the hole widened) as an applicator. To save money, purchase the glue in a large, gallon size.

● An alternative to white glue is paste, which is less messy but will not work as well with certain materials such as wood. A few small containers of paste could be passed around or children can have individual squares of paper with some paste on them. Each child can use a stick, brush, or their fingers to apply the paste.

Resources

Charner, K., and C. Barnes, eds. 2000. *The giant encyclopedia of arts and crafts activities*. Beltsville, Md.: Gryphon House.

Davalos, S. R. 1999. *Making sense of art: Sensory-based art activi-ties for young children, 3–5*. Shawnee Mission, Kans.: Autism Asperger Publishing.

Kohl, M. F. 1993. *ScienceArts: Discovering science through art experiences*. Bellingham, Wash.: Bright Ring Publishing.

———. 1994. *Preschool art: It's the process not the product*. Beltsville, Md.: Gryphon House.

———. 2000. *The big messy (but easy to clean up) art book*. Beltsville, Md.: Gryphon House.

Moomaw, S., and B. Hieronymus. 1999. *More than painting: Exploring the wonders of art in preschool and kindergarten*. St. Paul: Redleaf Press.

———. 1999. *Much more than painting: Exploring the wonders of art in preschool and kindergarten*. St. Paul: Redleaf Press.

Web Sites

Incredible Art Department
www.princetonol.com/groups/iad. Click on Lessons, then on
Early Childhood.

About Daycare
daycare.about.com. Click on Activities on the side bar, then
on Art Activities.

The Chalkboard
patricia_f.tripod.com. Click on Assorted Art Activities on the
side bar.

Earlychildhood.com
www.earlychildhood.com. Click on Arts and Crafts on the
side bar.

ECEOL-L Web Site
www.ume.maine.edu/ECEOL-L. Click on Curriculum and
Environments, then scroll down to Art area.

Kinder Art
www.kinderart.com

LessonPlansPage.com
www.lessonplanspage.com/ArtK1.htm

9. Safe Fun Outdoors or in the Gym

Large-motor (or gross-motor) play most often happens outdoors or in the gym. In this type of play, young children learn to coordinate their large muscles and increase their strength, agility, and understanding of how their bodies move. Developing these large-motor skills is as important to their overall healthy growth as practicing cognitive skills (learning colors, shapes) or small-motor skills (writing letters, doing puzzles).

Although it is tempting for teachers to use this time to "take a breather," your task is to provide children with many different and safe activities that allow them to practice balancing, jumping, running, climbing, hopping, ball handling, aiming, and more. Help them challenge themselves physically while staying safe.

Preventing Problems

● Schedule outdoor/gym time for at least thirty minutes each morning and thirty minutes each afternoon (for full-day or double-shift programs).

● Post outside or in the gym a list of activities that the children enjoy. Consider including the following on the list: hopscotch, hide-and-seek, playing gas station with tricycles, jumping rope, playing with a parachute, tossing beanbags into a box, dancing to taped music, painting with water and big brushes, pretending to be firefighters, and walking through an obstacle course. Include a variety of cooperative group movement games (see the resources on p. 29 for books of ideas).

● Use your list of activities to provide different things for the children to do each day. A limited number of choices or the same choices every day does not provide enough large-muscle growth and also leads to boredom. Accidents on the playground are often caused by bored children taking dangerous chances.

● If at all possible provide bike helmets to those riding tricycles. Helmets are required for those riding scooters or bikes. This helps them establish good safety habits, and will prevent the rare tricycle head injury.

● Most accidents in child care settings are caused by swings. If you have a swing set, create a visible marker around the outside of the swing area to signal children not to move too close so they won't be hit by a child swinging. Railroad ties work well as they are big enough that children will not trip on them, but not so big that they take up a great deal of space. They can usually be obtained inexpensively. A teacher should always be watching the swing area.

● Set a few firm playground/gym rules, relating to your particular equipment. You might use the following:

 ▶ "Go down the slide on your bottom."

 ▶ "Swing only while seated and stop swinging before jumping off."

 ▶ "Climb using two hands."

● Before going outside, assign each staff person a different part of the playground to supervise. Make sure all children can be seen easily and reached quickly by an adult.

Dealing with Existing Problems
Limited or Unsafe Play Equipment

If you have very little in the way of usable play equipment such as swings, slides, and climbers, and there is not a park nearby, you can still provide a good large-motor program.

● Hang a tire swing from a tree.

● Bring with you boxes of equipment that include balls, hoops, jump ropes, bubble blowing supplies, a parachute, balance beams, beanbags, shovels, pails, and frisbees.

● Fill boxes with props that relate to particular themes. For example, in a beach theme box, put shells, towels, sunglasses, empty plastic suntan lotion bottles, swim goggles, swim fins, inflatable pool toys, and so on. Use a wagon to haul the boxes.

● Include among your materials foam rubber sports equipment (tennis balls, baseballs, soccer balls). These are inexpensive, safe, and easy for young children to use, are easy to haul, and can be used indoors or out.

● Supply dress-up clothes and art activities for variety.

● Use large cardboard boxes for a variety of creative play activities. Invite the children to make forts, cars, stages, and more, from wooden boxes, boards, and old sheets.

● Put wheels on your water table so you can bring it outside on warm days.

● Use your list of fun activities (as described in "Preventing Problems") often. You will need to provide more structure if you have little usable equipment.

● Make a large sandbox with wooden boards. Supplied with shovels, funnels, and other creative sand toys, the sandbox will be a well-used and loved area of the playground. To keep out neighborhood pets, cover the sandbox with an inexpensive plastic tarp.

● If you have access to a gym but the equipment is designed for older children (high basketball hoops, tall volleyball nets), adapt to that equipment by using a large beach ball for a volleyball and a small rubber ball for a basketball.

● Check equipment at least weekly to determine if there are loose pieces, sharp edges or nails, splintered wood, or other problems. Children can help you find these problems and usually become aware of them before you do. At the first sign of an unsafe condition, keep children off equipment until it can be fixed or replaced. Rope off the equipment or have a similar highly visible marker to prevent children from using it. The children can help fix equipment in some cases

by sanding wood surfaces, hammering protruding nails, and painting rusted areas. Close adult supervision will be needed.

Wood, Concrete, or Paved Play Areas

● A hard surface under play equipment or where children run is extremely dangerous. Put mats, mattresses, or similar cushioning under and around any climbing equipment used in a gym. Surround outdoor structures with bark dust, pea gravel, sand, tire shreds, or similar loose materials. If possible, cover the entire play area, except where wheeled toys are used, with a cushioning material. Some programs have been able to get these donated from suppliers, as they can be quite expensive. In the long run, bark dust and sand can be more expensive than the more permanent materials, as they have to be replaced regularly. But consider that the cost to a program of one serious accident makes the cost of essential safety equipment worth the expense.

No Indoor Gym Space for When Weather Is Bad

If you live in a part of the country where children cannot go outside for very long for many months of the year, how can you provide your children with an adequate large-motor program?

● Unless the weather is severe, take your children outside for a short time every day. Start collecting a supply of extra boots, mittens, hats, and so on for children who do not come properly dressed. If heat is the problem, keep a supply of sunscreen and sun hats. Some fresh air and only ten minutes of running and playing will provide children with a satisfying experience. Afterwards, they will be better able and more willing to be involved in more restricted indoor play.

● If at all possible, move tables and shelves to provide room for children to move around within your room. Use records, tapes, or your own voice for movement games and exercises. Make sure the children have plenty of time to move on their own to music (creative dance), move freely to their own ideas ("Let's move like bees stuck in honey"), and be physical with each other (exercising with partners). Creative expression with their whole bodies provides a great emotional release for any strong feelings or anxiety children may have. The hassle of moving furniture out of the way and then back will be worthwhile, as you will prevent behavior problems and meet children's large-motor needs. Invite the children to help with moving.

Resources

American Academy of Pediatrics, American Public Health Association, and National Resource Center for Health and Safety in Child Care. 2002. *Caring for our children—National health and safety standards: Guidelines for out-of-home child care programs*, 2d ed. Elk Grove Village, Ill.: American Academy of Pediatrics.

Fromberg, D. P. 2001. *Outdoor play: Teaching strategies with young children*. New York: Teachers College Press.

Henniger, M. 1994. Planning for outdoor play. *Young Children* 49 (4): 10–15.

Miller, S. 1999. Balloons, blankets, and balls. *Young Children* 54 (5): 58–63

Pica, R. 1997. Beyond physical development: Why young children need to move. *Young Children* 52 (6): 4–11.

Poest, C., J. Williams, D. Witt, and M. E. Atwood. 1990. Challenge me to move: Large muscle development in young children. *Young Children* 45 (5): 4–10.

Portman, P. A., and L. Staley. 2000. Red rover, red rover, it's time to move over! *Young Children* 55 (1): 67–72.

Torbert, M., and L. Schneider. 1993. *Follow me too: A handbook of movement activities for three- to five-year-olds*. New York: Addison-Wesley.

Wilson, R., S. Kilmer, and V. Knauerhase. 1996. Developing an environmental outdoor play space. *Young Children* 51 (6): 56–61.

Web Sites

Links to numerous articles. Earlychildhood.com. www.earlychildhood.com/Articles/index.cfm. Click on Physical Education, Movement, Play, and Playgrounds.

National Program for Playground Safety www.uni.edu/playground

Outdoor Play. Various articles. www.nncc.org. Click on Articles and Resources, then on Activities and Learning, then on Outdoor Play and Sports.

Outdoor Activities. Various articles. daycare.about.com/cs. Enter "outdoor" in the search box.

Physical Education/Movement. Various articles. users.stargate.net/~cokids. Click on Teacher Pages, then on Physical Education/Movement.

Videos

NAEYC
1509 16th Street, N.W.
Washington, DC 20036-1426
www.naeyc.org
New Games for Child Care Settings (also available in Spanish), 28 min.
Structured Play: Gross Motor Activities for Everyday (also available in Spanish), 28 min.
Safe Active Play: A Guide to Avoiding Play Area Hazards, 35 min.

10. Peaceful Naptimes ———

Naptime can be a stressful time of day or a warm and relaxing time for both you and the children. Careful attention to the environment, to comforting routines, and to individual needs for rest and activity will help make naptime peaceful.

Preventing Problems

● Schedule naptime late enough so that most children are tired.

● Establish a routine such as reading a book or singing a song just before each naptime. Use the same song each time to establish a comforting ritual.

● Remind children of naptime rules (no more than two) that you have established, such as "Stay on your cot and use a whisper voice only."

● Have a transition period when children can lie down and look quietly at books for fifteen minutes.

● Reassure new children that they are not going to sleep for the night but just for a few hours and that they will be picked up by their parents later in the day.

● Leave at least three feet of space between each cot, and place children who are near to each other, head to toe. This prevents the spread of colds as well as minimizes talking.

● Start each naptime by doing a group physical exercise while children are lying on their cots or pads. Talk them through lifting one leg then the other, one arm then the other, one leg and one arm together, then the others, and so on. As it progresses use a quieter voice and slower movements. End by talking them through some deep breathing and muscle-relaxing exercises.

● Darken the room and play soft, soothing music throughout naptime. Use the same music each day. There are many recordings of lullabies, classical music, and New Age music designed to foster relaxation.

● Ask parents to bring in blankets, teddy bears, and other sleeping aids used at home.

● Gently rub backs or foreheads.

● As children want to do what adults do, lie down yourself for awhile.

Dealing with Existing Problems

Infants/Young Toddlers

Different Schedules: As most programs allow children under two to fall asleep when they are tired, you have the problem of almost always having some children sleeping while others are awake. In a week or two, most children will get used to sleeping through the noise. Create a separate sleeping room (ideally with a large glass window between it and the main room for easy viewing). If this is not possible, use a curtain to section off a portion of the room for sleeping.

Older Toddlers/Preschoolers

Squirmers: Some children need to squirm for about a half hour before they can relax enough to sleep. These are the children who do not settle down or relax when you rub their backs or foreheads. Let them get their wiggles out before trying to help them sleep.

Non-nappers: Some children are just not nappers. However, they still need a rest period in full-day programs. After they have rested for about forty-five minutes, arrange for these children to play in another place or allow them to do quiet activities in the room.

Noisemakers: Children who are deliberately loud and wake others up are usually either bored or enjoy the attention their disturbance brings. Try the prevention ideas and non-napper ideas listed above to prevent boredom and to encourage good behavior. If the problem persists, calmly place the child, with her cot or mat, just outside the room in the hallway or in an adjoining room (assuming the area is safe, not too hot or cold, and the child can be seen by an adult). Show no anger or frustration. Tell the child she can come back to the room when she can lie quietly. Repeat this procedure until the behavior stops. (See "Children with Challenging Behaviors" on p. 122 for more ideas.)

Socializers: Some children have a difficult time not talking and playing with their friends who are lying nearby. Place the cots or mats of such children behind shelves or other furniture so they can't see their buddies. Strategically place room dividers and rearrange the room to create as many private sleeping areas as necessary.

No Rewards: Tell the children who have followed the rules that they have done well: "Because you were quiet, naptime was peaceful, and all the children who wanted to sleep were able to." Do not reward children for sleeping, as it is not something most children can control.

Resources

Da Ros, D., and A. Wong. 1994. Caregivers corner: Naptime: A transition with ease. *Young Children* 50 (1): 69.

Koralek, D. 2000. Meet Maryanne Lazarchick—An accredited family child care provider. *Young Children* 57 (1): 25–26.

Siren-Tiusanen, H., and H. A. Robinson. 2001. Nap schedules and sleep practices in infant-toddler groups. *Early Childhood Research Quarterly* 16 (1): 453–74.

Soundy, C., and N. Stout. 2002. Pillow talk: Fostering the emotional and language needs of young learners. *Young Children* 57 (2): 20–24.

Web Sites

Naptime ideas submitted by teachers
www.perpetualpreschool.com/napideas.html

Taking the Nightmare Out of Naptime by Sandra Crosser, Ph.D.
www.earlychildhood.com/Articles/index.cfm. Click on Child Care, then scroll down and click on the article title.

Rest Time: The Key to Effective Rest Time Is Flexibility by Robert C. Mills
www.nncc.org. Click on Articles and Resources, then on Child Care Best Practices, then on Daily Schedules and Program Planning, then scroll down and click on article title.

11. Computer Center Concerns

There are three main issues to consider for an effective computer center: Managing it for "crowd control" and safety, keeping the computer from breaking or crashing, and making sure the children are using it for good purposes. The last concern may fall into the category I have called, "Problems you didn't know you had." It is not enough that children are busy and happy tapping away at a computer game or that it engages them for a long time (so do cartoons on TV!). Nor is it enough that they are learning "computer skills" like moving the mouse. They should be using the computer to create and learn in ways that no other tool or equipment in your classroom can do as effectively. The computer should support and add depth to your curriculum and goals for children, rather than be an "add-on." Most children's software are of the "drill and practice variety"—which are really just electronic worksheets— or they are mindless games. There are a few excellent programs, however, that allow children to be creative and efficient beyond what they can do with nonelectronic materials, which is why adults use computers after all. These include the ability to easily erase, re-create, save, and edit work; have easy access to a great deal of information (pictures and text) through reference programs and the Internet; do animations; create and play music; make professional-looking story books; and more.

Preventing Problems

● Treat the computer center just like other centers in the classroom, using a sign-up sheet for taking turns, making sure all who want a turn gets one. Encourage children who are not drawn to it to try it out. Make it one choice among many during your free choice time.

● Create a few clear rules about the use of the computer and post them with images and words. These may include the following: "touch only the keyboard," "ask for help as soon as there is a problem," and "keep food and drinks far away."

● Use special computer programs that prevent the children from accessing any parts of the computer system other than the software you have selected for them and that prevents them from accessing inappropriate Web sites.

● Make each computer an activity center for two children and help them collaborate. This will also help with the problem of many children wanting to use the computer at the same time. They will often remind each other of the rules. It will add a social dimension to the activity and there will be conversation and negotiation.

● If a particular child or children are skilled at using the computer and use it carefully, make them the class IT (information technology) specialist. Have them help other children when asked and direct other children with questions to them.

● Limit the software to just a very few open-ended, creative programs that allow children to make animated pictures, stories, and books, and to children's reference programs and Web sites that allow them easy access to visually accurate information. See the end of this section for some information about such programs and Web sites.

● Learn to use a simple authoring program like HyperStudio or one of the many Web site creators available (some are free). This will allow you to document, display, keep, and update children's work, class projects, field trips, and so on.

● If possible, purchase or use a scanner, a digital camera, and other technology tools that will allow you and the children to extend the computer's capabilities. You can use these tools with the children to document your classroom work and activities and increase communications with parents.

- Create a class Web site and use e-mail to communicate with families. A Web camera can allow parents to visually drop in on your classroom at their convenience and see the great things you are doing as they happen, creating much goodwill among parents.

- Take the time and effort to get some training on using computers. Learn how to defrag, update drivers, and perform routine maintenance. You will ultimately save time by using it much faster, preventing problems, and being able to fix simple problems.

- Make sure you have access to someone who really knows how to keep the computer running well, fix computer glitches, and make repairs. Buy extended warranties. Your computer will break down, crash, and need repair, even if it does not get heavy use (which is unlikely in preschool classrooms).

Dealing with Existing Problems

Children Who Do Not Use the Computer Correctly or Carefully

- Remind children of the rules. Make sure they understand and can follow the rules and provide instruction if they cannot. Tell them the consequence of breaking rules is that they will have to choose another activity. Follow through if necessary. Make sure they understand what they did wrong and what they will need to do before using the computer again. Repeat the conversation just before they will use it the next time.

- Children who continue to misuse the computer are showing that they are not ready for this type of activity. Show them other ways they can get their needs and interests met with more interactive, hands-on, sensory materials. Give them another opportunity to use the computer in a few weeks if they are interested. State the rules and consequences before they return to using it.

Too Many Users

- Avoid limiting the computer time to a very short time (such as five minutes) to allow more children to use it each day, as that will result in very unsatisfying experiences at the computer. Instead limit the number of children using it each day and have a rotating schedule so that half the children use it one day and the other half the next, or something similar.

- Develop projects that involve a number of children using the computer and other materials as part of the project. This could be a project involving making a dinosaur with information about dinosaurs obtained from the computer and documentation of its progress displayed and stored on the computer.

- Add additional, less expensive technologies such as digital cameras to expand the hardware available to children.

- Sometimes the popularity of the computer is due to its entertainment value because of the software chosen. Use programs as described previously. Help children use one or two open-ended programs in increasingly sophisticated ways and to go back and edit work they previously saved.

Children Who Do Not Want to Use the Computer

This is a similar problem to children who avoid other types of activities. Because it is important for children to have many kinds of experiences and gain skills in many areas, use of the computer should be as mandatory as listening to stories. As computer literacy is as vital to being fully literate as print literacy, it is important that all children gain computer skills.

- There is a tendency for girls to get less encouragement and support for using technology than boys (in general) resulting in unequal knowledge and skills starting in early childhood. Pay particular attention to any (unconscious) biases on your part or other staff. Pairing up girls adds a social dimension to the activity that many girls enjoy. Software that includes elements appealing to girls, or is at least gender neutral, will also help. These may include female characters or voice-overs and the ability to use it for communication and interacting with others.

- Using the rotating schedule described previously with a time slot for each child will provide opportunities for all children to use the computer. Do not allow children to cede their time to others; instead, find out why they are reluctant and what will engage them. They may need to learn some specific skills and practice them without fear of criticism or failure. They may need to try a different software program or be given a sense of purpose for using the computer, such as "Let's make a story about the restaurant you made in dramatic play today and you can take it home to show your family."

Pressure to Eliminate Computers in the Classroom or to Have More Computers or to Use Inappropriate Software

● As discussed earlier, it is important to have a balanced program with a broad array of activities and materials available for children. Access to one or two computers for every ten to fifteen children is sufficient and allows for ample time to work in other areas.

● Having no computers is an acceptable choice for many preschool classrooms, but should be an informed, deliberate choice on your part. It may unnecessarily limit the learning opportunities for your children. For children from low-income families who may not have computers at home, it is important to have computers in the classroom. A vocal group of people has firmly asserted that there is no place for computers in early childhood classrooms (see the Fools Gold report in the resource list below). My view is that computers do have a place in your classroom but, at best, it is a limited one for children who are not yet reading. There are challenges: it requires work and oversight and sometimes one-on-one guidance. However, when used well, the benefits outweigh the problems.

● Write a clear, one or two page philosophy and approach statement about computers to give to parents, supervisors, evaluators, and others who may be critical. Include the importance of variety and balance in the curriculum in your statement and draw on the resources at the end of this section. Include a rationale for using a limited number of open-ended and reference software as being in line with developmentally appropriate practices.

● If you work in a program that serves low-income families, it is particularly important to have a computer in your classroom to help provide experiences with a tool that is common to children from wealthier families. This unequal access to technology has been called the "digital divide" and preschools have an important role in closing that divide.

● Make sure that children sit at the computer in an "ergonomically" correct way, such as eyes level with the screen. Limit time on the computer to no more than fifteen minutes at a sitting. This should dispel any concerns about improper use or potential harm to children.

Resources

Anderson, G. T. 2000. Computers in a developmentally appropriate curricula. *Young Children* 55 (2): 90–93.

Haugland, S. 1999. What role should technology play in young children's learning? Part 1. *Young Children* 54 (6): 26–31.

———. 2000. What role should technology play in young children's learning? Part 2—Early childhood classrooms in the 21st century. *Young Children* 55 (1): 12.

Haugland, S., and J. Wright. 1997. *Young children and technology: A world of discovery.* New York: Allyn & Bacon.

Web Sites

Early Connections Web site of the Northwest Educational Technology Consortium (Northwest Regional Educational Laboratory)
www.netc.org/earlyconnections

Technology in Early Childhood Education: Finding the Balance
www.netc.org/earlyconnections/byrequest.pdf

Technology and Young Children. NAEYC Position Statement. 1996.
www.naeyc.org. Click on NAEYC Resources, then on View position statements, then on Improving program practices with children, then scroll down to article title.

Fools Gold: A Critical Look at Computers in Childhood
www.allianceforchildhood.net. Scroll down and click on article title.

Computer Ergonomics for Elementary School (concepts easily adapted to younger children)
orosha.org/cergos

Lesson plans on various subjects using computer or Internet-based strategies
www.lessonplanspage.com/CIK1.htm

Videos

NAEYC
1509 16th Street, N.W.
Washington, DC 20036-1426
www.naeyc.org
The Adventure Begins: Preschool and Technology, 10 min.
Your Preschool Classroom Computer Center: How Does It Measure Up? 20 min.

Software, Selection, and Reviews
Web Sites

Seven Steps to Responsible Software Selection
www.netc.org/software/eric_software.html

Way Cool Software Reviews
www.ucc.uconn.edu/~wwwpcse/wcool2.html

World Village Educational Software Reviews
www.worldvillage.com/softwarereviews

HyperStudio Software
www.hyperstudio.com

Kid Pix Software
www.kidpix.com

Ed Software
www.edsoftware.com

Part II

Classroom Concerns

1. Making the Classroom Environment Work for You —

How you organize the classroom environment and what equipment you place in it affect children's learning and behavior. Children who are bored, overstimulated, or confused by the environment will react by developing behavior problems. An appropriate environment will help reduce overactive, aggressive, and disruptive behaviors. It will also provide many fun learning opportunities for children.

Preventing Problems

● To avoid arguments, have several duplicates of toys, especially for toddlers. Include both push and pull toys, items that can be put in and taken out of containers, trucks to fill up, and low vehicles to ride on. Make sure that all the toys are too big for the children to put in their mouths.

● For all children, provide toys and games with a wide skill range so more able children will be challenged but less able or younger children will not be frustrated. For example, have four-piece, ten-piece, and twenty-five-piece puzzles.

● Arrange the furniture so that you have no long corridors that may invite running in the room. Place quiet areas (library, table toys) away from noisy areas (blocks, dramatic play).

● Rotate supplies and toys to avoid boredom. Provide many toys and activities that children can use without help from adults. To create calm, paint walls in pastel colors and display posters that are soothing to look at. Consider reproductions of famous works of art or scenes from nature. These can be obtained inexpensively by purchasing art or nature calendars when they go on sale in early January of each year. Avoid very busy, brightly colored rooms, which please adults but overstimulate children.

● Change the dramatic play area fairly often. Set up a post office for three or four weeks, then a restaurant for several weeks, then a campground. Have the children come up with other ideas.

● Label all shelves and counters with words and pictures so that children will be able to put materials in their proper places without adult help.

● To avoid arguments and safety concerns due to overcrowding, limit the number of children allowed in certain small areas of the room. To indicate the allowed number, put up picture signs that children can understand. A small water-play basin or a woodworking table may need to be limited to two or three.

● Make popular areas of the room, such as dramatic play and blocks, as large as possible to accommodate many children. Avoid putting number limits in these areas (unless the areas are very small) because children will feel frustrated if they are kept out. Setting number limits in these areas may cause more problems than it will solve.

● Balance the hardness in the room (chairs, tables, floors, walls) with things that are soft. For example, use beanbag chairs, large floor pillows, rugs that can be cleaned easily, wall hangings, and fabric draped from the ceiling.

● Create at least one private space where a child can choose to be away from others. For example, use a large, painted refrigerator box with pillows inside.

● Establish a place to store unfinished artwork and other projects to be completed later. Provide individual, personal storage areas where children can keep projects, notes, extra clothes, and stuffed animals from home.

Dealing with Existing Problems
Small Spaces

● If you have a small center or house with a number of small rooms, you can designate each room for certain activities. All groups of children then share all rooms on a rotating basis. One room can be for art, another for dramatic play, a third for group times, and so on. It is possible for several teachers to share such spaces by coordinating schedules and assigning themselves to a room to supervise, rather than supervising only their own groups of children.

● To increase usable space and make a creative and fun room, install a loft. Caution: ceilings must be high enough, and there should be enough money allocated to build a sturdy and safe loft.

Not Enough Storage Space

● Build shelves high up on the walls to provide valuable extra storage space. If closed cabinets are too expensive, consider covering open shelves with fabric to make the room look neater. This also helps solve the problem of children being attracted to the items on the shelves.

- Store large items that will not be used for a period of several months with a mini-storage company or perhaps, for less money (or free), with a local business or agency that has some extra space and is willing to help you out.

- See if a staff member with a good deal of extra storage room at home might be willing to store items there. In this case, post a list of every stored item at the center where the list will be accessible to everyone. When items are brought back to school, cross them off the list. Add newly stored items to the list. It is important to have the staff member who is providing the storage space sign a statement agreeing to the arrangement and agreeing to return all items at the request of the director, board president, or other supervisor.

A High Ceiling or Large Open Space

- Lower the ceiling by draping fabric or a parachute or by hanging umbrellas or other items. Be cautious: hang these securely. To avoid any fire danger, make sure the objects are not near light fixtures or heat sources. Before doing this, ask your local fire official if hanging material violates regulations.

- Because large spaces tend to get noisy and make children feel overwhelmed, partition them. If actual room dividers are not available, an inexpensive partition can be made using a 4 by 6 feet sheet of particle board and four metal brackets to hold it upright. Stringing fabric for a curtain can also work. Perhaps the unused area can be set aside for an indoor gym.

- Create several cozy spaces by draping attractive fabric between sets of bookshelves or cabinets. You can also cut door and window holes in cardboard refrigerator boxes and cover or paint them.

Little Money for Supplies or Equipment

- Teacher-made games are often the most used and best-liked materials in the classroom. Look in equipment catalogs for many items that you can make without much difficulty and for much less money than if purchased. Cover them with a clear adhesive paper or laminate them to make them last for years.

- Ask parents and staff to help you collect free materials, such as cardboard, cereal boxes, paper towel tubes, egg cartons, juice containers, disposable meat trays, and so on, that can be used to make different games.

- Host a party for parents during which they help make these games. Serve snacks and allow plenty of time to chat. Allow parents to make a game or two for home use.

- Check with manufacturers in your area. Often they can give you useful scrap materials, such as paper, wood pieces, plastic containers, and cloth.

- You can save hundreds of dollars a year on paper supplies by using paper scraps donated by local printers and by using old computer paper from a company such as your electric utility.

- Often a local carpenter, skilled parent, or friend can make classroom furniture and shelves for much less money than the equipment sold in catalogs.

- Check garage sales, used-furniture stores, and Salvation Army or Goodwill-type stores for usable items. These used items often need only some paint or a few screws.

Sharing Your Classroom

- To avoid problems, meet at least monthly with the teachers who share your room. Discuss expectations for use of materials and cleanliness. Define exactly what materials can be shared; what needs to be put away; and what, if anything, needs to be locked up. Having a supervisor at your meeting to mediate can help avoid an impasse and help determine what constitutes reasonable expectations. When you find the room left in good condition, leave notes thanking the other teachers.

- If you have to move furniture and put away supplies at the end of each day or each week, make your job easier by putting wheels on the bottom of all your furniture. Hinged shelving units that fold together and can be locked are very handy.

- As the end of the day approaches, enlist the help of the other staff and the children in putting things away gradually. Close areas of the room, one by one, so that at the end of the day you are in a space that is easy to clean. This avoids putting in extra hours of hard work after class, when you are already tired and eager to leave.

Resources

Cutler, K. 2000. Organizing the curriculum storage in a preschool/child care environment. *Young Children* 55 (3): 88–92.

Greenman, J. 1988. *Caring spaces, learning places: Children's environments that work.* Redmond, Wash.: Exchange Press.

Isbell, R., and B. Exelby. 2001. *Early learning environments that work.* Beltsville, Md.: Gryphon House.

Kielar, J. 1999. An antidote to the noisy nineties. *Young Children* 54 (5): 28–29.

Lowman, L., and L. Ruhmann. 1998. Simply sensational spaces: A multi-'S' approach to toddler environments. *Young Children* 53 (3): 11–17.

Packer, S. 2000. The effects of scarcity and abundance in early childhood settings. *Young Children* 55 (5): 36–38.

Ratcliff, N. 2001. Using the environment to prevent problems and support learning. *Young Children* 56 (5): 84–88.

Weinstein, C., and T. David. 1987. *Spaces for children: The built environment and child development.* New York: Plenum Press.

Web Sites

An Environment that Positively Impacts Young Children by Rebecca Isbell, Ed.D.
www.earlychildhood.com/Articles/index.cfm. Click on Learning Settings, Equipment, and Materials, then scroll down and click on article title.

Classroom Design and How It Influences Behavior
www.earlychildhood.com/Activities/index.cfm. Click on Learning Settings, Equipment, and Materials, then scroll down and click on article title.

Problems in the Block Corner? by Susan Miller, Ed.D.
www.earlychildhood.com/Activities/index.cfm. Click on Learning Settings, Equipment, and Materials, then scroll down and click on article title.

Tips for Furnishing the Learning Environment by Angie Dorrell
www.earlychildhood.com/Activities/index.cfm. Click on Learning Settings, Equipment, and Materials, then scroll down and click on article title.

Toys and Equipment by Lesia Oesterreich
www.nncc.org. Click on Articles and Resources and then on Activities and Learning (under Child Care Programming), then Toys and Materials, then on the article title.

Videos

NAEYC
1509 16th Street, N.W.
Washington, DC 20036-1426
www.naeyc.org
Places to Grow—The Learning Environment, 30 min.

2. Selecting and Using a Curriculum

There are basically two types of curricula. One consists of prescribed-activity ideas to use with children and the other consists of an approach to teaching (including a philosophy, general principles, and ideas for structuring your schedule and environment). In the teaching-approach curriculum, the teacher develops the actual activities or adapts them from resource books.

Purchasing a curriculum with prescribed activities is like purchasing a closet full of clothes. You may save a great deal of time and effort by not buying clothes, but many in the closet will not suit you and will not fit. Of course no one does this, yet many programs do purchase prescribed-activity curricula. A teaching-approach curriculum is like an empty closet with hangers, storage, shoe racks, and shelves. On these structures you can properly and conveniently place clothes of your own choosing. You will need to make decisions about what to buy and take the time and energy to do the purchasing, but the result will be more satisfying. Without question, teaching-approach curricula are better for children. The activities you develop can come out of the children's interests, immediate needs, and culture. No question, these activities require more planning time, work, energy, knowledge, and thought on your part.

If you are a beginning teacher and will not be provided with thorough training for using a teaching-approach curriculum, you might choose (or be required to use) a curriculum with prescribed activities. Be prepared, however, to change many of the prescribed activities and to drop some that do not work for your group. When you feel comfortable enough with your knowledge of how young children (and your group in particular) learn and which activities work well and which do not, you can switch to a teaching-approach curriculum.

The greatest benefit of a teaching-approach curriculum is that it will provide you with a sound theory or philosophy on which to base all your activities and interactions with children. This curriculum will give you a reason for doing what you do with children and help you determine how to do it most effectively.

Many curricula of both types include tools and strategies for assessing children on skills related to each particular curriculum's goals for children, and for planning activities. These can be very useful in tracking children's progress and helping you to meet individual needs.

At the end of this chapter, you will find sources for some prescribed-activity curricula. They are not described because they all are very similar. A number of teaching-approach curricula are described, however. Sources for additional information about these curricula are provided at the end of the chapter. Some of the best teachers do not use one particular approach but use parts of several. These teachers usually have had many years of experience and have a well-defined approach that they can clearly describe and smoothly carry out.

Themes

Themes, or units, are probably the most common curriculum approach found in preschool classrooms. Almost all prescribed-activities curricula use themes such as the following: community helpers, transportation, our neighborhood, fire safety, nutrition, spring, and so on. You can also use themes with many teaching-approach curricula, but you don't have to. A theme typically lasts for one or two weeks and provides the basis for art, math, science, literature, language, field trips, and other activities.

Like any curriculum, a theme-based curriculum can be done well or poorly. A shortcoming of a theme-based curriculum is that it does not come from your important theory base, unless it is used with a teaching-approach curriculum. Therefore, you may not know how to carry out the themes effectively. Also, themes may lead you toward using activities that you control and direct rather than toward using activities that children choose and direct themselves. There is a tendency for theme topics to be somewhat trivial or contrived. However, this can be corrected by observing children, knowing about their families and then developing themes from their lives, needs, and interests.

Being able to implement a particular theme as the interest or need arises is important. Too often themes are set well in advance leaving no room for spontaneity. For example, if two children in your class will be having new siblings in their families, you will want to do a theme about babies. Themes, like the activities themselves, should come from the needs, interests, and culture of the children. Some of the best themes are those that affect all children and are deeply important to them. Consider using the following themes, which include a few activity ideas as examples:

Separations

To grow, all people must separate from others and from situations. Children deal with separations every day and will deal with them for the rest of their lives. To develop a theme on separation, provide concrete activities that show children the difficulty and pain of separating, but also show the positive things that usually result from the separation, especially when proper nurturing and support is provided.

Science: Transplant shoots from a mature spider fern to show how they separate. Focus on the special care needed to help the shoot survive and grow. Chart the growth of the new shoots. Transplant one without fertilizer and water. Observe and chart what happens to it.

Cooking: Separate eggs and make something with the whites and a different dish with the yolks. Point out how one thing separated into parts can result in each part having very different but very wonderful qualities.

Literature: Read books about separation. "Hansel and Gretel" and many other fairy tales deal with separation. Create books about events that happened to you or to the children involving separation, such as getting lost but making a new friend in the process.

Fairness

Almost all children feel strongly that everyone should be treated equitably. They feel deeply hurt if they do not get their "fair share."

Math and Science: Strengthen counting skills by counting votes. Have children stand, at the same time, in one area of the room to have their vote counted for a particular choice, another area for the other choice, and a third area for undecided voters. This "forced choice" method eliminates the common problem of children voting for more than one choice. Use graphing to compare how many children voted for a particular choice or were undecided. Show fractions when food is divided up and simple division when toys are divided up. To assure that each child will get the same amount of an item, demonstrate weighing and measuring with a scale, ruler, unifix cubes, or a length of string.

Social/Cognitive: Discuss various ways of creating a list for the order in which children will take turns using a popular toy. Use some of the following ideas: alphabetical by first initial, picking names out of a hat, youngest first, tallest first, or rolling a die with the highest number going first. Ask children for their ideas. Vote on which idea is fairest and use the one that gets the most votes. Try the other ideas during the course of the next few days. Vote again after the children have seen all ideas in action.

Changes

Change is part of living and growing. Although often painful, changing means growing up. Examples of change are everywhere.

Cooking: List the qualities of uncooked eggs. Ask children to predict what they will look like when cooked various ways (fried, boiled). Cook them and observe changes as a result of heating. Eat them. Cook other foods that change when heated and compare them. Note that although eggs get harder when heated, vegetables get softer. Find out why.

Science: Show how water changes to its three states: solid (ice), liquid (water), and gas (steam). Talk about the unique and helpful properties at each state. Observe weather and track changes over a one-month period and record morning, midday, and afternoon temperatures each day. Discuss why these changes occur and the benefits and problems of the changes. Avoid unusual changes, like metamorphoses (tadpoles to frogs) as they are difficult for children (and adults) to understand and explain, or long-term changes (seasons and trees) which are difficult to observe.

Literature: Read *The Very Hungry Caterpillar*, by Eric Carle; *Changes, Changes*, by Pat Hutchins; *Love You Forever*, by Robert Munsch; and *Lifetimes*, by Bryan Mellonie.

Art: Let children experiment with mixing and changing colors. Provide a small plastic pitcher of water, clear plastic cups, eyedroppers, food coloring, and a basin to dump out cloudy water. Make available paper towels or watercolor paper to see how the colors change when dripped on the paper.

Consider other themes such as the following: Losing/Winning/Cooperating, Choosing and Making Decisions, Feeling Scared/Feeling Safe, and Angry Feelings and What to Do with Them.

Repeat or review the themes at various times during the year as issues arise in children's lives. If there is an unexpected event that is of high interest to the children—such as a sudden snowstorm or a child entering the hospital—cut short, delay, or run concurrently the theme you have been doing, to focus on this more important theme. Once the ideas and activities in a theme have become familiar to the children, integrate and use them throughout the year and at various times during the day. For example, have the children use the skills gained during the "Fairness" theme to solve daily conflicts.

Drawbacks of a theme-based curriculum are the following: It sets up a structure that can be artificial and arbitrary if not directly related to the needs and interests of the children; it may overload the children with more information than they can take in; the themes may never be referred to again after they have been used; the themes themselves may be trivial; and it can interfere with individualizing.

Teaching-Approach Curricula

The Creative Curriculum®

The Creative Curriculum is a teaching-approach curriculum, although activity ideas are also suggested. This curriculum revolves around the classroom environment. The curriculum focuses on eleven learning centers or interest areas, such as the block area, toys and games, art, sand and water, discovery, and so on. For each area there are guidelines for selecting and arranging equipment, examples of ways to interact with children to encourage meaningful play and learning, suggestions for setting reasonable limits, and many activity ideas. Themes can be used with this curriculum, or it can stand alone. The Creative Curriculum includes strategies for teaching content throughout the day and for teachers to respond to individual needs of children including those with challenging behaviors, special needs, and English-language learners. It incorporates an assessment system to help guide observations of children and plan for individual needs, with options for computer-based or online recording and reporting of children's progress.

Emergent Curriculum

"Emergent curriculum" is a teaching approach that encourages teachers to build curriculum ideas based on the emerging interests or needs of the children and sometimes the interests of the teacher, if appropriate. Other sources for curriculum ideas are "hot topics" in your community (pollution, a new animal at the zoo, a new building in town, and so on); other teachers or early childhood specialists; new or newly found books, tapes, or records; observations of people or places in the community; and unexpected events in the news. Curriculum ideas can change rapidly or last a long time, depending on the children's needs and interests.

Being keenly tuned in to the children's interests and concerns, and being flexible and responsive so you can act on those interests and concerns are all-important elements of emergent curriculum. Themes and projects are often used within emergent curriculum. An excellent illustration of this can be seen in the video, *Setting Sail* (Harvest Resources). The teachers observed that the children were playing out parts of the *Titanic* story during dramatic play. This happened before the movie was released; it came from a song and a book about the *Titanic*. The teachers then developed a long, complex project on the *Titanic* that included creating a model of the ship, reading various books, studying news articles about the recovery of the *Titanic*, and writing a letter to Robert Ballard, the adventurer who found the wreck of the *Titanic*. Important themes such as safety and danger, and lost and found were explored. A formal celebration marked the end of the project with children giving their families tours of their displayed work.

High/Scope

The High/Scope curriculum is also called the "cognitively oriented curriculum." Central to the High/Scope curriculum is that children need to be repeatedly exposed to fifty different key experiences. Some of these experiences are the following: classifying (such as separating jungle animal toys from forest animal toys), seriation (such as putting objects in order of shortest to tallest), spatial relationships (such as moving in a direction and describing if the movement was *to, from, into, toward, over, under,* or *away*), and time (such as drawing a picture of a past event and talking about it in the past tense).

This curriculum places a heavy emphasis on setting up an appropriate classroom environment, scheduling, and planning because most of the learning takes place through children choosing activities and doing them. The teacher assists children in their own learning but usually does not give direct instruction.

Another important part of the High/Scope curriculum is the idea of "Plan-Do-Review." Teachers help children plan what they will do; the children do it; and then, at some point afterward, the children review what they have done. For example, a child might decide she will play in the block area after circle time. When excused from circle, she will place her nametag on a hook below a picture of blocks. Later in the morning, in a small group, she will draw a picture of the block structure she made and tell the teacher and the other children about it.

Multiple Intelligences

Based on the theories of Howard Gardner, multiple intelligences is simply the idea that people have at least eight kinds of intelligence, all of equal value, and we all tend to be stronger in some than others. These include the following:

- Linguistic intelligence ("word smart")
- Logical-mathematical intelligence ("number/reasoning smart")
- Spatial intelligence ("picture smart")
- Bodily-kinesthetic intelligence ("body smart")
- Musical intelligence ("music smart")
- Interpersonal intelligence ("people smart")
- Intrapersonal intelligence ("self smart")
- Naturalist intelligence ("nature smart")

However, schools—particularly K–12 schools—tend to focus almost all teaching and learning activities on the first two of these intelligences. Although this is less true in early childhood programs, looking for multiple intelligences in our children helps us to see their strengths and potential more clearly. It also gives us ideas to present activities or teach concepts to meet a wider variety of learning styles.

The multiple intelligences concept is more commonly used to expand a curriculum than used as a stand-alone curriculum. It has been incorporated with Reggio Emilia and the Project Approach because of a natural fit; these approaches provide many opportunities for all the various intelligences of children to flourish.

The Project Approach

The Project Approach involves focusing at length on a specific topic that is well known and important to the children. Activities are developed based on discovering as much as possible about that topic. For example, in one school, the school bus was chosen as the focus because it was an object of fascination to the children and symbolized growing up. The children spent many weeks (unlike themes, project work units often last as long as six to seven weeks) discussing how to build a detailed school bus in the classroom, gathering materials, and building it. They used cardboard boxes, tinfoil, Styrofoam, paint, and so on. They interviewed the bus driver to obtain all the information they needed. When their bus started falling apart, repair crews fixed it. During this process, the teacher encouraged the development of reading (she read all the words that were found on an actual school bus), writing (the children made signs for the bus), social skills (the children took turns using popular tools), problem-solving skills (the children decided who would work on what part), and many more. Content areas (math, science, literacy, and so on) are integrated within and throughout the projects. Other project ideas that teachers have used successfully include the grocery store, ants, flowers, trucks, shoes, and bread.

Although the Project Approach does not directly address some of the important themes discussed previously (fairness, change, and so on), there is the potential for these to be a project topic or for the issues to emerge while working on a project. These themes can also be addressed during other parts of the day.

Reggio Emilia

Reggio Emilia, a town in north-central Italy, has been providing exceptional quality early childhood services to its families for more than fifty years. They have evolved a system that reflects the love of art in that community (and Italy) and combines in-depth projects that are highly creative and intellectually rigorous, beautiful environments and documentation of children's work, strong parent and community connections, and more. Each preschool has its own art teacher and a well-supplied art room. They believe that children have a "hundred languages" to express through various art media. The Reggio approach is a good example of just how wonderful an early childhood program can be when everything is done well and thoughtfully and there is great community support over time.

American educators have been particularly struck by the advanced artistic abilities of these young children, challenging our developmental expectations of what young children can do. As a result, many educators have begun to realize the tremendous impact of culture on children's development—in this case, a very rich and deep culture. American educators also have begun to realize that there is a place for teaching specific skills to children in early childhood classrooms, under certain conditions.

Much controversy surrounds the appropriateness of importing the Reggio Emilia approach to the United States. Most agree, however, that the spirit, intensity, commitment, and responsiveness to children and families that characterize the Reggio approach are the most important elements to import, but also the most difficult. The specifics of the approach, such as a focus on the visual arts, are easier to import, but result in a cultural mismatch. U.S. culture does not have that same advanced sense of aesthetics or attach as much importance to art, for example. American early childhood teachers can admire and learn much from Reggio Emilia, but we must be careful how we implement what we learn.

Vivian Gussin Paley's Approach

Over her many years as a kindergarten teacher, Vivian Gussin Paley developed and wrote eloquently about an approach that can be characterized as creating classrooms that are loving, inclusive, learning communities. Her approach has much in common with emergent curriculum as it involves carefully observing and understanding children and creating a curriculum that is responsive to them. Children create stories from dreams and events important to them and then they invite other children to act them out. These stories, over the course of the year, create connections among children and a unique community emerges. The teacher also develops stories—allegories that parallel the lives and issues of the classrooms. The teacher as an active learner and researcher is an important part of this approach. Several of her books deal with children with special needs and how she helped them become part of the classroom community through this approach. Critical thinking, play, literature, and creativity come together to create a challenging and full curriculum.

Resources

General

Bredekamp, S., and T. Rosegrant. 1992. *Reaching potentials: Appropriate curriculum and assessment for young children.* Vol. 1. Washington, D.C.: National Association for the Education of Young Children (NAEYC).

———. 1995. *Reaching potentials: Appropriate curriculum and assessment for young children.* Vol. 2. Washington, D.C.: NAEYC.

Curtis, D., and M. Carter. 1996. *Reflecting children's lives: A handbook for planning child-centered curriculum.* St. Paul: Redleaf Press.

Saracho, O. M., and B. Spodek. 2001. *Contemporary perspectives on early childhood curriculum.* Greenwich, Conn.: Information Age Publishing.

Schickedanz, J. A., M. L. Pergantis, J. Kanosky, A. Blaney, and J. Ottinger. 1997. *Curriculum in early childhood: A resource guide for preschool and kindergarten teachers.* Boston: Allyn & Bacon.

Seefeldt, C., ed. 1999. *The early childhood curriculum: Current findings in theory and practice.* 3d ed. New York: Teachers College Press.

Themes

Nunelley, J. C. 1990. Beyond turkeys, Santas, snowmen, and hearts: How to plan innovative curriculum themes. *Young Children* 46 (1): 24–29.

Web Sites

Animals and Occupations: Why Theme-Based Curricula Work by Sandra Rollins Hurley and Sally Blake
www.earlychildhood.com/Articles/index.cfm. Click on on Curriculum, then scroll down and click on article title.

Perpetual Preschool. Includes many ideas for themes and activities.
www.perpetualpreschool.com

Themes to Teach By by Renee Farrington
www.earlychildhood.com/Articles/index.cfm. Click on Curriculum, then scroll down and click on article title.

The Creative Curriculum®

Trister-Dodge, D. 2002. *The Creative Curriculum for preschool.* 4th ed. Washington, D.C.: Teaching Strategies, Inc.

Web Sites

The home page for the publisher of the Creative Curriculum www.teachingstrategies.com

Emergent Curriculum

Booth, C. 1997. The fiber project: One teacher's adventure toward emergent curriculum. *Young Children* 52 (5): 79–85.

Jones, E., and J. Nimmo. 1994. *Emergent curriculum.* Washington, D.C.: NAEYC.

Jones, E., K. Evans, and K. S. Renken. 2001. *The lively kindergarten: Emergent curriculum in action.* Washington, D.C.: NAEYC.

Pelo, A. 1997. Our school's not fair: A story about emergent curriculum. *Young Children* 52 (7): 57–61.

Schiller, M. 1995. An emergent art curriculum that fosters understanding. *Young Children* 50 (3): 33–38.

Workman, S., and M. C. Anziano. 1993. Curriculum webs: Weaving connections from children to teachers. *Young Children* 48 (2): 4–9.

Videos

Harvest Resources
P. O. Box 22106
Seattle, WA 98122-0106
www.ecetrainers.com
Setting Sail: An Emergent Curriculum Project, 19 min.
Thinking Big: Extending Emergent Curriculum Projects, 26 min.

Web Sites

A description of emergent curriculum
www.coopchild.org/emergent.htm

Multiple Intelligences

Carlisle, A. 2001. Using multiple intelligences theory to assess early childhood curricula. *Young Children* 56 (6): 77–83.

Chen, Jie-Qi, ed. 1998. *Project Spectrum: Early learning activities.* New York: Teachers College Press.

Gardner, H. 1993. *Multiple intelligences: The theory in practice.* New York: Basic Books.

———. 2000. *Intelligence reframed: Multiple intelligences for the 21st century.* New York: Basic Books.

Web Sites

Definition and explanation by Thomas Armstrong, Ph.D., author of numerous books and articles on the topic
www.thomasarmstrong.com/multiple_intelligences.htm

Developing Multiple Intelligences in Young Learners by Connie Hine
www.earlychildhood.com/Articles/index.cfm. Click on Multiple Intelligences, then scroll down and click on the article title.

Multiple Intelligences. Various resources. Early Childhood Educator's and Family Web Corner.
users.stargate.net/~cokids. Click on Teacher Pages then on Multiple Intelligences.

Multiple Intelligences from the American Education Network Corporation
www.aenc.org/KE-Intelligences.html

Multiple Ways of Knowing: Howard Gardner's Theory of Multiple Intelligences Extend and Enhance Student Learning by Marian Beckman www.earlychildhood.com/Articles/index.cfm. Click on Multiple Intelligences, then scroll down and click on the article title.

Project Approach

Helm, J., and L. Katz. 2001. *Young investigators: The Project Approach in the early years.* New York: Teachers College Press.

LeeKeenan, D., and C. P. Edwards. 1992. Using the Project Approach with toddlers. *Young Children* 47 (4): 31–35.

Web Sites

Issues in Selecting Topics for Projects by L. G. Katz and S. C. Chard. ERIC Digest. 1998. ericeece.org. Click on Publications, then on Digests, then on Title, then scroll down and click on the article title.

Project Approach in Early Childhood and Elementary Education home page www.project-approach.com

Project Approach. Various articles. Early Childhood Educator's and Family Web Corner. users.stargate.net/~cokids. Click on Teacher Pages then on Project Approach.

Videos

See Harvest Resources' videos under Emergent Curriculum on the previous page.

Teachers College Press
P. O. Box 20
Willliston, VT 05495-0020
www.tcpress.com
A Children's Journey: Investigating the Fire Truck, 25 min.

Reggio Emilia

Bredekamp, S. 1993. Reflections on Reggio Emilia. *Young Children* 49 (1): 13–17

Edwards, C. P., L. Gandini, and G. Forman. 1993. *The hundred languages of children: The Reggio Emilia approach to early childhood education.* Norwood, N.J.: Ablex.

Fraser, S., and C. Gestwiki. 2001. *Authentic childhood: Exploring Reggio Emilia in the classroom.* Clifton Park, N.Y.: Delmar Learning.

Gillespie, C. W. 2000. Six Head Start classrooms begin to explore the Reggio Emilia approach. *Young Children* 55 (1): 21

Project Zero and Reggio Children. 2001. *Making learning visible: Children as individual and group learners.* Reggio Emilia, Italy: Reggio Children.

Staley, L. 1998. Beginning to implement the Reggio philosophy. *Young Children* 53 (5): 20–25

Web Sites

ERIC-EECE. Clearinghouse on Elementary and Early Childhood Education. Reggio Emilia Resources. ericeece.org/reggio.html

Reggio Emilia: Some Lessons for U.S. Educators by R. S. New. ERIC Digest. 1993. ericeece.org. Click on Publications, then on Digests, then on Title, then scroll down and click on the article title.

Reflections and Impressions from Reggio Emilia: "It's Not about Art!" by Nancy B. Hertzog ecrp.uiuc.edu/v3n1/hertzog.html

Reggio Emilia. Various articles. Early Childhood Educator's and Family Web Corner users.stargate.net/~cokids. Click on Teacher Pages, then on Reggio Emilia.

The Reggio Emilia Approach. Reggio Emilia. Cyert Center for Early Education. Carnegie Mellon University. www.cmu.edu/cyert-center. Click on Reggio Emilia Approach on the side bar.

Vivian Gussin Paley's Approach

Hurwitz, S. 2001. The teacher who would be Vivian. *Young Children* 56 (5): 89–91.

Paley, V. G. 1991. *The boy who would be a helicopter.* Cambridge: Harvard University Press.

———. 1992. *You can't say you can't play.* Cambridge: Harvard University Press.

———. 1998. *The girl with the brown crayon.* Cambridge: Harvard University Press.

Wiltz, N. W., and G. G. Fein. 1996. Evolution of a narrative curriculum: The contributions of Vivian Gussin Paley. *Young Children* 51 (3): 61–68.

Videos

Ball State University and Indiana Center on Early Childhood Development available from NAEYC.
NAEYC
1509 16th Street, N.W.
Washington, DC 20036-1426
www.naeyc.org
Vivian Gussin Paley and The Boy Who Could Tell Stories, 30 min.

Prepackaged Curricula

Creative Discoveries
140 Union Street, Suite 310
Lynn, MA 01901
www.creativediscoverieskits.com

Early Beginnings Preschool Program
8536 B Cedarhome Drive
Stanwood, WA 98292
www.earlybeginnings.com

Early Start Preschool Curriculum (not affiliated with the federal Early Start Program)
P. O. Box 350187
Jacksonville, FL 32235
www.earlystartcurriculum.com

Funshine Express Early Learning Curriculum
1409 W. Villard Street
Dickinson, ND 58601
www.funshineexpress.com

High Reach Learning
P. O. Box 410647
Charlotte, NC 28241
www.highreach.com

3. Assessment and Accountability

Early childhood teachers working in all types of programs—from Head Start to private preschools—are under increasing pressure to be accountable. You are expected to show that your children are making progress, and that they are learning and growing. People want to know that they are getting something for their money, whether they pay through their tax dollars or directly from their purses. But even without this external pressure, good teachers want to track children's progress, to know each child's strengths and weaknesses so they can individualize, and to know if their teaching strategies are working. To do this, whether for accountability or not, requires some form of assessment.

Any assessment you use should be one part of a system, or cycle, of individualizing. The assessment provides the focus for the first parts of the cycle: observation and recording. It may also help you with the second part, which is analysis, or determining the meaning of what you observed and recorded. Are the behaviors or skills acceptable, excellent, or is there cause for concern? What are some reasons for the concern? This information is then used to set one or two goals for children. The goals become the basis for planning and implementing activities or actions to help children meet those goals. Then, observe again to see if your actions made a difference; if they helped children to reach those goals. The goals should be age and culturally appropriate for your group and include a range of broad abilities. They may include things such as, "In six months Makala will go from speaking two- or three-word sentences to five- or six-word sentences," or, "Jorge will learn to successfully enter into play with a group that is already playing."

The main differences among assessment tools are the criteria (or the items, which are usually in the form of questions) and their purposes. Some tools are designed to determine if children should be referred for more testing because they may have developmental delays (screening), while others are designed to help you plan instruction (curriculum-based checklists), and others are designed to compare children to their age-mates (norm-referenced, standardized tests).

The drive for accountability can sometimes result in practices that are not in agreement with good classroom assessment practices, as funders usually want quantifiable results from standardized tests on a narrow set of skills, while teachers want useful information about many aspects of their children's development. However, you can gather helpful information about children that also meets the need for accountability. It's not easy, but this should be your goal and you may have to advocate strongly for it.

Preventing Problems

● Be strong in your knowledge and belief that high-stakes testing of young children is wrong. High-stakes testing means that the results of an assessment are used to make lasting decisions about a child's placement or the fate of a program or a teacher. During the preschool years children are growing and changing so fast, and they can behave so differently in different situations or with different people, that assessment results are always questionable. However, you can and should be an advocate for appropriate uses of assessment results that will lead to children getting the kind of instruction and services that will help them grow to their full potential.

● Know some basic information about what makes a good or bad assessment or assessment process. A good assessment will match your goals for children and your curriculum. It will be valid—the developers will have done research to make sure that it measures what it is supposed to measure. It will also be reliable—the developers have done research to make sure that it *accurately* measures what it is supposed to measure.

● Know clearly the purpose of any assessment that you do and that it is appropriate for your purpose, then you can assure any concerned parents or others that it will be helpful and not harmful for children.

● Make sure that any assessment tool you have been asked to use is administered by observing children in natural, normal situations. These include routines (such as meals, transitions, washing hands, arrival), play (such as dramatic play, outdoor/gym play, doing puzzles, building with blocks), and typical interactions (negotiating a turn, singing with a group, listening to a story, asking for something from you). Assessments that require direct questioning of children in isolation or asking them to perform unusual or unfamiliar tasks will not give valid results.

- Check that language items are assessed in a child's first, strongest language by a native speaker of that language (unless it is an assessment for the particular purpose of determining a child's English-language abilities).

- Make sure the items apply to your particular children and your teaching approach. All assessments have a cultural bias—they reflect a particular culture, its knowledge base, and its values. Children should not be viewed as incapable because they lack the experiences of the dominant culture. For example, four-year-old children in the inner city may not know what a "lake" is, while rural children may not know what a "curb" is. In your teaching, you may spend a great deal of time promoting creative expression, problem-solving skills, kindness to others, respect for the environment, and appreciation of differences. However, many assessment tools do not measure such things. Even if your children may do fine on such assessments, they will fail to capture children's abilities and progress on many very important skills and fail to give an accurate picture of your classroom.

- Be proactive in informing parents about any assessment you will be doing with their children. Early in the year, share with parents the assessment tool and review some of the items and how you evaluate them. Tell them the purpose of the assessment and how the results will be used. Explain when and how often you will share the results with them.

- Know the strengths and limitations of any assessment you use; all assessments have both. Also know how to use it well. Any assessment tool requires extensive training, ongoing support, and access to a user's manual. A great deal of practice is necessary to use an assessment accurately, so it doesn't take too much time to administer. Ask for a year to "field-test" any new tool, which is a reasonable amount of time to gain accountability for using it fully and accurately. Most teachers don't feel fully capable with an assessment system until they have used it for two years.

- Get help from someone with expertise in assessment, but who also understands the particular needs and development of young children. Make sure this person can help you protect your children from harmful assessment practices due to accountability expectations and help you institute positive, helpful practices.

Dealing with Existing Problems

Inappropriate Assessment Tools

If you have been mandated to use a particular assessment or system that you think is not a good one, try some of these ideas:

- Gather additional information about skills and abilities that you believe are important but not measured by the assessment. If possible, use the same format as the mandated assessment to gather this information.

- If the mandated assessment only asks for a number rating on items, write down some anecdotal information, from observations of your children, related to the items (as well as to any additional items you think are important but are not on the assessment). This will give you a fuller picture of the child and information useful for planning.

- Try to find another assessment tool or system that will provide information similar to the mandated assessment but that is better suited to your children and your needs. Request that this more appropriate assessment be used instead.

- Minimize the importance of the assessment by showing evidence of learning and growth through a variety of ways. Over time, keep examples of children's artwork and writing, audio and video recordings, photos, stories of their activities, quotes of things they say, and more on a wide variety of abilities, knowledge, and dispositions. Share this information too when asked to reveal the assessment results.

Assessing Valid Skills

Resist feeling pressure to teach to the test (sometimes teachers impose this on themselves). Some tests, like screening tests, have items that are indicators of skills or knowledge and are not important skills to know specifically. For example, many such tests ask children to copy designs or stack small blocks. These items are assessing various small-motor and eye-hand coordination skills. These skills are best developed when children are engaged in similar activities that have meaning for them, where they have some choice (in play situations), and as part of everyday routines (pouring juice, for example). This way they are motivated to learn and are not put under pressure to perform. Having children practice the actual items on the test can lead to a boring and stressful curriculum. Teaching to the test also can lead teachers to try to break down their teaching into discrete, isolated subskills that can make their classrooms very alien to young children. If you teach to a high level and provide engaging activities (projects around children's interests) with opportunities for children to learn a variety of specific skills within those activities, children will learn very well the type of basic skills that are assessed on tests.

● Assessing certain items naturally through observations can sometimes be difficult. For example, some assessments ask if a child can seriate (put things in some order such as by shortest to tallest, largest to smallest, or lightest to darkest). It may be difficult to see children do this naturally in play. However, you can find or create materials or simple games that will lead children to do such an activity. Cut cardboard paper towel tubes in various lengths and place them in a container that will hold them upright. Or put twelve small rocks of various sizes or colors in an empty egg carton. If some children do not seriate on their own when given access, you can provide some playful guidance through strategies, such as asking, "I have put these rocks in a certain order, could you figure out what it is? Can you put them in a different order and see if I can guess?" At first, they may need assistance seriating; start from the left and move to the right, and/or from top to bottom.

● If you have some children who can do all or most items easily or some who cannot do many of the items, then the assessment does not have a broad enough range nor is it an appropriate tool for your group. If children start out by doing very well on the assessment, it is not sufficiently challenging to show growth and progress over the year. This is referred to as a "low ceiling." The items may be too easy and may need to be more difficult (such as addition up through twenty rather than ten) or categories of challenging items may not be included (such as early writing or reading ability, representational drawing, or solving conflicts fairly and independently). If children cannot answer most of the questions, then the "floor" is too high. It does not show you what children are capable of doing so you can build on their current strengths and abilities and set appropriate goals. Most assessments describe the age range for which they are designed. A range from 2.5 to 6 is typical and sufficient for most preschool groups. However, if you have some children with special needs, delays, or gifts, you will likely need an assessment with a broader range.

Talking with Parents

● Parents or others may ask you to tell them how well their children are doing compared to others in your group or program, or nationally. This drive to compare is fueled daily by the media. The most appropriate assessments for young children do not provide this type of information nor have it as their purpose. If it is collected, however, ask your supervisor *not* to give you access to the information, except for screening results, which usually put all children into one of two very broad categories: "refer for further evaluation" or "do not refer." Because screenings are made to be done quickly, they are not refined enough to make comparisons among children in any other way.

● Parents do, of course, have the right to full access to any assessment information on their children, but it may be helpful to everyone if the results from norm-referenced tests are given to parents by a supervisor or evaluation specialist, moving it away from the classroom level. Help parents understand the various kinds of assessments and their purposes. Parents appreciate hearing about their children in detail on a range of abilities—including social skills, creative and critical thinking, problem solving, and dispositions—along with the more typical, academic abilities. When given a rich story about their child and her progress, and the opportunity to see various examples of their child's work over time, parents often feel less need to make comparisons.

Resources

Bergan, J. R., and J. K. Feld. 1993. Developmental assessment: New directions. *Young Children* 48 (5): 41–47.

Curtis, D., and M. Carter. 2000. *The art of awareness: How observation can transform your teaching.* St. Paul: Redleaf Press.

Gronlund, G. 1998. Portfolios as an assessment tool: Is collection of work enough? *Young Children* 53 (3): 4–10.

Hemmeter, M. L., K. L. Maxwell, M. J. Ault, and J. W. Schuster. 2001. *Assessment of practices in early elementary classrooms (APEEC).* New York: Teachers College Press.

Hills, T. W. 1993. Assessment in context—Teachers and children at work. *Young Children* 48 (5): 20–28.

Leavitt, R. L., and B. K. Eheart. 1991. Assessment in early childhood programs. *Young Children* 46 (5): 4–9.

Lowenthal, B. 1997. Useful early childhood assessment: Play-based, interviews, and multiple intelligences. *Early Childhood Development and Care* 129: 43–49.

MacDonald, S. 1997. *Portfolio and its uses: A road map to assessment.* Little Rock, Ark.: SECA

Mindes, G., H. Ireton, and C. Mardell-Czudnowski. 1996. *Assessing young children.* Albany, N.Y.: Delmar Publishers.

Schweinhart, L. J. 1993. Observing young children in action: The key to early childhood assessment. *Young Children* 48 (5): 29–33.

Web Sites

Assessment. Numerous resources. Early Childhood Educator's and Family Web Corner.
users.stargate.net/~cokids. Click on Teacher Pages then on Assessment.

Assessment, Portfolios, and Observation. Various articles. Earlychildhood.com.
www.earlychildhood.com/Articles/index.cfm. Click on Assessment, Portfolios, and Observation.

Fighting the Tests: A Practical Guide to Rescuing Our Schools by Alfie Kohn
www.alfiekohn.org/teaching/ftt.htm

A Developmental Approach to Assessment of Young Children by Lilian Katz. Eric Digest. 1997.
ericeece.org. Click on Publications, then on Digests, then on Title, then scroll down and click on the article title.

Assessment Issues in Early Childhood Special Education. ERIC Clearinghouse on Disabilities and Gifted Education. ericec.org. Click on Frequently Asked Questions (FAQs), then scroll down and click on article title (under Early Childhood).

Issues of Assessment in Testing Children under Age Eight by Gwen G. Stevens and Karen DeBord. 2001.
www.ces.ncsu.edu/depts/fcs/pub/2001sp/stevens.html

Guidelines for Appropriate Curriculum Content and Assessment in Programs Serving Children Ages 3 through 8. NAEYC Position Statement. 1990.
www.naeyc.org. Click on NAEYC Resources, then on Position Statements, then on Improving practices with children, then scroll down and click on the article title.

New Assessment: Early Childhood Resources. University of New Mexico.
www.newassessment.org

The Portfolio and Its Use: Developmentally Appropriate Assessment of Young Children by Cathy Grace. 1992.
ericeece.org. Click on Publications, then on Digests, then on Title, then scroll down and click on the article title.

Portfolio Assessment. Links to resources and to ideas from teachers.
www.perpetualpreschool.com/portfolio_assessment.htm

Standardized Testing of Young Children 3 through 8 Years of Age. NAEYC Position Statement. 1987.
www.naeyc.org. Click on NAEYC Resources, then on Position Statements, then on Improving practices with children, then scroll down and click on the article title.

Trends in Early Childhood Assessment Policies and Practices by Lorrie A. Shepard, Grace Taylor, and Sharon L. Kagan. 1996.
www.negp.gov/Reports/ecms2.pdf

Selected Child Assessments (Curriculum-Based, Criterion-Referenced, and Standardized)

Creative Curriculum Assessment
Teaching Strategies Inc.
P. O. Box 42243
Washington, DC 20015
teachingstrategies.com

High/Scope Child Observation Record (COR) for Ages 2½ to 6
High/Scope Educational Research Foundation
600 N. River Street
Ypsilanti, MI 48198-2898
www.highscope.org/Assessment/cor.htm

Focused Portfolios™
Focused Portfolios™: A Complete Assessment for the Young Child
by Gaye Gronlund and Bev Engel
www.focusedportfolios.com
Redleaf Press
450 N. Syndicate, Suite 5
St. Paul, MN 55104

Oregon Assessment for Children 3–5 in Developmentally Appropriate Classrooms
Early Childhood Training Center/Portland State University
P. O. Box 1491
Portland, OR 97207
www.ectc.pdx.edu

The Work Sampling System
Pearson Early Learning
P. O. Box 2500
135 South Mt. Zion Road
Lebanon, IN 46052
www.pearsonearlylearning.com

Also:

Performance Assessment in Early Childhood Education: The Work Sampling System by Samuel J. Meisels. ERIC Digest. 1995.
ericeece.org. Click on Publications, then on Digests, then on Title, then scroll down and click on the article title.

4. Individualizing ————

Individualizing means your schedule suits each child's needs for action and rest. It means that the equipment, materials, and layout of your classroom enhance the growth of every child and that the activities you choose are good ones for each child. It also means that the way you present the activities makes each child feel successful but challenged. Is this possible? Well, probably not for every child at all times, but you can do a great deal to move closer toward that goal. You can do this by thorough planning and by observing children carefully during an activity so you can change and adapt your curriculum.

Individualizing is an important goal to work toward because the more you individualize, the smoother your classroom will run. Behavior problems will decrease and the amount of learning and growth will increase.

Preventing Problems

● Know as much as you can about your children's lives. How many brothers and sisters do they have and how old are they? What are each family's primary values? What does each family do for fun? Conduct home visits for each child, if at all possible. This will give you the greatest insight into their lives.

● Ask each parent at least these essential questions: What do I need to know about your child to be a good teacher for him? What are your child's interests, strengths, and unique characteristics? Which five adjectives best describe your child?

● Know your children's abilities well through assessing them, talking with parents, and observing children in action. Jot down notes about the children's strengths and weaknesses and keep your observations on file. Refer to the file at least weekly to refresh your memory about particular children, especially when you are planning. This will help you maintain realistic expectations about what each child can and cannot do. A more formal assessment system is discussed in the previous chapter, "Assessment and Accountability."

● Prepare for the unexpected. Assume that any given activity might not be successful, at least with some children, and plan for alternative ways of doing it or an alternative activity.

● Do all you can to get good volunteer help from the community, from parents, or wherever possible. Individualizing can be done much more effectively in small groups or one-on-one. Spend time informing your volunteers of what they can expect from particular children and train these volunteers to work effectively with those children.

● If you cannot get extra help, do activities in small groups while the rest of the children are doing free choice activities. If you have only one aide, divide the large group of children into two smaller groups. Each child can have much more individual attention and many more chances to talk in a small group.

● Individualize during free choice, which should last at least forty-five minutes. Move around the classroom and observe each child at play. Ask questions or begin a conversation that will extend the child's thinking or creativity, or help him do the activity at a more advanced level, if it will not interfere with his play. You might say, "Tell me about the picture you are painting."

● Add new equipment or materials to make the child's play more challenging or more fun. For instance, you might put out pieces of garden hose when the children start playing firefighter.

● Help the children solve any problems they may be having by asking questions and by having them generate solutions: "How can you get Sara to give you a turn with the puzzle without hurting her?"

● Provide a wide variety of equipment and materials. Have some simple three-piece puzzles as well as more difficult ones. Have some lightweight, easy-to-ride trikes as well as two-wheel scooters or small bikes, some with training wheels.

Planning for Individual Needs

● When you are planning, meet with as many members of your teaching team as possible, including volunteers. By doing this, everyone will have a good sense of what you hope to achieve through your activities and how you hope to achieve your expectations for each child. They also can provide additional ideas for ways to individualize.

● Develop a systematic way of planning for individual needs. If you plan an activity designed to be responsive to the needs and interests of one or two specific children each day, you will provide an individualized activity for each child in your group once or twice per month. Keep a checklist with the names of each child in your group, and the month and year at the top, to make sure that each child received at least one such activity every month.

● Review the activities of the previous week before you plan. Determine what was successful, what was not, and why. Pay particular attention to the children who have special needs and review what worked well for them and what did not. Use what you know to plan for successful experiences for those children.

● Consider that a great deal of important individualizing can happen only when you make it part of your planning. For example, you decide to plan an activity with small groups of children during which they will take turns following verbal directions, such as, "Please put the red block underneath the chair." During your planning you realize that several children will find this direction easy and can be given more complicated directions, such as, "Please put the blue block on the chair and the yellow block behind the chair." But some children will need simpler directions, such as, "Please put a block on the chair." Individualizing like this may require you to gather more or different materials for the activity ahead of time so that you are not limited in the ways you can individualize during the activity.

● As you plan such a verbal-direction activity, or any activity, go through your list of children and pay particular attention to those with special needs. This will help you get a good idea of how to individualize this activity. For example, you may realize that one or two children will have trouble waiting for a turn. Several options to deal with this are possible:

▸ Allow these children to have their turns early and then move on to another activity shortly after their turn.

▸ Do the activity with half the group while another adult does the activity with the other half in another room.

▸ Actively involve the children more, especially the ones you are concerned about. Let them take turns being the "teacher" and giving out the directions.

▸ Make the activity more physically active. You might say, "Hop to the chair and put the red block on it."

▸ Do the verbal-direction activity with children during a time other than group time, especially if it can be done as part of a real activity. For example, during free choice ask individual children to help set the table for a snack. Give them commands related to setting up the snack: "Please put the blue bowl in the center of the round table."

▸ Plan this activity so that it will relate directly to your particular children. The result, written on an index card or planning form, might look something like the following:

Small Group

Directions Game with Blocks and Chair

Me: Tiger group
Aide: Lion group in room 2
Mike and Jessica: Do puzzles if restless and help set snack later
Celia: Harder (three directions)
Debbie and Anthony: Easier
Jason: Sit by the teacher and hold the blocks

Individualizing on the Spot

● Because you will not be able to think of all the possible needs for all your children, you will have to observe them carefully during an activity. If many of the children are restless or bored, change your activity. Do something else or change the way you are doing the activity. Make it simpler, quicker, or involve the children more actively. If one or two children are restless or bored, give them something specific to do or to hold. If that is not successful, let them do a different activity that will not be disruptive.

● If a child is having a difficult time accomplishing the activity you planned, modify it for him or give extra help, unless this will cause embarrassment. Ask the child first if he wants help and give some choices: "Pouring juice is difficult. Would you like to pour from a smaller pitcher, wait until there is a smaller amount left, or ask a friend to do it for you?" Give encouragement to the child for what he can do. If he decides to wait, you might say, "You really have a lot of patience waiting for the juice pitcher to come back to you."

● Avoid highlighting a child's problem. If a child with gross-motor difficulties cannot do jumping jacks as well as the other children, ignore the differences, tell him about the abilities he does have, and provide help at a later time when you can be with the child privately. This will prevent him from feeling different and less able than other children. It also will enable you to provide direct and effective help.

● If a child can do your planned activity quickly and easily, add a challenge to the activity. For example, you discover during a cooking project that a child knows how to measure half a cup. For the next ingredient have him measure out one-fourth of a cup. If he has some trouble, talk him through this process. "One quarter is a half of a half. Can you find the line on the cup that is halfway between the bottom and the one-half line?"

● A great way to individualize on the spot is to include something specific and unique about each child during an activity. It could simply entail short statements such as, "It's Rafael's turn and he is waiting so patiently," or, "Sierra, your mother is coming home from her trip tonight. You must be very excited," or, "Look at DJ's picture. It has so much detail and such bright colors," or, "I don't know how to tell the difference between a seal and sea lion, so let's ask Kelly to ask her dad, as he is a marine biologist."

Individualizing the Physical Environment

The way you set up the classroom last year might have worked well for that group, but several children in your group this year wander about the room, are easily distracted, and do not settle into an activity. Use some of the following ideas to alter the physical environment to help those children and to benefit the other children as well.

● Provide at least one private, quiet space such as a refrigerator box with soft cushions inside.

● Create spaces and places suitable for various numbers of children. You can have a sand tray with small figures in it for a one-person activity, a small table for two with simple board games to choose from, a book-making area for three children, and so forth.

● Define the learning centers and other areas in your room clearly. Put up dividers or tape on the floor around the areas.

● Make a planning board for each area, where children can place their nametags after they have decided where they will play. Ask them to tell you their plans.

● Limit the busy-ness of the room. Cover storage areas; have a few large, soothing posters rather than many small, brightly colored pictures; take down mobiles; organize and label all shelves and counters.

Individualizing Your Daily Schedule

● You also may need to revise your schedule for your particular group of children this year. Several children may tire easily or have short attention spans. You will have to shorten group times; lengthen free choice time; and perhaps add an additional, short rest time.

● Several children in the same group, however, may have high cognitive abilities. Use the increased free choice time to provide challenging activities for these children. Invite them to do silent reading or writing (to the best of their ability) during the additional rest time, if they are not tired.

● You probably will need to revise your schedule one or more times during the year as the children change and grow and their behaviors are impacted by the seasons.

Resources

Cassidy, D., and C. Lancaster. 1993. The grassroots curriculum: A dialogue between children and teachers. *Young Children* 48 (6): 47–51.

Ferguson, C. 2001. Discovering, supporting, and promoting young children's passions and interests: One teacher's reflections. *Young Children* 56 (4): 6–11.

Hatch, T. 1990. Looking at Hank, looking at Ira: Looking at individual four-year-olds especially their leadership styles. *Young Children* 45 (5): 11–17.

McCormick, L., and S. Feeney. 1995. Modifying and expanding activities for children with disabilities. *Young Children* 50 (4): 10–17.

Walker, B., N. L. Hafenstein and L. Crow-Enslow. 1999. Meeting the needs of gifted learners in the early childhood classroom. *Young Children* 54 (1): 32–36.

Web Sites

Individualizing for Young Children. Child Care Plus Newsletter. www.ccplus.org/listof.htm Scroll down and click on article title (back issue 8.1)

Individualizing: A Plan for Success. Head Start Training Guide. www.headstartinfo.org. Click on Publications, then on Head Start Publications Online, then on National Training Guides, then click on the title.

5. Teaching Mixed-Age Groups

It is becoming increasingly common for early childhood educators to teach and care for a group of children whose ages range several years or more. Sometimes this is done just for expediency but it can have many benefits for children and teachers. There are some challenges, particularly if you have not worked with children who are younger (or older) before. However, after an adjustment period, most teachers find it so rewarding that they are reluctant to teach single-age groups again. Among the rewards are being with children over an extended period and helping them grow from being the "baby" of the group to a leader who the "babies" look up to. Siblings can be together, in some cases, adding to more of a family atmosphere than with single-age groups. A great deal of time and effort is saved by not teaching classroom rules and expectations to an entirely new group of children at the beginning of the year. Younger children gain advantages by engaging in more complex play and activities than they would on their own in a single-age group.

Preventing Problems

● Make sure that the age range is not too large. Infants and toddlers do not mix well with preschoolers, unless the group size is very small. There are basic safety concerns and it is too difficult to meet the needs of children across such a range. They need different types of materials and equipment, management strategies, and schedules.

● Have a written statement and know the compelling reasons why mixed-age groups are beneficial to children. Research indicates that older children are not disadvantaged in any way by being with younger children and younger children do better than children in single-age group classrooms. Children in mixed-age classrooms like school, themselves, and other children better than children in single-age classrooms. And children in mixed-age groups seem to be more empathetic and have more advanced social skills (Chase and Doan 1994; Mason and Burns 1966; Veenman 1996).

● Ask for the support you need to be effective with a mixed-age group, especially when starting. This may include training, purchasing new materials and equipment, extra planning time, time to observe an experienced teacher with a mixed-age group, and being observed and getting feedback from an experienced coach.

● Make the differences in abilities and skills among children work for you. Encourage children to help each other—ask older children to assist younger ones and younger ones to ask for assistance from older children. Have older children "read" to younger ones.

● Have an efficient, workable system for observing and assessing children, as the range of needs will be great. The assessment tool needs to be carefully selected to apply to a very wide age range, or you may need to use more than one tool. To meet the range of needs requires systematic, ongoing observations and planning.

Dealing with Existing Problems

● Some older children enjoy helping younger ones too much, speaking for them, and dominating them in various ways. On the other hand, some young children can be unreasonably demanding on older children. Teach younger children to seek help or attention from older children appropriately ("Wait until he stops talking and then use your words; you may need to wait awhile") and teach older children how to help without doing too much ("Show Lisa where the puzzle piece goes, don't do it for her"). Teach older children how to keep younger children from being too bothersome ("I can help you in a little bit, but not right now") and younger children to seek help from a variety of people. Teach younger children how to enter and take a role in the more complex play of older children and teach older children to include younger children in their play by helping them find an acceptable role. Make sure that the "acceptable" role is not always the dog or the baby or some other passive, subservient role. Do not allow exclusions from any play activity because of age (or any other reason), unless it is clearly an issue of safety.

● If an older child gives wrong or unhelpful information to a younger one, use it as an opportunity to teach both children the acceptable information or behavior. If it is a deliberate act of meanness on the part of the older child, treat it as you would any other aggressive behavior. Remind the older child of your classroom rule about being kind and respectful to everyone, have him make amends appropriate to the

problem ("Tell Jamie the correct rule for riding safely"), and give assistance to the victim ("Ask someone else for help next time"). More ideas are included in part V of this book.

● Age bias is common among children. That is, older children sometimes tease or bully younger ones. One great benefit of mixed-age grouping is the potential to counteract such bias. It does require effort and being proactive about it. Be clear that age bias is unacceptable just like any other type of biased or mean behavior. A strong classroom-wide focus on being kind and helpful to others through adult modeling and teaching positive ways to get needs met, helps to reduce age bias a great deal. The ideas above for not allowing exclusions and for helping older children find acceptable roles for younger children will also help.

● Younger children in mixed-age groups can feel overwhelmed and therefore may not fully participate in activities. They may feel inadequate or feel intimidated by the behaviors of older children. If a younger child is passively watching and it doesn't happen often or for long periods, it may be a healthy behavior through which he is learning how older children act. If it happens too often, be a mediator for awhile, helping the younger child find a role in the activity that he is comfortable with and helping the older children incorporate him into the activity so as not to be a problem. In addition have ample activities and materials that appeal to both younger and older children, so that there are many choices for each.

● If you are finding it difficult to meet individual needs across such a wide age/developmental range, try some of the following ideas:

 ▶ Seek extra volunteer help from parents or community agencies.

 ▶ Obtain more materials that are both easier and more challenging.

 ▶ Rework your daily schedule. This may mean more or less time spent on a particular part of the day (large motor, free choice, and so forth) or just a reordering.

 ▶ Allow more time for planning, taking into consideration the various and particular needs of individual children. Focus at first on the few children who seem to be having the most difficulty. See the previous chapter on individualizing for ideas.

 ▶ Develop an organized system for individualizing so that once or twice per month you plan and initiate an activity that is designed for each individual child in your class. They may be simple activities and involve a number of children, but they are built around the interests, needs, and learning style of one particular child. If you target one or two children per day, you will get to each child once or twice each month. Within a few months you will notice a difference in children's behaviors and the class will run smoother.

Resources

Chase, P., and J. Doan. 1994. *Full circle: A new look at multi-age education.* Portsmouth, N.H.: Heinemann Publishers.

Katz, L. G., D. Evangelou, and J. A. Hartman. 1990. *The case for mixed-age grouping in early education.* Washington, D.C.: NAEYC.

Mason, D. A., and R. B. Burns. 1966. Simply no worse or no better may simply be wrong: A critique of Veenmans' conclusion about multi-grade classes. *Review of Educational Research* 66 (3): 307–22.

Miller, B. 2001. *Children at the center: Implementing the mulitage classroom.* ERIC Clearinghouse for Educational Management,.

Paley, V. G. 1992. *You can't say you can't play.* Cambridge: Harvard University Press.

Theilheimer, R. 1993. Something for everyone: Benefits of mixed-age group for children, parents, and teachers. *Young Children* 48 (5): 82–87.

Veenman, S. 1996. Effects of multi-grade and multi-age classes reconsidered. *Review of Educational Research* 66 (3): 323–40.

Web Sites

The Benefits of Mixed-Age Grouping by Lilian Katz. ERIC Digest. 1995.
ericeece.org. Click on Publications, then on Digests, then on Title, then scroll down and click on the article title.

Caring for Multi-Age Groups by Lesia Oesterreich. National Network for Child Care.
www.nncc.org. Click on Search, then enter "multi-age" in the search box, scroll down and click on article title.

Mixed-Age Grouping: What Does the Research Say, and How Can Parents Use This Information? by Debbie Reese. 1998.
npin.org. Click on Parent News, then on 1998, then on May 1998, then click on article title.

Multi-Age Links from Multiage-Education.com
www.multiage-education.com/multiagelinks

Non-Graded and Mixed-Age Groupings in Early Childhood by Lilian Katz. ERIC Digest. 1992.
ericeece.org. Click on Publications, then on Digests, then on Title, then scroll down and click on the article title.

6. Field Trips Are Supposed to Be Fun

Field trips are an extremely important part of a program for young children. Although they can be costly and stressful, they are worth the effort because children get to see, smell, and touch firsthand the world around them (which is the way they learn best). After a field trip, children enjoy re-creating what they experienced when they return to the classroom. After a field trip to a city harbor, the children in one class made elaborate ships and docks with blocks, drew pictures of boats, and acted out riding on a ship for several weeks. A display or book of photographs from the trip, captioned with children's comments and memories, help extend the educational value and enjoyment of the trip. Providing opportunities for children to see and experience something new, followed by time to re-create it through play and art, is a powerful way to help children learn and grow.

If at all possible, plan one or more field trips a month. A field trip does not have to be very elaborate or go to an unusual place. You can show the children a new aspect of something familiar. A trip to a popular local restaurant where the children can see how the food is prepared and ask questions of the cook can be very rewarding. This can then provide the basis for some great play situations back in the dramatic play area, especially if you provide some playdough to "cook" with and paper and pens to make menus and take orders.

Preventing Problems

● Before a field trip, get parent permission forms signed and place large notices to remind parents of the trip.

● To allow time for preparation, arrange the field trip early in the week, but not the first day back after a weekend. Children are often more attentive early in the week, so take your field trip then. During the rest of the week you can provide activities in which the children play, talk about, and draw what they have experienced on their trip.

● Carefully scout out and plan your trip. Visit the place yourself before the trip so you will experience no unpleasant surprises. Make sure there are things to see and do that will hold the children's attention and interest. Places such as museums, which do not allow touching, will be frustrating for them. Request that the guide have some experience with young children. If no one is available, gather some basic information and do the tour yourself.

● Keep the trip short and simple. Avoid the temptation to visit several different places on the same day because they are near each other. Visit only two or three rooms of a large museum or only two sections of the zoo. Overstimulation caused by doing and seeing too much will make the children crabby and tired. If the field trip will be a long one, plan for at least one unstructured time when the children can freely play at a nearby park, playground, or gym.

● Before going, tell the children a little of what they can expect to see on the field trip. If possible, show some pictures of the place. Read a book and sing songs related to the trip. For example, you might sing "Johnny Works with One Hammer" and read *In Christina's Tool Box* (Homan 1981) before a trip to a hardware store.

● Set one or two rules for safety, such as "Walk at all times" and "Stay with the class." Ask the children to repeat the rules. If necessary, practice them by taking a short walk before the field trip. Set any special rules needed for a particular trip, such as "Stay back from the water."

● Put a button or tag on each child with the name and phone number of your center/school on it in case a child gets lost. Consider dividing the class into two smaller groups for a field trip. Line up extra help from responsible adults such as parents, your supervisor, or volunteers. Assign several children to each adult. The adult will then be responsible for those children throughout the trip. Ask for a "head count" from each adult about once an hour to make sure all the children are accounted for. Make sure each child has a partner with whom she will stay during the entire field trip.

● Consider using a long loop of rope with knots tied along it when walking on a field trip. Have each child hold onto a knot and one adult hold the front while another adult holds the back. Control the length of the rope, the spacing of the knots (so that children don't step on another's heels), and the walking pace. This provides the group control you need for safety while giving children some responsibility and autonomy.

- Bring along snacks and plenty of water, especially on hot days. Build time into your field trip schedule to allow for food or drink breaks. When children are hungry or thirsty, they learn little from a trip and may misbehave.

- Take along a first-aid kit and emergency numbers for each child, as well as tissues and some extra clothes.

- Record your field trip with photos and make a book of each one. Write text based on the children's descriptions and memories. Digital photos allow the possibility of putting your field trip stories on the Web or on CD-ROMs.

Dealing with Existing Problems

Active, Overly Excited, Unruly Group

- Start the year out with short, simple, nearby field trips. Get as many adults as possible to help. As the children gain skills and learn rules for field trips, increase the length and complexity of the trips.

- If the children become difficult to manage during a trip, consider cutting the trip short if possible. If transportation problems do not allow this, change your plans and walk to a nearby park or playground.

- If only one child typically makes your trips unpleasant and difficult, assign an adult to be with just that one child during the trip. As a last resort, consider leaving this child with another class for the day or making a similar arrangement. In any case, don't deprive the majority of your children the value of field trips because of one difficult child.

No Transportation or Budget for Field Trips

- Provide the valuable experiences gained from field trips by visiting nearby stores, businesses, services, and agencies. The special attention the children can get from an owner or worker and the "behind the scenes" look provide a very different experience from the one they get when they go to these same places with their parents as consumers. Visit some of the following places on your neighborhood trips: library, post office, fire station, police station, telephone company, newspaper publisher, office building, hospital, doctor, veterinarian, dentist, optometrist, other schools, lumberyard, florist, hardware store, auto dealership, repair shop, photographer's studio, radio station, recycling center, teachers' homes, motel, restaurant, construction site, bank, supermarket, service station, pet store, scrap yard, and carpenter's shop.

- Prepare children to look for certain items by giving them a set of pictures to match to things they will see on the trip. Encourage them to check off the picture when they see it. They will feel very grown-up carrying clipboards, pencils, and checklists, and you will provide a focus and a sense of purpose for them. Challenge them cognitively by asking them to look for some things they might not usually notice. Enhance their social and language skills by having two children work together on one list. This is a good way to make a familiar trip a unique experience.

- Take a walk around the neighborhood or to a nearby park as another alternative to an elaborate trip. A walk can have a particular theme or purpose and a great deal of spontaneous learning can happen. On your neighborhood walk, look for and identify or collect (if appropriate) items such as the following: leaves of various kinds, grasses and weeds, wildflowers, insects, animals, trees, colors, shapes, litter to recycle, simple architectural features (columns, steps, arches), working people, and smells. Note that the clipboard idea can work well for neighborhood walks when looking for items that cannot be collected. With this activity you will enhance the important cognitive skill of classification, especially if you are creating unique categories such as smells: sweet smells (candy store), polluting smells (cigarette smoke), food smells (deli), strong smells (gasoline). Remember that the younger the children, the simpler and more concrete the categories should be. When you are back in the classroom, discuss, sort, and graph what the children saw or collected.

- Make inexpensive clipboards by stapling paper to a stiff piece of cardboard and attaching a string with a pencil on the end of it. Store the pencil on the cardboard by gluing a small piece of Velcro on the pencil and by stapling the corresponding Velcro piece to the top of the board.

Resources

Homan, D. *In Christina's Tool Box*. Durham, N.C.: Lollipop Power.

Redleaf, R. 1997. *Open the door, let's explore more: Field trips of discovery for young children*. St. Paul: Redleaf Press.

Spears, J. 2000. *Field trip theme-a-saurus: The great big book of field trips with extended classroom activities*. Redding, Calif.: Totline.

Field trip ideas from various sources
www.preschoolbystormie.com/fieldtrips.htm

How to Plan a Field Trip. About Daycare.com.
daycare.about.com. Enter "plan a field trip" in the search box,
then click on article title.

Field Trips Worth Taking
www.edpsych.com/TeTips2.htm

Making a Book Using the Digital Camera. KidSmart.
www.kidsmartearlylearning.org. Click on Site Map, then scroll
down and click on article title in the Promising Practices box.

7. Toys from Home

Although most teachers have a rule that toys from home are not allowed in school, children still bring them in. They crave the security of a link from home and they enjoy showing off what they own. Children often use toys from home as a way to make friends when they are able to find others with similar interests and then connect through the object. Accommodate these needs in your classroom. Stifling them will only lead to frustration and frustration will lead to misbehavior. Consider some of the following ways to allow toys from home in the classroom while preventing the problems caused by them.

● At least once a week, give children an opportunity to share their toys during the day. You might do this through a "Show and Tell" session. To prevent "Show and Tell" from lasting too long, have some children share every Monday, others on Tuesday, and so on. Other ideas for making "Show and Tell" engaging can be found in the chapter on circle time on pp. 11–13.

● Allow children to play with their toys from home during the first fifteen minutes of free choice. If some toys cause conflicts or lead to hurtful or uncreative play, put reasonable limits on what toys can be brought from home such as no action figures or Barbie dolls.

● Provide many opportunities for children to make friends and engage with each other physically and socially. Find ways to incorporate interests from home into the classroom that are not related to commercial objects. For example, develop dramatic play or interest centers around the occupations or avocations of their parents, such as a fire station, music center, post office, hospital, or restaurant. Use some materials that are borrowed from the families. Even just adding single items from children's homes to an area can have a big impact. This may be a tortilla press in the kitchen area or a favorite book in the library. Suggest that children bring photos of parents, pets, homes, or favorite toys. These ideas will meet similar needs that motivate children to bring toys from home.

● Provide a special shelf where toys from home are kept. Establish a procedure whereby during free choice, children may play with the toy for a set amount of time (five to ten minutes), but first must ask the owner. The owner can refuse or agree to the request. This promotes language and social development, although it takes more work on your part to remind children to ask and to help them find the right words. Several months may pass before this routine works smoothly. It will work better with four- and five-year-old children than with younger children.

● Have a clearly written policy about toys from home for parents to read at the time they enroll their children. Include the specific limits you have set, the procedures for having and using toys at home in the classroom, and the reasons for the limits and procedures.

Resources

Dailey, K. 1997. Sharing centers: An alternative approach to show and tell. *Early Childhood Education Journal* 24 (4): 223–27

Oken-Wright, P. 1988. Show and tell grows up. *Young Children* 43 (2): 52–57.

Phillipoff, A. 1990. Caregivers corner. Themes for show and tell. *Young Children* 45 (4): 43.

8. Lost or Missing ————————————

Clothing and toys (or parts of toys) are the two most common items lost or missing in early childhood programs. In either case, the loss is very frustrating because clothing and toys are expensive and time consuming to replace, and the loss was probably preventable. When there are many lost items it is usually symptomatic of a disorganized program. Although lost or missing items will always be a reality for groups of busy adults and active young children, losses can be minimized by using some of the ideas in this chapter.

Preventing Problems
Clothing

• In your parent handbook and during new parent orientation, request that all clothing be labeled with the child's name. Also state that in spite of all the care you take, clothing will occasionally get lost or be taken home accidentally by another child, never to be seen again. This creates a realistic expectation that if the child is in the preschool for more than a few months there is a good chance that some item will get lost. Ask the parents to please check all clothing their child brings home to make sure it indeed belongs to their child. Remind them that many children have clothing that looks similar to those belonging to another child.

• Include in your parent handbook a statement making clear whether the program will reimburse parents for lost clothing. If the program will reimburse parents, state how the rates are determined.

• Encourage parents to purchase a laundry marker pen and put their child's initials on the inside label of her clothing. Ask parents to do this at school if they are unable to do it at home. Only do this marking yourself as a last resort.

• Bring a box outside or have a very specific place designated where children are required to put any clothing that they remove when they're outside.

• Make sure each child has her own cubby or box where she can keep her personal belongings. Be very consistent about requiring the child to put in her cubby any clothing she removes when inside.

• Give a quick check of cubbies before the children go home each day and before leaving any area (field trip site, playground) where children may have removed jackets or sweaters.

• Keep a "Lost and Found Box" in a place where it cannot be ransacked too easily. Keep a supply of clothing that has been donated or purchased cheaply from secondhand stores. If you can replace an item of lost clothing with a reasonable facsimile, you may be able to reduce the parents' unhappiness.

Toys or Toy Parts

• Put the name of your class on any item that may be used in another classroom, but that belongs in your room. Put the name of your school on any item that is shared by various programs or sites. Make an inventory. List every item in your class on a sheet of paper so that you will know if anything is missing. Update this list at least once a year. Add any new toys or equipment to the list. Remove from the list any item that has been discarded.

• Most cardboard toy boxes will not hold up very long under constant use in a preschool classroom. Start to build a collection of sturdy plastic containers (the clear ones are best as they make it easier for a child to find the one he is looking for). These regularly go on sale at discount department stores. Transfer the toy or game into the container when you bring it to the classroom. Pieces of a toy are much less likely to be lost in one of these than in a dilapidated box.

• Keep a file of addresses and phone numbers of toy companies listed on the boxes or wrappers of items you purchased. If the item has a model number or specific name, note that with the company list, if you are no longer keeping the box. Most companies will replace missing pieces of games or toys for a small fee. You may have to wait a number of weeks, however, before you receive the part. Many companies also have toll-free numbers for you to call to find out if the part can be replaced and the cost.

• Label all your shelves and containers. Always require that toys and games be put back where they belong when each child is finished playing with them.

• Code your puzzles and all the pieces. For example, on the back of a puzzle, write the number 1 with a permanent marker and write the same number on the back of each of the pieces of that puzzle. Code your next puzzle number 2, the next 3, and so on. If pieces from various puzzles get mixed together (not uncommon in preschools), you can separate them easily by finding the code number.

Dealing with Existing Problems

When Clothing Is Missing

● Enlist the help of the children and other staff in tracking down the item. Form a search party and make a game out of it.

● As you know, clothing is a major expense to parents, and so the loss of any clothing is upsetting. Explain to the parents the program's policy about missing clothing and show it to them in writing. Describe what you have done to locate the item. Assure them that you will continue to look for it. Send a note home to all parents in case the missing item mistakenly went home with another child. Place a note on your parent bulletin board about the missing item. Knowing that you are concerned, that you take the problem seriously, that you tried your best to find it, and that you will continue to do so will usually satisfy most parents.

(For ideas on dealing with parents who are irate about lost clothing, see the chapter on complaining parents on pp. 169–171.)

When a Toy or Part Is Missing

● Check your shelves at the end of free choice time to make sure all items are back where they belong. Check puzzles and games to make sure all the pieces are still there. If any pieces are missing, take the time to have every child look for the missing piece before the class does anything else. In looking for the piece, move shelves, tables, chairs, rugs, and other furnishings as necessary. Check in the trash cans and sort through all the toy containers. Ask all the children to check their pockets and cubbies.

● Do this all-out search for a number of reasons: First, the longer you wait, the less likely you are to find a missing piece. Second, you are teaching the children that the supplies are valuable and must be taken care of. They will be much more diligent about not losing pieces after one or two such searches.

● If the piece is still not found, ask the janitor (if you have one) to look for the piece when cleaning. If it does not show up in a day or two, write to the company for a replacement as described previously. Have the children help you write the letter so they can appreciate the process necessary to obtain a new piece.

● If a replacement can be made, do so. If the missing item or piece is something the children can make themselves or help someone else make, then involve them. Puzzle pieces can be made from wood scraps with a band saw or jigsaw, from "plastic wood," or from cardboard. Layer cardboard pieces or use cardboard from packing boxes to make them thicker. Laminate the pieces for durability.

9. Coping with Accidents and Emergencies

Nothing is more frightening than a hurt child. Not only are you concerned about the health of the child, but you are worried about appeasing anxious parents and perhaps an upset boss. Although you can do many things to prevent problems, an accident will occasionally happen even in the best program. Any time large numbers of children are in one place along with climbing equipment and room to move, accidents will occur. Although preventing and avoiding injuries is one of your most important tasks, allowing children to take some risks is a vital part of helping them learn and grow. Making risk taking as safe as possible is a difficult balancing act. Every insurance company would love centers or schools without playgrounds, but children's need to develop themselves physically far outweighs the risks.

Most injuries happen on playgrounds or gym equipment. Swings are the cause of most serious playground accidents. (For safety ideas, see the chapter "Safe Fun Outdoors or in the Gym" on pp. 27–29.)

Some of the anxiety of coping with the inevitable injury can be lessened when you are secure in your knowledge of what to do for a variety of emergencies and injuries and that you have quick access to first-aid supplies and professional assistance if necessary.

Preventing Problems

● Before a child enrolls in your classroom, obtain from her parents the name of their doctor to call and permission (an emergency release form) to take their child to the nearest hospital in case of an emergency. Update the form every six months and make a copy of it. Put the original in the child's file and keep all the copies together to take on field trips.

• In your classroom, post an escape plan, which consists of written instructions and a map with red arrows showing the quickest way out, as well as alternative exits. Use different colored arrows on your map.

• Keep emergency phone numbers clearly posted by each phone. Include fire, police, ambulance, and poison control (unless you have a centralized system accessed by dialing 911). Also keep a sign with your program's address on it near the phone so it can be quickly recited in an emergency.

• Role-play with the children what you will do and what they should do when a child gets hurt outside, on a field trip, or inside.

• Set a few inside and a few outside rules related to safety. Among your inside rules, you might include the following:

  ▸ "Always walk inside the classroom."

  ▸ "Throw only soft things and throw them away from people."

  ▸ "Build blocks only as high as your nose."

  ▸ "Pick toys up from the floor after you have finished playing."

  ▸ "Touch other people only after you have their permission."

For your outside rules, you might include the following:

  ▸ "Swing only when seated."

  ▸ "Go down the slide on your bottom."

  ▸ "Climb using two hands."

  ▸ "Wear a helmet when riding your bike."

• Enforce these rules consistently. Focus your energy and attention on the children when they are following the rules. Give them information about their behavior: "When you build the blocks lower than your nose, they can't fall on your head. You're keeping yourself safe." Practice the rules by role-playing in small groups.

• Keep your first aid and CPR cards current. First-aid training is available through most Red Cross chapters. However, it is important to request and receive first-aid training that directly relates to young children and to medical emergencies typically seen in preschools.

• Have a first-aid kit available where you can get to it quickly. Keep in it at least the following: adhesive strip bandages (various sizes), adhesive tape, sterile gauze pads and bandages (various sizes), disposable and sterile plastic gloves, syrup of ipecac, a thermometer, and tweezers. Check with your local health department for additions to your kit. On field trips take a first-aid kit as well as emergency release forms for each child. Periodically check expiration dates on items such as syrup of ipecac.

• Have a number of "blood spill" kits, separate from first-aid kits. They can be bought prepackaged or you can put one together. These typically include latex gloves, a disposable plastic scoop, a mild bleach solution in a spray bottle (or a manufactured EPA-approved HIV and HBV disinfectant), a disposable absorbent towel, and a disposable biohazard plastic bag.

• Have a readily accessible copy of an up-to-date book about what do to in various childhood emergencies. See the end of this chapter for some recommendations.

• Keep several ice packs in the kitchen freezer. Bags of frozen peas work well because they are pliable. Make sure, however, that they will not be used for food.

• To prevent choking, do not give popcorn, peanuts, or whole grapes to children under three years old, or peanuts to children under four years old. Do not give balloons to any child.

• Keep any poisonous or dangerous substance in a locked cabinet with a "Mr. Yuk" sticker on it. Tell the children what the sticker means. Keep your poison control phone number posted by the telephone and keep a bottle of syrup of ipecac available (in a locked cabinet) in case you need to induce vomiting. All drugstores sell this syrup. Be sure to check the expiration date regularly.

• Cover all electrical outlets with childproof safety covers. Check with your local child care licensing agency to determine which type of outlet covers are best to use.

• Remove from outside the building, as well as from inside the classroom, any plants and shrubs that are toxic. Replace them with nontoxic plants.

• Provide plenty of water for the children to drink, particularly outside on hot days. If there is no water fountain outside, take a thermos of water and paper cups outside with you. On hot days, put sunblock specifically made for children on them to prevent sunburn. Obtain parent permission first and ask them to supply the lotion.

How to Make Risk Taking Reasonably Safe

● After you have established safety rules and the children understand them well, provide opportunities for the children to take physical risks while minimizing the possibility of injury. Most children love to take risks, which is one reason they disobey safety rules. If they know they will have many opportunities to take risks, they are more likely to obey the established rules.

● The following is one example of structuring safe risk taking: Bring out mats to put under a climbing structure. One at a time, allow children to hang from their knees, do flips, swing with one hand, or do something similar, depending on each child's ability. Be the "spotter" to make sure the children do not fall too hard. Teach the children to break their falls with their arms. If needed, add additional safety equipment such as more mats, kneepads, and a bike helmet. If the bars are not too high, teach the children to be spotters for each other. Allow only one child on the equipment at a time and put a short time limit on each turn, as accidents are more likely to happen when the children are tired. By structuring and monitoring a risky activity such as just described, you will help children learn that risks can be taken, that they are fun, but that there are sensible ways to take a risk.

● Using a similar structure, try other activities such as the following: tumbling games and handstands, wrestling, jumping from reasonable heights, and swinging on a rope.

● Invite an older child to the class who is a good skateboarder. Before this older child demonstrates tricks, have her talk about all the safety equipment she wears and why she wears it. Encourage her to talk about the hours of training she did before she could do tricks and about the cautions she takes.

Successful Fire Drills

● At least quarterly, have an expert check your fire extinguishers, smoke detectors, and sprinkler system to make sure they are in good working order.

● Invite to your classroom a fire safety specialist from your local fire bureau to give you help on establishing safe classroom procedures and equipment use. If she talks directly to the children, make sure she can speak at their level of understanding (without being condescending).

● Practice a fire drill at least once a month with your class. Early in the year, before the first actual fire drill, slowly walk through a fire drill several times. Talk to the children about what they are doing and why. Tell them about the loud bell and what to expect. Make sure each adult knows her specific duties for fire drills. Time your fire drills with a stopwatch. Set a goal with the children for reducing the time they need to evacuate the room and work together toward this goal.

● Remind the children periodically of the fire drill rules: "Be silent." "Walk quickly." "Follow the teacher's directions."

● Make sure they know and can find the specific destination where the class will meet outside, such as "Along the fence behind the big climber."

● Take your class attendance list with you and account for each child once you all arrive at the outside destination.

● Shut off the lights and close the doors when leaving the room. This will slow the spread of a fire if one actually happens.

● When the children and adults are safely outside, briefly discuss how much time the evacuation took, what went well, and what can be improved.

● If you do not have a formal fire alarm bell, use a special whistle or handbell that is loud and is used for no other purpose. In order for the children to respond quickly, they must associate this sound with a fire alarm and with nothing else.

● Hold fire drills at various times of the day, including when children are outside.

● When the children are proficient at fire drills, change a part of the drill. Block one of the exits or doorways and use another way to go outside. In a real fire, your quickest exits may be blocked by heat or smoke.

● Have children practice "Stop, Drop, and Roll" in case their clothes catch on fire. Tape a large cloth or paper "flame" to their clothes to make the experience more concrete.

Keep Track of Injuries

- After an injury has occurred, write a note (or fill in a preprinted form) to give to parents, explaining what happened and describing the treatment you gave. Sign the note yourself and have the parent sign it. Make a copy for your own records. This will keep all information clear and straight and will protect you and the parents from liability.

- At the end of every month and every year, look back over the records to determine the most common injuries. Set a goal to reduce those injuries by making specific changes such as fixing or removing certain equipment, setting some new classroom rules, rearranging furniture or materials, or starting a fund-raising campaign for a new playground surface.

Resources

American Academy of Pediatrics. 2002. *Caring for our children: National health and safety performance standards: Guidelines for out-of-home child care programs.* 2d ed. Elk Grove, Ill.: American Academy of Pediatrics.

Emergency First Aid Books

Bosque, E., and S. Watson. 1997. *Safe and sound: How to prevent and treat most common childhood emergencies.* New York: St. Martin's Press.

Enzig, M., ed. 1992. *The baby and child emergency first aid handbook: Simple step-by-step instructions for the most common childhood emergencies.* Minnetonka, Minn.: Meadowbrook Press.

National Safety Council, ed. 1997. *Infant and child CPR.* Sudbury, Mass.: Jones & Bartlett Publishing.

Web Sites

A Parent's Guide to First Aid, Children's Healthcare of Atlanta www.choa.org/first_aid/default.shtml

First Aid for Children. About.com. pediatrics.about.com/cs/firstaid

Learn CPR. You Can Do It. University of Washington. depts.washington.edu/learncpr/index.html

Resources for Educators and Parents from the Federal Emergency Management Agency (FEMA). Includes a link to "Earthquake Preparedness: What Every Childcare Provider Should Know." www.fema.gov/kids/teacher.htm

Environmental Protection Agency (EPA) Resources for Teachers www.epa.gov/teachers

Health and Safety Topics. National Network for Child Care. www.nncc.org/Health/health.safe.page.html

Agencies and Organizations

Consumer Product Safety Commission (800-638-2772). Call or use their Web site to report an unsafe toy or product, or to get safety information about a particular toy or product. www.cpsc.gov

National Center for Injury Prevention and Control www.cdc.gov/ncipc

National Institute for Occupational Safety and Health Safety and Health Topics www.cdc.gov/niosh/toplst.html

National Resource Center for Health and Safety in Child Care. At this site, you can download the full text of American Academy of Pediatrics. 2002. *Caring for our children: National health and safety performance standards: Guidelines for out-of-home child care programs.* nrc.uchsc.edu

American Academy of Pediatrics www.aap.org

American Public Health Association www.apha.org

Occupational Safety and Health Administration (OSHA) www.osha.gov

10. Children Who Are Ill and Other Health Concerns

There is a great deal of concern about children in early childhood programs becoming sick more frequently and with more serious illnesses than other children. Although some evidence indicates that this may be generally true, in programs where reasonable health precautions are taken and where teachers are aware of the causes of and ways to prevent common illnesses, the threat to children's health should be no greater than anywhere else.

Preventing Problems

- Stay home when you are sick. Because you may get little sick leave and substitutes are hard to find, you probably feel obligated to be at work unless you are practically dying! If you do this, however, you may infect some children, who will infect other children, who will then infect you again. This cycle of sickness is not uncommon in preschools.

- Make sure all children are fully immunized. You can obtain information about immunization schedules from your local health department.

• Before children enroll in your program, require that they receive a physical examination from a physician clearing them to participate fully in all preschool activities or explaining any limitations.

• Require parents to fill out a health and medical history form. This can be very helpful if, for example, you notice spots on a child that look like chicken pox. The form will tell you if the child has already had chicken pox. Thus, you can determine the nature of the spots more easily. If the program keeps these files in a central location, make sure you know how to find them for the children in your class and that you see the form for each new child.

• Wash your hands thoroughly with warm water and disinfectant soap. Note that this is the single most important thing a teacher can do to prevent a wide variety of illnesses and diseases. Wash your hands after diapering, using the toilet yourself, helping a child with toileting, helping a child blow his nose, blowing your own nose, and before serving and/or eating food. If you are outside or in a place that is not accessible to a sink, carry a small plastic tube or bottle of "waterless" hand disinfectant sanitizer.

• Supervise children's handwashing carefully. Make sure they thoroughly wash when arriving at school from home; after toileting; after blowing their noses; before meals and snacks; and after playing with dirt, sand, paint, and so on.

• Keep spray bottles of diluted bleach water handy (one tablespoon of bleach to one quart of water; one part bleach to ten parts water for blood spills). Keep this out of children's reach. Use bleach water to wipe off surfaces (especially changing tables after diapering), toilets and sinks once during the day, and classroom tables before and after meals and snacks.

• Wash toys regularly and spray plastic toys with a bleach solution. Put toys through the kitchen sanitizer/dishwasher twice a week, especially infant and toddler toys that are often "mouthed." Many infant and toddler toys need to be cleaned on a daily basis. Sanitize only those toys that will not be ruined by high heat or bleach. Or, wash toys in the water-play table with warm, soapy water. Most children enjoy doing this.

• To prevent the possible spread of the HIV virus that causes AIDS, use sterile, disposable latex gloves (to avoid direct skin contact with blood from cuts or

wounds) and the blood spill kit discussed in the previous chapter. To prevent the spread of hepatitis and other diseases, use plastic sterile gloves when serving food.

• Exclude children from attending your program if they show signs of any infectious disease (caused by a virus, bacterium, fungus, or parasite), communicable disease (easily spread), diarrhea, or if they feel too sick to participate in activities. Fever is not a good indicator of a child's condition or contagiousness, so judge by the child's behavior, actions, and symptoms. If a child becomes ill while in school, notify parents (or the emergency contact person the parents have designated if they cannot be reached) to pick him up. Make sure your program has a written policy, which parents receive upon enrollment, stating that this will happen. Notify the parents of all children who came in contact with a child who has an infectious or communicable illness. Notify your local health department and find out what actions need to be taken.

• For the most common illnesses, have preprinted forms that list the symptoms, suggested treatment (if confirmed by a physician), and when the child can return to preschool. Give this form to the parent when he comes to pick up his child. Make clear that you do not know definitely what the child has but that based on the symptoms, you are stating what you suspect.

• Keep trash, especially soiled diapers and used tissues, in a container with a secure lid. Keep the container covered. Empty the trash daily in half-day programs and at least twice a day in full-day programs.

• Provide at least three feet of space between cribs, cots, or mats. Place children "head to toe" so that their faces are not close to each other during naptime. These measures will prevent colds from spreading.

• See that each child has his own toothbrush. Store the brushes in such a way that the bristles of any brush never touch anything. Do not let children touch any brush but their own. Use some of the following ways to accomplish this: plastic travel covers, hooks in individual cubbies, a rack with separators between each brush. Sterilize toothbrushes frequently with mild bleach water (and then thoroughly rinsed) or in the dishwasher.

• Provide a "get well" space where a child can lie down on a cot if he is not feeling well. Set up this space away from other children, but within eyesight of an adult. Have the children who are waiting to be picked up by parents because of illness use this area.

• Contact your local health department for information and charts on common contagious illnesses and suggested policies for your center.

• Ask parents to ask their physician for clear criteria for when the child can return to the group care after an illness. It may be a certain number of days or the lack of certain symptoms. Provide clear criteria for returning after colds and flus where the child is likely not to see a doctor. Many programs require the child to be free of fever or diarrhea for twenty-four hours and feel well enough to fully participate in activities before she can return.

Allergies: Food and More

At intake, ask parents about any allergies their children may have. Keep a posted list of children with food allergies and the foods they are allergic to in the classroom and in the kitchen. Some children are so allergic to certain foods that it may be necessary to ban the food from the classroom or program completely. Peanuts are the most common food that may cause such a severe reaction in some children.

Six foods account for about 90 percent of all food allergies in children: peanuts, tree nuts, milk, eggs, wheat, and soy. Ask parents for information from their child's doctor about exactly which foods she must avoid, what can be substituted, what symptoms to look for, and what do if the child has a reaction. Enlist their support and help in making sure that their child is safe. Practice for a potential emergency as you would a fire drill. A response to a severe reaction may require a trip to the emergency room, so prepare accordingly.

Keep a bee sting kit on hand and learn how to use it. Some children are highly allergic to bee stings and require an injection to keep them breathing if they are stung. Ask each parent when they enroll if their child is allergic to bee stings. Take the kit on any outings or field trips if you have an allergic child in your class.

Some children are allergic to dust, various animals, and toxins from cleaning products, paint, perfumes, and other sources. It may be necessary to remove any class pets you have and minimize the number of pillows and stuffed animals (or make sure that they are washable and are washed weekly) and reduce the amount of carpeting. There are many nontoxic cleaners and products now available that can be substituted for standard products. If any linens are used, these should be washed weekly in very hot water.

The air quality in your classroom is an important consideration. Daily dusting (damp rag) and vacuuming of any carpeting with a professional machine with a high-quality filter will be very helpful to children with allergies. Filters in the heating and air conditioning system should be very high quality and be replaced or cleaned at least monthly. An additional air filter and dehumidifier, if there is dampness, adds additional protections.

Children with Asthma

Asthma has become the most common chronic health problem among children, and the number of affected children is growing rapidly. When a child has an asthma attack, she has trouble breathing due to swelling of the air passages in the lungs and a build up of mucous. It can be triggered by a common illness, too much strenuous activity, or an allergic reaction (see above). Most children with asthma can participate normally in activities, but some cautions and restrictions may be necessary, such as having more rests and breaks than other children.

Most children with asthma will have some medication, typically in the form of an inhaler, that is either taken regularly or when an attack occurs. One of the biggest problems with young children is forgetting to take their medication with them wherever they go. You and the child's parents must assist. As with all medications, make sure you have clear directions on its dosage and use and a phone number to call with any questions.

Each child with asthma should have her own written plan that is kept in her file (and taken on field trips) describing potential triggers, what to do in case of an attack, and other pertinent information. As the child's teacher you should know this and not have to rely on looking in the file. Know how to use the child's inhaler, nebulizer, or other equipment. If a child has an attack, help keep her calm by being calm yourself and talking in a soothing voice. Have her sit upright and rub her back as you implement the treatment plan and get any necessary help. Make sure other staff members know how to access information about what to do if a child has an asthma attack in case it happens when you are absent or away.

Head Lice

Head lice are tiny reddish-brown, wingless insects. Their eggs or nits attach to strands of hair close to the scalp and are grayish and oval shaped. They survive on human blood and can't live without a human host for more than a day. They do not spread disease, but are extremely itchy and annoying and can spread quickly to others. They can be difficult to get rid of and some lice are developing resistance to some of the chemicals used as treatments.

As lice do not jump or fly, there is much you can do to prevent an outbreak of lice. Do not let children share hats, combs, pillows, hair ties, and similar items. As soon as you see a child scratching her head, check for lice using an approved method.

When a child has lice, parents will need to get an over-the-counter treatment (shampoo with pesticide specifically for lice) or prescription from a doctor, do a thorough washing of clothes and bedding in hot water, and vacuum any carpeting. In classrooms, it is necessary to vacuum and check all the children. There is no need to bag clothes and stuffed animals or spray with a pesticide. Treatment of lice often requires removal of nits with a special comb and vigilant checking and rechecking. The shampoo treatment alone rarely completely gets rid of them.

There is some controversy over whether children can return to a group setting while still having nits in their hair. This is a concern because some children can be out quite a few days until the nits are completely gone. A study conducted by the CDC found that when there are just a few nits left, most children do not become reinfested, especially if they are more than a quarter of an inch above the scalp. However, the American Pediculosis Association recommends a strict "no nit" policy.

At enrollment, make sure that parents know your policy about excluding children with head lice and, if it occurs, provide them with helpful information to treat their child.

Giving Medication

This often causes problems for teachers as they sometimes have to remember to give medication to several different children at various times during the day. A missed dose may harm the child and will undoubtedly be of great concern to parents.

● Use an electronic "pill reminder" alarm. They are very small and relatively cheap. A parent may be willing to purchase or lend you one if it means not missing a dose of medicine.

● Administer only prescription medications with written orders from the doctor and the parent's signature. This will limit the number of medicines given out. Don't give over-the-counter medications to children at the request of parents. Insist on permission from the doctor.

● Ask if the parents will provide the same medication or a similar one that requires two or fewer daily doses so it can be given at home. This can be done with many drugs and usually can be arranged over the phone with the doctor and/or pharmacist.

● If a parent works or lives nearby, request that he come to the class and administer the medicine.

● Ask the parents to have the pharmacist provide a small, extra, labeled bottle to use at preschool. This will eliminate the hassle for parents of picking up and bringing in the medicine daily and relieve you from having to return it to them at the end of each day.

● Post a log sheet near where the medicine is locked and write down each dose of medication you give. This will help you remember if and when you gave it. Provide a separate sheet for each child.

Children Who Come to School Dirty

Cleanliness can be a personal or cultural issue. Some people and some cultures accept body odor more and have different standards of cleanliness than main-stream Americans. In many cases those standards are related to the limited availability of water, soap, towels, washing machines, dryers, and so on, because of poverty or other circumstances. A reasonable amount of cleanliness is necessary, however, for children to stay healthy and to be pleasing enough for other children to want to play with them. If the lack of cleanliness creates a real problem for a child in your class, consider the following:

● Meet with the parents to determine their perspective on cleanliness. Help them find resources or easy methods for cleaning clothes and children if necessary. Let them know objective reasons for your concern (the child is not making friends or a cut became infected). Explain that in the classroom setting a higher standard of cleanliness is needed for the child to stay healthy because so many children are close together for long periods. Remember that health habits at home are not your main concern, unless the child's health is seriously threatened.

● If conditions are extremely bad and the child's health and well-being are truly at stake, refer the family to your local social service agency. Follow your program's policies on referrals. Usually a supervisor will make the call. (See "Parents Who May Be Abusive to Their Children" on pp. 176–179.) The agency may provide the family with a home health worker who is trained to help with these matters.

● Help the child to clean himself at school soon after he arrives. Assist with this, if necessary. Offer the child a clean set of clothes for him to use (donated or secondhand) if he desires. Do this discreetly to avoid embarrassment. Most children who do this prefer to change back into their clothes from home before they leave school at the end of the day.

● Help the other children maintain respect and consideration for the child. Remind them of the rule about being kind and respectful. Support the child who gets ridiculed and help him stand up for himself. "Michael is a kind person and a good friend. That is much more important than what his clothes look like."

Resources

American Academy of Pediatrics. 2002. *Caring for our children: National health and safety performance standards: Guidelines for out-of-home child care programs.* 2d ed. Elk Grove, Ill.: American Academy of Pediatrics.

Dooling, M., and M. S. Ulione. 2000. Health consultation in child care: A partnership that works. *Young Children* 55 (2): 23–26.

Goldberg, E. 1994. Including children with chronic health conditions: Nebulizers in the classroom. *Young Children* 49 (2): 34–37.

Kendrick, A. S., and R. Kaufmann, eds. 1995. *Healthy young children: A manual for programs.* Washington, D.C.: NAEYC.

Rice, J. A. 1997. *Those mean nasty dirty downright disgusting but . . . invisible germs.* St. Paul: Redleaf Press.

———. 1998. *Those itsy-bitsy teeny-tiny not-so-nice head lice.* St. Paul: Redleaf Press.

Schmitt, B. D. 1991. *Your child's health: The parents' guide to symptoms, emergencies, common childhood illnesses, behavior, and school problems.* New York: Bantam Books.

Web Sites

Information on Common Childhood Illnesses. Links to dozens of sites with information from Allergies to Warts. KinderStart. www.kinderstart.com. Click on Health/Medical/Dental, then on Common Illnesses.

Centers for Disease Control. Various topics. www.cdc.gov/health

Health and Safety. Numerous articles including Asthma Management in Child Care by Will Evans and Head Lice: Those Itchy Little Bugs by Charlotte Hendricks. www.earlychildhood.com/Articles/index.cfm. Click on Health and Safety.

Health and Safety—Tips from teachers www.perpetualpreschool.com/health_&_safety_ideas.htm

Health and Safety Topics. National Network for Child Care. www.nncc.org. Click on Articles and Resources, then on Health and Safety.

HeadLice.org—Web site of the National Pediculosis Association Includes clear photos to help you distinguish lice and nits from other hair debris. www.headlice.org

National Resource Center for Health and Safety in Child Care At this site, you can download the full text of *Caring for Our Children: National Health and Safety Performance Standards: Guidelines for Out-of-Home Child Care Programs.* nrc.uchsc.edu

What You Should Know about Asthma in the Child Care Setting www.cdc.gov/health

Agencies and Organizations

California Child Care Health Program www.childcarehealth.org

American Academy of Pediatrics www.aap.org

American Public Health Association www.apha.org

Occupational Safety and Health Administration (OSHA) www.osha.gov

Part III

Children with Particular Needs

1. Suspected Disabilities ———

As you are the first teacher for most of your children, you will come in contact with some who have mild disabilities that have not been detected. Sometimes this happens because no one has yet realized that a problem exists, but sometimes parents deny that their child has a problem or the family physician says that the child will grow out of it.

A child in your class who is clumsy and has many accidents on the playground may have large-motor coordination or sensory integration problems and should be looked at by a physical therapist. A child (over three-and-a-half) who has difficulty putting together simple puzzles, drawing simple shapes, getting dressed, or eating a meal without making a mess may have fine-motor coordination problems, and should be looked at by an occupational therapist. A child who never seems to listen to you or seems lost in her own world may have problems hearing and should be seen by a physician; an audiologist; or an ear, nose, and throat specialist (ENT). A child who bumps into things and has trouble concentrating may not be seeing well and should be seen by an ophthalmologist. A child who says very little or talks in "baby talk" may have speech or language problems (the most common disability in young children) and should be seen by a speech therapist.

How do you know if the child really has a problem that needs professional help? Observe the child carefully, talk to her parents (to be sure the behaviors do not just occur at school), and give a screening test. These are designed to be quick and easy to administer, and they let you know if the child needs to be referred for a professional assessment.

If your program has policies and procedures in place regarding screening, observing, diagnosing, and serving children with disabilities, follow these procedures. Use the information in this chapter to determine if the practices are good ones and to strengthen them if needed. If your program has no set policies and procedures, use the information in this chapter to help develop them.

Observing

Write down exactly what you see the child do without interpreting it. Do not include your judgments. For example, you might write the following:

Chris 2/20/03

8:45 Tripped and fell when entered class.
9:00 Slid off chair.
9:05 Knocked over milk glass.
9:20 Bumped into table while running to circle. Bruised leg.

This observation report provides clear evidence of the child's difficulties. Show this list to parents and specialists.

To help you observe more systematically, use observational assessments as described in the chapter, "Assessment and Accountability" on pp. 44–47. If you are concerned about an area of development, you can supplement a general assessment with an additional checklist tool. There are checklists for behavior, social/emotional development, language, speech, and more. Checklists often list behaviors you may not think of looking for or may not consider part of the problem. They provide further evidence of real concerns about the child.

Screening

A screening test gives a general profile of a child's strengths and weaknesses. It cannot be used to determine if a child has a certain disability, but only to determine if a child should receive further testing by a specialist.

● Use a screening test that is valid and reliable for the age of your children. (See list at the end of this chapter.) Most screening tests take fifteen to twenty minutes, are easy to give, and do not require much special training. If you do not feel able to give the test yourself, find a person who can teach you or who can do it for you. Most school districts use screening tests and have personnel who are trained to give them.

● Obtain written permission from parents to give a screening test to their child. A screening test usually consists of questions for you to ask a child or skills, called items, for you to observe a child doing. Many now include questions for parents, especially for an infant and toddler screening test. These items are commonly divided into six areas of a child's development: language, social/emotional, cognitive, self-help, fine motor, and large motor. Some screening tests are designed for just one particular area of development, which will give a more detailed, accurate assessment for that area, because there are many more items. These are typically in the language and social/emotional/behaviorial areas. The following is a list of items, one in each of the six areas of development, typically found on screening tests for four-year-olds:

Language	Can use past tense and future tense when talking.
Social/emotional	Engages in dramatic play, e.g., plays house, pretends to be animals.
Cognitive	Counts four objects and tells how many.
Self-help	Uses toilet independently.
Fine motor	Copies a square.
Large motor	Stands on one foot for eight seconds.

A child who is weak in one or several areas of development should be taken to a specialist by her parents. The specialist will then give her more in-depth tests called diagnostic tests. These will determine if a problem exists and the extent of the problem. The specialist will then develop a plan for helping the child. Make certain that ideas for you to help the child in class are included in this plan.

● Use screening tests with caution. They sometimes will identify a child as needing further evaluation who is really not in need (perhaps she is shy or does not speak English well) and fail to identify a child who actually does need further evaluation (the test may not be sensitive enough or it might catch a child on a "good" day). These tests are most accurate when used in conjunction with careful classroom observations of the child (across situations and over time), with information from parents, and with observations made by other adults.

Preventing Problems

● Screen all your children. This avoids the problem of singling some children out from others, which may upset some parents or make those children feel different. This procedure will also help you catch any problems that you may have overlooked. Health related screenings—height, weight, vision, hearing, sensory integration functioning—should be done by an appropriate health professional or under the close direction and supervision of one.

● Screen early in the year or soon after any new children enter your class, but give yourself enough time to get to know the children well and for them to feel comfortable with you. Children must feel supported and relaxed when being tested to get accurate results. Don't wait too long, however. Act on your concerns about a child as quickly as possible. Note that getting an appointment with a specialist and starting a treatment program often takes months.

● Keep a list of specialists (speech therapists, physical therapists, occupational therapists, pediatricians, ENTs, opthamologists, and audiologists) in your area for referral to parents. Include those specialists who are good with children and with whom other parents have been happy. Write down their addresses and phone numbers.

● Give all parents a written policy on observing, screening, and referring children to specialists. Ask them to sign permission forms for this when they enroll their children. Then they will not be surprised when the time comes to discuss the results of the screening and observation with them. Include the following in your written policy: information about the screening test you use; the reason for screening and observation; a personal account about how a child was helped by your screening and referral; and an assurance of confidentiality.

● Schedule regular conference times with parents at least twice a year. Hold the first one soon after the child is enrolled and screened. Hold the second one toward the end of the program year. This creates a situation where meeting with parents is a given. If there is a concern about the child, a special meeting will not have to be arranged. Asking parents to attend a special meeting may cause them great anxiety and they may refuse to come or just not show up.

● If at all possible, do home visits with all your families. This will give you great insight into each child and family. You may see very different behaviors at home than at school. Use the home visit as a time to form a bond and strengthen your relationship with each family, especially the first one. Don't have a big agenda or specific educational goals in mind. Build trust and observe for the purpose of getting to know and understand the child and family more thoroughly and deeply.

Dealing with Existing Problems

Parents Who Deny There Is a Problem

Some parents do not know enough about child development to recognize that their child has a problem. However, once they are shown concrete evidence of the problem, they will usually be very concerned and interested in doing whatever is necessary to help their child.

Some parents may refuse to recognize that their child has a problem, even when they have the knowledge and the evidence. Usually they have good motives for doing this, such as not wanting their child labeled or considered an outcast, not wanting to feel responsible for the problem or overwhelmed by it, not wanting to admit their own similar weaknesses or problems, or wanting their child to be normal, liked, and treated with respect.

● Do not bring up the issue of your concerns with parents until you have won their trust. Be very supportive, friendly, and helpful. Ask questions and consider them the experts on their child. During this time, gather information about the child by observing and screening, as discussed earlier, and by reading more about the particular disability you suspect. By winning parents' trust and confidence, you accept as valid their motives for denying the problem. When they feel you have their child's best interests at heart, they will be ready to listen to your concerns.

● If parents avoid talking to you informally, set up a meeting with them. Tell them that the purpose of the meeting is to chat and to find out more about each other. Spend this time just listening, asking questions, and discussing positive things about their child. It is important not to "make up" things. Always be honest and up-front. You may need several meetings like this before you can bring up your concerns.

● When you are able to state your concerns, do so by telling the parents only what you have observed. Do not make judgments. Simply say something like the following: "I have seen that Chris falls down and bumps into things quite a bit. Here are some specific examples from notes I took on February 20." Include information from the screening test. State your own lack of expertise about what this means and ask them to let you have someone who knows more observe and test their child. Assure them that nothing will be done without their knowledge and permission. If you will be arranging the evaluation, ask the parents to

sign a permission form (this is required by law) to have a trained professional observe and evaluate their child. Also request permission for you to receive the results and to discuss them with the specialist.

● Remember that you have a professional responsibility to inform parents of concerns you have about their children no matter how hard this is to face. (See "Telling Parents about the Difficult Behavior of Their Children," on pp. 173–175, for effective ways to do this.)

Other Professionals Who Believe There Is No Problem

Some physicians, pediatricians, or other health professionals will occasionally downplay a child's problems. They may even state flatly that there is no problem to be concerned about. "The child will outgrow it" is a typical phrase you might hear.

A health professional will do this because she firmly believes that focusing attention on the problem may make it worse if the problem is not that serious. She believes that the child will be able to compensate for it, especially if the child is strong in other areas of development, and that calling attention to the problem may make the child feel different, damaging her self-esteem.

But if the child's problems are addressed in a positive way by building on her strengths, and the teachers and professionals are sensitive, the child can improve and also feel very good about herself. Children can often overcome a problem much more quickly and easily as preschoolers than they can when older. Many problems will get worse if left untreated. It makes little sense to ignore a problem when you can help the child overcome it, prevent the possibility of it getting worse, and also make the child feel good about herself.

● If you are uncertain that a problem exists, get a second opinion from another professional, if possible. If the second professional agrees there is no problem, then leaving the situation alone is probably safe. Throughout this process, write down reports of all meetings and phone conversations, and keep these in a safe place. If at a later time the child's problem reappears, gets worse, or another teacher has similar concerns, you will have a record of what you have done.

● If you are still convinced that the problem is a real one that should not be ignored, you may need a third opinion from another professional. If the second professional you consult agrees with you, follow her recommendations. If, however, she also believes that there is no problem or if it is not possible to get a third opinion and the child's parents also feel there is no problem, keep a record of everything you have done as described previously. You can still do many things in the classroom to help the child in a supportive way, without violating her parents' wishes. Doing those things is just part of individualizing, which all good preschool teachers do. Read as much as you can about the child's particular problem and about ways to help. In the following chapter, you will find more ideas about helping children with disabilities.

Difficulty in Finding or Affording Professional Services

● If you work in a program that has no access or funding for the services of a health professional and the parents cannot afford the services, consider other options such as the following:

▶ Many service and religious organizations, such as the Kiwanis, Elks, Lions, Salvation Army, National Council of Jewish Women, Shriners, Easter Seals, and so on, can help out with costs of diagnosing a potentially disabled child.

▶ You may tap the services of your local school district, although the response varies greatly among school districts. Many are happy to help while others are overwhelmed with the children they currently serve. However, school districts are required by law to at least determine, for any child who lives in their district, if she needs to be seen by a specialist. They may use your observation records to help make that determination, so make sure your notes are complete. Most school districts go beyond the minimum requirements and will refer a child in need to a specialist for evaluation and provide services if needed. Contact the special education coordinator.

▶ County or state mental health departments or health departments can also be a source for finding specialists. People in these agencies can also inform you of the laws in your state. Many states have laws that mandate services to young children with disabilities. A federal law mandates that all states provide a free, appropriate, public education to all children with disabilities through state education agencies.

Screening Tests
Global

Ages and Stages Questionnaires (ASQ). Parent administered for children four months to five years. Includes items in communication, gross motor, fine motor, problem solving, and personal-social. In English, Spanish, French, and Korean. Available from Paul H. Brookes Publishing, www.pbrookes.com.

Developmental Indicators for the Assessment of Learning—Third Edition (DIAL-3). For children ages 3.0 to 6.11 in English and Spanish. Includes the domains of motor, language, concepts, self-help, and social. Available from American Guidance Service, agsnet.com.

Early Screening Inventory—Revised (ESI-R). Consists of two instruments, one for three- to four-and-a-half-year olds and other for four-and-a-half- to six-year-olds in English and Spanish. Includes a parent questionnaire. Available from Pearson Early Learning, www.pearsonearlylearning.com.

FirstSTEP. For children 2.9 to 6.2 years of age. Cognition, communication, and motor domains are addressed. Optional Social/Emotional Scale and Adaptive Behavior Checklist. Available from the Psychologic Corporation, www.psychcorp.com.

Infant-Toddler and Family Instrument (ITFI). For children six months to three years and their families. Includes caregiver interview questions in the areas of home and family life, child health and safety, and family issues and concerns. Also a developmental map in the areas of gross/fine motor, social/emotional, language, coping/self-help. Available from Paul H. Brookes Publishing, www.pbrookes.com.

Language

Preschool Language Scales—Fourth Edition (English and Spanish). Includes receptive and expressive language in the areas of attention, play, gesture, vocal development, social communication, semantics, language structure, integrative language skills, and phonological awareness. Available from the Psychological Corporation, www.psychcorp.com.

The Fluharty Preschool Speech and Language Screening Test—Second Edition. For children ages three years old and six to eleven. Areas include articulation, expressive/receptive vocabulary, and composite language. Available from American Guidance Service, agsnet.com.

National Institute on Deafness and other Communication Disorders (NIDCD) Checklist of Speech and Language Milestones. Available at the NIDCD Web site: www.nidcd.nih.gov. Click on Voice, Speech, and Language under Health Information.

Social/Emotional

Ages and Stages Questionnaires: Social-Emotional (ASQ:SE). Parent administered for children six months to five years in English and Spanish. Includes areas of self-regulation, compliance, communication, adaptive functioning, autonomy, affect, and interaction with people. Available from Paul H. Brookes Publishing, www.pbrookes.com.

Devereux Early Childhood Assessment (DECA). A scale of resiliency for children ages two to five. It includes the domains of initiative, self-control, attachment, and behavior concerns.

More information can be found at www.devereuxearlychildhood.org and purchasing can be done through Kaplan Early Learning Company at www.kaplanco.com.

Resources

Curtis, D., and M. Carter. 2000. *The art of awareness: How observation can transform your teaching.* St. Paul: Redleaf Press.

Gullo, Domnic F. 1994. *Understanding assessment and evaluation in early childhood education.* New York: Teachers College Press.

Meisels, S. J, and S. Atkins-Burnett. 1994. *Developmental screening in early childhood: A guide.* 4th ed. Washington, D.C.: NAEYC.

Meisels, S. J., and E. Fenichel, eds. 1996. *New visions for the developmental assessment of infants and young children.* Washington, D.C.: Zero to Three National Center for Infants and Toddlers.

Schweinhart, L. 1993. Observing young children in action: The key to early childhood assessment. *Young Children* 48 (5): 29–33.

2. Children with Disabilities in Your Class

Many teachers worry about having a child with a disability in their class. They worry that they do not have the proper training or expertise to help the child or to deal with the child's problems. They worry that the child will take up so much extra time and energy that the rest of the class will suffer. These are real and valid concerns. However, most teachers find that when they actually have a child with a disability in their class, the joys far outweigh the problems, real or imagined. When this doesn't happen, the child is either misassigned (perhaps he is too severely disabled to benefit from a regular classroom) or the teachers have not received the information and support they need.

If you are already using good early childhood practices (an individualized, active, social, playful, child-focused classroom), you will not have difficulty caring for and teaching a child with a mild or moderate disability. You will have to stretch some of the things you already do, but your basic approach and routines will not have to change. For example, many children with developmental delays or mental disabilities have very short attention spans and experience difficulty focusing in group situations. Undoubtedly you already have a few children who fit this description, but the child with a disability may have an even shorter attention span and experience more difficulty focusing. Lower your expectations slightly, but keep challenging the child. Use the same techniques you already use—small groups, short group times, alternative quiet activities during group times for some children, seating the child next to you, involving all children actively—but employ these techniques sooner, more often, and very consistently for a child with a disability.

Young children are usually very open and accepting of children with disabilities, even very severe disabilities. Most have not built up many prejudices or misconceptions yet. This makes your job easier, in a way, than the job of teachers of older children.

You will quickly find that children with disabilities are children, first and foremost. The similarities between them and children without disabilities are far greater than the differences.

Preventing Problems

● Read books and view films with the children about children with a variety of disabilities. The best ones do not make disabilities the central focus but include children with disabilities as part of a good story. Use these to talk about individual differences and similarities.

● Read articles or books on the disability of the child in your class particularly as it impacts young children. The Internet can be very helpful in finding resources. Often the parents of the child have done this reading and have insights on how the disability impacts their child.

● Answer the questions (which are often painfully honest) that children ask about disabilities with direct, simple, and factual responses. If you are unsure or don't know the answer, say so, and seek the answer together from books or professionals. If a child asks, "Why can't he walk?" respond by telling him to ask the child. If the child cannot or will not respond, give a simple answer to the best of your ability: "When he was born his legs didn't work. He gets around very well using his wheelchair, though." Many children are not just curious but are worried that this disability might happen to them or that they will "catch it." They need some reassurance.

● Show children concretely and in a variety of ways how different everyone is from each other, but how ultimately we are more similar than different. To do this, you might want to graph the height of the children. On the graph, draw a human figure to represent each two-inch increment in height. Next to each make a column of dots, one for each child whose height is in that range. Invite the children to measure and graph each other; then do the same for a group of children two years older and a group two years younger. (See below.)

Two-Year-Olds

30" or less 1 child	32" 2 children	34" 7 children	36" or more 7 children
1	2	7	7

Four-Year-Olds

37" or less 1 child	39" 2 children	41" 3 children	43" or more 8 children
1	2	3	8

Six-Year-Olds

44" or less 2 children	46" 5 children	48" 5 children	50" or more 6 children
2	5	5	6

- Point out that in spite of great individual differences between the children in the same class, most of the children are taller than the younger children and shorter than the older children. Note that all children are growing, and that the older ones were once as short as the younger ones and the younger ones will someday be as tall as the older ones.

- Take an active approach to replacing children's misconceived stereotypes about disabilities with notions based in reality. Do this through concrete activities such as these:

  - Invite people with disabilities who will talk openly about their disabilities to spend time in the class.

  - Correct misconceptions as soon as you hear children say them.

  - Show specific examples (through films, books, and on field trips) of people with disabilities functioning in a variety of self-sufficient ways and situations.

(See the chapter on "Children Who Are Culturally or Physically 'Different' and Biased Behaviors" on pp. 81–87 for more ideas.)

- Make sure you are part of the team of people who meet to determine the child's goals and services. This is usually called the interdisciplinary or multidisciplinary team and the goals and services are written in a plan called the IEP (individualized educational plan) or IFSP (individualized family service plan). If this has already happened, request the parents' permission to become part of future team meetings and to read the plan. Ask questions to make sure you fully understand the plan. Make sure you have a copy of the plan.

- If you are part of the planning team, request that educational goals or objectives are written that can be easily met in your active, child-centered classroom. An objective such as "Angie will stack six blocks with 80 percent accuracy" implies direct teaching, boring repetition, isolating skills, and little choice for Angie. A goal such as "Angie will use blocks daily for creative play and stack them on the storage shelf when done" develops the same skills as the first objective but in a fun and creative way, integrates the skills into routines, and gives choices to Angie.

- If possible, meet with all team members (which may include the parents, a physical therapist, occupational therapist, speech pathologist, and other health professionals) individually and before the child is in your class. Discuss their goals for the child, their expectations of you, your concerns, and how the team members can help you. Make sure that the logistics of when and how they will provide therapy to the child are clear and that these logistics will not cause problems for your schedule or routines. Get the phone numbers of the team members so you can contact them quickly if necessary.

- Set up a regular system for communicating with therapists to discuss the objectives they are working on and how you can help the child meet those objectives in the classroom.

- Reach a clear understanding that you would like the child in your class on a trial basis to start with. Set up in advance a meeting time (four to six weeks after the child starts) to discuss any problems, concerns, or successes you might have. Be honest and forthright, but reasonable, about what you need for the child to be successful in your class. If you cannot get those needs met, then the child might be better off in a different placement.

- Make adjustments to the room, furniture, and equipment before the child enters your class, if possible. If the class has already started, enlist the help of the children and explain what you are doing and why. Show them a photo of the child and tell them all you know about him, not just about his disabling condition.

- Provide a wide variety of equipment and materials that span a broad range of skill levels. For example, have three-piece puzzles as well as twelve-piece puzzles.

- Maintain daily communication with the parents. Meet regularly to discuss the child's problems and progress.

Dealing with Existing Problems
Conflict with Therapists or Other Specialists

Conflict between teachers and others who serve the special needs of a child with a disability often arise because each views the child from a different angle. A teacher might see the child's strengths and abilities, whereas a specialist might be more focused on fixing what is wrong with the child. They also have been trained very differently and even use different jargon. Miscommunication can happen easily.

Conflict over Educational Approach. A common area of conflict is over the educational approach. You may, for example, provide many opportunities for children (including a child with a disability) to learn math skills by manipulating objects, playing dice games, setting the table for the correct number of children, regulating on their own the number of children allowed at the sand table, and graphing. A special educator might approach math development by drilling a child with a disability on counting beads and reinforcing correct answers with a reward, while keeping careful data by tallying all responses. These two very different approaches may not be easily reconciled.

● Find areas of commonality. You both want to help the child learn and grow, your goals for the child are the same, and you agree on the child's strengths and problems. Build on those commonalities and discuss ways in which you can agree to help the child. For example, the specialist can sit with the child during a math game and help her count the dots on the dice, figure out when her turn is, and record her progress. If this fails, at least agree to disagree. The child will not be harmed by being served in two different ways.

● Be patient and understand that the special education or therapeutic approach is designed to be precise, clear, and scientific. The therapist was trained in this approach, which comes from good intentions to help the child. This approach often gets good short-term results and children with severe disabilities benefit greatly from it. However, continue to use and advocate your approach even though you may get negative feedback on it from someone who has a more formal education than you do. Children with mild to moderate disabilities benefit greatly from learning to be self-initiating, especially for long-term growth. They are young children first and foremost and, like all young children, they learn best through playful, active, integrated activities.

Fortunately, many special educators and therapists are changing to this approach. More is being written about it and you can give them some of this written information to support your views. (See the resources at the end of this section.)

Conflict over Managing Behavior. Conflict also occurs over the use of reinforcement (reward and punishment) systems. Most early childhood professionals manage behavior through setting a stimulating environment, providing an active schedule, encouraging positive behavior, giving children many chances to be successful, using logical consequences, and redirecting children. They do not use punishment. They sometimes reluctantly use rewards as a last resort, but these are curtailed as soon as possible. Even then the results may not be very good and the means do not justify the ends. Some special educators, however, use reinforcement systems through rewards (stickers, stars, food, tokens) or punishment as the first method to deal with a problem. Many self-contained special education classroom teachers use an ongoing reward and punishment system as part of their routine group management. For some very disabled children, these systems work well and may, indeed, be appropriate.

● Some preschools have set policies stating that rewards, especially food and tokens, are not allowed. This frees the teacher to reject the use of a reinforcement system, without having to defend her position.

● Work with the special educator to set a specific, written plan about how you will help the child by using a wide variety of methods—teaching correct behaviors, redirection, child choice, logical consequences, and so on. Agree together to try this out before using a reinforcement system. If this plan fails and a reinforcement system seems necessary, set a very specific plan to fade out the reward as soon as possible.

The Overly Involved Parent

Parents of children with disabilities care deeply about their children, are very concerned about their growth and development, and tend to be very involved in their lives. If they can afford to stay at home, mothers of children with disabilities are less likely to work than other mothers. Because of this concern, commitment, and available time, a parent might want to spend a great deal of time in your classroom. While this can be extremely helpful, it can also create problems. The child might not get enough time to be independent and the parent may at times be more of a hindrance than a help. She may interact poorly with the other children or with her own child, or she may demand your attention when you need to give it to the other children.

● Meet with the parent, preferably before she starts volunteering, to discuss potential problems, to inform her of your approach, and to make expectations clear. Agree to a regular schedule of volunteer hours. Make it clear that you may ask her to curtail her involvement if it does not work out. Meet regularly, at least monthly, to discuss any concerns and to make plans for improvements. Give informal feedback more frequently. Clarify your roles and do quick training sessions about your methods. Ask her to work with other children to give her child time to be independent. Express your appreciation and give specific, positive feedback about what she does well. Provide very specific, factual information about the problems: "This morning you cut Julia's food for her. I then asked you to let her cut it herself. A few minutes later you went back to cutting it for her. Tell me what happened and let's figure out how to solve the problem."

The Child Who Takes Too Much Time and Energy

A child with a disability requires more time and energy than other children. If the situation becomes too much, however, then you are not getting the support you need. Many children with disabilities need an aide (at least part-time), and often the local school district or early intervention program will provide one. This can be a great help to you and the child, especially if the aide is capable and hard-working. If you have an aide who is not, and you cannot train and motivate her, make sure you provide objective information about her job performance to her supervisors. A year in the life of a young child is too important for her to receive less than excellent services.

● Enlist the assistance of other children to help the child with a disability. Most will be eager to help if the task is reasonable. Children can push a wheelchair; help a child clean up; assist her with puzzles, zipping, buttoning, or tying; and even teach a simple skill. This will also encourage responsibility and altruism, while freeing time for you. However, make sure that other children do not do things for the child with a disability that she can do for herself. The child needs to develop independence.

● Part of the problem may be that you are not getting the information or the equipment you need to be effective. You must have access to a competent professional, who can observe you and the child in the classroom and recommend methods or materials to use that will save time, increase efficiency, and allow the child to be more independent. This person is usually one of the health professionals on the child's team, but she could be a specialist from a hospital, social service agency, or university.

The Child with a Disability Who Does Not Play with Others

For many children with disabilities, playing with other children does not come naturally. This happens because they have had few opportunities to do so, because their verbal skills are poor, or because they have not developed positive social skills. Most young children with disabilities can learn to play with others, however, if a caring teacher helps. Usually the teacher has to provide direct and specific assistance.

● Involve the child as fully as possible in all group games and activities. Physically guide a child with a developmental delay through all the actions in a group movement game. See that the child has a turn just like everyone else.

● Teach the child to pretend. Play pretend games with the child, starting with you pretending to be an animal. Then encourage the child to pretend to be an animal with you. After he feels comfortable, bring in another child and pretend together, eventually pulling yourself out of the game.

● Teach the child to imitate. To encourage imitation, involve him in simple imitative games such as noncompetitive "Simon Says." Let other children lead the imitation games so he will get used to imitating children.

● Teach the child the right words and actions to use to join children in play. You may need to say them for him and show him how, until the child can do it on his own. Note that the best method of joining play is to start by imitating, in some way, what the children are already doing.

● Mediate a play situation. When the child with a disability is playing alongside another child and they are using the same materials, encourage them to play together by suggesting a slight variation or by introducing a new item: "Sara is building a road and so are you. You can hook your roads together to make a big, long road. There are more cars on the red shelf."

● Set out play materials that are of particular interest to the child with a disability.

● Encourage another child to play with her by providing a special game or unique toy that only two can use.

● Adapt toys and equipment to make them easier for the child with the disability to use. For example, add straps to the pedals of a trike to make it possible for a child with a mild physical disability to use it. She can then be part of the active outdoor play along with the other children.

● Encourage the child with a disability to bring in favorite toys from home, including popular commercial toys, to help her form friendships. Put some limits on the use of these toys as discussed in "Toys from Home," p. 55.

● Help him expand his play skills by imitating what he does and then doing something slightly different. For example, if the child is stacking small blocks, do the same thing until you have his attention, and then stack the blocks by alternating big and little ones.

Resources

Allred, K. W., R. Briem, and S. J. Black. 1998. Collaboratively addressing the needs of young children with disabilities. *Young Children* 53 (5): 32–36.

Beckman, P. J., ed. 1996. *Strategies for working with families of young children with disabilities.* Baltimore: Paul H. Brookes.

Blaska, J. K., and E. C. Lynch. 1998. Is everyone included? Using children's literature to facilitate the understanding of disabilities. *Young Children* 53 (2): 36–38.

Brown, M. H., R. Althouse, and C. Anfin. 1993. Guided dramatization: Fostering social development in children with disabilities. *Young Children* 48 (2): 68–71.

Chandler, P. 1994. *A place for me: Including children with special needs in early care and education settings.* Washington, D.C.: NAEYC.

Diamond, K. E., L. L. Hestenes, and C. E. O'Connor. 1994. Research in review. Integrating young children with disabilities in preschool: Problems and promise. *Young Children* 49 (2): 68–75.

McCormick, L., and S. Feeney. 1995. Modifying and expanding activities for children with disabilities. *Young Children* 50 (4): 10–17.

NAEYC and DEC (Division for Early Childhood of the Council for Exceptional Children). 2000. *Including all children: Children with disabilities in early childhood programs.* Washington, D.C.: NAEYC; Denver: DEC.

Odom, S. L., ed. 2000. *Widening the circle: Including children with disabilities in preschool programs.* New York: Teachers College Press.

Ostrosky, M., and S. Sandall, eds. 2001. *Teaching strategies: What to do to support young children's development.* Denver: DEC.

Russell-Fox, J. 1997. Together is better: Specific tips on how to include children with various types of disabilities. *Young Children* 52 (4): 81–83.

Sandall, S., and M. Ostrosky, eds. 2000. *Natural environments and inclusion.* Denver: DEC.

Sandall, S., M. McLean, and B. Smith. 2001. *DEC recommended practices in early intervention/early childhood special education.* Denver: DEC.

Stewart, S. 1999. Good questions to ask: When a child with a developmental delay joins your class. *Young Children* 54 (5): 25–27.

Wolery, M., and J. S. Wilbers, eds. 1994. *Including children with special needs in early childhood programs.* Washington, D.C.: NAEYC.

Children's Books

Bunnet, R. 1993. *Friends in the park.* New York: Checkerboard Press. (Various disabilities)

————. 1996. *Friends at school.* New York: Star Bright Books. (Various disabilities)

Caseley, J. 1991. *Harry and Willy and Carrothead.* New York: Greenwillow. (Physical disability)

Condra, E. 2002. *See the ocean.* Nashville: Eager Minds Press. (Visual impairment)

Cowan-Fletcher, J. 1996. *Mama zooms.* New York: Scholastic. (Mother in a wheelchair)

Fleming, V. 1993. *Be good to Eddie Lee.* East Rutherford, N.J.: Putnam Publishing. (Down's syndrome)

Lakin, P. 1994. *Dad and me in the morning.* Morton Grove, Ill.: Albert Whitman & Co. (Hearing impaired)

Millman, I. 1998. *Moses goes to a concert.* New York: Farrar, Straus & Giroux. (Hearing impaired)

Osofsky, A. 1994. *My buddy.* New York: Henry Holt & Co. (Child with muscular dystrophy and his dog)

Powers, M. E. 1987. *Our teacher's in a wheelchair.* Morton Grove, Ill.: Albert Whitman & Co. (Physically disabled male child care teacher)

Quinsey, M. B. 1986. *Why does that man have such a big nose?* Seattle: Parenting Press. (Physical differences)

Rabe, B. 1988. *Where's Chimpy?* Morton Grove, Ill: Albert Whitman & Co. (Down's syndrome)

Rogers, F. 2000. *Extraordinary friends: Let's talk about it.* New York: Puffin.

Videos

NAEYC
1509 16th Street, N.W.
Washington, DC 20036-1426
www.naeyc.org
Child Care and Children with Special Needs, two tape set
Early Intervention: Natural Environments for Children (Also in Spanish), 28 min.

Fanlight Productions
4196 Washington Street, Suite 2
Boston, MA 02131
www.fanlight.com
When Parents Can't Fix It, 58 min. (Five families with children that have disabilities.)

Web Sites

Children with Special Needs. Numerous articles from the National Network for Child Care Web site related to both general issues and specific disabilities.
www.nncc.org. Link to Articles and Resources, then Children with Special Needs.

Effective Practices for Preparing Young Children with Disabilities for School by C. L. Salisbury and B. J. Smith. ERIC Digest. 1993.
www.eric.ed.gov. Click on Digests and enter the title in the search box.

Inclusion. National Child Care Information Center.
www.nccic.org. Click on Selected Resource Lists, scroll down and click on Inclusion.

Inclusion in the Preschool Setting by Deanna Jordan
www.earlychildhood.com/Articles/index.cfm. Link to Inclusion.

Integrating Children with Disabilities into Preschool by Karen E. Diamond, Linda L. Hestenes, and Caryn O'Connor. ERIC Digest. 1994.
www.eric.ed.gov. Click on Digests and enter the title in the search box.

NAEYC Position Statement: Inclusion
www.naeyc.org. Link to NAEYC Resources, then Position Statements, then Improving Practices with Young Children.

Selected Conditions of Young Children with Disabilities. Developmental-Behavioral Pediatrics Web site. Direct access to information on dozens of conditions.
www.dbpeds.org/conditions

3. Gifted or Talented Children

About 5 percent of all children, regardless of family income, age, or race, are gifted or talented. If not nurtured, their abilities will not be fully realized and they may develop behavior problems. In fact, a child in your class with behavior problems may be a gifted child who is unchallenged and bored. By identifying gifted children and providing for their needs, you will help them as well as yourself.

Although a small percentage of children have unique, above ordinary abilities, which we call gifts or talents, all children have strengths, interests, and proclivities. An important job of teachers and parents is to recognize these in each child and provide active support, resources, and guidance to help them to fully develop.

As with other children with special needs, providing a good program for gifted children is not hard if you already have an active, child-centered, individualized classroom. You will just need to provide some additional challenges and opportunities within your current curriculum and routines.

You will find that the suggestions in this chapter can work well with almost all children, not just the gifted. However, for their basic needs to be met, gifted children require these approaches.

Preventing Problems

● Provide many opportunities for all children to be creative through open-ended art activities (not crafts that result in a specific, finished product), music, creative dance and movement, story writing, and creative dramatics. A talented child will be excited when participating in his area of interest.

● Make available a wide variety of creative materials, which any child can use for any purpose (within reasonable limits) during free choice. Include many different kinds of blank paper, streamers, pieces of foam, different sizes of cups and containers, wood scraps, cotton balls, cloth, buttons, foil, colored chalk, pens, colored pencils, glue, paste, staplers, scissors, tape, and so on. Keep these items in separate boxes.

● Know the interests of the children in your class. Give them many opportunities to talk about and pursue their interests. Although some gifted children are very capable across all areas of development, most have one or two specific areas of talent and interest and are normal in other areas. By giving all children opportunities to pursue interests you will be able to determine which children are gifted and to nurture those gifts.

● Ask the parents of any new child if their child has any particular talents, skills, interests, or strengths. Parents are usually good judges of their child's abilities, particularly if they have a checklist to use, such as the one that follows. As with any child with special needs, much contact and good communication with parents is necessary to avoid problems and provide the best possible services.

• Understanding the eight different intelligences (described in more detail in "Selecting and Using a Curriculum," pp. 40–41) can help you to see and nurture a broad range of gifts and talents. These are: linguistic intelligence ("word smart"), logical-mathematical intelligence ("number/reasoning smart"), spatial intelligence ("picture smart"), bodily-kinesthetic intelligence ("body smart"), musical intelligence ("music smart"), interpersonal intelligence ("people smart"), intrapersonal intelligence ("self smart"), naturalist intelligence ("nature smart"). Value them equally and provide many opportunities in your classroom for them all to be expressed and developed.

• Teachers and parents have a critical role in helping gifted and talented children reach their full potential. Although such children have within themselves these abilities, it requires a good deal of effort on the part of the adults in the children's lives to make sure that they are fully realized. We all know someone who has great talent and ability that he or she is not using! The adults need to assure that these children have a good balance of healthy activities (time for active play and to be with friends) and emotional support, and to make certain that their needs and weaknesses are not overlooked. The adults also need to provide access to high-quality resources and assistance they need to nurture their talents. For example, a child with visual artistic talent will need to have a special teacher or two, usually found through art schools. However, finding the right teacher is important and difficult. A teacher should understand the developmental needs of young children, challenge without putting too much pressure on the child, and nurture the particular strengths of the child.

Identifying Gifted and Talented Children

The following is a list of characteristics of young children who are gifted and/or talented. Most gifted children have a number of these characteristics but not all.

A gifted child . . .

- Has a very good memory, especially long-term memory
- Has a very good vocabulary
- Can concentrate for long periods
- Retains information easily
- Observes keenly and is very curious
- Has strong interests
- Shows early compassion for others
- Is interested in books
- Exhibits a high energy level
- Is often a perfectionist
- Prefers to play with older children or to be with adults
- Does simple math problems easily and enjoys them
- Is very persistent
- Has a good sense of humor
- Uses common items in uncommon ways
- Shows leadership ability and good social skills
- Shows a strong interest in any or in several of the arts
- Is very sensitive

As most children have at least one area of strength, take a wide view of giftedness or talent. A child may be gifted in the area of social skills and leadership (could she be a future politician?), large-motor skills (a future athlete?), empathy toward others (a future psychologist?), small-motor skills (a future craftsperson?), or verbal skills such as persuasion and negotiation (a future lawyer?).

• When planning your activities, devise ways to make them more challenging for gifted children. If, for example, you will be playing a memory game during small group time, plan to add additional items when your gifted children have a turn. For instance, for most children you would place four items on a tray and take one away (while you cover the items so they can't see which one is removed). Then you would invite a child to guess which one is gone. For gifted children you might place six items and take two away. Plan this ahead of time so the activity will run smoothly. For all the children, including gifted children, increase the difficulty of the activity slightly, once they can do it with little effort. However, start and end with activities that are not too difficult, so that all the children will feel competent and successful.

- Ask gifted children for their suggestions about changing aspects of an activity and follow through on reasonable ideas. This will stretch their thinking skills and provide valuable feedback about their thoughts and needs.

- Give gifted children many opportunities to make real choices and to be leaders: "You can dismiss the children from circle. How would you like to do it—by first initials, by colors of shirts, or in some other way?"

- Allow gifted children to pursue their own interests as far as they can go. Encourage them by providing books and materials related to their interests. Many gifted children are particularly attracted to computers because they enable them to stretch their skills and knowledge beyond what they can do on their own. Computers also have challenges inherent in them; there are always new things to do on the computer and more sophisticated ways of doing them. (See the chapter "The Computer Center" on pp. 31–33 for more ideas.)

- Give all children, but especially gifted children, a five-minute warning, at least, before they have to end their activity and move on to the next routine.

- Ask gifted children about how they came up with a particular response. Although some children will not be able to tell you, others will. For example, if a child says to you, "I think that sign says 'Open,'" ask her how she knows that. Her response will give you great insight into how her mind works and help you to plan for her needs. She might say, "I see it every time we go into the store" or "My mother read it to me yesterday" or "I sounded out the letters." The first response indicates that she is a very receptive, quick, and self-directed learner; the second indicates a good visual and auditory memory; and the third reveals an analytical thinker.

- Be prepared to modify an activity while you are doing it to make it more challenging. Or, provide an alternative, although you did not plan for it. For example, if you notice that a gifted child is bored during a story that the other children are enjoying, let her choose to look at another book by herself or leave off words at the end of some sentences and have the child verbally fill them in.

- Because most gifted children are very active and have broad interests, provide a wide variety of choices including challenging games, puzzles, dramatic play situations, and table toys.

- Give gifted children many opportunities to generate ideas through brainstorming rather than through answering questions that have one right answer. (Read the chapter on "Individualizing" on pp. 47–50 for more ideas.)

Lack of Access to Support and Resources

This is a problem for all teachers and parents of gifted children, but it is particularly acute for families with low incomes and those in rural areas.

- Maintain a list of good teachers and resources in the community as you become aware of them related to specific talents. A child with musical ability may be better off with a good piano teacher than with a poor violin teacher because that is her (or the parents) preferred instrument.

- Some teachers will take children on a scholarship. Help parents ask, if necessary. Some communities have music centers or programs that assist with the cost of renting or purchasing a musical instrument. In many communities, you will find clubs for various interests—astronomy, computers, photography, dance, theater, or drawing, for example—and that have adults who really enjoy nurturing the interests and talents of young children.

- Help find a mentor for the child. This can be an older child or teen with similar talents who will help the child—emotionally as much as with skills—by taking a strong interest in her.

- The Internet can be a great resource to connect with a community of similarly talented children, and parents and teachers of such children, who can provide advice and support.

Problem Behaviors of Some Gifted Children

Because of their uniqueness, gifted children have a tendency toward certain behaviors that can cause problems for themselves, yourself, their parents, or their classmates. Use the suggestions in the table on the following page to minimize these problems.

Problems	Suggested Solutions
Bored, acts silly, acts out.	Provide more stimulating and challenging activities. Give the child opportunities and ample time to pursue her own interests at her own pace.
Invents her own methods or systems of doing things, which conflict with yours or the way these things need to be done.	Provide many opportunities for the child to do things her own way when it will not cause a problem. When something must be done your way, be firm about the need do it your way, but explain your reasons clearly. Help her generate ways to meet both her needs and those of the group.
Gullible, easily fooled, and swayed.	Appreciate the child's sense of wonder, trust, and curiosity that results in him being gullible. Respect him by not teasing about his gullibility. Point out calmly the truth of the situation. Support and validate his feelings so that he will continue to be open and trusting. Stop others from teasing him.
Perfectionist, discouraged, critical of self and others.	Continue to encourage the child's attempts: "You feel you can do better and you will. You tried hard and worked hard, which is something to be very proud of." Also: "Look how much better you did this time than last time." Tell her specifically what she does well and why it is good. Support and validate her feelings of frustration at the shortcomings of others: "Some children find things more difficult than you do, but everyone has some things they do very well. Let's appreciate how much people try."
Gets impatient or angry at interruptions.	Allow plenty of time for the child to work on things of his own choosing. Give plenty of warning before he has to finish an activity. Have a way and a place for him to save his work to finish at another time. Make sure that he can keep his work safe in this place.
Dislikes repetitious activities or games.	When the child is bored with an activity, offer her an alternative. Help her express her discomfort in a socially appropriate way: "When you are restless ask me for something else to do."
Resists directions.	Give the child many opportunities to have control over her time and routines. Explain thoroughly the reasons for your directions. Give her plenty of advanced warning before changes.
Very active and energetic, talks too much, and dominates discussions.	Provide long free choice times with a wide variety of active choices. Redirect the child's energy into activities that are creative and constructive. Limit the amount of time any child can talk in a group setting. When he wants too much of your time, tell him that you will listen to him for one more minute (set a timer), but that you will listen again at a specific time (such as "as soon as we go outside").
Overlooks details and skips routines; impatient with things that are not important to her.	Give the child some slack by not putting too much emphasis on formalities and routines. Remind her when she needs to do something for health or safety reasons and explain why: "Tie your shoes so that you don't trip over your laces." You will have to do this often but say it calmly. The child is not forgetful, simply disinterested.

Resources

Galbraith, J., and P. Espland. 1998. *The gifted kids' survival guide for ages ten and under.* Minneapolis: Free Spirit Publishing.

Karnes, M., and L. J. Johnson. 1989. Training for staff, parents, and volunteers working with gifted young children, especially those with disabilities and from low-income homes. *Young Children* 44 (3): 49–56.

Smutny, J. F., ed. 1998. *The young gifted child: Potential and promise: An anthology.* Cresskill, N.J.: Hampton Press.

Walker, B., N. L. Hafenstein, and L. Crow-Enslow. 1999. Meeting the needs of gifted learners in the early childhood classroom. *Young Children* 54 (1): 32–36.

Walker, S. Y., and S. K. Perry. 1991. *The survival guide for parents of gifted kids: How to understand, live with, and stick up for your gifted child.* Minneapolis: Free Spirit Publishing.

Winebrenner, S., and P. Espeland, eds. 2000. *Teaching gifted kids in the regular classroom: Strategies and techniques every teacher can use to meet the academic needs of the gifted and talented.* Rev. ed. Minneapolis: Free Spirit Publishing.

Wolfe, J. 1989. The gifted preschooler: Developmentally different, but still three or four years old. *Young Children* 44 (3): 41–48.

Web Sites

ERIC Clearinghouse on Disabilities and Gifted Education. ericec.org. Click on Frequently Asked Questions (FAQs) for links to many articles.

A Gifted Child. A Center for Evaluation of Gifted Children. www.a-gifted-child.com

Gifted Children: Identification, Encouragement, and Development. For the Parents of Children with Great Promise. www.gifted-children.com

Gifted Children Have Special Needs Too by Nancy Symmes Sweeney www.earlychildhood.com/Articles/index.cfm. Link to Children with Special Needs.

GT World. Online community for parents of gifted and talented children. www.gtworld.org

Pre-K Smarties: Teach Your Children. Links to articles and resources. www.preksmarties.com/gifted.htm

National Association for Gifted Children www.nagc.org

Nurturing Giftedness in Young Children by Wendy C. Roedell. ERIC Digest. 1990. www.eric.ed.gov. Click on Digests and enter the title in the search box.

Teaching Young Gifted Children in the Regular Classroom by Joan Franklin Smutny. ERIC Digest. 2000. www.eric.ed.gov. Click on Digests and enter the title in the search box.

4. Children Who Are Culturally or Physically "Different" and Biased Behaviors

Culture is how we live our lives. It is what we eat, how we dress, how we talk, the way we communicate, what we believe in, what we hope for, how we raise our children, the music we listen to, and so on. Everyone is part of a culture or several cultures.

Seeing culture broadly is important in order to help children and to create a supportive classroom. Our society has many cultures. A culture of poverty, a culture of wealth, a male culture, a female culture, gay and lesbian cultures, racial and ethnic cultures, regional cultures based on what part of the country one comes from, cultures based on what language a person speaks (including a Deaf culture whose members share American Sign Language), and more.

In many classrooms there are one or two children whose families are from a culture different from the other children. Whether they are the only African American children in a predominantly white classroom, the only white children in a predominantly Hispanic classroom, the only girls among boys, the only Deaf children among hearing children, or the only poor children among upper-middle-class children, they will need some special attention to feel included and accepted.

Similarly, a group of children who are all different from the predominant culture around them (for example, a class of all Asian children, whose families recently immigrated to Seattle) will need a curriculum and teaching approach that addresses their particular needs.

Children whose cultural backgrounds reflect the predominant culture around them (in many places this is every child in the class) need to learn about other cultures and people who are different than them. This broadens their view of the world and teaches them to accept and appreciate the similarities and differences of others.

All children receive great benefit from learning to actively counteract stereotypes and to move beyond judgments from surface appearances. In many class-

rooms the biases or prejudices of some children toward others are not based on cultural or ethnic differences, but on appearance, age, or gender. Physically attractive children tend to be liked and physically unattractive children tend to be not liked based on appearance alone. Girls and boys tend to stick with their own gender and exclude the other sex from their play. Older children tend to exclude younger children. These biases, found in most classrooms, are a good place to start to help children develop tolerance and compassion for others and to help children who may be victims of bias stand up for themselves. They are immediate and real.

Teachers need to employ a wide variety of methods to help children change misguided beliefs or to prevent the development of those beliefs. This chapter discusses concrete ways to replace stereotypes with truth.

Preventing Problems

● Meet with parents to determine their cultural preferences for their children, their goals, concerns, and hopes.

● Upon enrolling their children, make sure parents know your policies and procedures about celebrating cultural diversity, your approach to holidays, and your methods of counteracting bias. This should be in writing in a parent handbook.

● Establish a classroom rule: "Only words that don't hurt people can be used." Include here teasing, name-calling, and excluding others because of what they look like or who they are.

● Provide books, puzzles, pictures, and artwork that reflect a variety of cultures and show people of different races, skin colors, physical attributes, and abilities.

● Invite people with disabilities into your classroom and take field trips to visit people wth disabilities at their places of work. This way, children can see people with disabilities being capable and productive, as well as learn about adaptations.

● Invite to your class or visit people who have jobs that defy stereotypes. For instance, when doing a health unit, invite to the classroom a male nurse or a Hispanic dentist. Invite a female firefighter when doing a unit on community workers.

● Invite people to your classroom who can share their cultural traditions—stories, songs, dance, dress, and food. Make sure the children know what these people do and how they dress during a typical day. Make clear the differences between costumes or historical dress and daily dress, and between rituals and daily routines.

● Involve children in traditions from other cultures. For example, during Halloween, tell children how it is celebrated in other countries. Role-play some of these traditions. Invite the children to tell you a joke for an apple or a nickel as the children in Scotland do on Halloween. Because real bonfires on almost every street corner are another Halloween tradition in Scotland, gather the children around a pretend bonfire (piled up branches and wood on top of flashlights, decorated with paper flames in a slightly darkened room) and listen to stories. Share your own traditions with the children.

● Use holiday celebrations as a basis for counteracting stereotypes. Tell the story of Thanksgiving from the perspective of Native Americans and use cultural activities that represent actual practices rather than stereotypes. Show examples of Native American stereotypes (readily found at Thanksgiving time) and explain why they are not accurate.

● Use a bicultural and bilingual (if appropriate) curriculum with a class consisting of children who are culturally different from the predominant society. Many are available. In this approach children learn the values, language, and customs of their own culture as well as those of the predominant one.

● Answer questions about people with differences openly and honestly. For example, if a child asks, "Why does that man walk funny?" answer by saying, "He was probably born with legs that work differently from most people, although I don't know for sure. He uses crutches and metal braces on his legs to help support his legs so he can walk for himself. You may ask him yourself politely if he's not busy."

Dealing with Existing Problems
When You See Bias Happening

Children will not change their misguided beliefs about differences (learned from parents and/or assimilated from media and society in general) simply by seeing and hearing positive images of different cultures or by celebrating cultural holidays (Martin Luther King Jr.'s birthday, Hanukkah, Kwanza, Chinese New Year, Cinco de Mayo, and so on). To change their beliefs or to minimize the likelihood that they will develop negative beliefs, it is necessary to address the bias directly.

● Give children correct information as soon as they hear stereotypical statements (whether from children or adults) or see biased behavior. Say something like the following: "It hurts deeply inside to be told you can't play because of the color of your skin (or how much you weigh, and so forth). This goes against our class rule of using words that do not hurt. People have to get to know each other before they can really tell if they like or don't like each other. Let me help you find a way to play together."

● Help the offended child stand up for himself. Support his hurt feelings and then help him say such words as "I'm proud of my skin color and I can play here if I want to." Continue to encourage nonbiased behaviors in the offending child: "You had a lot of fun today with Maria whose skin is different from yours. Many different children can enjoy each other." Don't try to force friendships or deny a child's feelings of dislike or repulsion. Set up opportunities for friendships to develop through play and mutual interests.

● Develop activities that actively counteract the stereotype that was acted upon. Write stories with the children about classroom events in which biases were overcome (such as two culturally different children who didn't like each other at first but then became good friends). Use puppets to make up stories about incidents of bias and how people can deal with them effectively.

● When you or the children notice examples of prejudice, show them ways to do something about it. For example, on a field trip to a museum, you realize that the museum has many steps and is not wheelchair accessible. Ask the children, "Can all people get up these steps? Which people can't? Can they get into the museum? How would it make you feel if you couldn't go to the museum? What can be done about it?" If they have trouble developing solutions, suggest some, such as talking to the person in charge of the museum or writing a letter to him. Follow through on the idea as a class and share the response. Sometimes you can get dramatic and satisfying results. Your actions may result in the building of a ramp! If this happens, take several trips to watch the ramp being built.

● Meet with the parents of the child who often expresses bias. Explain how you are dealing with this trait in the classroom and discuss your views on it. Listen carefully to their views and develop a plan together. If they disagree with you and support their child's biases, make clear that in your class you still will not allow the voicing or acting out of biases. (They may choose to use a different program.) Have a parent meeting where all parents can listen and discuss these issues. You may gain good support this way.

Differences in Learning Styles and Priorities Due to Culture

Different cultures emphasize certain values and abilities over others. While some cultures strongly value education, others value hard work and physical labor. Some cultures value promptness, others value a relaxed attitude about time. The visual sense is very important in some cultures (colorful art and clothing) while other cultures place more emphasis on the auditory sense (music, discussion, and literature). Seeing the strength of what each culture values and recognizing how it may be different from those in your classroom is important. A clash between a child's own culture and the culture of the school will result in his feeling less able, less willing to participate, different, and odd.

● Once you have recognized the differences between your values and the values of a family (discovered through home visits, meeting with parents, inviting parents to share aspects of the culture in the classroom, reading, and listening to the child), help the child by being flexible about your values and by supporting his. For example, in the culture of the urban poor in America, many families view time as very flexible and flowing. (There are many exceptions to this and to any generalizations about a culture.) The family may have no set meal times, bedtimes, bath schedules, and so on. When the child enters your class, he confronts a set schedule with specific times for everything. This is very different from what he has always known and therefore internalized as his sense of what time means. Review your schedule with the children and give frequent reminders about what happens and when, give ample warnings before the next routine on your schedule, allow children to finish projects or save them to finish later, allow plenty of time for children to play and choose from a wide selection of activities, and alter your schedule occasionally. This will enable you to help all children develop a sense of time and order (which is highly valued in mainstream society) while supporting the child whose culture views time differently. Apply a similar approach to other cultural issues.

Multiracial or Multiethnic Children

The numbers of children of mixed race/ethnicity is growing faster than the numbers of single-race children. You may even have a multiracial/multiethnic child in your class and not realize it. They have different needs than children of one race/ethnicity (whether a minority race or Anglo). Their needs often get overlooked, even with teachers who have very multicultural curriculum and environments, as they are more complex. Every multiracial/multiethnic child has a different situation and parents can view their children's ethnicity very differently.

● Have conversions with the parents about how they view their child. Some feel strongly that their child should identify with a particular racial identity, while others may feel that the child should identify with both (or all) races. Still others may feel strongly that they should have no firm identification with any race or the child should eventually choose. Also find out how they combine their cultures. Do they celebrate all holidays associated with both (or all) cultures, or do they celebrate none? Are most of the family's friends and relatives of one particular race or are they diverse?

● Most families want and most children need to have their particular combination of identities recognized and appreciated. When talking about winter holidays, for example, you might say, "In Paula's house they celebrate Christmas and Hanukkah." Or during a meal, "Ken eats with chopsticks sometimes and a fork at other times in his house." Or when discussing Martin Luther King Jr.'s birthday and around St. Patrick's Day, "Kylie is proud both of her African heritage and her Irish heritage."

● Many multiracial/multiethnic adults talk about feeling, as children, that they belong to no group or are "in-between." They also report being teased a great deal and feeling ashamed. As a clear sense of identity is important to growing up healthy, this is of great concern. You can do many things to help multiracial/multiethnic children feel visible and valued. There are some excellent picture books to help you, listed in the resources. Although doing many things to celebrate the diversity around us is an important part of this effort, it is not enough. It is also vital to talk about the diversity *within* us. Almost all of your children (as well as teachers and staff) have some mixed heritage. We also have different characteristics, some of which are more like our fathers and some more like our mothers. Make books about these and talk about them.

● There are also many children who are single-race but have been adopted into a family of a different race. Their needs are similar in that they usually have multiple racial or ethnic identities and should feel proud of both of them. However, they have the additional needs of children who have been adopted.

● Ask for training and resources. Almost all communities have a sensitive, knowledgeable person who can provide insight into the particular needs of multiracial/multiethnic children and how teachers can help meet them. Read more on the issue. There are some good books and Web sites on this topic listed in the resources.

Children with Gay or Lesbian Parents

This is also a growing population, as birth technologies improve and more gay or lesbian parents adopt children. Among gay or lesbian parents, there is much diversity. Some are very open and will actively help you to meet their child's needs and to talk about their family with the class. Others are more careful and want you to make no special mention of their families. Make sure that you maintain ongoing communication with them to know how (or if) they want their family to be discussed with their child and with the class.

● Most teachers who are not gay or lesbian have a high level of discomfort dealing with this issue, in part because they have a hard time separating "sex" from the issue of sexual orientation. They also have a hard time feeling comfortable talking about anything related to sex with young children who are not their own. The simplest way of talking about sexual orientation with young children is not to deal with sex at all, but focus on what is visible: some families have two mommies, some have two daddies, some have one mommy or one daddy, and some have a mommy and a daddy.

● There are now more images and books available (see the resources) that show male couples with children and female couples with children. This is important in helping these children feel that their families are not so different from other families. Children's healthy development (including sexual and sex-role development) is much less contingent on the sexual orientation of their parents than other factors, like how nurturing and supportive the child's parents and teachers are. However, as with other "differences," these children are vulnerable, if for no other reason than that they will get so much negativity from other children and adults who are biased. These children will need a bit more support, assurance, protection, and self-esteem building than most other children. Make sure you intervene if you see any bias from others by using the strategies discussed previously.

Children Who Have Been Adopted

Include adoption whenever talking about birth, babies, and families. It is now more common for children who are adopted to be told so by their parents, but many parents still do not tell their children. While it is true that if the child does not know, chances are you do not know, it is important not to assume that if you know, the child knows. Telling a child he has been adopted is a delicate matter that should only be done by parents. If parents are unsure about what and when to tell their child that he is adopted, refer them to some of the resources listed at the end of this chapter.

● Adoption is one way that families are made, however, and it should be part of your exploration of families with your children even if you have no adopted children in your class. As with all complicated issues, give a modest amount of information at a level young children can understand. Focus on the joy of being "chosen" and bringing happiness into the lives of the new parents. The child, after all, makes the family. There are a number of excellent picture books listed in the resources to help you send clear, positive messages.

Children from Religious Minorities

Some families are part of a religious group, such as Buddhist, Jehovah's Witnesses, or Jewish, and have many values and practices that may be very different from the common practices in your classroom. Make sure all families know your approach to celebrating holidays and birthdays when they enroll. Meet with parents from religious minorities to negotiate any altering of your approach that is acceptable to both of you. This may involve inviting a Jewish parent to show the children how Hanukkah is celebrated or supporting parents who are Jehovah's Witnesses who decide to keep their child home during Halloween. If a fair compromise cannot be worked out, the parents may feel more comfortable placing their child in a program affiliated with their particular religion.

● Help parents recognize that many religious holidays have secular aspects to them. Dyeing eggs and egg hunts at Easter and Santa Claus and trees at Christmas have become mainstream American cultural symbols and events, although they have religious origins. Almost all children know about and enjoy these activities and traditions. To deny their existence by never doing these activities nor displaying traditional decorations in a center does children a disservice because they are so important to children. However, limit the amount of time you spend celebrating traditional holidays in typical ways because the children get exposed to them from many other sources. Expand children's cultural understanding and awareness by presenting a wide array of holidays and ways that they are celebrated in different places. Use children's excitement about holidays to foster learning and growth in all areas of development. Invite the children to classify and match Easter eggs of various patterns or make books for Christmas presents. Consider your classroom a place where all children's interests and values are supported and then deepened and expanded.

Resources

Beaty, J. J. 1997. *Building bridges with multicultural picture books for children 3–5.* Upper Saddle River, N. J.: Merrill Prentice-Hall.

Derman-Sparks, L., and the A.B.C. Task Force. 1989. *Anti-bias curriculum.* Washington, D.C.: NAEYC.

Elswood, R. 1999. Really including diversity in early childhood classrooms. *Young Children* 54 (4): 62–66.

Freeman, M., S. Foster, N. Peddle, and L. Burnley. 1995. God revels in diversity: Converting the faithful to anti-bias education. *Young Children* 50 (2): 20–25.

Garcia, E. E. 1997. Research in review. The education of Hispanics in early childhood: Of roots and wings. *Young Children* 52 (3): 5–14.

Gray, D. D. 2002. *Attaching in adoption: A practical guide for parents.* Indianapolis: Perspectives Press.

Grieshaber, S., and G. Cannella, eds. 2001. *Embracing identities in early childhood education: Diversity and possibilities.* New York: Teachers College Press.

Hunt, R. 1999. Making positive multicultural early childhood education happen. *Young Children* 54 (5): 39–42.

Johnson, H. H. 1994. The Bodyworks: Inside me—Another approach to alike and different. *Young Children* 49 (6): 21–26.

Jones, E., and L. Derman-Sparks. 1992. Meeting the challenge of diversity. *Young Children* 47 (2): 12–18.

Kendall, F. 1995. *Diversity in the classroom: New approaches to the education of young children.* New York: Teachers College Press.

Koeppel, J., and M. Mulrooney. 1992. The Sister Schools Program: A way for cildren to learn about diversity when there isn't any in their school. *Young Children* 48 (1): 44–47.

Mallory, B. L., and R. S. New, eds. 1993. *Diversity and developmentally appropriate practices.* New York: Teachers College Press.

Matiella, A. C. 1991. Positively different. *Creating a bias-free environment for young children.* Santa Cruz, Calif.: ETR Associates/Network Publications.

Morrison, J. W., and L. S. Rodgers. 1996. Being responsive to the needs of children from dual heritage backgrounds. *Young Children* 52 (1): 29–33.

Ramsey, P. G. 1998. *Teaching and learning in a diverse world: Multicultural education for young children.* 2d ed. New York: Teachers College Press.

Root, M. P. P., ed. 1996. *The multiracial experience.* Newberry Park, Calif.: Sage.

Seng, S. H. 1994. *Educating young children in a diverse society.* ERIC, ED 377981.

Thompson, B. J. 1993. *Words can hurt you: Beginning a program of anti-bias education.* Reading, Mass.: Addison-Wesley Publishing Company.

Wardle, F. 1990. Endorsing children's differences: Meeting the needs of adopted minority children. *Young Children* 45 (5): 44–46.

———. 1999. *Tomorrow's children: Meeting the needs of multiracial and multiethnic children at home, in early childhood programs, and at school.* Denver: Center for the Study of Biracial Children.

Watkins, M. 1995. *Talking to young children about adoption.* New Haven, Conn.: Yale University Press.

Wickens, E. 1993. Penny's question: I will have a child in my class with two moms—What do you know about this? *Young Children* 48 (3): 25–28.

Wright, M. A. 2000. *I'm chocolate, you're vanilla: Raising healthy black and biracial children in a race-conscious world.* San Franscisco: Jossey-Bass.

Children's Books

Combs, B. 2001. *123 a family counting book.* Ridley Park, Pa.: Two Lives Publishing. (Various gay and lesbian families)

———. 2001. *ABC a family alphabet book.* Ridley Park, Pa.: Two Lives Publishing. (Various gay and lesbian families)

Curtis, J. L. 1996. *Tell me again about the night I was born.* New York: Harper Collins Juvenile. (Adoption)

Davol, M. W. 1993. *Black, white, just right!* Morton Grove, Ill.: Albert Whitman & Co. (Biracial child finds strengths in her dual identity)

Edmonds, B. L. 2000. *Mama eat ant, yuck!* Eugene, Ore.: Barby's House Books. (Two moms)

Gordon, S. 2000. *All families are different.* Amherst, N.Y.: Prometheus Books.

Kates, B. J. 1992. *We're different, we're the same.* Sesame Street Picturebacks. New York: Random House.

Katz, K. 1997. *Over the moon: An adoption tale.* New York: Henry Holt. (Foreign adoption)

———. 2002. *The colors of us.* New York: Henry Holt & Co.

Kissinger, K. 1997. *All the colors we are: The story of how we get our skin color.* St. Paul: Redleaf Press.

Koehler, P. 1997. *The day we met you.* New York: Aladdin Paperbacks. (Adoption)

Morris, A. 1993. *Bread, bread, bread.* Around the World Series. New York: Scott Foresman.

———. 1994. *Loving.* Around the World Series. New York: Mulberry Books.

———. 1994. *On the go.* Around the World Series. New York: Scott Foresman.

———. 1995. *Houses and homes.* Around the World Series. New York: Mulberry Books.

———. 1998. *Shoes, shoes, shoes.* Around the World Series. New York: Mulberry Books.

———. 1998. *Tools.* New York: Mulberry Books.

———. 2000. *Families.* New York: HarperCollins Juvenile.

———. 2000. *Hats, hats, hats.* Around the World Series. New York: Mulberry Books.

Quinsey, M. B. 1986. *Why does that man have such a big nose?* Seattle: Parenting Press. (Good responses to questions about physical differences)

Schuett, S. 1994. *Beginnings: How families come to be.* Morton Grove, Ill.: Albert Whitman & Co. (Six children learn how they came to be with their families—biologically, adoptions into diverse families, and living with a relative after the death of a parent)

Videos

Educational Productions
900 SW Gemini Drive
Beaverton, OR 97008
www.edpro.com

Starting Points: For Educators of Culturally and Linguistically Diverse Young Children. (Set of three videos)

Web Sites

Adoptive Families Magazine. Link to Adoption in the Classroom, a two-page guide for teachers, and other articles and resources.
www.adoptivefamilies.com

The Center for the Study of Biracial Children
www.csbc.cncfamily.com

Children of Lesbians and Gays Everywhere. COLAGE.
www.colage.org. Click on Resources for access to many articles, book lists, and more.

Creating Optimal Learning Environments for All Children: Culturally Responsive Curriculum and Materials. NWREL Child and Family E-Newsletter.
www.nwrel.org/cfc. Link to archived newsletter: Vol. 1, No.11.

Evaluating Multicultural Children's Picture Books. Facts in Action Early Childhood Clearinghouse.
factsinaction.org. Click on In the Classroom: Putting Research into Practice.

Examining Multicultural Picture Books for the Early Childhood Classroom: Possibilities and Pitfalls by Jean Mendoza and Debbie Reese. Early Childhood Research & Practice (ECRP). Volume 3, No. 2., Fall 2001 (online only). ecrp.uiuc.edu/v3n2/mendoza.html

Gay Parent Magazine www.gayparentmag.com. Click on Articles to access many articles on the topic of being gay and a parent.

Gender and Culture in Picture Books. Resources compiled by Kay E. Vandergrift, Rutgers University. www.scils.rutgers.edu/~kvander. Link on Gender and Culture in Picture Books.

Great Owl Books' Butternut collection of books for the biracial community www.viconet.com/~greatowlbooks

Lesbian and Gay Parenting. The American Psychological Association Web site. www.apa.org/pi/parent.html

Meeting the Needs of Multiracial and Multiethnic Children by Francis Wardle www.earlychildhood.com/Articles/index.cfm. Enter "multiracial" in the search box.

Multicultural Picture Books for Children. Booklist for Children from the Boston Public Library. www.bpl.org/kids/booklists/multic.htm

National Adoption Center's "The Learning Center" www.adoptnet.org. Click on Information Resources for access to articles and other resources.

National Adoption Information Clearinghouse. U.S. Department of Health and Human Services. www.calib.com/naic

Picture Books/Young Readers. Clearinghouse for Multicultural/Bilingual Education of Weber State University departments.weber.edu/mbe. Link to Clearinghouse Index, then Books.

Preparing Children for a Multicultural World by Melia Franklin. Action Alliance for Children. www.4children.org. Click on Search and enter "multicultural" in the search box.

Responding to Linguistic and Cultural Diversity. NAEYC Position Statement. 1995. (Also in Spanish) www.naeyc.org/resources. Link to Position Statements and then Improving Practices with Young Children.

Serving Children in Biracial/Biethnic Families. A Training Curriculum. California Childcare Health Program. www.childcarehealth.org. Click on Training Curricula.

Teaching about Diversity. Educators for Social Responsibility. www.esrnational.org/diversity.html

Teaching Young Chidren to Resist Bias. 1997. National Parent Information Network. npin.org. Click on Virtual Library, then on Full Text Resources, then on the "T" in the alphabet list, then scroll down to article title.

Working with Culturally and Linguistically Diverse Families by D. A. Bruns and R. M. Corso. ERIC Digest. 2001. www.eric.ed.gov. Click on Digests and enter the title in the search box.

5. Children Who Are Learning English

English language learners (ELL) are also called children who have "English as a second language" (ESL), and the somewhat negative, "limited English proficient" (LEP), as well as other terms. The number of such children has increased rapidly in recent years and will continue to do so in all parts of the United States. Among the challenges we face are helping them understand basic rules of the classroom, helping them communicate with other children and make friends, communicating with their parents, and helping them feel like an equal member of your classroom community.

Your general, long-term goal is to help these children become bicultural and bilingual. That means putting a high value on home language and culture while supporting new skills and abilities in learning English and U.S. culture. It is challenging to help children learn a new set of behaviors—some of which may be in opposition to those learned and valued at home—and to do this while not diminishing the importance of the home culture. But it is achievable and necessary if we are to help ELL children to be successful. For example, in many cultures, looking down while an adult or higher status person is talking is a sign of respect. However, in mainstream U.S. culture, looking directly in the speaker's eyes is considered respectful. If this happens you can tell the child that you appreciate that she is being respectful, that it is good to do this at home, but most American adults want you to look them in the eyes when they talk to you. This "teaching" mode is a good strategy for helping children learn to be bicultural while being supportive of their home cultures. Many adults who once learned English in American classrooms talk about how "different" and "inferior" they felt at the time. They also report that their teachers often did things that contributed to these feelings, rather than to help make things easier for them. Of course there also are many positive stories of supportive, caring teachers. This section includes ideas for making life better for these children and smoothing the transition while they learn English language and American culture.

Preventing Problems

● Become aware of what constitutes American middle-class cultural practices and values, which operate in most schools and programs, that are distinct from other cultures. This will help you see where children and families may differ. Teachers in most American classrooms foster individualism and independence (such as "do your own work"). Children from many other cultures often mistake this for coldness, a lack of personal connectedness, and an uncaring teacher.

● Learn some basic words and phrases in the child's language, especially those that may comfort her in times of stress. Also learn some phrases that will help you to communicate with parents. Do this while continuing to learn as much of the language as you can.

● The most important and strongest parts of communication are nonverbal. Creative teachers find many ways to support and connect with children with whom they do not share a language by being emotionally responsive and sensitive. Smiles, hugs, encouraging nods, gestures, observing for needs, and helping them meet those needs—all go a long way to supporting children without knowing their home language.

● If you have a number of children in your group who speak the same language and the rest speak English, strive toward a bilingual classroom if you or an assistant can speak both languages. This puts equal value on English and the other language and helps the English-speaking children by introducing them to a new language. Start with teaching everyone songs, finger plays, and "functional dialogue"—such as words and phrases used during meal times—in the second language and then expand.

● Find ways to communicate with families, such as having notes translated. Assist families in linking with resources in the community that help immigrant families and to classes that teach English to adults. If families feel connected and valued by the school or center, they will be supportive of you and their child's growth and development.

● Find out some of the unique aspects of the children's cultures including styles of communication, popular foods, beliefs, routines, songs, dances, games, and folktales. Use this information to add to your curriculum and materials that support their home culture in the classroom.

● If you have a diverse group of English language learners who speak a number of different languages, find some commonalties among them to connect them with each other. In one preschool class the teacher found that dramatic play around a restaurant theme was very successful because many of the children's families were involved in the restaurant business. Common things across cultures are slightly different in each, such as the tools we use to eat (chopsticks, forks, fingers), types of bread we eat (tortillas, sliced loaves, nan), kinds of hats we wear, and the way we carry things.

Dealing with Existing Problems
Subgroups of Children Who Speak the Same Language

It is fairly common to have a number of children in the same class who speak the same (non-English) language. Some of these children may even be related, typically as cousins. They tend to stick together closely and form a tight-knit group. The problem is that they set themselves apart socially from the other children and it can delay their access to learning English and American culture. Using the bilingual approach described previously can help greatly with this problem. Take steps to bring those children into the group and connect other children with them. The walls that segregate a classroom into two parts can be invisible, but still very formidable. Provide specific help to all children to get them to play and interact with each other. Teach both groups of children some basic words and phrases, gestures, and social cues (eye contact, gentle touching) and help the children to use them. Connect children with each other through their mutual interests or skills, for example block building, cars/trucks, drawing/painting, music/singing, or science.

Problems with a Bilingual Aide

Many times the assistant teacher or aide speaks both the language of a number of the children in the class and English. She is expected to help children who are monolingual or just beginning to learn English to understand what is happening, and to assist you, as the teacher, to speak to them. However, in some cases the bilingual aide may not have much education or professional experience in early childhood education and this may result in some clashes between you and her.

● Try to prevent such clashes by giving her a thorough orientation and rationale to your teaching approach. Also explain why you are doing what you do as you go, as much as possible.

● Advocate for training opportunities for her from your school or agency.

● Enlist her help and support in pursuing the goal of bicultural and bilingual competence for all children as discussed previously. This will help avoid a common problem where the aide speaks her native language to those children who understand it, almost all the time and nearly exclusively.

● Sort out which of the aide's behaviors that concern you are culturally related and which are due to lack of training. It may be necessary to ask some questions and have a discussion with her to determine the difference, such as, "I want to understand your approach, tell me about your discussion with Carlito this morning." Do this when she does good things as well as things that concern you. You also might need to ask other people of the same cultural group about the behaviors to determine what is cultural and what is just practice. Be flexible with the culturally related behaviors and use the other behaviors as opportunities to teach your aide new skills.

● Choose your battles carefully. If you are instructing and correcting too often, you will undermine your relationship. Start by working on one specific concern that is likely to meet with success. Tell her what she does particularly well so not all your feedback is negative.

The Child Who Won't Speak at All

The "silent stage" is a common phase in the course of learning a new language. Most people (of any age) who are newly immersed in a foreign language environment go through it. During this stage, the person is learning by listening intently and is waiting to feel more confident before speaking publicly. In young children it typically lasts one or two months but can last longer, especially for children who are shy. If it goes on for much longer seek the help of a speech and language pathologist who knows about children who are learning a new language. Often such children will first communicate with a particular person with

whom they feel safe, usually another child or a teacher. Typically these first communications will be in a very soft, quiet voice. Support and assist them, but don't push them to speak. Provide some alternative ways for them to communicate, like pointing, gesturing, sign language, and picture boards, but not to the extent that it becomes an easy way out of speaking. Seek ideas from the children's parents and use some of the strategies recommended later in this book for children who are shy.

Resources

Ballenger, C. 1998. *Teaching other people's children: Literacy and learning in a bilingual classroom.* New York: Teachers College Press.

Garcia, E. E., and B. McLaughlin, with B. Spodek, and O. N. Saracho, eds. 1995. *Early childhood yearbook series: Meeting the challenge of linguistic and cultural diversity in early childhood education.* New York: Teachers College Press.

Genesee, F., ed. 1994. *Educating second language children: The whole child, the whole curriculum, the whole community.* New York: Cambridge University Press.

Genishi, C. 2002. Research in review: Young English language learners: Resourceful in the classroom. *Young Children* 57 (4): 66–72.

Tabors, P. O. 1997. *One child, two languages: A guide for pre-school educators of children learning English as a second language.* Baltimore: Paul H. Brookes.

Sources for Multilingual Children's Books

America's Stir-Fry
www.americas-stirfry.com

Bilingual Books for Kids, Inc.
www.bilingualbooks.com

Bookswithoutborders.com
bookswithoutborders.com

Web Sites

The Center for Multilingual, Multicultural Research at University of Southern California
www.usc.edu/dept/education/CMMR

Clearinghouse for Multicultural/Bilingual Education at Weber State University
departments.weber.edu/mbe

NAEYC Position Statement: Responding to Linguistic and Cultural Diversity—Recommendations for Effective Early Childhood Education. 1996.
www.naeyc.org/resources. Click on View Position Statements, then click on Improving practices with children, then scroll down to Responding to Linguistic and Ethnic Diversity.

The National Clearinghouse for English Language Acquisition and Language Instruction Educational Programs (formerly, National Center for Bilingual Education)
www.ncbe.gwu.edu. For a vast number of excellent resources click on the Online Library. Find links to the helpful NCRCD-SLL Publications, Educational Practice Reports, particularly #14: *Fostering Second Language Development in Young Children:*

Principles and Practices by Barry McLaughlin (1995). Also link to the NCBE Parent Guides: *If Your Child Learns in Two Languages* (available in five languages: English, Spanish, Vietnamese, Chinese, and Haitian Creole) and ERIC Digests.

NWREL Early Childhood E-Newsletter: ELL/Bilingual Education
www.nwrel.org/cfc/newsletters/vol1_is5.html

6. TV/Video-Obsessed Children

Some children spend a great deal of time watching television or videos at home. Although it may be only the older preschool children who spend time playing video games, all young children are influenced by them. In many cases adults do not limit what is watched or played, counteract the values promoted, nor help children understand what they see. Children in this situation will often engage in play that is derivative of TV shows, resulting in aggressive, repetitive, low-level, or dangerous play.

However, when children share a mutual interest based on toys and play from a TV show or video game, it can help them make friends. As this can be very helpful for a child who is new, shy, or "different," do not eliminate all such play. Instead, put reasonable limits on the play, as discussed in this chapter.

Preventing Problems

● Watch the popular shows and videos most often viewed by your children to understand who the characters are and what their appeal is.

● Have readily available dramatic play materials that encourage play not related to TV characters. Some examples: fire hats and pieces of garden hose; stethoscopes, crutches, bandages, and other hospital supplies; stamps, envelopes, paper, mail bags, hats, and other post office supplies.

● If you have action figures in your class, use generic ones that cannot be identified with currently popular shows. Provide small plastic dinosaurs, lions, bears, and other scary animals with which children can safely play out fears and aggression.

● Offer many opportunities for children to be involved in cooperative games and activities such as building projects and group art activities.

● Talk to parents about the importance of limiting, monitoring, and discussing what children view.

Because of the availability of videos in almost all homes, many children are watching adult films that confuse and even terrify them.

● Teach media literacy. Provide specific activities that teach children how to watch critically and not be fooled by advertisers or children's TV developers. Help children understand that advertisers want you to want things, most of which are bad for you, so that you will beg your parents for them. The advertisers will make these things look better than they are: more fun, more exciting, or tastier. See the resources at the end for media literacy activities.

Dealing with Existing Problems

Noncreative Play

● If some children insist that others play according to a particular TV script, talk to them about how the TV show was written by a person who made it up. Explain that children have ideas just as good as these adult writers. Help the children rewrite the script or create new ones.

● Ask questions and provide suggestions that help them get deeper insights behind characters' personalities and motivations: "What might have made the bad guy bad? What power can you use to change the bad guy? How can you use cleverness (brain power) rather than physical strength (body power) to stop the bad guy?"

Aggressive Play

Play that imitates TV often is a problem because of its aggressive nature. Be aware that in this kind of play, children may get hurt or may be dominated by others. However, remember that many children need to act out issues related to good and evil or power and weakness. The play tends to be loud, physical, and boisterous, which is very satisfying to many children. Give them ample opportunities to play out these themes and do loud physical play in acceptable ways. Adding play props outdoors based on themes such as firefighting, hunting for dinosaur bones, and emergency medical technicians, can help meet this goal.

- Set up rules to avoid problems and make sure that roles are rotated. Such rules might include the following: use only gentle contact and any child can call a time-out to leave the game or switch roles.

- Put a reasonable limit on the amount of time children can spend in play that is based on TV shows or videos. After that time, redirect them by suggesting other choices they can make. (See "War, Gun, or Violent Play" in "Hitting and Aggression" on p. 145 for ideas on dealing with action figures and other aggressive play from TV.)

Resolving Conflicts

- Conflicts that arise from this type of play provide excellent opportunities for you to help children learn conflict resolution skills. Encourage the children to talk through problems and help them negotiate compromises. (See "Helping Children with Difficult Behaviors" on pp. 123–126 and "Hitting and Aggression" on pp. 143–144 for conflict resolution ideas.)

Barbie Doll Play

Even if these types of dolls are not available in the classroom, many girls (and a few boys) will find opportunities to play out their ideas of "teenage adventures." This is disturbing because it usually reflects stereotypical behavior. It is the female version of boys' war play, as females are taught to gain power for themselves by attracting the "right man" (power by association). We know that this course is dangerous because it discourages self-reliance and intellectual growth. Many more women are hurt by it than win by it. To see young girls practicing behaviors whose only goals are to become popular with boys is cause for concern. However, stopping this type of play is difficult because the messages in the media are so strong.

- Tell the children about your concerns in simple terms: "Real teenagers like to dress up, but they also spend a lot of time reading and learning and working, so they can take care of themselves and their families when they are grown-ups."

- Put a time limit on the play and then redirect the children into an activity that is equally compelling, such as pretending to be teenagers working in a restaurant with many props and dress-up clothes.

- Provide a wide variety of active, hands-on choices. Stimulate the children's thinking and challenge their imaginations so that they will not need to play with Barbie dolls. (See "Toys from Home" on p. 55 for additional suggestions.)

Resources

Boyatzis, C. J. 1997. Of Power Rangers and v-chips. *Young Children* 52 (7): 74–79.

Cantor, J. 1998. *Mommy, I'm scared: How TV and movies frighten children and what we can do to protect them.* New York: Harvest Books.

Carlsson-Paige, N., and D. E. Levin. 1995. Viewpoint #4. Can teachers resolve the war-play dilemma? *Young Children* 50 (5): 62–63.

DeGaetano, G. 1996. *Watch it: Media literacy activities for young children.* Redmond, Wash.: Train of Thought Publishing.

Grossman, D., and G. DeGaetano. 1999. *Stop teaching our kids to kill: A call to action against TV, movie, and video game violence.* New York: Random House.

Levin, D. E. *Remote control childhood? Combating the hazards of media culture.* Washington, D.C.: NAEYC.

Levin, D. E., and N. Carlsson-Paige. 1994. Developmentally appropriate television: Putting children first. *Young Children* 49 (5): 38–44.

Levine, M. 1998. *See no evil: A guide to protecting our children from media violence.* San Francisco: Jossey-Bass.

Minow, N. N., and C. Lamay. 1996. *Abandoned in the wasteland: Children, television, and the First Amendment.* New York: Hill & Wang Publishers.

Winn, M. 2002. *The plug-in drug: Television, computers, and family life.* New York: Penguin USA.

Web Sites

Action for Media Education
www.action4mediaed.org

Articles on television and media. Kaiser Family Foundation. www.kff.org. Link on Television in the Browse by Topic area

The Center for Media Literacy
www.medialit.org. Click on Reading Room to access many articles.

Children Now. Children and the Media.
www.childrennow.org/media

Coalition for Quality Children's Media
www.cqcm.org

Guidelines for Family Television Viewing. ERIC Digest. 1990. (Available in Spanish and Chinese)
www.eric.ed.gov. Click on Digests and enter the title in the search box.

Media Violence in Children's Lives. NAEYC Position Statement. 1990, 1994.
www.naeyc.org. Link to Resources, then Position Statements, then Improving Program Practices with Children.

National Institute on Media and the Family
www.mediaandthefamily.org

Television Violence: Content, Context, Consequences by Amy Aidman. ERIC Digest. 1997.
www.eric.ed.gov. Click on Digests and enter the title in the search box.

Visual Media and Young Children's Attention Span by Gloria DeGaetano. Early Childhood Educators' and Family Web Corner. users.stargate.net/~cokids. Link to Articles and then New Articles, scroll down to Education.

7. Children with Extreme Fears

Most preschool children have common fears, such as a fear of the dark, snakes, or being left alone. These are healthy fears (they protect children) as long as they do not get in the way of children's abilities to play, have friends, and be reasonably independent for their age. These fears are healthy as far as they are connected to reality; that is, if some possibility of danger or harm really exists. Extremely fearful children will be obsessed by their fear. They will talk about it or show anxiety about it often and at times when no cause is apparent.

Possible Causes

Fears develop because preschoolers have active imaginations and are becoming aware of cause-and-effect relationships: "If it is dark then dangers can't be seen, and if they can't be seen then I can't protect myself." They have an increasing awareness of how many ways they can be hurt, they have conflicts within themselves over being independent but still needing adult protection, and they are egocentric (they see themselves at the center of the world and therefore believe dangers are directed at them).

Some gifted children can develop extreme fears (for example, of pollution, fire, or diseases) because, while they have an advanced intellect, they still have emotions typical of a young child. They understand certain facts and cause-and-effect relationships but lack the ability to put these in proper perspective.

Fears of monsters can represent children's anxieties about not being able to control their own aggression. (See part V, "Children with Challenging Behaviors," on p. 122 for ideas on teaching self-control.)

For toddlers or developmentally delayed children, some fears develop because the world is still an unsure place: "Is my brother with a mask on still my brother or is he somebody else?" The ability to know that something is still there even if it cannot be seen is called *object permanence*. It develops gradually and is why peek-a-boo is fun for children. They also have not developed a good sense of relationships (size, weight, and so on). They think that being washed down the drain along with the bath water is possible.

Extreme fears can develop as a result of the factors discussed above and the added experience of a trauma. In most cases, extreme fears are linked directly to a troubling experience, such as fear of fires after seeing a neighbor's house burn or fear of water after a near drowning. In other cases, the connection is less clear. Extreme fears can result from a more general anxiety or insecurity. A child who has witnessed a violent act may become extremely fearful of the dark, for example, although darkness was not connected to the event. A neglected or abused child may have a number of extreme fears, although none are necessarily related to a particular trauma.

Preventing Problems

● When the family enters the program, make sure they fill out an intake form that asks about any stressful events in the child's life and about fears the child has.

● Maintain regular communication with parents so that they will inform you of any problems or traumatic events in their children's lives.

● Create a sense of security for all children by having a consistent daily schedule, comforting routines, and a child-controlled environment (many appropriate choices, child-size furniture and materials, and equipment accessible on low shelves). Whenever possible, make children aware of all changes before they happen. Remind them of the next event in the schedule. Children feel safer when they can predict what will happen next.

● Support and validate the feelings of all children, even if you can't support the behaviors: "I can hear that you are very angry. You have a right to be angry, and I would be angry, too, if someone teased me. Let me help you talk to him about it."

● Provide many opportunities for children to safely express their feelings and fears through a wide variety of methods. Children can talk about fears during a sharing circle, draw on blank paper, make up stories that adults can write down for them, use dress-up clothes and props for dramatic play, play with small figures of people and animals, and act out short stories (such as "The Three Little Pigs") that involve fearful events.

● Play games that help strengthen the children's sense of knowing something is still there even if it can't be seen (object permanence). Include peek-a-boo, hide-and-seek, "what's missing?" and similar games.

● Read children's literature dealing with fearful events that children overcome. Original fairy tales do this better than most other forms of children's literature. Stories such as "Little Red Cap" and "Mama Goat and the Seven Little Kids" put children or young animals in extremely dangerous circumstances but through their own abilities, they come out of these adventures alive and even better off. These stories are very healing.

Dealing with Existing Problems

● Children with extreme fears will usually benefit from professional counseling. Recommend this and with the parents' permission, ask the counselor for advice about helping the child in the classroom. Counseling will be of most benefit if the whole family is involved. Provide suggestions for finding counselors who are skilled in working with young children.

● Support the child's feelings no matter how irrational they seem to you. Avoid the temptation to say something like the following: "Come on, there's nothing to be afraid of." Remember that the fears are very real to the child. Do not make the child do something that he is terrified of. Support him by saying: "I know dogs are frightening to you. You can hold my hand, and you don't have to pet her. I will protect you."

● Join the child's fantasy about the fear and help him overcome it. For example, if a child is afraid to go into a closet for some art materials because there is a monster in it, go into the closet with him to get rid of the monster. Follow his lead by asking, "What can we do to get rid of the monster?" Perhaps you will both need to catch the monster, put it in a garbage bag, and throw it in the dumpster.

● Most counselors help people overcome their fears by very gradually introducing the fearful element and letting the person get used to it slowly. You can do the same. For example, you can help a child overcome a

fear of water through the following steps, moving on to the next step only when he feels comfortable and in control:

1. Have him play in a gentle sprinkler or hose aimed at the feet and hold his hand.
2. Hold only his little finger.
3. Let go and have him play on his own.
4. Gradually raise the level and intensity of the water.
5. Have him stand in a small wading pool and hold his hand if needed.
6. Have him stand on his own.
7. Have him sit down in the wading pool while you hold his body.
8. Have him sit while you hold his hand.
9. Have him sit while you hold his little finger.
10. Have him sit on his own.
11. Take him to a large pool and have him wade in the shallow end while you hold his body.
12. Hold only his hand.
13. Hold only his little finger.
14. Have him play on his own.
15. Gradually increase the water level.

- Be aware that some children can move through these steps more quickly than others or may not need every step to be successful while other children may need even smaller steps. Make sure the child controls the process: "If you need my hand back again, just tell me."

- If the child talks about his fears very often, give only minimal attention to his comments and limit them. Say something like the following: "I'll listen carefully to you for one more minute (set a timer), and then you need to do something else." Respond so he will know you listened and then redirect him into active play with other children.

- Give the child many opportunities to be in control: "You can be in charge of turning the lights off and on when we leave and enter the room."

- Make up stories or read books directly related to the particular fear the child has that tell how a child overcame the fear.

- Provide specific, factual information about the object of the fear and ways to deal with it. For example, help a child who is very afraid of dogs by explaining that, "Most dogs will not chase you if you don't run. Most dogs will go away if you say 'Go' in a loud, firm voice and stamp your foot. Pet only a dog whose name you know and if the owner tells you it's okay."

- Talk with the parents. Find out if they know where the fear comes from. In one case, a child's intense fear of insects was a result of his mother's similar fear. The teacher helped the mother realize that until she was able to overcome her own fear, her child's fear would probably not diminish. Reassure the parents that with support most children grow out of most irrational fears.

Resources

Brett, D. 1988. *Annie stories*. New York: Workman.

Garber, S. W. 1993. *Monsters under the bed and other childhood fears: Helping your child overcome anxieties, fears, and phobias*. New York: Villard Books.

Grimm, J., and W. Grimm. 1944. *Grimm's fairy tales*. New York: Pantheon Books.

Hyson, M. C. 1986. Lobster on the sidewalk: Understanding and helping children with fears. In *Reducing stress in young children's lives*, edited by J. B. McCracken. Washington, D.C.: NAEYC.

Rapee, R. M., ed. 2000. *Helping your anxious child: A step-by-step guide for parents*. Oakland: New Harbinger Publications.

Children's Books

Blegvad, L. 1987. *Anna Banana and me*. New York: Aladdin Paperbacks. (Fears in general)

Crary, E. 1996. *I'm scared (Dealing with feelings)*. Seattle: Parenting Press. (Fears in general)

Hazen, B. S., and T. Ross. 1992. *The knight who was afraid of the dark*. New York: Penguin USA.

Howe, J. 1990. *There's a monster under my bed*. New York: Aladdin Paperbacks.

Marcus, I. W. 1991. *Scary night visitors: A story for children with bedtime fears*. Washington, D.C.: Magination.

Mayer, M. 1987. *There's an alligator under my bed*. New York: E. P. Dutton.

———. 1992. *There's a nightmare in my closet*. New York: E. P. Dutton.

———. 1992. *There's something in my attic*. New York: Puffin.

Polacco, P. 1997. *Thunder cake*. New York: Paper Star. (Fear of thunderstorms)

Rand, T. 1993. *Once when I was scared*. New York: Puffin. (Grandfather tells of how he braved the woods in a storm)

Sendak, M. 1988. *Where the wild things are*. New York: Scholastic. (Max confronts the monsters within)

Tomlinson, J. 2001. *The owl who was afraid of the dark*. Cambridge, Mass.: Candlewick Press.

Viorst, J. 1987. *My Mama says there aren't any zombies, ghosts, vampires, monsters, fiends, goblins, or things*. New York: Aladdin Paperbacks.

Web Sites

Childhood Fears: What Children Are Afraid Of and Why (Parts 1 and 2 of a two-part series) by Sandra Crosser, Ph.D. www.earlychildhood.com/Articles/index.cfm. Enter "fears" in the search box.

Children and Anxiety. The Anxiety Panic Internet Resource. www.algy.com/anxiety/children.html

Coping with Anxiety, Fears, and Phobias. KidsHealth Web site. kidshealth.org/parent. Enter "fears" in the search box.

Coping with Fears and Stress by Edward Robinson and Joseph C. Rotter. ERIC Digest. 1991. www.eric.ed.gov. Click on Digests and enter the title in the search box.

Facing Childhood Fears by Eleanor Reynolds, M.A. www.earlychildhood.com/Articles/index.cfm. Enter "fears" in the search box.

Soothing Children's Fears. FamilyFun Web site. family.go.com/raisingkids/child. Link through Raising Kids, then Children, and then Your Child's Development.

8. The Sexually Precocious Child

This is the child who knows a great deal about sex, acts sexually or provocative, or tries to involve other children in games that simulate sexual activity or include touching each others' genitals. It goes beyond the typical behaviors of young children who are curious about what other people's bodies look like and want to play doctor. This child is sophisticated, manipulative of others, and wants to do the activities often.

The child who exhibits these behaviors may do so because of the following:

● *She has learned that she can get certain children to like her, play with her, and pay attention to her, through the behaviors.*

● *She is imitating the behaviors she observes from parents, older siblings, baby-sitters, or neighbors.*

● *She has a low self-image and this behavior is a way to get attention, control others, see herself as "grown-up," and feel in control.*

● *She has been sexually abused and sees herself as worthwhile primarily because of her sexuality.*

Preventing Problems

Most teachers of young children feel unsure of themselves when dealing with sexual issues with their children. There is great fear of being misunderstood by parents or others who may mistake a healthy openness about sexuality with perversion. We live in a society that is uncomfortable with sex and sexuality in general. This attitude, contrary to popular opinion, most likely increases sexual deviance (including sex crimes against children) rather than decreases it. Our society is intensely ambivilant about sex. We have a popular teen female rock idol that acts and dresses overtly sexual while proclaiming a commitment to virginity. However, healthy sexual development begins at birth and is part of a teacher's responsibility—and parents', of course—as with all other areas of development.

● In a natural, relaxed way, provide opportunities for children, who are all naturally curious about bodies, to see what bodies look like. Have boys and girls share bathrooms. At about five years of age children begin to want some privacy, and that should be respected. Give older preschoolers the option of sharing a bathroom or having privacy. Supervise the bathrooms carefully to make sure that no child is being manipulated by a sexually precocious child. A relaxed atmosphere about bodies will help them understand that the human body and its natural functions, such as elimination, is different from sexuality. It will also reduce the desire and need to explore bodies through playing doctor or other games.

● Talk to children about protecting themselves from sexual abuse and the importance of getting help if they are being sexually abused. Many good curricula that deal with the issue in a nonthreatening and very concrete way are available. (See "Parents Who May Be Abusive to Their Children" on p. 178 for a list of these curricula.) Children can best protect themselves by telling the adult perpetrator that they will tell their teacher (or mother or other specific authority figure) on them. Saying no is usually not enough. Be available and approachable so that a child who is being sexually abused will tell you about it.

● Talk about bodies and use the appropriate names for body parts—*penis, scrotum, testicles, vulva, vagina, clitoris, urethra, anus*—in a relaxed, matter-of-fact way. This helps desexualize these body parts and gives children the vocabulary they need to describe the abuse if they are victimized.

● Provide pictures, puzzles, anatomically correct dolls, and picture books that reflect a relaxed, open attitude about bodies and bodily functions.

● As all children are bombarded with many images of subtle and overt sexuality from movies, TV, and advertising, do not ignore this. Tell the children that these behaviors are okay for adults but that they are not okay for children, much like driving a car.

● Give all children lots of attention for who they are and for appropriate things they say and do. Build the self-esteem of all your children with this type of attention. Note that the absence of a great deal of positive attention from adults can create an atmosphere in which children seek attention from other children or accept attention from abusive or manipulative adults. When children seek attention from other children, the result is a classroom of children with behaviors that are difficult to manage, such as acting out, silliness, and the controlling of some children by others.

● Give minimal attention or praise for how they look or what they wear. If a child comes in with a new dress, screeching with delight, "Look what I'm wearing," respond by saying, "It looks lovely on you, but I like you no matter what you are wearing."

• Get to know parents, siblings, and family routines, so that you can get a sense of where the behaviors might be coming from.

• Assure all the children in your class that you will not allow any child to force another child to do what she does not want to do. "This is a safe classroom. I won't let anyone hurt you and I won't let you hurt anyone."

Dealing with Existing Problems

Questions about Sex

• Most questions about sex reflect a healthy curiosity about how babies are made, about relationships between men and women, and about the human body. Give honest, short, straightforward answers to these questions. However, make sure that you fully understand what the child actually wants to know. For example, if a child asks how a man and woman make a baby, ask her questions to determine if she wants to know what they do physically to make a baby before assuming that this is what she wants to know. She may really want to know about the birth process. Also ask her how she thinks a man and woman make a baby. This will tell you her level of understanding. If you determine the question does pertain to the sex act, say something like this: "When a man and woman love each other very much, they lie in bed and hug and kiss. If they want to, the man puts his penis inside the woman's vagina and that feels really good for both of them. Tiny sperm come out of the man's penis, and if one meets a tiny egg inside the woman's body, a baby will start to grow" (Gordon and Gordon 1974).

• A sexually precocious child may ask questions that reflect an adult knowledge of sex or of unusual sexual practices. This is cause for concern. Try to determine where and how she has gained that knowledge, in case it is through direct experience. (See below, "Determining if the Child Is Being Sexually Abused.")

Mutual Exploration

• If you see play where children are exploring each other's genitals and they are both mutually involved and interested (there doesn't appear to be any manipulation), tell them, "It is important to keep your clothes on in the classroom and keep hands or objects away from each other's genitals. This is because our genitals and anus are very delicate and can easily get hurt or sore." Support their interest in knowing what bodies look like and help the children find some books to learn more.

The Manipulative Child

• Intervene calmly in the situation where a child is getting others to do what she wants them to do. Help the child who is being controlled by the sexually precocious child to stand up for herself. Give her specific words she can use to assert her right not to be taken advantage of: "I don't have to do whatever you tell me to do if I don't want to. Friends do what both want to do." Have both children come up with acceptable ways to play together. Tell the manipulative child that forcing herself on others will not be tolerated. Let her know that the consequences of doing this again will be that she will have to play by herself. Give her positive feedback often when she interacts with others positively: "Thank you for playing fairly. It makes our classroom a fun and safe place for everyone."

Grown-Up Play in the Dramatic Play Area

• If a child spends a great deal of time in the dramatic play area acting out sexually advanced behavior, limit the amount of time any child can stay in that area. Provide materials and a starting structure for the dramatic play area to be a restaurant, office, or a store. This may be less conducive to the behavior than a house or a kitchen area. Spend time playing with the children in this area and redirect the play if it goes in a sexual direction by asking for other ideas or bringing in a new, attractive item with which to play.

Appropriate Affection

• Provide the sexually precocious child with a great deal of positive attention when she is acting age appropriately. Give her hugs and safe physical affection (stroke her hair, hold her hand) so that she will learn how normal relations between adults and children should and could be. Let her know that she is worthwhile and loved even when she is not being sexual.

Determining if the Child Is Being Sexually Abused

• Use a sexual abuse prevention curriculum and read books written for young children about sexual abuse. Provide opportunities for the child to draw pictures and dictate stories about her fears and concerns. Create some secure, private time for the two of you so that she can talk about any abuse that may be happening. If it is happening, tell her that you can help her make it stop. Tell your supervisor about the child's statements so that the appropriate actions can be taken. If a social service agency is involved with the family, ask someone in the agency if she has knowledge that sexual abuse has occurred recently. Ask any of the social service or health professionals involved for advice about how to help the child. (See "Parents Who May Be Abusive to Their Children" on p. 176 for further information.)

Fairy Tales Can Help Heal

● Read original Brothers Grimm fairy tales, such as "Little Red Riding Hood" and "Hansel and Gretel," to your children. These can be very therapeutic as they deal with children overcoming the abuse and manipulation of adults.

Resources

For curricula for children to prevent sexual and physical abuse, see the chapter, "Parents Who May Be Abusive to Their Children" on p. 178.

Adams, C., and J. Fay. 1992. *Helping your child recover from sexual abuse.* Seattle: University of Washington Press.

Corbett, S. 1991. Children and sexuality. *Young Children* 46 (2): 71–77.

Fausto-Sterling, A. 2000. *Sexing the body: Gender politics and the construction of sexuality.* New York: Basic Books.

Furman, E. 1987. More protections, fewer directions. Some experiences with helping children prevent sexual abuse. *Young Children* 42 (5): 5–7.

Good, L. A. 1996. When a child has been sexually abused: Several resources for parents and early childhood professionals. *Young Children* 51 (5): 84–85.

Gordon, J. 1999. *Raising your child responsibly in a sexually permissive world.* Avon, Mass.: Adams Media Corporation.

Hagans, K. B., J. Case, and K. Brohl. *When your child has been molested: A parent's guide to healing and recovery.* San Francisco: Jossey-Bass.

Honig, A. 2000. Psychosexual development in infants and young children: Implications for caregivers. *Young Children* 55 (5): 70–77.

Jordan, N. H. 1993. Sexual abuse prevention programs in early childhood education: A caveat. *Young Children* 48 (6): 76–79.

Koblinsky, S., and N. Behana. 1984. Child sexual abuse: The educator's role in prevention, detection, and intervention. *Young Children* 39 (60): 3–15.

Kraizer, S. 1996. *The safe child book: A commonsense approach to protecting children and teaching children to protect themselves.* New York: Fireside.

Rothbaum, F., A. Grauer, and D. J. Rubin. 1997. Becoming sexual: Differences between child and adult sexuality. *Young Children* 52 (6): 22–28.

Children's Books

Bassett, K. 1982. *My very own special body book.* Redding, Calif.: Hawthorne Press.

Brenner, B., and G. Ancona. 1973. *Bodies.* New York: E. P. Dutton.

Brown, L. K., ed. 2000. *What's the big secret?: Talking about sex with girls and boys.* New York: Little Brown & Co.

Freeman, L. 1984. *It's my body.* Seattle: Parenting Press.

Girard, L. W. 1992. *My body is private.* Morton Grove, Ill.: Albert Whitman & Co.

Gordon, S., and J. Gordon. 1992. *A better safe than sorry book.* Amherst, N.Y.: Prometheus Books.

———. 1992. *Did the sun shine before you were born? A sex education primer.* Amherst, N.Y.: Prometheus Books.

Harris, R. H. 2002. *It's so amazing: A book about eggs, sperm, birth, babies, and families.* Cambridge, Mass.: Candlewick Press.

Hindman, J. 1983. *A very touching book.* Ontario, Ore.: Alexandria Association.

Kehoe, P. 1987. *Something happened and I'm scared to tell.* Seattle: Parenting Press.

Kleven, S. 1998. *The right touch: A read-aloud story to help prevent child sexual abuse.* Bellevue, Wash.: Illumination Arts.

Spelman, C. 1997. *Your body belongs to you.* Morton Grove, Ill.: Albert Whitman & Co.

Stinson, K. 1988. *The bare naked book.* Toronto: Annick.

Zipes, J. 1992. *The complete fairy tales of the Brothers Grimm.* New York: Bantam Books.

Web Sites

The Expected and the Dysfunctional: Dealing with Child-to-Child Sexual Behavior by Francis Wardle, Ph.D. www.earlychildhood.com/Articles/index.cfm. Enter "sexual behavior" in the search box.

National Clearinghouse on Abuse and Neglect www.calib.com/nccanch

Questions and Answers about Sex. KidsHealth Web site. www.kidshealth.org/parent. Enter "sex" in the search box.

Sexual Development—Talking about Sex, Playing "Doctor," and other articles. iVillage Web site. www.ivillage.com/topics. Link to Parenting, and then Sexual Development.

Warning Signs of Sexual Abuse by Kathleen Reagan. Parenthood.com Web site. www.parenthoodweb.com. Enter "sexual abuse" in the search box.

9. Children Who Identify with the Opposite Sex and Sex-Bias Issues

In a typical class you will have children with a wide variety of sex-role and gender attitudes about themselves and others. Most feel very comfortable about being a boy or a girl and accept a wide variety of behaviors from others. Some may act very masculine or very feminine with exaggerated and stereotypical behaviors and may also put other children down when they do not act similarly. Occasionally you will have a child in your class who sees himself or herself socially as a member of the opposite sex.

The child who identifies with the opposite sex usually knows his/her own biological sex by the age of three, but aspires to jobs and roles typical of the other sex (a boy wants to be a nurse; a girl wants to be a truck driver), prefers to dress up in clothes and accessories associated with the other sex, wants to be a character for Halloween who is the opposite sex (a witch for a boy, Superman for a girl), and prefers to play with groups of children of the opposite sex. The girl may choose block play almost exclusively; the boy only dresses up.

All healthy children who feel good about themselves will exhibit these behaviors at times. You need to encourage both boys and girls to feel comfortable in a variety of roles and experience a wide variety of activities. The child who identifies with the opposite sex, however, exhibits these behaviors often and consistently. This child may also exaggerate the behaviors by picking up on broad stereotypes, such as a boy who spends a great deal of time imitating a cheerleader or a girl who often engages others in rough-and-tumble play. Ideas for responding to this type of behavior follow.

The child's language will give you important clues to how he/she perceives him/herself. A boy might make a statement such as, "Teacher, we girls chased the boys all around the playground, and we caught them!" A girl who identifies with the opposite sex might pick many fights and say things such as, "Me and the other boys are the drivers; you girls be the riders."

The reasons for this development are not totally understood, but they appear to be primarily physiological, due to prenatal hormone levels, among other factors. What is known, and what is important for teachers to understand, is that the child does not choose to identify with the opposite sex. It is not a sign of a problem, disease, or sickness that can be corrected. About 5 percent of children have these characteristics. This has been documented throughout history and in all cultures. Your goal is to make sure the child feels supported, feels good about him/herself, and is respected by other children. Although these are goals for all children, they are more difficult to achieve with the child who identifies with the opposite sex, because of all the ridicule that child receives. When the child feels more secure, supported, and accepted, some of the exaggerated, stereotyped behaviors will diminish.

The same is true for boys who act "macho" and girls who act "prissy." The usual cause of such behaviors is insecurity. Adhering to rigid stereotypical behaviors makes it clear and easy to know how to act in any situation. Social interactions, which are complex even in preschool, can become less scary. If you make these children feel more secure by giving them opportunities to be coddled and cared for, and build their self-esteem, the exaggerated behaviors will diminish.

Preventing Problems

The following ideas are designed to help you create a classroom atmosphere where a broad range of sex-role behavior will be accepted and supported. The result will be that the child who identifies with the opposite sex will feel less different and more free to be who she/he is. Boys who exhibit "macho" behaviors and girls who act overly feminine will feel less need to engage in such behaviors. As there will always be a range of sex-role behaviors within any group of children, implement these ideas even if you do not currently have a child in your class who identifies with the opposite sex or one who exhibits exaggerated sex-role behavior.

● In your classroom or your teaching, eliminate anything that points up artificial differences between boys and girls. For example, avoid forming a boy's line and a girl's line.

● Avoid counting numbers of girls and numbers of boys during role call. Count children sitting on the left side and those on the right side or just count all children.

● Avoid complimenting children when they dress up. Compliment all children for appropriate preschool dress: "Those jeans will be perfect for playing in the sandbox."

● Teach children the real differences between the sexes. Boys and men have penises. Girls and women have vaginas. Differences between girls and boys are basically physical ones and are not related to ability and skill. Tell the children that girls can do anything boys can do and that boys can do anything girls can do. Show and display pictures of girls/women and boys/men in a wide variety of jobs, hobbies, and roles, such as female athletes and men feeding babies.

● Actively encourage boys and girls to play with each other, form friendships, and accept a wide range of behaviors from each other.

● Include in the dramatic play area a variety of materials and clothing such as plastic tools, ties, sport jackets, and men's and women's shoes.

● Place the block area next to the dramatic play area to encourage play between these two areas.

● Read stories that include strong female characters and males who nurture. Avoid stories that reinforce stereotypes or leave out female characters.

● Include females in songs and finger plays. For example, each children's finger during "Where Is Thumbkin?" can be "ma'am" as easily as "sir." It also can be a gender neutral "friend." In the same way, the monkeys jumping on the bed can be female as easily as male, and the doctor who is called when they are all off the bed can be a woman doctor.

Dealing with Existing Problems
Building Self-Esteem

● Remind the child of his abilities and strengths. Approve of the child's desire to do any activity. If an activity is not appropriate for school, request that it be done at home or put limits on the time and place for the behaviors, while respecting the child's desire to do it. Inappropriate behavior at school (such as the cheerleading and the rough-and-tumble play examples already given) are inappropriate for all children, not just children who identify with the opposite sex, macho boys, or prissy girls.

● Intervene when another child rejects, teases, or pokes fun at the child who identifies with the opposite sex. Help him to verbally stand up for himself with statements such as, "I have a right to play whatever I want. If you don't like it, play somewhere else." Have him practice saying this. Tell the child who is doing the teasing that you would help him if he were being teased and tell the teaser that you will not tolerate hurtful words. Explain that a consequence of teasing, if it happens again, could be not playing with any children for a while. Explain to him the importance of respecting everyone, especially those who do things differently from most people. When you see him interacting positively with the teased child later, let him know how well he is doing.

Exaggerated Sex-Role Behaviors

● Deal with exaggerated sex-role behavior by limiting the time the child spends in such activities (as you would any uncreative, repetitive activity) and redirecting him into a more creative and varied but similar activitiy. You can also extend and deepen the activity by adding variety and challenge. Cheerleaders, male or female, can learn new tumbles and movements. They work hard at stretching and exercising. The routines are often complicated.

● Children who engage in exaggerated sex-role behavior need to know that it is acceptable to be a little child. Some teachers found that if they encourage them to act like a "baby" in dramatic play, it meets an emotional need and reduces the amount of sex-typed behavior. Also do many other things to build self-esteem: support strengths, give positive feedback to appropriate behaviors, engage in playful interactions, give them physical affection if they enjoy it.

Helping Parents

Almost all parents of a child who identifies with the opposite sex know that their child is different. Some parents will try to deny this, and some will want to find out how to help. Parents of girls may be more accepting because "tomboy" behavior is tolerated by society. Parents of boys may have a harder time because society is less willing to tolerate effeminate behavior, which is wrongly associated with homosexuality by many people. The word "sissy" has a much more negative connotation than tomboy.

● Assure all parents that you accept and care about *all* children regardless of individual differences in behavior or physical appearance. Assure them that all children are unique—they all have strengths and weaknesses. Let parents know that you will not tolerate teasing and meanness in your class and that children will be taught to be supportive and positive toward others.

- Talk with and write notes to the parents often about the positive aspects of their child: "He has a great attention span." "She's a motivated learner." "He's a champ at putting together puzzles." Let parents know that you are willing and able to help and are available to talk whenever they have any questions or concerns. (See "When You See Bias Happening" on p. 82 for ideas on dealing with sex-biased remarks or behaviors.)

Resources

Cahill, B. J., and R. Theilheimer. 1999. Can Tommy and Sam get married? Questions about gender, sexuality, and young children. *Young Children* 54 (1): 27–31.

Johnson, H. H. 1994. The Bodyworks: Inside me—Another approach to alike and different. *Young Children* 49 (6): 21–26.

Marshall, N. L., W. W. Robeson, and N. Keefe. 1999. Gender equity in early childhood education. *Young Children* 54 (4): 9–13.

Money, J. 1981. *Love and love sickness: The science of sex, gender difference, and pair bonding.* Baltimore: Johns Hopkins University Press.

Money, J., and A. A. Ehrhardt. 1996. *Man and woman, boy and girl: Gender identity from conception to maturity.* Northvale, N.J.: Jason Aronson Publishers.

Pollack, W. 1999. *Real boys: Rescuing our sons from the myths of boyhood.* New York: Owl Books.

Powlishta, K. K. 1995. Research in review: Gender segregation among children: Understanding the "cootie phenomenon." *Young Children* 50 (4): 61–69.

Sheldon, A. 1990. "Kings are royaler than queens": Language and socialization. *Young Children* 45 (2): 4–9.

Wellhousen, K. 1996. Girls can be bull riders, too! Supporting children's understanding of gender roles through children's literature. *Young Children* 51 (5): 79–83.

Children's Books

Gordon, S. 1991. *Girls are girls and boys are boys. So what's the difference?* Amherst, N.Y.: Prometheus Books.

Waxman, S. 1976, 1989. *What is a girl? What is a boy?* New York: Thomas Y. Crowell.

Web Sites

Boys Will Be Boys: But Parents and Caregivers Can Help Them Avoid Growing into Harmful Stereotypes by Claudia Miller www.4children.org. Click on Search and enter "gender" in the search box.

Developmental Psychology—Gender Development. Links to numerous articles from the PsiCafe Web site of Portland State University. www.psy.pdx.edu/PsiCafe. Enter "gender" in the search box.

Dolls, Trucks, and Identity Educators Help Young Children Grow beyond Gender by Sehba Zhumkhawala www.4children.org. Click on Search and enter "gender" in the search box.

Gender and Culture in Picture Books. Resources compiled by Kay E. Vandergrift, Rutgers University. www.scils.rutgers.edu/~kvander. Link on Gender and Culture in Picture Books.

Real Boys: Rescuing Our Sons from the Myths of Boyhood www.williampollack.com. Link to an introduction and synopsis of the book or to articles by Dr. William Pollack.

Capsule Descriptions of Children's Books: Shattering Stereotypes: Courageous Girls, Ballet-Loving Boys by Joy Shioshita www.4children.org. Click on Search and enter "gender" in the search box.

Talking with Preschool Children about Sex by Lorie Selke www.4children.org. Click on Search and enter "sex" in the search box.

Two Moms, Two Dads: When Young Children Ask Us Questions about Gay and Lesbian Families, We Can Give Age-Appropriate and Supportive Explanations by Claudia Miller www.4children.org. Click on Search and enter "two moms" in the search box.

10. Children Who Are Too Responsible

These children do not show behavior problems in the typical way, and therefore, you can easily overlook them. They are the children who take care of others' needs beyond what is expected or reasonable for young children. They may focus on other children whom they see as weak and vulnerable and "parent" them. They may focus on adults and show unusual concern for their feelings and needs. On the surface, these behaviors are altruistic and positive. However, when these behaviors happen too often and too consistently, when others don't want or need the children's help, and when their own needs are denied, the children have serious problems. These are children who are being robbed of their right to grow up free of adult responsibilities and their right to be taken care of by adults.

Possible Causes and Consequences

Typically, overly responsible children are growing up in homes where roles are reversed. The children are taking care of their parents, psychologically, if not actually. Whether the parents are not functioning well because of alcoholism (most common), drug dependency, poor health, emotional problems, mental illness, or other reasons, the effect on children is similar. They learn to take on the parent role in the household for their own survival. These children often are the oldest child in the family or have no siblings.

Children who feel they are worthless because of years of negative feedback also can exhibit these behaviors. They have found that they can get positive feedback and satisfaction from doing something that comes easy to them—putting themselves last.

Most often, these children are girls, because these behaviors are more socially acceptable in females and modeled more by females. In fact, women who spend their lives sacrificing for their families and years volunteering in service organizations are considered to be exemplary people. Some are, because they truly enjoy the work and can afford it. But many others bury their own dreams, desires, and needs.

If this pattern of behavior continues, it will have a profound effect on the children's lives. They will continue to deny their own needs and may develop destructive behaviors, such as never questioning authority, dropping out of school, marrying abusive spouses, having more children than they can handle, living with poor health, or abusing drugs or alcohol.

Preventing Problems

● Make the development of self-esteem a vital part of your curriculum and integrate it throughout all parts of the day. During lunch, discuss the children's accomplishments that day. Help them evaluate themselves in positive ways by asking what they have done that makes them proud of themselves. One of the best self-concept building strategies is to challenge children without pushing or pressuring them. This sends the following message: "I believe you are smart and capable."

● Help children switch roles in dramatic play situations. This will reduce the amount of time some children dominate others or some children spend in inferior roles, such as the "baby" or the "dog."

● Inform the children through books, puppets, and plays about the appropriate roles of adults and children. Show situations where children are told to do unacceptable things, such as a five-year-old being told to care for younger siblings for several hours. Make sure the children know that this behavior is not acceptable. Tell them how they can get help by talking to a caring adult, such as yourself, or by using the telephone for help if they are frightened or if they are facing an emergency.

● Serve as a role model of an appropriately responsible adult. Explain how some responsibilities in their classroom belong to the children (using toys correctly), some to the teacher (providing safe toys), and some to both the children and the teacher (developing a new dramatic play area).

● Show children how to be helpful without completely doing things for others. For example, explain that they can help another child with a puzzle by doing one or two pieces and letting her finish, or by showing her how to match the color of a puzzle piece to the color on the puzzle frame.

● Meet with parents regularly and do home visits if at all possible. This will give you great insight into family situations, values, and problems.

Dealing with Existing Problems

● Intervene when you see overly responsible behaviors. Tell the child that you appreciate her helpfulness (these are children with fragile self-concepts) but that she needs to play. Redirect her into a more appropriate situation and spend a few minutes making sure she is on the right track.

● Help the child who is the focus of the caretaking behaviors by giving her the words she needs to assert her independence: "I can do it myself, thank you." The child also may need to learn to negotiate dramatic play roles to be more equal: "Let's both be doctors, and the doll can be the patient."

● Set up games that involve children taking turns and participating in equal relationships. Board games or lotto games, store bought or teacher made, are good for this. Make sure the games are easy enough for children to do on their own but challenging enough to make them inviting. Guide the overly responsible child to these games and try to have her play with a child who will stand up to her but not dominate her.

● Work on the root of the problem. If you discover, for example, that the child lives with an alcoholic or drug-abusing parent, seek help from local agencies that deal with helping alcoholic/substance abusers. In almost all cases, these agencies will suggest ways to assist the family and the child without violating trust or scaring them off. Read to the whole class children's books about alcoholic/substance abusing families and use puppets to role-play situations specific to these families. All children can relate to and benefit from learning about how children can get help and be healed from difficult situations.

● Find quiet time to spend with the child that is not too near other children. Read a book or make up a story related to (but not specifically about) her problem. Establish rapport and be open, empathetic, and ready to listen so she will talk about her situation. Remember that this will take much time and patience as most young children have difficulty knowing that they have a problem (they assume everybody lives the same way). Articulating this problem is very difficult for them.

Resources

Brett, D. 1988. *Annie stories.* New York: Workman Press.

Hasting, J. M., and M. H. Typpo. 1994. *An elephant in the living room: A leader's guide to helping children of alcoholics.* Minneapolis: CompCare.

Jesse, R. C. 1990. *Healing the hurt: Rebuilding relationships with your children: A self-help guide for parents in recovery.* Washington, D.C.: Johnson Institute.

Robinson, B. E. 1990. The teacher's role in working with children of alcoholic parents. *Young Children* 45 (4): 68–73.

Children's Books

Black, C. A. 1997. *My dad loves me, my dad has a disease: A child's view: Living with addiction.* Bainbridge Island, Wash.: MAC.

Davis, D. 1984. *Something is wrong at my house.* Seattle: Parenting Press.

DiGiovanni, K. 1986. *My house is different.* Center City, Minn.: Hazelden.

Hasting, J. M., and M. H. Typpo. 1994. *An elephant in the living room: The children's book.* Minneapolis: CompCare.

Moe, J., and D. Pohlman. 1989. *Kids' power: Healing games for children of alcoholics.* Dallas: ImaginWorks.

Wood, B. L. 1992. *Raising healthy children in an alcoholic home.* New York: Crossroad/Herder & Herder.

Web Sites

National Association for Children of Alcoholics
www.nacoa.net

Substance Abuse and Mental Health Services Administration. An agency of the U.S. Department of Health and Human Services.
www.samhsa.gov

Part IV

Children Who Must Cope with Major Changes

1. New to Your Class

2. Divorce and Remarriage

3. New Sibling

4. Hospitalization

5. Death of a Loved One

6. Tragedies

7. Moving On to the Next Class

1. New to Your Class

Almost all new children will have a hard time at first, especially with separating from parents at the start of the day. Usually this gets better within a few weeks when the child knows she will be picked up regularly and when she is familiar with the new surroundings and with you, her new teacher.

Preventing Problems

● If at all possible, visit the child in her home before she starts in your class. Leave a picture of yourself or snap a picture of her and you to leave or to send when developed.

● Invite the child and her parents to visit the class for about an hour before her first full day. Put no pressure on her to participate in any way. Respect her need to observe. If possible, have her visit several more times, gradually increasing the visiting times until her first full day.

● Request that a parent (or relative or friend) stay in the classroom the first few times the child attends, if at all possible. Ask the parent to sit quietly on the sidelines and not push the child into participating.

● Encourage the new child to bring in favorite toys from home to help her form friendships. Put some limits on the use of these toys as discussed in "Toys from Home" on p. 55.

● Make sure family members have ample information about your program and classroom so they can answer any questions their child may have before she begins. Provide a list of FAQs (Frequently Asked Questions) and answers. Some FAQs may include: "What do I call my teacher?" "What will we do all day?" "Do I take a nap?" "What can I bring from home?" "What if no one wants to play with me?"

Dealing with Existing Problems

● Recommend to parents that they drop off and pick up their child at the same time each day. This will establish a clear routine, and routines create security.

● Encourage the parents to arrange for their child to spend time outside of school hours with another child who is in the class. This will help the child establish a special bond with a classmate and help her look forward to coming to the new program.

● Read children's books dealing with the issue of starting school and/or moving. See the resources at the end of the chapter.

● The child who still has separation problems a month after being in the program with the same teacher(s) has a problem most likely due to causes other than the newness. Ask yourself if the child is gaining anything by the behavior, such as extra attention. Can you change things so that the child will gain extra attention by separating easily and joining the activities quickly? (The attention can be in the form of encouraging remarks, smiles, and hugs.) Meet with the parents to discuss possible causes and brainstorm solutions together. Determine if the child has excessive fears. Ask about the child's situation before entering the class and about major changes at home (a new sibling, divorce, or remarriage) that you can help the child work through. Face the possibility that the child might be better off in a different child care arrangement, such as family child care or fewer days of preschool, for now. See "Starting the Day Off Right" on p. 9, for additional ideas on helping a child who is having trouble separating from her parents.

The Child Who Has Recently Moved

● If the child has recently relocated, read books about moving and provide many opportunities for her to talk about her move. Ask her to show pictures, if she has them, of her old house and her friends from her former neighborhood. Help her write letters or draw pictures for these old friends.

● Help the child's parents learn about activities and resources for families in the area. These can include fun parks and playgrounds, places to swim, short hikes, zoos, museums, libraries, campgrounds, amusement parks, skating rinks, restaurants that welcome children, community centers, health clinics or pediatricians, social service agencies that help families, and family-oriented organizations from Parents without Partners to the YMCA.

● Provide all families with a list of other classmates and schoolmates with their addresses and phone numbers. Get permission from each family first to be included on the list, as some want to keep their addresses and phone numbers private. Help new families locate neighbors on the list that they can connect with to ask questions, car pool, or share transportation. The children may want to spend time playing together outside of school.

Resources

Balaban, N. 1985. *Starting school: From separation to independence.* New York: Teachers College Press.

Jalongo, M. R. 1985. When young children move. *Young Children* 40 (6): 51–57.

Jervis, K., and J. Berlfein, eds. 1984. *Separation: Strategies for helping two- to four-year-olds.* Washington, D.C.: NAEYC.

Leavitt, M. 1987. *Starting school: Happy beginnings.* ERIC, ED 282619.

Linke, P. 2000. *Home is where the family is: Moving house with children.* AECA Research in Practice Series 7 (3). ERIC, ED 448877.

Prestine, J. S. 1997. *Helping children cope with moving.* Parsippany, N.J.: Fearon Teacher Aids.

Children's Books about Starting a New School

Ahlburg, J., and A. Ahlburg. 1990. *Starting school.* New York: Puffin.

Cohen, M. 1989. *Will I have a friend?* New York: Aladdin Paperbacks.

Penn, A. 1993. *The kissing hand.* Washington, D.C.: The Child Welfare League of America.

Rankin, J. 2002. *First day.* New York: Margaret McElderry Books.

Tompert, A. 1988. *Will you come back for me?* Morton Grove, Ill.: Albert Whitman & Co.

Children's Books about Moving

Viorst, J. 1998. *Alexander, who's not (Do you hear me? I mean it!) going to move.* New York: Aladdin Picture Books.

Williamson, G. 1999. *What's the recipe for friend?* New Orleans: Peerless Publishing.

Web Sites
Starting School

Starting Child Care: What Young Children Learn about Relating to Adults in the First Weeks of Starting Child Care. Early Childhood Research and Practice. Fall 2000, Volume 2, Number 2. Online only.
ecrp.uiuc.edu

Starting School: What You Should Know about Your Kid's New Life as a Student
www.americanbaby.com. Enter "starting school" in the search box.

Starting School. American Academy for Child and Adolescent Psychiatry. Facts for Families #84.
www.aacap.org. Click on Facts for Families.

Parenting Skills: Starting School and Saying Goodbye
family.go.com. Enter "starting school" in the search box.

Preparing for School. Child Care Source.
www.childcaresource.org. Click on Ages and Stages on side bar, then scroll down to the article.

Moving

Children and Family Moves. American Academy for Child and Adolescent Psychiatry. Facts for Families #14.
www.aacap.org. Click on Facts for Families.

Understanding Children: Moving to a New Home by Lesia Oesterreich. National Network for Child Care.
www.nncc.org. Click on Articles and Resources, then Child Development, then scroll down to article under Emotional and Social.

2. Divorce and Remarriage

Although divorce has become an almost commonplace experience for children today, the emotional effect of divorce on a child is no less devastating. When a child experiences a divorce, you will most likely see behavior changes, such as moodiness, defiance, a short temper, increased aggression, nervous habits, more toileting "accidents," shorter attention span, temper tantrums, whining, and crying.

Children who fare best under this difficult situation are those whose parents remain civil and mature toward each other, do not play "tug of war" with their children or with their children's loyalties, speak well of the other parent to their children, keep in close contact with the children, and help them realize that they are not responsible for the divorce.

As the child's teacher, you may not have a big role in influencing these factors, but you can give parents this information. You can also be a great support, a source of stability, and someone who clarifies information for the child. You can certainly help him realize that the fault for the divorce is not his.

Preventing Problems

● The chances are good that at least one child in your class will experience divorce during the year, so discussing the topic any time will be helpful. Use children's books, stories, puppets, and films. Several children in your class are probably dealing with this problem. They can be helped by this and can contribute to the discussion.

● Provide information through books and pictures about many different kinds of families. Let the children know that children are loved and cared for in families with a wide variety of configurations: single moms, single dads, gay parents, joint custody, grandparents, foster parents, adoption, and so on. Discuss the different family arrangements of the children in your class.

• Give children helpful information about changing and about separating, through concrete experiences. See the section on themes in "Selecting and Using a Curriculum" on pp. 38–39.

• Provide many outlets for the children to express their feelings and emotions. This includes drawing, painting, sand play, water play, play with clay and play-dough, creative movement, and making up stories.

• Set up places in your classroom where children can have privacy and quiet.

• Allow many opportunities throughout the day for children to have control in appropriate ways. They can make many choices and decisions regarding books to browse, activities to engage in, materials to use, and more. This will ease one of the negative results of a major change in a child's life: the feeling of having no control.

• Make sure children know that your classroom is a safe place to express strong feelings, including anger, and how to redirect their anger and frustration in nondestructive ways. Help them learn how to calm themselves and get comfort from others. When a circumstance like divorce or remarriage happens they will have the tools they need to deal with their intense emotions.

Dealing with Existing Problems

After their parents separate, many children go through a grieving process over the loss of their family and/or a parent who has left. Children in foster care go through this repeatedly. The stages in this process are the following:

Denial	They deny the divorce is really happening.
Anger	They show their anger through misbehaviors.
Hope	They try to bring their parents back together.
Sadness	They begin to accept the reality of the situation and express their feelings.
Acceptance	They find ways to be at peace with themselves and their new situation and return to their usual behaviors.

• Be aware of these stages so that you can help children move through them at their own pace. Accept their feelings but help the children express these feelings appropriately. In the anger stage do not deny their need to express their anger but help them direct the emotion in a way that does not hurt others or themselves. You might say the following: "I can't let you hit another person, but would you like to pound clay or hammer nails?" Some of these feelings will emerge again for the child whose parent is remarrying.

• Make clear to the child that the divorce was not his fault and nothing he could have done or not done would have prevented it. Use books and stories to reinforce this message. Be aware that a child coping with a remarriage needs assurances that his parent does not love him any less because of the new spouse and perhaps new stepchildren. Assure the child that adults, like children, can love many people and love them all in different ways.

• Give the child many ways to express his feelings through open, creative activities. Ask him if he would like to write a story with you about a bunny who loses his parents. Using animal characters helps give the child some distance from the issue, allowing him to risk expressing his inner feelings. Ask him if he would like to draw pictures about what he is feeling.

• Help the child see the positive side of the divorce: "Your parents will be happier if they are not fighting so much. If they are happier, then it will be more fun to be with them and easier for them to make you happy." Do not deny the pain and the negative feelings the child is experiencing, but present another perspective. Point out that remarriage holds the possibility of more loving grown-ups to care for the child and maybe new brothers and sisters with whom to play.

• Avoid overprotecting or overindulging the child because of his pain. Remember that he will be better off with clearly defined, consistent limits. Give him support for appropriate behavior and redirect him toward this behavior. The last thing he needs now is to feel "different" because of being treated differently from the other children.

• Be loving and empathetic but do not allow a dependent relationship to develop between you and the child. Make sure he spends most of his time engaged with other children and not clinging to you. If this happens, say something like the following: "I'll give you one great big hug, and then you need to go play."

● All children and families undergoing this major change could benefit from professional counseling. Recommend this to parents as a way to ease the stress for everyone and to prevent future problems. Increasing lines of communication with parents by meeting and talking more often is crucial at this time.

Resources

Brett, D. 1988. *Annie stories.* New York: Workman.

Trozzi, M., and K. Massimini. 1999. *Talking with children about loss: Words, strategies, and wisdom to help children cope with death, divorce, and other difficult times.* New York: Perigee.

Divorce

Feeney, S., S. Riley, and K. Kipnis. 1988. Ethics case studies: The divorced parents. *Young Children* 43 (3): 48–51

Freeman, B. B. 1993. Separation and divorce: Children want their teachers to know. *Young Children* 48 (6): 58–63.

Kalter, N. 1991. *Growing up with divorce: Helping your child avoid immediate and later emotional problems.* New York: Fawcett Books.

Lansky, V. 1996. *Vicki Lansky's divorce book for parents: Helping your children cope with divorce and its aftermath.* Minnetonka, Minn.: Book Peddlers.

Ricci, I. 1997. *Mom's house, Dad's house: Making two homes for your child.* New York: Fireside.

Rogers, F. 1996. *Let's talk about it: Divorce.* New York: Philomel Books.

Sammons, W., and J. Lewis. 2000. What schools are doing to help children of divorce. *Young Children* 55 (5): 64–65.

Skeen, P., and P. C. McKenry. 1986. The Teacher's role in facilitating a child's adjustment to divorce. In *Reducing stress in young children's lives,* edited by J. B. McCracken. Washington, D.C.: NAEYC.

Teyber, E. 2001. *Helping children cope with divorce.* Rev. ed. Hoboken, N.J.: John Wiley & Sons

Remarriage and Stepfamilies

Fox, K. 1998. *Making the best of second best: A guide to positive stepparenting.* Rapid City, S.D.: Foxcraft, Inc.

Shomberg, E. F. 1999. *Blending families: A guide for parents, stepparents, and everyone building a successful new family.* New York: Berkley Publishing Group.

Children's Books about Divorce, Remarriage, and Stepfamilies

Benjamin, A. 1995. *Two's company.* New York: Viking Children's Books.

Jukes, M. 1999. *Like Jake and me.* Minneapolis: Econo-Clad Books.

Lanksy, V. 1998. *It's not your fault, Koko Bear: A read-together book for parents and young children during divorce.* Minnetonka, Minn.: Book Peddlers.

Masurel, C. 2001. *Two homes.* Cambridge, Mass.: Candlewick Press.

Quinlan, P. 1987. *My dad takes care of me.* Willowdale, Ontario: Annick Press.

Ransom, J. F. 2000. *I don't want to talk about it.* Washington, D.C.: Magination

Rogers, F. 1997. *Let's talk about it: Stepfamilies.* New York: Philomel Books.

Spellman, C. 1998. *Mama and Daddy Bear's divorce.* Morton Grove, Ill.: Albert Whitman & Co.

Thomas, P. 1999. *My family's changing: A first look at family break up.* Hauppauge, N.Y.: Barrons Juveniles.

Venable, L. A. 1999. *The not-so-wicked stepmother. A book for children and adults.* Birmingham, Ala.: L. A. Venable Publishing.

Zipes, J. 1992. *The complete fairy tales of the Brothers Grimm.* New York: Bantam Books.

Web Sites

Divorce

Activities for Helping Children Deal with Divorce by Sharon Leigh and Janet A. Clark. University of Missouri-Columbia Extension. 2001. muextension.missouri.edu. Click on Search tab, enter "divorce" in the search box.

Children and Divorce. The Better Divorce Network. www.betterdivorce.com. Click on Children & Divorce on the side bar.

Children and Divorce. American Academy of Child and Adolescent Psychiatry. Facts for Families #1. www.aacap.org. Link through Publications and then Facts for Families.

Children and Divorce. divorcesouce.com. divorcesource.com. Click on Children & Divorce under Info Categories.

Divorce Matters: A Child's View by Lesia Oesterreich. National Network for Child Care. www.nncc.org. Link through the Articles and Resources tab, then Child Development, then scroll down to Emotional and Social.

Focus on Kids: The Effects of Divorce on Children by Karen DeBord, Ph.D. National Network for Child Care. www.nncc.org. Link through the Articles and Resources tab, then Child Development, then scroll down to Emotional and Social.

Helping Children Understand Divorce by Sara Gable and Kelly Cole. University of Missouri-Columbia Extension. 2000. muextension.missouri.edu. Click on Search tab, enter "divorce" in the search box.

Helping Your Child Cope with Divorce. Child Care Source. www.childcaresource.org. Click on Ages and Stages on side bar, then scroll down to the article.

ParentSoup.com. iVillage. Numerous articles. parentsoup.com. Click on Parenting A–Z, then on Divorce.

Remarriage and Step Families

Interventions That Work for Stepfamilies. American Psychological Association. helping.apa.org. Link through Family and Relationships.

Stepfamilies. ParentSoup.com. iVillage. Numerous articles. www.parentsoup.com. Click on Stepparenting.

Stepfamilies and Parenting. Iowa State University Extension. www.extension.iastate.edu. Click on Search, then enter "stepfamilies" in the search box.

Stepfamily Association of America. Many articles from various publications. www.saafamiles.org. Link through Educational Resources tab and then Selected articles from the archived quarterly *SAA Families*.

Stepfamily Problems. American Academy of Child and Adolescent Psychiatry. Facts for Families #27. www.aacap.org. Link through Facts for Families.

Stepping Stones for Stepfamilies. Online home study program in six lessons. Iowa State University Extension. 2000. www.extension.iastate.edu. Click on Search, then enter "stepfamilies" in the search box.

Tips for Successful Stepfamilies. Child Care Source. www.childcaresource.org. Click on Ages and Stages on side bar, then scroll down to the article.

3. New Sibling

Whether by birth, remarriage, or adoption, a new sibling in the family will mean major changes. Children who have good preparation for this will weather the changes more easily, minimizing the feelings of uncertainty, jealousy, and insecurity that can develop. You, the teacher, can be a great source of information and comfort.

Preventing Problems

● Keep your children informed about how babies are made and are born. Many good books are available to help you do this in a simple, appropriate way for young children. Some teachers like to do this in the spring when farm animals are giving birth, but doing it occasionally throughout the year is important because new siblings can come at any time.

● Discuss the wide variety of family configurations, including adoption. Tell the children why people adopt children and how this process works.

● Use terms such as *uterus* or *womb* to explain where the baby grows, as many children believe the child grows in the stomach, which can confuse and disturb them.

● Make sure that the children understand that a long time passes before a baby grows old enough to be much fun to play with. Explain to the children that babies require a great deal of care so adults tend to fuss over babies and ignore older siblings.

Dealing with Existing Problems

● The main need of a child who has a new sibling is for attention. Parents are intensely focused on the needs of the baby and are exhausted. She is no longer getting as much attention at home as she did before the baby came. You, as the teacher, can help by increasing the amount of attention and affection you give the child. Do not wait until the child acts out for attention. Provide attention by talking and doing things with her based on her interests, rather than around her role as a big sister or discussing the baby.

● Give her specific ways to get attention without making others angry or annoyed. Help her practice questions she can ask her parents, such as, "Can you read to me when the baby is napping?" "Can you take me to the park while Daddy watches the baby?"

● Inform the parents of the child that the more they involve their child in all aspects of the preparation, birth, and caregiving, the more the child will feel needed and important. This reduces feelings of being displaced. Some families print out birth announcements that read: "Amy Rubin would like to announce the birth of her new baby brother, Angelo James, on July 26, 2002."

● Discuss the important jobs that a big brother or sister has, such as helping to make sure that the baby is safe and happy. The most important job is teaching by example: being strong and caring, being responsible, and getting needs met appropriately.

● Parents also need to know the importance of giving special time just to the older sibling. Although giving this time on a regular, scheduled basis is hard because new babies are so unpredictable, striving for this is wise. Perhaps parents could have a story time with the older child each time the baby naps.

● Give the child many opportunities to proudly share the progress of the baby's prenatal growth, birth, and care. Follow the progress of the fetus by showing the children photos or pictures in a book depicting the growth inside the womb, such as Nilson's *How Was I Born?* (see resources for complete listing). Invite the mother and father to come to class, as often as they can, so that the children can see the mother's expanding middle and ask questions about the pregnancy and birth. Have the parents bring the baby into the class and teach the children about diapering and baby care. Let the older sibling take the lead, as much as she can, in showing how to care for the baby. Invite the child to make books about the new baby and her concerns as well as her good feelings. Have her illustrate the book with pictures.

● Accept any feelings of jealousy or hatred that the child has toward the new baby. Be aware that soon after the new baby arrives, many children want to "give the baby back." Offer the child many outlets to express her feelings in a way that will not hurt herself or others. Include drawing, throwing a beanbag at a large target, talking about or drawing pictures of her feelings or writing about them, pounding play-dough or clay, dramatic play with dolls, and sand and water play.

Resources

Dunn, J. 1995. *From one child to two: What to expect, how to cope, and how to enjoy your growing family.* New York: Fawcett Books.

Koblinsky, S., J. Atkinson, and S. Davis. 1986. Sex education with young children. In *Reducing stress in young children's lives,* edited by J. B. McCracken. Washington, D.C.: NAEYC.

Leonard, J. 2000. *Twice blessed: Everything you need to know about having a second child—Preparing yourself, your marriage, and your firstborn for a new family of four.* New York: Griffin Trade Paperback.

Children's Books

Baker, S. 1999. *Before I was born.* Swindon, England: Child's Play International, Ltd.

Brown, M. T. 1990. *Arthur's baby.* New York: Little Brown & Co.

Cole, J. 1997. *I'm a big brother.* New York: William Morrow & Co.

———. 1997. *I'm a big sister.* New York: William Morrow & Co.

Davis, J. 1998. *Before you were born: A lift-the-flap book.* New York: Workman Publishing Company.

Douglas, A. 1998. *Baby science: How babies really work!* Toronto: Owl Communications.

———. 2000. *Before you were born: The inside story.* Toronto: Owl Communications.

Hoban, R. 1993. *A baby sister for Frances.* New York: HarperTrophy

Lewison, W. C. 1996. *Our new baby.* New York: Grosset & Dunlap.

Manushkin, F. 2002. *Baby, come out!* New York: Star Bright Books

Mayer, M. 1985. *The new baby.* New York: Golden Books.

Mayle, P. 2000. *Where did I come from?* Secaucus, N.J.: Lyle Stuart.

Murkoff, H. E. 2000. *What to expect when your mommy's having a baby.* New York: HarperCollins Juvenile Books.

Nilson, L. 1996. *How was I born?* New York: Bantam Doubleday Dell Publishers.

Rockwell, L. 2000. *Hello baby!* New York: Dragonfly.

Rogers, F. 1996. *The new baby. A Mister Rogers' first experience book.* New York: Paper Star.

Scott, A. H. 1992. *On Mother's lap.* New York: Clarion Books.

Ziefert, H. 1998. *Waiting for baby.* New York: Henry Holt & Co.

Web Sites

Helping Children Adapt to a New Sibling by Laurie Kramer. National Network for Child Care.
www.nncc.org. Link through Articles and Resources, then Guidance and Discipline, then scroll down to Stressful Life Events.

Preparing Your Child for a New Sibling. KidsHealth. kidshealth.org. Enter "new sibling" in the search box.

Preparing Your Child for a Sibling. Child Care Source. www.childcaresource.org. Click on Ages and Stages on side bar, then scroll down to the article.

Preparing Your Child for a Sibling's Birth. BabyCenter. www.babycenter.com. Enter "sibling's birth" in the search box.

Siblings and the Adopted Child by Renee Dubucs. FAIR (Families Adopting in Response). www.fairfamilies.org. Link through News from FAIR Archives, then Talking about Adoption, then scroll down to article in the Family section.

4. Hospitalization

Because young children typically have experiences in the hospital due to emergencies, it is important to present this topic even if you do not have a child in your class who is scheduled to enter a hospital.

A hospital experience can be very traumatic to a young child because he may be in much pain, the environment is so different from anywhere else (strange equipment, unusual smells, workers in masks and uniforms), the atmosphere is formal and rule-bound, and many hospitals are not very child-oriented.

Preventing Problems

● Read books about hospitals and answer questions children have that the books raise.

● Make sure the children understand that for most illnesses that are treated in hospitals (appendectomy, having ear tubes put in), children are not at fault and did not cause the problem.

● Visit a hospital. Prepare for the field trip well in advance and make sure that the children receive a tour from someone who relates well with young children. Have a paramedic visit the classroom with an ambulance the children can tour. Visit a doctor's office to give the children additional information about health care. See "Field Trips Are Supposed to Be Fun" on p. 53 for more information.

● Set up a hospital dramatic play area. Include cots, blankets, bandages, stethoscopes, pads of blank paper and pens, old X-rays, pictures of hospitals and doctors' offices, several toy doctor's kits, and crutches. Extend the play by having the children build an ambulance and role-play paramedics.

● Have small toy ambulances as part of your set of cars and trucks. Provide props that can be used with small figures of people to play out hospital scenes. Do this inexpensively by making small stretchers, beds, operating tables, surgical masks, and so on, out of cardboard, wooden craft sticks, and cloth.

Dealing with Existing Problems

● If you find out that a child in your class will be hospitalized, do the activities described above unless you have done them very recently. If more than six weeks has gone by, repeat the activities.

● Create opportunities for the child who will be hospitalized to talk about his concerns, make books about his concerns, draw pictures, and listen to picture books about hospitals. Meet with the child's parents to gain a full understanding of why, when, and for how long he will be hospitalized. Ask them what you can do to help their child.

● Provide parents with information, or at least access to information, about talking with children who are going to the hospital. See the resources at the end of this chapter.

● Make up a package for the child in the hospital. Include pictures of the class on field trips and at school, an audiotape or videotape made by the children and a tape of favorite songs from records, drawings made by the other children, new marking pens, and blank books to write and draw in. Present this package to him in the hospital or just before he leaves for the hospital.

● For long stays, provide regular (perhaps weekly) packages to the child with pictures of what the children did that week, materials to do an art project that was done in the class during the week (which may have to be modified for the hospital setting), some books, and pictures and letters from the class to the child.

● Provide information to other parents so that they can take their children to visit the child in the hospital.

● Visit or call the child while he is in the hospital. If possible, call from the classroom so that all children can talk to him.

- When a child returns to the classroom after a hospital stay or emergency room visit, provide many chances for him to share his experiences with the other children. Set up a hospital dramatic play area if this was not done before the stay. In one classroom a child's real experiences with a broken arm in the emergency room led to rich and exciting dramatic play, which led to investigating bones and skeletons, which then led to exploring organs and the inside of the body.

Resources

Fassler, D. 1986. The young child in the hospital. In *Reducing stress in young children's lives,* edited by J. B. McCracken. Washington, D.C.: NAEYC.

Keene, N. 2002. *Helping your child in the hospital: A practical guide for parents.* 3d ed. Cambridge, Mass.: O'Reilly & Associates.

Trawick-Smith, J., and R. H. Thompson. 1984. Preparing young children for hospitalization. *Young Children* 39 (5): 57–62.

Wallinga, C., and P. Skeen. 1997. Siblings of hospitalized and ill children: The teacher's role in helping these forgotten family members. *Young Children* 51 (6): 78–83.

Children's Books

Bridwell, N. 2000. *Clifford visits the hospital.* Clifford the Big Red Dog Series. New York: Scholastic.

Dooley, V. 1996. *Tubes in my ears: My trip to the hospital.* New York: Mondo Publishing.

Duncan, D. 1994. *When Molly was in the hospital: A book for brothers and sisters of hospitalized children.* Windsor, Calif.: Rayve Productions.

Hautzig, D. 1985. *A visit to the Sesame Street Hospital.* New York: Random House.

Johnson, M. 1998. *Let's talk about going to the hospital.* New York: Powerkids Press.

Lansky, V. 1990. *Koko Bear's big earache: Preparing your child for ear tube surgery.* Minnetonka, Minn.: Book Peddlers.

Moses, A. 1997. *At the hospital.* Field trip series. Chanhassen, Minn.: Children's World.

Pace, B. 1995. *Chris gets ear tubes.* Washington, D.C.: Gallaudet University Press.

Reit, S. 1984. *Jenny's in the hospital.* Racine, Wisc.: Western.

Rey, M. 1966. *Curious George goes to the hospital.* New York: Houghton Mifflin Co.

Rogers, F. 1997. *Going to the hospital.* First Experiences Series. New York: Paper Star.

Web Sites

Hospitalization—Preparing Your Preschooler. Children's Hospital of St. Louis. www.stlouischildrens.org. Enter "hospitalization" in the search box.

Children and Hospitalization by Jacob L. Driesen, Ph.D. www.driesen.com. Click on Search Our Site and enter "children and hospitalization" in the search box.

Pediatric Preparation Guidelines—Preschool (3–6 Years). New York University School of Medicine. www.med.nyu.edu. Enter "preschool" in the search box.

Pediatric Preparation Guidelines—Toddlers (1–3 Years). New York University School of Medicine. www.med.nyu.edu. Enter "toddlers" in the search box.

Preparing the Preschooler for Surgery. MUSC Children's Hospital. www.musckids.com. Enter "preschooler surgery" in the search box.

Preparing Preschoolers for Hospitalization. MUSC Children's Hospital. www.musckids.com. Enter "preparing preschoolers" in the search box.

Preschoolers Reactions to Health-Care Settings or Medical Procedures. Gillette Children's Specialty Healthcare. gillettechildrens.org. Enter "preschoolers reactions" in the search box.

5. Death of a Loved One ——

When a loved one dies, most children will go through a grieving process that can last a year or more, depending on the importance to the child of the person who died. Be aware of where the child is in the process so you can help in a meaningful way. Many children are deeply upset by the death of a beloved pet, nearly as much as a relative or friend. The anniversary of the death often brings the return of strong feelings and grief.

The following details the steps of the grieving process:

Denial	The child believes the dead person (or pet) will come back.
Anger	The child expresses strong feelings of being abandoned and rejected by the person who has died. The child may express these feelings through misbehaviors and acting out.
Grief	The child mourns over the loss. She cries often and feels despondent.
Acceptance	Gradually the child returns to more typical behaviors and attitudes. She comes to a new understanding of herself and her place in the world.

Preventing Problems

● Read books about death to all the children occasionally. Allow time for children to process the ideas and to ask questions. Many original versions of fairy tales, such as "Cinderella," deal with the death of a parent and the healing that comes from grieving. More contemporary versions tend to leave out these important details.

● Read simple versions of tales and myths that deal with death, from a variety of cultures and lands. Point out how different people believe different things about what happens to people when they die. Discuss how people cope with loss. A beautiful American Indian legend/dance is about a shrouded widow—the cocoon of a caterpillar who mourns for a year. She then realizes all she is missing in life and removes her shroud to reveal the colorful butterfly underneath.

● Talk about famous people when they die. The children will usually be aware of the death from the news and adult conversation. Explain in simple terms what made them important or famous and how their deeds will live on after them.

● Many (traditional) children's songs are about death—"Blue," "Who Killed Cock Robin?" "Go Tell Aunt Rhodie," "The Ruben James," "The *Titanic* (It Was Sad When the Great Ship Went Down)", and others. Sing these songs with the children so that death does not become a taboo subject.

● When a child finds a dead insect or small animal, use it as an opportunity for the children to learn what death means in concrete terms. Even very young toddlers can understand that death means no movement, stiffness, silence, and no response.

● Take a field trip to a cemetery. Get parent approval and prepare the children well for what to expect and what you will do there. Before going, talk with a friend so you can work through your own discomfort or anxiety about visiting a cemetery. If legal, make stone rubbings at the cemetery and take photographs. Bring flowers to lay on gravestones. This will bring out many questions about death and give the children a fuller understanding of how society deals with death. For more ideas on a field trip to a cemetery, see S. S. Riley's article, "Pilgrimage to Elmwood Cemetery" in the January 1989 issue of *Young Children*.

Dealing with Existing Problems

● If you find out that a child in your class has experienced a recent death in her family, do the activities described above. Ask the child's parents or guardians for ideas for helping the child in the classroom. Explain your approach and ask for their approval and ideas for improvements. Negotiate any activities that they feel uncomfortable with or would like to see included. Assure them that young children are aware of death and greatly benefit from information and outlets for expressing themselves, provided they are not pushed or given more information than they can handle.

● Ask the child's permission before talking about the death with the whole class. Take your cues from her about how much detail to go into. Have children direct questions to the child, unless she would prefer that you do the talking. Check each response you give with the child for accuracy and approval.

● Be aware that all children and families who have recently experienced the loss of a loved one, especially if the death was sudden and unexpected, could benefit from the help of a professional counselor. Recommend this to the family. Give them some of the resources listed at the end of this chapter.

● Because young children cannot put their feelings into words and because they usually act on their feelings, you will likely encounter challenging behaviors. Help the children express their feelings without hurting themselves or others. Provide them with outlets for expression such as drawing, pounding clay or playdough, hammering nails, climbing, running, and riding.

● Help children to soothe and calm themselves. They can generate their own ideas and/or you can suggest that they listen to music, sing, look at a book, talk, draw, or play with sand or water.

● Write books about the person who died and the wonderful things he or she did while alive. Be aware, however, that some children cannot or prefer not to talk about a recent death. Respect the child's feelings and instead write stories about young animals who have lost a loved one. This will be less threatening and will be very healing.

● Use the words "death" and "dead" instead of euphemisms such as loss, gone to sleep, passed away, and so on.

- If the death was due to an illness, be sure to help the children understand that ordinary illnesses do not result in death.

- Help parents see the importance of including the child in the funeral and in all aspects of the death and mourning. This is the only way they can know and benefit from the rituals and ceremonies our society has for death.

Questions about Death

- Answer questions simply and honestly. If a child asks, "What happens to people when they die?" answer by saying, "No one knows for sure. Different people believe different things, and when you are older, you can learn about it and decide for yourself. We do know that their bodies become stiff and cold, and the person can never talk, play, laugh, or move again. This makes us very sad because we will miss them."

- Be aware that children who ask questions about death often and regularly are working through the issue and may have had a recent experience with death. In some cases, the questions reflect a general insecurity or anxiety or fear related to other issues. As your best approach, provide loving reassurance to the child. Try to determine the actual cause of the anxiety. If she asks, "When will I die?" respond with, "I hope you live a very long time because you bring joy to everyone and many people love you a lot." If the questions and concern continue for more than a few weeks, talk to the parents about getting help from a professional counselor.

- The causes of death are of great interest to most children. This is natural, as they are trying hard to understand all aspects of the world around them. If they ask a blunt question to a grieving child or parent about the cause of the death when the person is not ready to talk about it yet, help by saying (if you don't know the cause yourself), "Julia isn't ready to tell you now because it makes her very sad. Maybe in a few days, if she's ready, she will tell us." If you do know the cause, give a brief explanation, "Julia's father was in a car accident. Let's talk more about it after circle time, because it makes Julia uncomfortable to talk about it now."

Death of a Classroom Pet

- The death of a classroom pet provides an excellent opportunity to explore the subject of death with your children, so don't minimize the event. Let each child hold the dead pet so she can learn concretely what death is. Encourage her to feel the stiffness, coldness, and lack of response of the animal. Compare that to how the animal used to be. Take plenty of time to read books about death, sing songs, and talk about feelings and beliefs. Have a ceremonious funeral and bury the pet outside under a marker. Invite each child who desires to do so to say something about the pet. Put together a book of remembrances. Plant something in memory of the pet.

Resources

Brett, D. 1988. *Annie stories.* New York: Workman.

Christian, L. G. 1997. Children and death. *Young Children* 52 (4): 76–80.

Dougy Center. 1999. *35 ways to help a grieving child.* Portland, Oreg.: Dougy Center for Grieving Children.

Essa, E. L., and C. I. Murray. 1994. Research in review. Young children's understanding and experience with death. *Young Children* 49 (4): 74–81.

Furman, E. 1986. Helping children cope with death. In *Reducing stress in young children's lives,* edited by J. B. McCracken. Washington, D.C.: NAEYC.

———. 1990. Plant a potato—Learn about life (and death). *Young Children* 46 (1): 15–20.

Goldman, L. E. 1996. We can help children grieve: A child-oriented model for memorializing. *Young Children* 51 (6): 69–73.

Greenberg, J. 1997. Seeing children through tragedy: My mother died today—When is she coming back? *Young Children* 51 (6): 76–77.

Hofschield, K. A. 1991. The gift of a butterfly. *Young Children* 46 (3): 3–6.

Hopkins, A. R. 2002. Children and grief: The role of the early childhood educator. *Young Children* 57 (1): 40–47.

Johnson, J., and M. Johnson. 1998. *Children grieve, too: Helping children cope with grief.* Omaha: Centering Corp.

Kroen, W. C. 1996. *Helping children cope with the loss of a loved one: A guide for grown-ups.* Minneapolis: Free Spirit Publishing.

MacIsaac, P., and S. King. 1989. What did you do with Sophie, teacher? *Young Children* 44 (2): 37–38.

Riley, S. S. 1989. Pilgrimage to Elmwood Cemetery. *Young Children* 44 (2): 33–36.

Silverman, J. 1999. *Help me say goodbye: Activities for helping kids cope when a special person dies.* Minneapolis: Fairview Press.

Trozzi, M., and K. Massimini. 1999. *Talking with children about loss: Words, strategies, and wisdom to help children cope with death, divorce, and other difficult times.* New York: Perigee.

Children's Books

Amery, H. 2002. *Greek myths for young children.* Newton, Mass.: EDC Publications.

Mellonie, B. 1983. *Lifetimes: The beautiful way to explain death to children.* New York: Bantam Doubleday Dell Publishers.

Mills, J. C. 1993. *Gentle willow: A story for children about dying.* Washington, D.C.: Imagination.

Munsch, R. 1988. *Love you forever.* Toronto: Firefly Books.

Polaccio, P. 2001. *The keeping quilt.* New York: Aladdin Paperbacks.

Rogers, F. 1998. *When a pet dies.* First experiences. New York: Paper Star.

Simon, N. 1992. *The saddest time.* Morton Grove, Ill.: Albert Whitman & Co.

Varley, S. 1992. *Badger's parting gifts.* New York: Mulberry Books.

Viorst, J. 1976. *The tenth good thing about Barney.* New York: Aladdin Paperbacks.

Wilhelm, H. 1989. *I'll always love you.* New York: Crown.

Zipes, J. 1992. *The complete fairy tales of the Brothers Grimm.* New York: Bantam Books.

Web Sites

The Child's Loss: Death, Grief, and Mourning. How Caregivers Can Help Children Exposed to Traumatic Death by Bruce D. Perry and Jana Rubenstein (also available in Spanish). Child Trauma Academy.
www.childtrauma.org. Click on CTA Materials on the side bar, then on Caregivers, scroll down to article.

Children and Grief. American Academy of Child and Adolescent Psychiatry. Facts for Families #8. 1998.
www.aacap.org. Link through Facts for Families and scroll down to article.

Dealing with Sadness and Loss by Charles A. Smith. National Network for Child Care.
www.nncc.org. Link through Articles and Resources tab, then Guidance and Discipline, then scroll down to article under Stressful Life Events category.

It Lets the Sad Out: Using Art to Help Children Express Deep Emotions by Barbara Rodriguez
earlychildhood.com/Articles/index.cfm. Link through Reading Room, enter "sad out" in the search box.

Grieving Kids Need Guidance by Naomi Naierman
earlychildhood.com/Articles/index.cfm. Enter "grieving" in the search box.

Learning to Live Through Loss: Helping Children Understand Death by Carolyn Wilken and Joyce Powell. National Network for Child Care.
www.nncc.org. Link through Articles and Resources tab, then Guidance and Discipline, then scroll down to article under Stressful Life Events category.

When a Pet Dies. American Academy of Child and Adolescent Psychiatry. Facts for Families #78. 2000.
www.aacap.org. Link through Facts for Families and scroll down to article.

6. Tragedies

Because of intense media coverage of events like those of September 11, 2001, school shootings, child abductions, and wars, many young children are repeatedly exposed to tragedies in graphic detail. Such events are difficult for us, as adults, to understand or to cope with. For young children it is even more difficult. Children's responses will vary, but basically all children want to be reassured that they are safe, that adults are protecting them from harm, that the world is predictable, and that people are basically good. Although we may not always have these positive feelings (which is the goal of terrorism, after all), children need to have them to grow up healthy.

Preventing Problems

As adults who care for children, we need to understand that growing up today involves complex challenges that are at least equal to but different than the challenges that faced children in previous generations. The main task is the same: protecting children from harm and helping them thrive. Yesterday's challenges for children centered more around basic physical health and safety, while today's challenges center more on psychological health and safety. Surviving childhood was the main concern previously. Injury and death from fires, accidents, poisoning, and so on were common and real. Much of our earliest children's literature involved moral tales focused on safety (Andersen's "Little Match Girl" and the Brothers Grimm's "Little Red Riding Hood"). Today we must protect our children, and help them learn to protect themselves, from the assault on their minds and hearts. Sophisticated advertisements and pop culture bombard them from ever-larger, increasingly ubiquitous video screens, such as computers, TVs, and video games. Seeing inappropriate content—frightening images aimed at adults—is almost unavoidable.

● Make sure your classroom is emotionally supporting to children. They need to be told and shown often that they are cared about, important, and unique. Establish a clear expectation that they will care for each other: "I won't let anyone hurt you (inside or out) and I won't let you hurt anyone." Actively teach the skills of caring—negotiating, turn taking, asking for what you need, asking about others' needs, being respectful, offering help to others, and comforting each other.

- Keep pop culture out of your classroom and minimize the pop culture that children bring in to the classroom. Make it a sanctuary from the commercial world. Display photographs (particularly of the children and their families) and art (particularly the children's work). Have plenty of high-quality children's literature available.

- Talk to parents about the importance of limiting all TV/video viewing, especially shows for adults, like the news and scary movies.

- Do not discuss events or issues among adults in front of children that are difficult for them to comprehend or may be frightening. Talk to parents about the importance of limiting discussion at home. Wait for the children to go to bed.

- Teach children some basic media literacy skills using the ideas and resources in the "TV/Video Obsessed Children" chapter on pp. 90–92.

Dealing with Existing Problems

- Make sure you spend ample time sorting out your own feelings. Talk at length with empathetic people who can help you deal with the outrage and fear that can be overwhelming. Remain calm and informed in order to help children. They will pick up and mirror your emotional state more readily than the words you say.

- Increase the amount and variety of calming activities. Match the activities with particular children. Some will find music soothing, others enjoy being held, some need to talk, while others will want to listen to stories or look at beautiful picture books.

- Add more sensory activities and give children more time to engage in them. These include sand and water play and playdough and clay.

- Provide a wide variety of art materials and media. Encourage children to draw pictures about what they have seen or how they feel.

- Avoid discussing the event with other adults in front of the children.

- Watch children carefully for how they are reacting to the event. Look for signs of stress and changes in behavior. Talk with and comfort those children who seem to be more stressed.

- Observe their spontaneous dramatic play to see how they may be "playing out" the events. Build on and redirect the play (if necessary) toward roles that offer help in emergency situations.

- Ask children what they know, have seen, or heard about the event. This will give you insight into what they are feeling and how they are thinking about it. Immediately clear up any misconceptions or wrong information they may have. Hearing their concerns and interpretations will help you know what to say and not say to them about the event.

- Validate and support their feelings. Tell them no more than they need to know in as simple terms as you can: "It was very scary, but now we are safe." "We all feel very sad and worried, but I and many others will work hard to see that it doesn't happen again." Overexplaining only causes confusion and may extend their anxiety.

- In discussions with children, follow the advice of Fred Rogers (Mr. Rogers) and "focus on the helpers." Even in tragedies of epic proportions, such as the Holocaust, there were numerous (even if not enough) helpers such as Oscar Schindler, Miep Gies, and the Danish people whose boat lift saved nearly all of Denmark's Jews. During the events of September 11, 2001, there were firefighters and police who saved many lives. This gives us hope and faith in others, which helps counteract the fear and hatred we have of the perpetrators.

- Feel comfortable saying, "I don't know, but I will try to find out and tell you later" or "no one knows at this time." If you are unsure how to answer a difficult question, it's good to say you don't know. This will give you time to figure out the best way to answer it.

- Tell children, "I and your parents will take care of you. We will protect you." Tell them this before they even ask for comfort as well as after. Tell them even if you have some doubts about your ability to do it.

- Keep your routines consistent. Children find assurance in sameness during times of stress. This is not the time to make major changes or go on a field trip to an unfamiliar place.

- Avoid assigning blame and generalizing it to a group. For every terrorist or murderer there are many more people from the same ethnic group or religion who are very caring and who are working hard for peace.

• Read stories to them about children (or small animals) who come safely through scary and traumatic events. Some of the original versions of the Brothers Grimm's fairy tales do this better than most contemporary stories. These include "Hansel and Gretel," "Mama Goat and the Seven Little Kids," "Tom Thumb," "Rapunzel," and many others. Stick to the stories that have strong girls and children, who are saved by their own cleverness and the help of an empathetic adult rather than merely saved by a stranger as in "Little Red Riding Hood," "Snow White," or contemporary versions of "Cinderella."

Resources

Greenman, J. 2001. *What happened to the world? Helping children cope in turbulent times.* Watertown, Mass.: Bright Horizons.

Gross, T., and S. Clemens. 2002. Painting a tragedy: Young children process the events of September 11. *Young Children* 57 (3): 44–51.

Russell, R., and J. Greenman. 2001. *What happened to the world? Facilitators guide.* Watertown, Mass.: Bright Horizons.

Zipes, J., trans. 1992. *The complete fairy tales of the Brothers Grimm.* New York: Bantam.

Web Sites

Behind the Headlines. Resources for Educators on the September 11 Tragedy and the Response. Teaching for Change. www.teachingforchange.org/Sept11.htm

The Child's Loss: Death, Grief, and Mourning. How Caregivers Can Help Children Exposed to Traumatic Death by Bruce D. Perry and Jana Rubenstein (also available in Spanish). Child Trauma Academy. www.childtrauma.org. Click on CTA Materials, then on Caregivers, scroll down to article.

Dealing with Sadness and Loss by Charles A. Smith. National Network for Child Care. www.nncc.org. Link through Articles and Resources tab, then Guidance and Discipline, then scroll down to article under Stressful Life Events category.

Helping Children Cope with Disaster. NAEYC. www.naeyc.org/coping_with_disaster.htm

Helping Young Children Cope with Tragedy. Wake County [N.C.] Public Schools. www.wcpss.net/parent-tips. Scroll down to link to article.

Helping Parents, Teachers, and Caregivers Deal with Children's Concerns about Violence in the News by Fred Rogers with Hedda Bluestone Sharapan pbskids.org/rogers. Link on Parents and Teachers.

It Lets the Sad Out: Using Art to Help Children Express Deep Emotions by Barbara Rodriguez earlychildhood.com/Articles/index.cfm. Enter "sad out" in the search box.

A National Tragedy: Helping Children Cope. Tips for Parents and Teachers. National Association of School Psychologists. www.nasponline.org/NEAT/terrorism.html

The Needs of Children during Traumatic Times: Being Responsive and Proactive. Issue of Child and Family E-Newsletter. Northwest Regional Educational Laboratory. www.nwrel.org/cfc. Link to archived newsletters, Volume 1, No. 7.

War, Terrorism, and America's Classrooms: Rethinking Schools. A Special Report. www.rethinkingschools.org/sept11

Various resources on helping children cope with violence from Mr. Rogers. Family Communication, Inc. www.misterrogers.org/early_care

7. Moving On to the Next Class

Helping children make a successful transition to the next grade or age level will be a great benefit to the children and to their next teacher. It will also help you by reducing the anxiety the children may have, especially as the end of the year approaches. Whether children are excited and feel big, or are worried and scared, moving to the next class is a major change and will affect everyone.

You also need to help the teachers and the children who are in the classes or age groups below yours to ease the transition into your class. You can implement the ideas in this chapter both for your children who are going into the next class and for the children who will be entering your class. Show care and interest in those children. They will feel positive toward you and feel happy to be in your class. When children start out with a positive attitude, you prevent many behavior problems.

Many early childhood teachers are concerned that by following good practices—giving children choices with active, hands-on materials in classrooms with self-directed learning centers—they are doing children a disservice. In the next grade, children may be required to sit at desks for long periods, take directions from the teacher, do paper and pencil tasks, and line up. While this may be true in many cases, it makes no sense to subject children to a program that does not meet their needs and will cause stress and misbehaviors because of what they may face next year. Children who feel good about themselves, are self-motivated learners, and have learned self-control will do better when faced with a stressful curriculum than will children who do not possess these qualities. However, you can smooth the transition by helping children prepare for what they will encounter, especially if it will be very different.

Preventing Problems

● Set up field trips to visit some of the classrooms your children will be attending. Invite teachers from the next level to visit your classroom and talk with your children. Prepare the children to ask questions of the teachers. Invite several children who were in your class last year to talk to your current group about what it is like being in the next room.

● With the permission of parents, send information to the next teacher about the children in your class. Stress their strengths and abilities. Express any concerns objectively and cautiously. You do not want the new teacher to prejudge the child, as he might act very differently in the new class or mature a great deal by then.

● Talk to several teachers of the next age grouping to understand their expectations for children. This does not mean you will change your curriculum to meet what may be inappropriate expectations. You may find, however, that the expectations are more appropriate than you anticipated. You may learn some helpful information, such as the style of writing used in that grade. To ease the transition for your children, use this style when printing names and writing stories.

● Organize a few meetings during the year when all the teachers in your grade/age level meet with all the teachers in the next level. Exchange information, coordinate, and clarify philosophies and goals.

● Read books and create stories about children who go to a new class.

● Develop a dramatic play area that includes the materials and equipment used in the next grade. Observe the spontaneous play that develops for misconceptions about what the children believe will happen in the next grade. Allow them to freely work through their concerns or their excitement.

● At the end of the school year, role-play situations the children are likely to encounter in the next class. Help them learn the actions and words to use to get their needs met, without causing problems. For example, if a child is given a math worksheet to complete, he can raise his hand and ask if he can use his crayons to figure out the problem. Most teachers will not object, if children ask politely. Children can also ask for materials to use to make projects more creative and for blank sheets of paper for writing stories during transition times.

● At the end of the school year, practice some of the routines or rules that are used in the next school or class. This may include the "lining-up routine." Explain the reasons for the rules or routines: "It may not be fun, but it is necessary because the new school has many more children than our school and fewer teachers in each class." Help them find ways to deal with the stress that may cause. "Let's think of things you can do while waiting quietly and still for a long time. I like to sing a song to myself inside my head."

● With parental permission, give all the children and their families class lists with addresses and phone numbers so that friendships can be maintained. Give all the children a class photo.

● Meet with parents to discuss the importance of helping their children move to the next grade. Invite a teacher or the principal to meet with the parents and to answer questions they have about the new class or school. Request that the guest bring a copy of the report card used in the next grade, if there is one. Help parents with ways to cope with different expectations and levels of involvement in the new school or class by providing specific information: "At Jefferson School, taking your concerns to the school's parent advisory committee is best. Make positive suggestions rather than complaints." Brainstorm together strategies to help their children get the most out of their new program.

● Provide all parents with information about transitioning children. Many good resources are listed at the end of this chapter.

Dealing with Existing Problems

● For children who are expressing fears and concerns about going into the next class, try the following ideas:

▶ Determine, if possible, who the teacher will be and talk with her about the child. Set a time for the child to visit the teacher and the classroom. Fear of the unknown is often the worst fear.

▶ Set up a time when a child from the next class can talk to the child in your class about what he can expect.

▶ Determine, if possible, the specific concerns the child has. You may be able to clear up some misconceptions easily.

▶ Role-play with the child situations he might encounter in the next grade. Having a chance to practice some new skills, before facing the real situation, always helps. See the examples above.

▶ Help the child stay in touch with at least one good friend from the class. Talk with his parents to arrange a photo exchange and to share addresses and phone numbers. Encourage the parents to set up visits with the other child.

Conflicting Styles and Expectations among Various Teachers in the Next Grade

● If your children are going to a number of different classrooms with teachers who all are very different, the transition from your class to the next can be very confusing. In some cases, the teachers' educational approaches may differ radically from one another. The best approach is to role-play and discuss two or three (at the most) of these approaches, particularly those most different from your own. Note that all children benefit from learning that different adults have different expectations and styles.

● If, for example, a variety of writing styles are used, pick the one to use in your class that you believe is the most appropriate for young children. Base your decision on the ease children will have in writing and reading it. If you have no preference, choose the one that is most common.

Celebrations Not Graduations

In many programs a great deal of time, energy, and money is spent on graduations. Most of these events are designed to meet the needs of the parents and put the children under stress. The children often have to spend too much time sitting and they have to perform as a group. Young children do neither very well. However, parents consider graduation from preschool to be a major milestone in their children's lives and like to mark it in some way.

● Meet the needs of both the parents and children by having an informal celebration. Prepare a special snack with the children and serve it to their parents at a short, early evening gathering. Make "graduation caps" with the children that they decorate. Present a short (fifteen minute) videotape or slide show of some of the highlights of the year. Have the children sing a few favorite songs that they have been singing all year and ask the parents to join in. Do an activity of movement games that involves the children and the parents together.

● Send a "diploma" to each child in the mail. Children love receiving mail and rarely get any, so your sending the "diploma" will make it very special.

● Plan your celebration with parents so they will understand your goal of involving the children in a meaningful, enjoyable occasion. Work out compromises and accept the good ideas of the parents. Be aware that they will take more responsibility for organizing the event if the ideas come from them.

Resources

Karr-Jelinek, C. 1994. *Transition to kindergarten: Parents and teachers working together.* ERIC, ED 371858.

Maxwell, K. L., and S. K. Eller. 1994. Research in review. Children's transition to kindergarten. *Young Children* 49 (6): 56–63.

National Association for the Education of Young Children (NAEYC). 1985. Ideas that work with young children: Graduation programs. *Young Children* 40 (3): 17.

Pianta, R. C., and M. Kraft-Sayre. 1999. Parent's observations about their children's transitions to kindergarten. *Young Children* 54 (3): 47–52.

Pianta, R. C., and M. Cox. 1999. *The transition to kindergarten.* Baltimore: Paul H. Brookes.

Ryan, B. 1996. *Helping your child start school: A practical guide for parents.* Secaucus, N.J.: Carol Publishing Group.

Vermont Department of Education. 2000. *Off to kindergarten: A booklet for parents, caregivers, and schools.* Montpelier, Vt.: Vermont Department of Education. ERIC, ED 454964.

Walmsley, S. A., and B. B. Walmsley. 1996. *Kindergarten: Ready or not? A parents guide.* Portsmouth, N.H.: Heinemann.

Ziegler, P. 1986. Saying goodbye to preschool. In *Reducing stress in young children's lives,* edited by J. B. McCracken. Washington, D.C.: NAEYC.

Children's Books

Howe, J. 1995. *When you go to kindergarten.* New York: Mulberry Books.

McGhee, A. 2002. *Countdown to kindergarten.* Orlando, Fla.: Silver Whistle.

Rankin, J. 2002. *First day*. New York: Margaret McElderry Books.

Rogers, J. 2002. *Kindergarten ABC*. New York: Cartwheel Books/Scholastic.

Schwartz, A. 1991. *Annabelle Swift, kindergartner*. London: Orchard Books.

Slate, J. 2001. *Miss Bindergarten gets ready for kindergarten*. New York: Puffin.

Videos

Family Communications, Inc
4802 Fifth Avenue
Pittsburgh, PA 15213
www.misterrogers.org
Going to School (Mr. Rogers)

NAEYC
1509 16th Street, N.W.
Washington, D.C. 20019
www.naeyc.org
Building Bridges to Kindergarten: Transition Planning for Children, 16 min.

Web Sites

Beyond Transition: Ensuring Continuity in Early Childhood Services by Joan Lombardi. ERIC Digest. ericeece.org. Link through Publications tab on side bar, then Digests, then Title, then scroll down to article.

Easing the Transition from Preschool to Kindergarten: A Guide for Early Childhood Teachers and Administrators. Head Start Information and Publication Center. www.headstartinfo.org. Click on Search and enter "transition to kindergarten."

Kindergarten Readiness and Transition. Daycare at About.com. daycare.about.com. Enter "kindergarten transition" in the search box.

Robert Pianta Talks about Kindergarten Transition. Family Involvement Network of Educators (FINE) Forum e-Newsletter. Issue 4—Spring 2002. gse.harvard.edu/hfrp/index.html. Click on FINE network on the side bar, then on e-newsletter, then on Issue 4, Spring 2002, then Questions and Answers.

Starting School: Effective Transitions by Sue Dockett and Bob Perry. *Early Childhood Research and Practice.* Fall 2001. Volume 3, Number 2. Online only. ecrp.uiuc.edu

Transition from Preschool to Kindergarten. Early Childhood Educators and Family Web Corner. users.stargate.net/~cokids/articleslist.html. Scroll down to the Education section.

Transition to Kindergarten. National Center for Early Development and Learning. Frank Porter Graham Child Develoment Institute. University of North Carolina. www.fpg.unc.edu. Scroll down to search bar and enter "transition."

Part V

Children with Challenging Behaviors

1. Helping Children with Challenging Behaviors

You may have noticed that a child who is challenging to deal with seems to act much better in one teacher's class than in another. You also may have observed that some teachers seem to have many children with behavior problems and some teachers seem to have few or none. The difference is not luck. Teachers do specific things that can make problem behaviors worse, keep them the same, or make them decrease. The chapters in this section reveal some of the strategies good teachers use to decrease behavior problems.

Your Goal: Teaching Self-Control and Acceptable Behaviors

Always keep in mind that your ultimate goal in helping young children with behavior problems is to teach them to control their own actions and reactions and to find alternative, more positive ways to get their needs met. With any challenging behavior, assume ignorance rather than malice. Although young children are certainly capable of malice, by taking a "teaching" approach to the problem, you will keep yourself calm and avoid power struggles with the child. You will have a positive, proactive approach to helping solve the difficult behavior.

● Before a problem occurs, discuss choices children can make about how to act. If several children usually argue over one particular trike, help them to figure out various ways to solve the problem just before they go out to use the equipment.

● Remind the children of the reason behind any rule or consequence to a behavior at the time the rule is being enforced. Have them repeat the reason back to you: "Kicking can seriously hurt a person. It only makes people angry and does not get the problem solved." Ask them to list some other ways to deal with the problem. Help them with ideas if necessary.

● If a child is given a consequence—such as having to choose a solitary activity because of hitting another child—tell her that she can join the other children when she feels able to use her voice to express her feelings. Respect her internal time clock even if it lasts only a few seconds. Repeat the consequence if she repeats the negative behavior.

● Actively teach children how to make friends, keep friends, and be liked by others. For example, when a group of children are playing together, a child may be able to enter the group by listening to the play and figuring out a role to take that will fit in. She should then ask to join by taking that role: "I'll be the sister, okay?" Barging in, changing the direction of the play, demanding a leadership role, or being too unassertive will result in rejection. Help children to negotiate solutions to conflicts. Sit with them and repeat the ideas they generate: "You both want the same toy so what can happen that will make you both happy?" Ask them to think through the consequence of each idea: "What might happen if you grab it? If you ask for it? If you ask me for help? If you wait for it?" Summarize and then ask the children to agree on a solution they both like.

● Teach problem solving, negotiation, and conflict resolution skills during small group activities, not just when there is a conflict. Role-play, use puppets, and read books. Elizabeth Crary's Children's Problem Solving Books are great for helping you do this. (See the resources on p. 125.)

Use Alternatives to Reinforcement Systems

Rewards (stickers, stars, and so on) for good behavior or negative reinforcement for bad behavior (time-out) do not teach children self-control or different behaviors. They are tempting to use because they can be very effective at changing behaviors quickly, but they give all the control to the teacher. Teaching skills, redirection, logical consequences, prevention strategies, and other techniques (described in this and subsequent chapters) will teach self-control better than reinforcement techniques and will effectively reduce problem behaviors. Although it may take more time to see dramatic changes in behavior, they will change the behaviors over the long term and permanently.

A danger of reinforcement systems is that they are so effective that teachers never fade them out to allow children to act appropriately on their own. Another problem with them is that the children who are not getting rewards feel cheated. This sometimes leads teachers to have a reinforcement system for the whole class, even though it is not really needed.

On its own, praise, such as "Good work," is a teacher-controlled form of reinforcement. It is a verbal reward system rather than a tangible reward system, but it is really no different from stickers and so on. In classrooms where teachers use a great deal of praise, children tend to be less cooperative with others and are more unsure of themselves.

However, social or verbal encouragement is something everyone needs. This entails letting children know what they are doing well by giving them specific information that is helpful: "You picked up the blocks quickly and neatly. They will be easy to find and play with tomorrow and everyone enjoys being in a clean room."

Modifying behavior through reinforcement systems can be useful with children with moderate to severe disabilities. However, use this reinforcement as a starting strategy (with the intention of eliminating it as soon as possible) and with the advice and support of a professional psychologist or special educator. Most children who have these conditions will not be served best in a regular early childhood program unless there is a great deal of support, such as a full-time, skilled aide. However, they may be included part of the time with the intention of integrating them fully (with continued support services) as their behaviors improve.

Reinforcement systems are powerful manipulators of children. However, your job as a teacher is to empower children, not to manipulate them.

Use Child Choice, Not Time-Out

Time-out—placing a child off by herself for a period of time—rarely works because the consequence is not related to the misbehavior. After a minute the child has forgotten why she is there. She is also angry because she is being punished and humiliated. She may be using "time-out" to think of ways to get back at you!

If a child needs to be removed from an area because of being continuously disruptive, let her choose a quiet activity away from others. This is called "child choice." Before doing this, give her at least one chance to improve her behavior by telling her that she will have to choose a different activity if she continues to be disruptive. If she does have to be removed, tell her that she can return when she feels calm and ready to attend. Help her learn and develop the skills she needs to do the appropriate behavior. Give her verbal encouragement when she does well. Child choice eliminates the punishment aspect of time-out and gives control to the child.

Try to Determine the Cause of the Problem

A cause exists for all behaviors. However, if the cause is not apparent (known abuse, a recent loss, overexcitement about a birthday, and so on), determining what it is can be challenging. Meeting with parents to support their efforts in dealing with their child's behavior problems can open the door to discovering the cause. If possible, request a home visit. A great deal is often revealed during a home visit. Family values, priorities, approaches to discipline, and attitudes about food and toileting can all become evident. Parents are more likely to open up when they feel comfortable on their own turf.

The most common causes for challenging behaviors are to get attention or to get an important need met (and not being able to get it met in an appropriate way). Other causes include anger, lack of knowing another way of behaving, or the child believing that he is "bad" and taking on that identity. Most children with challenging behaviors feel very powerless, invisible, and not in control of their lives—although their actions in the classroom may make you feel that they have total control! They need to take control whenever and however they can (sometimes even knowing that they will be punished) to compensate for those inadequate feelings. This is why it is very important to avoid punishments and to give them lots of attention and affection, for just being themselves as well as for "good" behaviors. It is also important to give them the skills they need to get their needs met and to get attention in appropriate ways.

The root causes of inadequate feelings or anger or the vital need that is not being met can be varied, but usually come down to complex problems at home. You may need to provide families with support, access to help and resources, and information about parenting skills, child development, and more, to help the child.

Physical or biological problems are other possible causes. Check the child's files for any medical information that might tell you something. Possible physical causes include certain kinds of allergies, mild autism, sensory integration problems, strong temperamental traits, and more. Request a medical checkup, as it may reveal the possible causes of the behavior problems. This is often a good place to start the process of helping the child because it takes the blame off the parents, the child, or you for the behaviors.

In one case, a three-and-a-half-year-old child had a problem of occasionally but regularly biting other children very hard. He was a wonderful child in every other respect. His parents were concerned, cooperative, and at a loss at what to do. The teachers tried everything they could think of to eliminate the behavior. They blamed themselves for not being consistent enough. They felt frustrated and as if they were failures. Eventually the child was referred to a special agency that dealt with emotionally disturbed children. During the interview process, it was discovered that the child was on medication for a physical problem. The medication was changed, and the biting stopped.

Continue to work on determining possible causes for problem behaviors while you work on changing the behaviors in the classroom and helping parents change the behaviors at home. Although you may not be able to solve the behavior problems by determining the cause, you will gain useful insights that will make you more empathetic to the child's problems. If you cannot find the cause, you can still do many things to help the child and to reduce the behaviors, as discussed in subsequent chapters.

Resources

For resources specific to parents and parenting, see the resource list at the end of the chapter, "Telling Parents about the Difficult Behavior of Their Child" on pp. 174–175.

Bakely, S. 2001. Through the lens of sensory integration: A different way of analyzing challenging behaviors. *Young Children* 56 (6): 70–76.

Betz, C. 1994. Beyond time-out: Tips from a teacher. *Young Children* 49 (3): 10–14.

Daniel, J. 1995. New beginnings: Transitions for difficult children. *Young Children* 50 (3): 17–23.

Eaton, M. 1997. Positive discipline: Fostering the self-esteem of young children. *Young Children* 52 (6): 43–46.

Fields, M. V., and C. Boesser. 2001. *Constructive guidance and discipline: Preschool and primary education.* 3d ed. New York: Prentice Hall.

Flicker, E. S., and J. A. Hoffman. 2002. Developmental discipline in the early childhood classroom. *Young Children* 57 (5): 82–89.

Gartrell, D. 1995. Misbehavior or mistaken behavior? *Young Children* 50 (5): 27–34.

———. 1997. Beyond discipline to guidance. *Young Children* 52 (6): 34–42.

———. 1997. *A guidance approach for the encouraging classroom.* Clifton Park, N.Y.: Delmar Learning.

———. 2001. Replacing time-out: Part one—Using guidance to build an encouraging classroom. *Young Children* 56 (6): 8–16.

———. 2001. Replacing time-out: Part two—Using guidance to maintain an encouraging classroom. *Young Children* 57 (2): 36–43.

Greenberg, P. 1991. *Character development: Encouraging self-esteem and self-discipline in infants, toddlers, and two-year-olds.* Washington, D.C.: NAEYC.

Greenspan, S. 1996. *The challenging child: Understanding, raising, and enjoying the five "difficult" types of children.* Cambridge, Mass.: Perseus Publishing.

Heath, H. 1994. Dealing with difficult behaviors—Teachers plan with parents. *Young Children* 49 (5): 20–24.

Kaiser, B., and J. Rasminsky. 1999. *Meeting the challenge: Effective strategies for challenging behaviors in early childhood environments.* Ottawa, Ontario: Canadian Child Care Federation.

Kohn, A. 1996. *Beyond discipline: From compliance to community.* Alexandria, Va.: Association for Supervision and Curriculum Development.

———. 1999. *Punished by rewards: The trouble with gold stars, incentive plans, A's, praise, and other bribes.* New York: Houghton Mifflin Co.

Kranowitz, C. S. 1998. *The out-of-sync child: Recognizing and coping with sensory integration dysfunction.* New York: Perigee.

Quinn, M. M., D. Osher, C. L. Warger, T. V. Hanley, B. D. Bader, and C. C. Hoffman. 2000. *Teaching and working with children who have emotional and behavioral challenges.* Longmont, Colo.: Sopris West.

Reinsberg, J. 1999. Understanding young children's behavior. *Young Children* 54 (4): 54–57.

Rodd, J. 1996. *Understanding young children's behavior.* New York: Teachers College Press.

Sandall, S., and M. Ostrosky, eds. 1999. *Practical ideas for addressing challenging behaviors.* Denver: Division for Early Childhood.

Scarlett, W. G. 1997. *Trouble in the classroom: Managing the behavior problems of young children.* San Francisco: Jossey-Bass.

Schreiber, M. 1999. Time-outs for toddlers: Is our goal punishment or education? *Young Children* 54 (4): 22–25.

Children's Books

Bang, M. G. 1999. *When Sophie gets angry—Really, really angry . . .* New York: Scholastic.

Crary, E. Children's Problem Solving Books and Dealing with Feelings Books. Includes: *I'm frustrated; I'm mad; I'm furious; I'm excited; I'm scared; Mommy don't go; I'm lost; I want it; I can't wait; I want to play; My name is not Dummy.* Seattle: Parenting Press.

Everitt, B. 1995. *Mean soup.* New York: Voyager Books.

Surat, M. M. 1989. *Angel child, dragon child.* New York: Scholastic.

Viorst, J. 1987. *Alexander and the terrible, horrible, no good, very bad day.* New York: Scott Foresman.

Training Curricula for Teachers (some are also for parents)

The Incredible Years. Teachers, Parents, and Children Training Series.
www.incredibleyears.com

Project SUCCEED: Supporting and Understanding Challenging Children's Emotional and Educational

Development. Portland State University. Regional Research Institute for Human Services. www.rri.pdx.edu

TLC: Teaching and Leading Children. American Guidance Service. www.agsnet.com

Videos

Educational Productions
9000 SW Gemini Drive
Beaverton, OR 97008
www.edpro.com
Preventing Discipline Problems. Three topics, two 25 minute videos for each topic (one teaching and one practice video). Reframing Discipline Series. Three topics, two 25 minute videos for each topic. Also available in Spanish.

NAEYC
1509 16th Street, N.W.
Washington, DC 20019
www.naeyc.org
Discipline: Appropriate Guidance of Young Children. 1988. 28 min. *Painting a Positive Picture: Proactive Behavior Management* (Also in Spanish). 2001. 28 min.

Web Sites

Behavior Support/Social Skills Development. Various articles from Early Childhood Educators' and Family Web Corner. users.stargate.net/~cokids. Click on Teacher Pages, then Behavior Support/Social Skills Development.

Bonding and Attachment in Maltreated Children: How You Can Help by Bruce Perry. Scholastic.com. teacher.scholastic.com. Link on Search. Enter "bonding and attachment" and scroll to article.

Center for Mental Health in Schools. UCLA. Many resources to access. smhp.psych.ucla.edu

Challenging Behavior in Preschool Classrooms: Linking Research to Practice. National Center for Early Development and Learning. University of North Carolina. Frank Porter Graham Child Development Center. In *Early Developments*, Winter 2002. Volume 6, #1. www.fpg.unc.edu/~ncedl. Scroll down to search box and enter "challenging behavior."

Discipline. Earlychildhood.com. Various articles. www.earlychildhood.com/Articles/index.cfm. Click on Discipline.

The Division for Early Childhood (DEC) Concept Paper on the Identification of and Intervention with Challenging Behavior. www.dec-sped.org. Scroll down to and click on DEC Policies, Position Statements, and Concept Papers, then scroll down to Challenging Behavior and click on Concept Paper.

Guidance and Discipline. National Network for Child Care. Many articles on a wide variety of related topics. www.nncc.org. Click on Articles and Resources tab, and then click on Guidance and Discipline.

Managing Inappropriate Behavior in the Classroom. ERIC Digest. 1990. www.ericeece.org. Click on Publications, then Digests, then Title, then scroll down to the article.

Mental Health for Young Children: Experiencing the World in a Positive Way. Action Alliance for Children. www.4children.org. Click on Search and enter "mental health young children."

Recognizing Difficult Behavior in the Preschool Child by Patricia Woodbury. Earlychildhood.com www.earlychildhood.com/Articles/index.cfm. Click on Curriculm, then scroll to article.

Positive Discipline. ERIC Digest. 1990. www.ericeece.org. Click on Publications, then Digests, then Title, then scroll down to the article.

2. Preventing Behavior Problems

If you have many children with challenging behaviors, or seem to be dealing constantly with such behaviors, chances are that there is a problem with your "program," not with the children. You will probably need to change aspects of your program; that is, the physical environment of the classroom, your schedule and curriculum, and your own attitudes, actions, and reactions. These are prevention strategies (or indirect guidance), which are your most powerful tools for changing challenging behaviors. Once you have made these changes, children who come into your class with intense emotional needs that they usually express through negative behaviors, will have almost no need to do so.

Because previous chapters of this book dealt with making the environment, daily schedule, and curriculum responsive to children, this chapter focuses on your attitudes, actions, and reactions.

Your Own Attitudes, Actions, and Reactions

Attitude: Focus on the Positive

Feel positively toward the child with behavior problems. View him as a valuable gift, as he will provide you with an opportunity to learn a great deal. You may learn about the causes of behavior problems, new approaches to helping, the nature of your own biases, new parenting skills, and the availability of community agencies and resources. He will provide you with a chance to help turn a life around for the better.

A child with challenging behaviors also can help you improve your program. A highly active child may be the first (or the only one) to let you know that your activity is boring. A child who cries often can tell you that you may not have enough inviting things to do (he probably has too much time to think about his unhappiness). Although you may feel that this challenging child has come into your life just to make you miserable, he has not. He is acting the best and only way he knows how. Understanding the challenging child will help you feel positive, empathetic, and loving toward him, which may be the single most important thing you can do to reduce the behaviors.

Attitude: The Child Can Do Better

Believe that you can help the child improve and be happier, although in some extreme cases years of treatment by a professional counselor, a special education program, or intervention by a social service agency may be necessary. Even if you are the person who only starts the process, you will have done something important. Don't be tempted to pass a problem off as a phase. Although it might actually be a phase, such as biting, you can still help improve the behavior. Don't shrug off the problem as being due to the child's terrible parents, over whom you have no control. Many children learn to behave positively at school while acting differently at home. They come to see themselves as worthwhile because of a loving teacher. Don't ignore the problem hoping that it will go away, that the child will move, or that nine months will pass quickly. Too many children get passed on this way and never get the help they need. Often they grow up to be troubled teens and adults who cause serious problems for society. Changing problem behaviors when the child is young is much easier than waiting until later. Believe in the child and your own ability to help him.

Attitude: Parents Are Doing the Best They Can under Difficult Circumstances

Parenting today is a great challenge, even for families with access to many resources and money to be able to spend long periods of quality time with their children. However, these families are very rare. For most parents, life is very stressful and there is little support for parents and children from society at large. All children need many positive interactions with caring, responsive adults every day to grow up mentally healthy. The reality of life today makes this difficult, which results in many children with emotional needs.

Almost every parent wants to be good to her children and wants her children to be capable, well liked, and happy. However, every parent struggles with being relaxed enough and having the time, knowledge, and skills to make this happen. As a teacher, it is important not to blame parents, but to help them in their very difficult task. Just having an empathetic attitude toward parents, especially those struggling most, will go a long way toward creating positive relations and developing a partnership for the benefit of the child.

Action: Have a Positive Classroom

● Make many more positive statements, and make them more energetically, than admonishments or corrections. Catch children doing well, and let them know that they are doing well. For children with intense emotional needs, catch them just "being" and let them know they are cared about. At the same time, give them useful, specific information about their behavior, without judging their characters. "Good boy" is a judgment. Saying, "You cleaned up the blocks so quickly and thoroughly; it makes our class look neat and it will be easy to find all the blocks tomorrow" is helpful. Tell them often how much you enjoy them, but only if you can be honest about this sentiment: "I love seeing each of your sweet faces every morning. You are so much fun to be with; thank you for sharing part of your day with me."

Action: Make Expectations Clear and Reasonable

● Establish few rules and enforce them consistently. One important rule to have is the following: "Use your body and words without hurting others inside or outside their bodies." To make this rule work you must deal with behaviors that violate it almost every time they happen. If a child breaks the rule ten times and is "called" on it only one of the times, the child will only be confused and angry and not likely to follow it. After a rule has been established well enough that the behavior is rarely seen, add a new, more sophisticated one if necessary. For example: "Ask if it is okay before you hug someone" or "You can be angry without being mean to others."

● Remind children of rules ahead of time: "Please walk when we get inside the room." Let your expectations be known immediately before the event. Remember that young children have short memories and are primarily interested in the here and now: "After you hang up your coat, please sit on the circle."

• State all rules and expectations positively because young children behave better when they know what to do. Instead of saying, "Don't yell," say, "Please use a quiet voice." Instead of saying, "Don't run," say, "Please walk."

Action: Make Sure the Children Feel Important and Respected

• Give all the children many chances to do jobs vital to the running of the classroom. Create a job chart where children's names are displayed next to the names and pictures of their jobs. Rotate the names daily. Examples of jobs are listed in the box on this page. Create as many jobs as possible. If possible, have one job for each child every day.

• Give children many chances to make real decisions such as what song to sing, what book to listen to, or what movement game to play. If necessary, give a choice between two or three songs, books, or games, as some choices may not be acceptable to you. Ask an individual child to make the choice, as opposed to the whole group, if you do not want to take the time to vote or decide by consensus. Make this the task of the "Teacher" on the job chart. You may want to have several "Teachers," "Environmentalists," and other jobs.

• Make sure that the children have easy access to sponges and soapy water to clean up messes after themselves, easy ways to put toys where they belong when the children are finished playing, and simple methods to dress and take care of themselves. Even a two-year-old can put her own coat on by laying it flat on the ground, front of the coat facing up, standing behind the top of the coat, putting her arms in the sleeves, and flipping it over her head. Encourage the children to help each other with buttoning, zipping jackets, putting on mittens, and so on. Remember that anything you can do to give children responsibility over themselves or each other, with little or no adult assistance, will make children feel powerful and will reduce behavior problems that stem from feelings of insecurity and powerlessness.

Action: Provide for Success

• Give each and every child many opportunities to be and feel successful and challenged. Individualize games and activities. For example, ask a child who does not yet name colors to match colors during a color/shape lotto game; ask a child who can name colors to find the color on his card; ask a child who can name colors and shapes to find the square that has both attributes. When all play together, the less able or the younger children learn from the more able or the older ones. To make this work, look at the card you are holding. If the child who can name colors and shapes has a picture that matches it, ask, "Who has a red triangle?" without showing him the card. If the child who can name colors but not the shapes has the picture, ask, "Who has a red shape with three sides?" (Draw a triangle if she can't get the shape.) If the child who can match colors has the picture, hold up the card for him to see and ask, "Who has this card?"

Job Chart	
Zookeeper 1	Feed the fish.
Zookeeper 2	Feed the guinea pig.
Waiter	Set the table.
Weather Reporter or Meteorologist	Draw or place a symbol of the day's weather on the calendar.
Dentist	Lead the toothbrushing and collect the toothbrushes.
Environmentalist	Turn off the lights each time the class leaves the room; collect litter off the playground; recycle paper rather than throwing it out.
Teacher	Decide what song we will sing; lead the song; dismiss the children from the circle.
Custodian	Wipe the tables and sweep the floor.
Librarian	Choose a book to read, distribute books that children request for book browsing, collect and account for all books.
Mathematician	Count the number of days since school began; count the number of children present and absent.

(He can then match it.) Once children can be successful with little effort, challenge them with a slightly harder task.

- Another way to ensure feelings of success is to provide sand and water play daily. Have fun equipment in each, such as plastic bottles, funnels, tubing, spoons, and measuring cups. Give children plenty of time to play. These activities are satisfying because children cannot fail at them; there is no right way or wrong way to do it. The smoothness, softness, and texture of sand and water are very soothing to young children. They help comfort and relax them. Keep a small broom and large dustpan (for sand) and large sponges and a bucket (for water) nearby so children can clean up after themselves.

- In addition, provide open-ended art and building materials daily, including blocks with accessories, playdough with many plastic or wooden tools, and drawing materials with different kinds of paper and pens.

Action: Meet Individual Needs

- Children who have intense emotional needs often come into your classroom in the morning nearly or fully depleted of positive feelings about themselves and in need of attention. Be proactive. As soon as such a child comes in the door (if not before) give him a great deal of attention and affection. Do not wait for him to express his needs, as it is likely to be expressed inappropriately. To use a car metaphor, if they come with their "tanks" nearly or completely on empty, fill them up before they run out and stall.

- A child who needs extra attention and asks for it in a positive way should get extra attention from you. If a child is having a rough day because his mother went out of town, permit him to spend more time on your lap than other children do. Let him know that you are doing this today because you know he feels sad, but that tomorrow you will do it less. Let the other children know you would do this for them if they were sad. Be aware that you do not have to provide the same kind of attention for the other children. Being fair with young children means meeting their individual needs, not treating every child exactly the same.

- Do not neglect any child's needs. However, be aware that a child who demands an unreasonable amount of attention cannot be accommodated because you will be depriving other children of their needs. This is a hard balancing act. You might need help from another teacher or your director to determine what is an unreasonable need for attention. In classrooms where children know they will get their share of attention, especially when they need it most, competition for attention by acting out is greatly reduced.

Action: Actively Teach and Promote Cooperation

- In the absence of a strong set of cooperation skills, aggression and competitiveness in children flourish. Set the following classroom rule: "Ask three before you ask me." This requires children to learn to seek help from and give assistance to their classmates. Some children will need your help initially to learn how to ask for help in a way that will get a positive response and to give help without doing everything for the other child.

- Use cooperative games often. "Islands" is an example of one. Lay down about ten rug squares or pieces of cardboard. Explain to the children that the object of the game is for everyone to help each other get on the islands (rug squares) quickly and be safe. When the music plays, invite the children to "swim" (walk) all around the islands, but when it stops tell them that they must get out of the water and onto an island quickly, or the fish will nibble their toes. Before you start the music again, remove two or three rug squares. Keep repeating the game until only one square is left. This game has no winners and losers, but it offers a challenge and a great deal of fun (Schneider and Torbert 1995).

- Modify existing games and equipment to make them more cooperative. For example, play "Farmer in the Dell" with two farmers and two of each character. Add more characters if needed so that everyone can be in the circle by the end. Here the "Cheeses" stand in the middle at the end and invite everyone else to make a circle around them. Sing "The cheese has lots of friends," instead of "The cheese stands alone," and have the "Cheeses" move around the circle shaking everyone's hands.

- Promote cooperation when situations arise in the classroom. Ask a child to help another child who has broken a class rule: "Everett, please tell Amelia the rule about running in class and give her ideas about how to remember it."

- Set up a dramatic play situation involving exciting adventures where all children work together against a shared problem. Fire fighting, rescue squad activities, catching a big fish, and working in a hospital are some examples. To avoid chaotic or silly play, provide many safe materials and guide the action at first, if necessary.

Action: Use Your Voice Effectively

All teachers with good control of their classrooms have mastered the art of voice control. If you speak in a moderate voice most of the time, the very few times that you do raise your voice slightly or lower it, you will immediately have a big impact on the children.

- Bring the noise level down in a room by starting out with a loud voice and by gradually bringing your voice down in volume as you speak.

- Vary your voice greatly. Get louder and faster when children start losing attention; use a deep, slow voice when making an important point; and talk softly to set a quiet, peaceful tone. Remember that voice variety keeps children from being bored and tuning you out, which can lead to misbehaviors.

- Use a tone and words that convey respect for children. You can check this by asking yourself if this is how you would talk to an adult friend. Expressions like "Use an indoor voice" or "You need to clean up now" are contrived and patronizing, while "Please speak quietly" and "Please pick up the toy" are more respectful. The use of an exaggerated, overly sweet tone of voice condescends to children. If you show respect for children, they will respect you. Mutual respect will eliminate many potential discipline problems.

Reaction: Mistakes Are Okay

- Treat mistakes and errors children make as a natural part of their learning. If a child drops a container of milk, calmly say, "It's all right. You can get the sponge and wipe it up. I'll help you if you need help." Later, ask him, "What can you do the next time to avoid a spill?" Offer a few suggestions if he has no ideas.

- Tell children about mistakes you make (such as scheduling a field trip to the zoo on the day it is closed), so they will know that adults still learn from their mistakes. Tell them what you did to correct the mistake or to try to make sure it will not happen again.

- Strive for the ideal of a supportive classroom in which all the children will thrive. Remove barriers that prevent children from being successful. A child who has a challenging time sitting still during an art project can stand and work on it or lay on a soft pillow and work on it, as long as safety precautions are taken. Perhaps he can work on a different activity. Encourage children to think of these solutions themselves. Be flexible, avoid arbitrary rules, and focus on helping, not fixing, children.

- When you create a classroom atmosphere where failing is difficult, even very discouraged children can feel good about themselves. Once children feel competent, challenge and encourage them to take risks. When children feel both challenged and secure, they will be motivated, engaged, and display few behavior problems.

Reaction: Validate Feelings

- When a child acts inappropriately—defiant or aggressive, for example—first respond by letting the child know that his feelings are acceptable. Say something such as: "I can see that you are angry and frustrated. It's okay to be angry here." Then move on to talking about the behavior itself: "I can't let you hurt yourself or others. This is a safe classroom. Let's figure out what you can do with your anger instead." This lets the child know that you are on his side and that you care about him and his needs. It will make it much more likely that he will cooperate with you in changing the behaviors.

Reaction: Help Children Calm Themselves

- In many situations, children are too upset to be reasoned with and to be helped to change behaviors. First they need to be calmer. Different children need different strategies to do this. Help each child figure out which calming strategy will work best and have a variety of strategies available. These include looking at a book, drawing a picture, listening to music or a story, being held, being stroked, hugging a pillow or toy animal, crying for a while, and more. Once you and the child know the most effective calming strategy, use it right away each time there is a need.

Reaction: Teach the Correct Behavior

- If a child grabs a toy, hits another child, crashes his trike into another's, or does some similar problematic behavior, assume that the child does not know the correct behavior. Continue to tell and show the child the appropriate behavior, even if you have done this several times. Young children need repetition to learn, and they do not carry over information from one situation to another very easily. A child may know not to crash his trike into another trike but may not realize that crashing his trike into the fence is not okay. At the same time that you remind him of the rules (keep yourself and others safe) and use child choice (if it happens again you will have to choose another activity), continue to teach correct behavior: "Ride the trike only on the track and stop before you hit something. I'll watch you in case you need some help."

● Teach a child words he can use and strategies to get a turn, rather than grabbing a toy, such as trading or setting a timer. Help him to generate ideas for getting what he wants if he has trouble thinking of any on his own. Make yourself available if additional help is needed. Give only as much assistance as is necessary so that the children work out solutions on their own.

Reaction: Redirect Behaviors

● Redirecting behaviors means helping a child follow her impulse or need, but in an acceptable way. For example, if a child is angry with another child she may not hit her, but she can express her anger in words or work with clay to release her feelings. A child who starts throwing blocks must be stopped, but she can be given a soft ball to throw instead. The key to successful redirection is to stay calm and find an activity that is very similar to the one the child is doing, but safe or socially acceptable. If you express anger or use redirection as punishment, your attempts to change behavior will not work. When done well, redirection lets children know that their feelings are valid and that they can act on their feelings. It teaches them that they can make choices as to how to act on their feelings in acceptable ways.

Reaction: Logical Consequences

Logical consequences are responses to problematic behaviors in which the natural result of doing the behavior is allowed to occur. If a child misuses a piece of equipment, the logical consequence is that she will help fix it, if possible, and then not get to use that piece of equipment for a period of time. The logical consequence of tripping another child is to help the hurt child get up and to get a bandage for her.

● The key to making logical consequences successful is to have the consequence be immediate (not going

outside tomorrow, because of misbehaving on the playground today, will not work for young children) and to make the consequence relate directly to the misbehavior. Always tell the child she is free to return to any activity when she feels ready to act correctly.

● Remember: logical consequences must never be punishment or retribution. Logical consequences should be used only as a last resort when repeated attempts at teaching correct behaviors or redirection are not working well. Before using any logical consequences, tell the child what the consequences will be the next time she misbehaves in the same way. She must know these ahead of time so that she has an opportunity to work on avoiding them. Continue to teach correct behavior and use redirection while also using logical consequences.

Reaction: Stay Calm Yourself

● Always react calmly to negative behaviors. Many young children with challenging behaviors are used to getting a big response from adults as a result of their behaviors. They thrive on the attention, excitement, anger, and chaos they can create. If they see that you will react the same way, you will experience difficulty getting them to change their behaviors. If they see you are not reacting strongly, they might step up the behaviors at first (to make sure you have seen them), but eventually they will give them up. This will happen faster when you also use all the strategies discussed above and in the chapters ahead.

Resources

Beatty, J. J. 1998. *Prosocial guidance in the preschool classroom.* New York: Prentice Hall.

Cherry, C. 2002. *Please don't sit on the kids: Alternatives to punitive discipline.* Belmont, Calif.: Fearon/Janus/Quercus.

Crary, E. 1984. *Kids can cooperate: A practical guide to teaching problem solving.* Seattle: Parenting Press.

Dreikurs, R., and V. Stolz. 1991. *Children: The challenge.* New York: Plume.

Eisenberg, N. 1995. Prosocial development: A multifaceted model. In *Moral development,* edited by W. Kurtines and J. Gewirtz. Boston: Allyn and Bacon.

Ginott, H. G. 1995. *Teacher and child: A book for parents and teachers.* New York: Collier Books.

Goffin, S. 1987. Cooperative behaviors: They need our support. *Young Children* 42 (2): 75–81.

Hitz, R., and A. Driscoll. 1988. Praise or encouragement? New insights into praise: Implications for early childhood teachers. *Young Children* 43 (5): 6–13.

Honig, A. S., and D. S. Wittmer. 1996. Helping children become more prosocial: Ideas for classrooms, families, schools, and communities. Part 2. *Young Children* 51 (2): 62–70.

Keenan, M. 1996. They pushed my buttons: Being put up against myself. *Young Children* 51 (6): 74–75.

Marshall, H. H. 1995. Beyond "I like the way . . ." *Young Children* 50 (2): 26–28.

McClellen, D. E., and L. G. Katz. *Fostering children's social competence: The teacher's role*. Research into practice, vol 8. Washington, D.C.: NAEYC

Mize, J. 1995. Coaching preschool children in social skills: A cognitive-social learning curriculum. In *Teaching social skills to children and youth: Innovative approaches*. 3d ed. Edited by G. Carteledge and J. F. Milbum. Boston: Allyn and Bacon.

National Association for the Education of Young Children (NAEYC). 1988. Ideas that work with young children. Avoiding "me against you" discipline. *Young Children* 44 (1): 24–29.

Oken-Wright, P. 1992. From tug of war to "let's make a deal": The teacher's role. *Young Children* 48 (1): 15–20.

Ratcliff, N. 2001. Use the environment to prevent problems and support learning. *Young Children* 56 (5): 84–88.

Rogers, D. L., and D. D. Ross. 1986. Encouraging positive social interaction among young children. *Young Children* 41 (3): 12–17.

Schneider, L. B., and M. Torbert. 1995. *Follow me too: A handbook of movement activities for children*. New York: Pearson.

Slaby, R. G., W. C. Roedell, D. Arezzo, and K. Hendrix. 1995. *Early violence prevention: Tools for teachers of young children*. Washington, D.C.: NAEYC.

Staub, E. 1995. The roots of prosocial and antisocial behavior in persons and groups: Environmental influence, personality, culture, and socialization. In *Moral development*, edited by W. Kurtines and J. Gewirtz. Boston: Allyn and Bacon.

Trawick-Smith, J. 1988. Let's say you're the baby, OK: Play leadership and following behavior of young children. *Young Children* 43 (5): 51–59.

Tudge, J., and D. Caruso. 1988. Cooperative problem solving in the classroom: Enhancing young children's cognitive development. *Young Children* 44 (1): 46–52.

Whitehouse, E., and W. Pudney. 1996. *A volcano in my tummy: Helping children to handle anger: A resource book for parents, caregivers, and teachers*. Gabriola Island, British Columbia: New Society Publishers.

Whitin, P. 2001. Kindness in a jar. *Young Children* 56 (5): 18–22.

Wittmer, D. S., and A. S. Honig. 1994. Encouraging positive social development in young children. *Young Children* 49 (5): 4–12.

Social Skills Curricula

First Step to Success. Preschool Edition. Sopris West. www.sopriswest.com

Second Step (Preschool/Kindergarten Curriculum). Committee for Children. Committee for Children. www.cfchildren.org

Stop and Think Social Skills Program. Sopris West. www.sopriswest.com

Web Sites

Aggression and Cooperation: Helping Young Children Develop Constructive Strategies by Jan Jewett. ERIC Digest. 1992. www.ericeece.org. Click on Publications, then Digests, then Title, then scroll down to the article.

Be More Specific Than You're Terrific by Jane Pratte. Earlychildhood.com. www.earlychildhood.com/Articles/index.cfm. Click on Child Development, then scroll down to the article.

Encouraging Social Skills in Young Children: Tips Teachers Can Share with Parents by Jacquelyn Mize, Ph.D., and Ellen Abell, Ph.D. www.humsci.auburn.edu/parent

Having Friends, Making Friends, and Keeping Friends: Relationships as Educational Contexts by Willard W. Hartup. ERIC Digest. 1992. www.ericeece.org. Click on Publications, then Digests, then Title, then scroll down to the article.

Do You Know How I Feel? Empathy and the Young Child by Sandra Crosser, Ph.D. Earlychildhood.com. www.earlychildhood.com/Articles/index.cfm. Click on Child Development, then scroll down to the article.

Emotional/Social Development. Access to many articles on various related topics. National Network for Child Care. www.nncc.org. Click on Articles and Resources, then Child Development, then Emotional/Social.

The Magical I-Message by Eleanor Reynolds. Earlychildhood.com. www.earlychildhood.com/Articles/index.cfm. Click on Child Development, then scroll down to the article.

Preventing Violence through Anger Management by Mary Drecktrah, Ph.D., and Amy Wallenfang. Earlychildhood.com. www.earlychildhood.com/Articles/index.cfm. Click on Child Development, then scroll down to the article.

Threat or Consequence: What's the Difference? by Eleanor Reynolds. Earlychildhood.com. www.earlychildhood.com/Articles/index.cfm. Click on Child Development, then scroll down to the article.

Understanding and Facilitating Preschool Children's Peer Acceptance by Kristen M. Kemple. ERIC Digest. 1992. www.ericeece.org. Click on Publications, Digests, then Title, then scroll down to the article.

Young Children's Social Development: A Checklist by Diane McClellan and Lilian G. Katz. ERIC Digest. 1993. www.ericeece.org. Click on Publications, then Digests, then Title, then scroll down to the article.

3. Children with Severe Behavior Problems

Some children have behavior problems so severe that they endanger the safety of the other children, themselves, or you. Severe behavior problems usually reflect serious emotional problems.

The child with severe emotional problems

- Destroys property for no apparent reason
- Acts very withdrawn and unresponsive
- Has extreme fears and phobias
- Has extreme and frequent mood swings
- Obsesses about a particular detail or item
- Plays with feces
- Eats items that are clearly not food
- Kills or tortures animals
- Displays unusual emotions such as laughing when hurt
- Has unusual and intense habits such as hair pulling, rocking, head banging, or excessive masturbation/self-stimulation
- Runs away regularly
- Makes suicidal statements
- Places herself in physical danger
- Hurts herself
- Takes pleasure in hurting or being cruel to others
- Singles out another child to victimize
- Often manipulates others in very sophisticated ways, sexually or otherwise

---

Although many children will exhibit one or more of these behaviors on occasion, when they occur regularly or often and intensely, they are cause for great concern. There may be an organic reason for these behaviors, such as birth trauma or autism, or the child may have been traumatized by abuse, neglect, or a violent event.

Logic, reason, redirection, consequences, and all your tried-and-true guidance techniques that work with most children, are not effective with these children. Sometimes the behaviors seem very deliberate, clearly planned to get others to dislike them and to get themselves in trouble.

Unless you or an assistant is specially trained to help a child with severe behavior problems and have professional support services, you may be doing a disservice to the child by keeping him in your class. You also may be spending so much time helping this one child, that the needs of the other children in your class will not be met. If the child is in a treatment program and the behaviors are improving, integrating him into your class may be appropriate, but perhaps not on a full-time basis. Usually the most appropriate placement for a child with severe emotional problems is in a therapeutic preschool or a treatment center, and getting individual and family therapy. A regular group setting is only a good place for the child if it is part of his individualized educational plan, there is intensive support (such as a full-time, skilled aide), you have on-site and ongoing support from your supervisor and the child's parents, and you have training by and access to mental health specialists. When these supports are in place, integrating a child with serious emotional or behavioral problems can be very successful and rewarding for you, the child, and the other children in the class. It is, after all, the best place for the child to learn to get along with her typically developing peers.

Many children who exhibit these extreme behaviors are getting special education services and have a diagnosis, such as behavior disorder, conduct disorder, oppositional defiant disorder, attention deficit/hyperactivity disorder (ADHD), post-traumatic stress disorder, reactive attachment disorder, emotionally disturbed, severely emotionally disturbed (SED), depression, sensory-integration dysfunction, bipolar disorder, and obsessive-compulsive disorder, among others. However, there are many, many children with these extreme behaviors who are not getting the special services they need. The reasons are numerous, from the reluctance to put such a stigmatizing label on a young child to the lack of money for services or the lack of availability. This is especially true in smaller, more rural communities. The major barrier to services, however, is the failure to view serious behavior or emotional disabilities as requiring the kind of support that is provided to children with serious cognitive disabilities (mental retardation, for example) or physical disabilities (spina bifida or juvenile arthritis, for example).

- Do everything you can to convince the parents that their child needs to be referred for evaluation and placement. Keep detailed and objective notes of the behaviors you observe in the classroom to help other professionals determine the best placement for the child. (See "Observing" in "Suspected Disabilities" on p. 67.) In most places, your local school district serves as the place to make a referral. For other sources of help, check with your local department of special education, mental health organization, health advocacy organization, or the county, city, or state agency that deals with services to families and children.

● If the parents refuse or deny there is a problem, keep written, dated records of your conversations. There have been cases where parents have successfully sued preschool programs for failing to make them aware of their child's problem while she was attending. For the benefit of the child, you are obligated to tell parents what you have observed about the child and to seek a referral. If you can get no evaluation, support, special education services, and assistance from a mental health professional, have your supervisor help the family to find a better placement for their child.

Resources

Bakely, S. 2001. Through the lens of sensory integration: A different way of analyzing challenging behaviors. *Young Children* 56 (6): 70–76.

Greene, R. 2001. *The explosive child: A new approach for understanding and parenting easily frustrated, chronically inflexible children.* New York: HarperCollins.

Hughes, D. A. 1999. *Building the bonds of attachment: Awakening love in deeply troubled children.* Northvale, N.J.: Jason Aronson Publishing.

Karr-Morse, R., and M. S. Wiley. 1998. *Ghosts from the nursery.* New York: Atlantic Monthly Press.

Kranowitz, C. S. 1998. *The out-of-sync child: Recognizing and coping with sensory integration dysfunction.* New York: Perigee.

Magid, K., and C. A. McKelvey. 1990. *High risk: Children without a conscience.* New York: Bantam Doubleday Dell.

Paley, V. G. 1991. *The boy who would be a helicopter.* Cambridge: Harvard University Press.

Riley, D. A. 2002. *The defiant child: A parent's guide to oppositional defiant disorder.* Cutton, Calif.: Taylor Publishing.

Taylor, J. F. 2001. *From defiance to cooperation: Real solutions to transforming the angry, defiant, and discouraged child.* New York: Prima Publishing.

Web Sites

Bipolar Disorder (Manic-Depressive Illness). American Academy of Child and Adolescent Psychiatry. Facts for Families #38. www.aacap.org. Link through Facts for Families, and scroll down to the article.

Center for Mental Health in Schools. UCLA. Many resources to access. smhp.psych.ucla.edu

Conduct Disorder. American Academy of Child and Adolescent Psychiatry. Facts for Families #33. www.aacap.org. Link through Facts for Families, and scroll down to the article.

Council for Children with Behavior Disorders. Many resources to access. www.ccbd.net

The Depressed Child. American Academy of Child and Adolescent Psychiatry. Facts for Families #4. www.aacap.org. Link through Facts for Families, and scroll down to the article.

Educating Students with Emotional/Behavioral Disorders; Emotional Disturbance; Interventions for Chronic Behavior Problems; and other resources. National Information Center for Children and Youth with Disabilities. www.nichcy.org. Link through Our Publications tab on side bar, enter "emotional" in the search box.

Emotionally Disturbed. Parent Pals.com Special Education Resources. www.parentpals.com. Click on Emotionally Disturbed under Resources.

Obsessive-Compulsive Disorder in Children and Adolescents. American Academy of Child and Adolescent Psychiatry. Facts for Families #60. www.aacap.org. Link through Facts for Families, and scroll down to the article.

Oppositional Defiant Disorder. American Academy of Child and Adolescent Psychiatry. Facts for Families #72. www.aacap.org. Link through Facts for Families, and scroll down to the article.

Posttraumatic Stress Disorder. American Academy of Child and Adolescent Psychiatry. Facts for Families #70. www.aacap.org. Link through Facts for Families, and scroll down to the article.

4. Active and Distracted ———

Almost every classroom has at least one child who has difficulty concentrating or sitting still for a short time, compared to other children his age. The causes for this are many and varied.

Most children like this have little control over their problem, although they want very much to control it. At the extreme, such children may have ADD (attention deficit disorder) or ADHD (attention deficit/hyperactivity disorder). A combination of drug, individual, and family therapy can be very helpful. (See the chapter "Suspected Disabilities" on p. 67 and "Children with Severe Behavior Problems" on p. 133).

Medication (Ritalin is most common) is controversial because many people feel it is overused for the convenience of teachers and school systems. It is very effective at reducing active behaviors, however, which is why it may have become overused. If prescribed, use this medicine in conjunction with making changes in the classroom and the home to improve the child's ability to thrive there. The goal should be to help the child come off the medication as soon as possible.

This chapter offers numerous ideas for helping active and distracted children feel successful and gain some self-control and self-respect.

Preventing Problems

● To avoid a classroom that is overstimulating for the children, reduce the busy-ness in your room, while keeping it aesthetically pleasing. Use warm, soft colors; cover or store teacher supplies and materials; arrange things neatly. Reduce the number of pictures (and choose soothing ones like nature photos and reproductions of Impressionist art), mobiles, and signs hanging from ceilings and walls.

● Label all shelves and containers. See that everything has its proper place in the classroom. This will help the active or distracted child as he often has trouble organizing himself and his surroundings.

● Inform all children of what to expect ahead of time. Tell them, "We will be going outside for thirty minutes. When the bell rings, we will come inside for snack. Now put your coat on and walk to the door." Note that this is of particular help to the active child.

● Set up and follow daily routines and rituals. Make your daily schedule essentially the same every day, with active times and sitting times alternating. A "good morning song" to start each day is an example of a ritual. This provides a sense of security to a child whose world feels unsteady.

Dealing with Existing Problems

● Use a small, freestanding cardboard divider to keep visual distractions from interfering with an active child's attention while he works at a table activity. Use a large divider during nap or rest times.

● Physical contact helps some active children feel more in control of themselves. To help a child attend better during circle time have him sit on an adult's lap, touch or rub his back gently, or hold his hand.

● Appreciate the positive aspects of having an active or easily distracted child in your class. Look at the child as being very attracted to the wonderful things you have provided. Use the active child as your barometer for determining if your activity has gone on too long or is not very interesting to the children. A high activity level can be a great asset, especially for adults, who can accomplish a great deal in a shorter time than most people.

● Provide a curriculum and activities that do not require a great deal of sitting or paper and pencil tasks. Have at least forty-five minutes of free choice and thirty minutes of outside or gym play for every three-and-a-half hours of class time.

● Keep group times short and meet in small groups. Many active children have a hard time concentrating in groups, but do much better when receiving individual instruction.

● Give instructions clearly and specifically for any task you are requiring children to do. Do not give more than two or three directions at a time. Reinforce the directions visually by demonstrating them and by drawing a picture to which the children can refer frequently while carrying out the activity.

● Some children benefit from individual, specific instructions. Tell the child specifically how to attend and remind him often: "Look at the line on the paper, put your scissors on top of the line, and then cut."

● For the overly energetic child, provide many outlets that will not cause problems. Give him beanbags to throw and a gym mat to roll around on. Stroking a stuffed animal or squeezing a foam ball while sitting in a group can help him release some extra energy, without disrupting the activity.

● Change your expectations. Allow the child to spend less time at activities and to move around during some activities. He can stand or play with a quiet activity at a table nearby during circle time.

● Whenever possible, substitute items that are easier to use or less likely to get the child in trouble. If he can't keep his chair still while seated at the table, let him sit on a beanbag chair that is not easily moved around.

● Use redirection to give the child a nondestructive or even positive outlet for his energy. A child who can't sit still during a flannelboard story can place the flannel figures on the board and move them around.

● As often as you can, catch the child when he is calm and let him know when his overactive behavior is improving: "You've been listening for a long time. You must feel very proud of yourself."

● Provide more direction, and verbal and physical assistance, through tasks and routines than you do for other children.

● Although many in the medical community claim there is no proof of a link between food and behavior, many teachers and parents have seen clear evidence that certain foods, food additives, chemical substances, or even some synthetic fabrics affect behavior. An allergist or pediatrician can test for these reactions. Working on changes in the diet often makes for a positive first step for teachers and parents to help a child. There is no blame on anyone and positive, direct action is being taken. Some diets can be very challenging to maintain, however, and will require great effort and vigilance. A dietary approach to dealing with active behavior should be used along with the other approaches discussed. If a child is on a modified diet and his behavior does not change, help the parents seek family counseling and work on other solutions.

Resources

Barkely, R. 2000. *Taking charge of ADHD*. Rev. ed. New York: Guilford Press.

Budd, L. 2002. *Living with the active, alert child: Groundbreaking strategies for parents*. Seattle: Parenting Press.

Flick, G. L. 1997. *ADD/ADHD behavior-change resource kit: Ready-to-use strategies and activities for helping children with attention deficit disorder*. San Francisco: Jossey-Bass.

Ingersoll, B. D. 1995. *Distant drums, different drummers: A guide for young people with ADHD*. Melbourne, Fla.: Cape Publications.

Rich, B. A. 1993. Listening to Harry (and solving a problem in my kindergarten classroom). *Young Children* 48 (6): 52.

Ricker, A. 2001. *Bad attitude: Reverse your child's rudeness in one week—with food*. Emmaus, Pa.: Rodale Press.

Taylor, J. F. 1999. *Helping your hyperactive/ADD child*. New York: Prima Publishing.

Zimmerman, M. 1999. *The ADD nutrition solution: A drug-free thirty-day plan*. New York: Owl Books.

Children's Books

Gehret, J. 1996. *Eagle eyes: A child's guide to paying attention*. New York: Verbal Images Press.

Web Sites

Attention Deficit Hyperactivity Disorder. Child Care Source. www.childcaresource.org. Click on Ages and Stages and scroll down to article.

Children Who Can't Pay Attention/ADHD. American Academy of Child and Adolescent Psychiatry. Facts for Families #6. www.aacap.org. Link through Facts for Families, and scroll down to the article.

Guidance Techniques for Distractible Children. Parenting Press's Tip and Tool of the Week. June 9, 2001. www.parentingpress.com. Click on Tip Archive, then Guidance and Discipline, then scroll down to article title.

The Hummingbird Syndrome: Children Who Flit About during Play Time by Sandra Crosser. Earlychildood.com. www.earlychildhood.com/Articles/index.cfm. Click on Child Development, then scroll down and click on the article title.

Is It Temperament or Attention Deficit? Parenting Press's Tip and Tool of the Week. September 30, 2000. www.parentingpress.com. Click on Tip Archive, then Temperament, then scroll down to article title.

5. Biting

Children who bite usually do so because they are frustrated or angry. Typically, they want a toy or a privilege that another child has. They bite less out of aggression toward the other child than as a way to get what they want. They often act quickly and impulsively, too young or immature to think through other choices. The age when biting is most frequent is between thirteen and twenty-four months. Some children bite because their language skills are not good enough to say what they want. Teething can also be a cause of biting. Frustrations due to overcrowding and too many children in one classroom can lead to biting as well. Your essential task is to help the child find another way to express frustration or anger and to get her needs met.

Preventing Problems

● Have at least two of each toy for toddlers. This prevents disputes over particular toys, which causes frustration. Make sure you have an ample supply of toys that are interesting to toddlers.

● Create a setting with few frustrations by doing the following: Give children easy access to many materials, set clear limits but few absolute requirements, offer a great deal of time for free choice, set regular routines, and provide a flexible schedule and activities.

● Attend to the teething needs of toddlers through use of individual teething rings and other safe, soothing things to bite on.

● Provide many ways for children to express their feelings and frustrations by providing toys to pound, nails to hammer, clay or playdough to mold, sand and water play to experiment with, and beanbags to throw. Provide ample time and space for gross-motor play outdoors and indoors.

● Help children calm themselves down when they are upset. Children often know what activities will calm them down. If not, you can suggest that they listen to music, look at a book, sing, talk, draw, or ask to be held.

● Help children express their feelings with words or vocalizations for very young children or children with language disabilities. Interpret their words to other children for them, if necessary: "Rosa, Sara is saying 'Me. Me.' She is telling you she would like a turn."

● Provide a great deal of individual attention and affection. Some children bite out of the frustration of feeling "invisible."

Dealing with Existing Problems

● Toddlers are often too young to connect a negative consequence (time-out, having a toy removed, and so on) with the biting that preceded it, which is why any type of punishment rarely works. Instead, comfort the child who has been bitten and say in a sharp voice to the biter, "That hurts." Use a stern face so she will know that you disapprove. Be brief so as not to give the child who has bitten too much attention and then enlist the biter in comforting the bitten child.

● Watch the child who bites carefully to determine what, if anything, causes this behavior. Check for times of day, interactions with certain other children, or particular situations. If at all possible, catch the child just before she is going to bite. Stop her and say in a sharp voice, "That would hurt." If the biting was not provoked or connected to a frustrating situation, give her a teething ring to bite on. Move her quickly away from other children and give her an engaging toy.

● If the biting was about to occur because of a frustrating situation, such as a toy being grabbed from her, help the child vocalize her needs: "Use your voice" or "Tell him want you want." Help her to say the words or sounds if necessary. Then help resolve the dispute by doing one of the following things: give the child who grabbed the toy away another toy, set a timer for turns, present a toy they can use together, or give the two children two different toys. Remember that even screaming when frustrated is far preferable to biting. Encourage the child whenever she vocalizes and doesn't bite: "Using words is a great way to get what you want." Work on the screaming to gradually reduce the volume and ultimately to have her use actual words.

- If the child seems to bite only one particular child, keep them separated. Consider moving the child to another class. When a child who bites is with children who are slightly older, the biting often stops because they won't let her do it.

- Make changes in your routines or schedule. If biting happens most often close to lunchtime, make sure the child has a midmorning snack to ward off hunger or have lunch a little earlier.

- In extreme cases, you may have to help the child's parents find another program, perhaps temporarily. Some children do not thrive in a large group setting and may stop biting when attending a program with fewer children or a more relaxed schedule.

- The solution to biting, unfortunately, usually involves very careful, persistent, and tireless observation of the child who bites, something that is challenging for teachers to do with other children and activities to attend to. You must be able to step in as soon as you see any sign of frustration (or other sign that biting might occur), before the biting happens. Then you can redirect the child to a nonviolent outlet such as a pounding bench, or teach her to use words or take a turn, depending on her age or ability. The more skilled staff people in a classroom, the easier the task will be. Capable volunteers can be a big help in such cases.

Resources

Kinnell, G. 2002. *No biting: Policy and practice for toddler programs.* St. Paul: Redleaf Press.

National Association for the Education of Young Children (NAEYC). 1997. Using NAEYC's Code of Ethics. Who is the biter? *Young Children* 52 (2): 54–55.

Solomons, H. C., and R. Elardo. 1989. Bite injuries at a day care center. *Early Childhood Research Quarterly* 4 (1): 89–96.

Children's Books

Katz, K. 2002. *No biting!* New York: Grosset & Dunlap

Minarit, E. H. 1978. *No fighting, no biting.* New York: HarperCollins.

Web Sites

Biters: Why They Do It and What to Do about It (Also in Spanish). KinderStart search engine. www.kinderstart.com. Link on Child Development and then Behavior: Biting.

Biting. Child Care Source. www.childcaresource.org. Click on Ages and Stages and scroll down to article.

Biting Hurts! by Lesia Oesterreich. National Network for Child Care. www.nncc.org. Click on Articles and Resources, then Guidance and Discipline, then to article title under Techniques and Strategies.

Biting in the Toddler Years by Linda Passmark. The Natural Child Project. www.naturalchild.com. Click on Search and then enter "biting" in the search box.

Fighting and Biting. American Academy of Child and Adolescent Psychiatry. Facts for Families #81. www.aacap.org. Link through Facts for Families and then scroll down to article title.

Safety First—Biting in the Childcare Setting www.healthychild.net. Enter "biting" in search box.

When Children Bite by Christine M. Todd. National Network for Child Care. www.nncc.org. Click on Articles and Resources, then Guidance and Discipline, then to article title under Techniques and Strategies.

6. Clingy, Dependent, and Won't Participate

Clingy and dependent behaviors are normal for children who are new to a program or who are going through a stressful change. However, some children are clingy and dependent because they have learned that it gets them what they want and lets them avoid what they do not want! In some cases, what they do not want is to do something new or take even a small risk, as this causes anxiety. This can be a way to cover up a lack of skill or weakness. For example, difficulty with small-motor tasks or, more likely, lack of social skills or fear of being rejected by other children. In any case, indulging the behaviors is not helpful to the child. The ideas in this section will help you to be supportive without being indulgent, and to balance the needs of the clingy and dependent child with the needs of the rest of your group.

Preventing Problems

- Provide a wide variety of fun, active, hands-on activities, which are open-ended and have no right or wrong way to do them. Give the child plenty of time to make choices from those activities.

- Move around the classroom during free choice time. Spend some time with each of the children, but spend more time with those who have greater needs for attention and affection.

- Reduce the children's insecurities by letting them make choices and have control by setting a predictable schedule and by helping them keep track of this schedule.

- Meet children's individual needs as much as possible because this will reduce insecurities. (See "Individualizing," on pp. 147–150, for further information.)

- Promote responsible (age appropriate) behavior by teaching the children self-help skills and by giving them many jobs, access to sponges and materials to clean up after themselves, and easy ways to put away materials when done using them.

- Teach all children the skills needed for making and keeping friends. Do not allow children to exclude other children from playing with them. Observe children's play carefully so that you can assist children to effectively play with others.

- Try to find out why the child is clingy or dependent. Are there family changes, such as a new baby, a recent move, a parent's illness, or a recent death? Is there a problem or weakness he is avoiding dealing with?

Dealing with Existing Problems

- If the child is facing temporary stressful changes in his life, give him extra attention and affection for a while. When you give attention before it is asked for, you reduce the need for inappropriate behavior to get attention. Ask him to request this attention in acceptable ways, such as by using words or signaling you. Let the child know that you are giving him extra support temporarily.

- Put a strict limit on the amount of time the child can spend by your side. Set a timer and say, "In two minutes I will give you a hug and help you find a place to play."

- Create a simple system for taking turns for children who would like to sit next to you at a meal or during a circle time. Post a list of the children's names (have them write their own if they are able) and have them cross off their names when they have had a turn. This is a concrete way for those children to know that they will get to be near you, to visibly see when that will be, and to know that the system is equitable.

- Don't reinforce the child's dependency by hugging or holding him too much. Give him very little attention when he is clinging, and physically guide him to an area in which he can play. Don't push or drag him, as this will only increase his insecurity. Give him specific feedback when he is playing away from you.

- If the child interrupts your interactions with others often, tell him that he can wait or find something to do and you will come to him when you are finished. If he chooses to wait, place your hand gently on his arm while you are talking (so that he will know you have not forgotten him) and tell him that when you remove your hand and turn around you will be ready to talk to him, but not before. If you do this consistently, he will learn not to interrupt, as he will feel secure that he will get your attention.

- Engage him in a game or a more social, positive interaction with you. Tell the clingy child, "Sit (or stand) across from me. That way I can see your sweet face and hear you better." Guide him across from you. Play with table toys or do a board game together. Move away when other children join or when he is happily playing on his own.

- Try to connect the child with one other child who would make a good playmate. Find a common interest between them and help them start playing together. Remove yourself when you see they are playing on their own.

- Guide him and another child to an activity that is specifically designed for two, such as a board game.

- Meet with the child's parents to discuss together possible causes of the problem and ways to deal with it. Suggest that they arrange to have their child spend time outside of class with a child from the class. This usually establishes friendships and will give the child an incentive to move away from you and play with another child.

Resources

Also see resources at the end of the chapter, "Shy and Withdrawn" on p. 152.

Web Sites

Keys to Living with the Quiet, Easily Discouraged Child. Parenting Press's Tip and Tool of the Week. December 13, 1997. www.parentingpress.com. Click on Tip Archive, then on Dealing with Temperament, then scroll down to article title.

Living with the Sensitive, Cautious Child. Parenting Press's Tip and Tool of the Week. September 5, 1998. www.parentingpress.com. Click on Tip Archive, then on Dealing with Temperament, then scroll down to article title.

Sara Won't Try by Sandra Crosser. Earlychildhood.com. www.earlychildhood.com/Articles/index.cfm. Click on Child Development, then scroll down to article title.

7. Cursing, Name-Calling, and Hurtful Language

This is a challenging problem for many teachers because they do not want to ignore foul language, yet they know paying attention to it may make it worse. Children use swear words because it gets a big response and this makes them feel powerful. For girls especially, name-calling and hurtful language can be a very powerful form of aggression (boys tend to use physical aggression). For this reason, it is important to deal with the behaviors. The key to eliminating the behavior is to take away the power of the words, to make children feel powerful in acceptable ways, and to teach better responses to anger or frustration.

Some parents are concerned that their children will learn foul language from other children. The reality is that most of your children heard these words before they came to your class but they may now be of an age when they are interested in trying them out. You can reassure parents that you are taking a multifaceted approach to preventing and reducing the problem, as described in this chapter.

Preventing Problems

● Establish a classroom rule that only words that do not hurt other people can be used. Periodically remind children of this rule.

● Talk about the words that go with negative feelings, such as *frustrated, embarrassed, hurt, put down, angry, humiliated,* and so on. These are socially acceptable expressions and alternatives to cursing. Encourage children to talk about what makes them feel this way. Give them practice in saying the words.

● Let them know that negative feelings are okay and that everyone has them.

● When children express their feelings by using appropriate phrases such as "I'm angry because she pushed me" or "You really make me mad," praise them energetically. Say, "It's great that you used words that let us know how you feel. Now we can help you solve the problem."

Dealing with Existing Problems

Usually, a child uses swear words for one of the following reasons:

▶ To get attention by causing adults to focus energy and time on correcting or admonishing them, or to get attention from other children by making them laugh, look at her, or talk to her.

▶ To empower herself by causing adults or other children to get upset, agitated, concerned, or excited.

▶ To empower herself by putting down others. This is especially true of racial slurs.

▶ Unintentionally: the words are an automatic response when she gets angry or frustrated or about someone who is different than her. She hears her parents and/or siblings use these words at home, has learned to do this too, and has no reason to do otherwise.

▶ To act and sound like an adult.

You can usually tell which of these reasons causes cursing by examining how she does it. Is she looking or waiting for a response from you or other children? Does she increase the volume of her voice? Is it targeted directly at another child? Or does she just say the words in a matter-of-fact way? Base your approach to dealing with the problem on the reason.

● If the goal of the swear words is attention seeking or self-empowerment, ignore the language as much as possible. If other children respond by "telling you" about what was said, say to them calmly, "I heard the words. I am ignoring them, and you can ignore them too." Show no agitation or anger, as this is just what the child wants. If you have to, gently remove the child from the other children to talk to him. Preferably, wait a few minutes and then talk to him about the "respectful language" rule. Tell him how much you appreciate him using good words because they tell you how he is feeling and they don't make other people angry. Help him find other words he can say instead and find strategies to solve or prevent his frustration or anger.

- If she is saying these words to get other children to laugh and get excited, she can make up silly rhymes, tell simple jokes, or lead an active movement game instead.

- If saying these words involves hurting others, help the child practice expressing her feelings and concerns using different, acceptable words and teach her strategies for solving conflicts respectfully. Talk with the other child involved in the altercation about his options. This child can practice saying, "If you call me names, I won't play with you," and then walk away.

- If using these words is unintentional (an automatic response or an imitation of adults), intervene quickly but calmly. Tell the child to use different words because those words can hurt and upset others. Ask her, "What other words can you use?" Recommend some if she can't think of any. Have her practice saying the more appropriate words out loud. As you will be helping her break an established habit, you may need to intervene many times before she will use better language.

Complaints of Parents about Swear Words

If a parent complains that her child learned bad language from other children in your class, you can involve the parent in solving the problem.

- Don't contradict the parent or act defensively because, after all, the allegation may be true.

- Tell the parent that you are concerned about cursing and hurtful language in the classroom and explain your approach and strategies for dealing with this behavior.

- Ask for the parent's help and suggestions for dealing with the problem.

- Ask the parent what you can do to help her child.

- Brainstorm ways that you can help each other and ways to use similar methods for dealing with the problem so there is consistency between home and school. (See "Complaining Parents," on pp. 169–171, for more ideas.)

Resources

Froschl, M., and B. Sprung. 1999. On purpose: Addressing teasing and bullying in early education. *Young Children* 54 (2): 70–72.

Children's Books

Crary, E. 1992. *My name is not Dummy.* Seattle: Parenting Press.

Henkes, K. 1996. *Chrysanthemum.* New York: Mulberry Books.

Web Sites

Dealing with Name-Calling. Parenting Tip and Tool of the Week. Parenting Press. January 6, 2001. www.parentingpress.com. Click on Tip Archive, then Problem Solving, then scroll down to article title.

Helping Your Child Respond to Teasing. Parenting Tip and Tool of the Week. Parenting Press. January 6, 2001. www.parentingpress.com. Click on Tip Archive, then People Skills, then scroll down to article title.

Name-Calling: When Do You Step In? by Eleanor Reynolds. EarlyChildhood.com. www.earlychildhood.com/Articles/index.cfm. Link on Discipline, then scroll down to article title.

Those Four-Letter Words by Christine M. Todd. National Network for Child Care. www.nncc.org. Click on Articles and Resources, then Guidance.

What to Do When Children Use "Bathroom Language" by Timothy Jay. Earlychildhood.com. www.earlychildhood.com/Articles/index.cfm. Link on Discipline, then scroll down to article title.

When Young Children Use Profanity: How to Handle Cursing and Name-Calling by Timothy Jay. Earlychildhood.com. www.earlychildhood.com/Articles/index.cfm. Link on Discipline, then scroll down to article title.

8. Excessive Crying or Whining

This behavior is more common in children who are new to the center. (See "New to the Class," on p. 105, and "Starting the Day Off Right," on pp. 9–11, for ideas on helping a new child.) Children who are very sensitive or fragile by temperament will cry and whine more than other children, and you should adjust your expectations for these children. However, you can help them (as well all the children) by teaching them new coping behaviors.

Try to determine the root cause of the behavior as it may be an attention-getting strategy, but there may be a more serious reason, such as chronic pain or a recent stressful event. Whining is so common among children because it is very effective. Adults find it so annoying that they will give in to the child, or at least pay attention to him. In one situation, a three-year-old cried often and regularly at her child care center from her first day to long past the time most children feel safe and comfortable and stop crying. In talking with her mother, she reported that the child talks happily at home about all the activities at the center and sings all the songs and finger plays. This gave the teachers the information they needed. They stopped indulging the behavior, would say firmly, "You're okay. You don't need to cry," and then guide her to an activity. The crying stopped quickly.

Preventing Problems

● Provide individual attention and a great deal of affection to all children.

● In all you do, strive for a healthy balance between security (making children feel loved and safe) and challenge (engaging environment and activities that stretch children's brains and muscles a bit).

● Give little attention to any negative or inappropriate behavior. Give a great deal of energy and attention to acceptable behaviors. Help children learn words and strategies that help them get their needs met in ways that are positive.

● Help children learn to prevent getting themselves into situations that will cause frustration, anger, or humiliation. They may need to choose to play with certain children rather than others; choose certain toys or games rather than others.

● Use many cooperative games and activities. Eliminate competition. Almost all young children have a very difficult time dealing with losing and the stress of competition. More fragile children fare even worse. Teaching the skills of cooperation and negotiation provides children alternatives to interacting with others competitively.

● Deal directly and effectively with all acts of aggression (including manipulation and passive aggression) and hurtful behaviors and language among children. Make sure that children interact with others positively.

Dealing with Existing Problems

● Give minimal attention to the crying or whining of children age two years and older. Tell the child kindly: "Use words I can understand and I'll be glad to help you." Support the child's feelings while redirecting his behavior.

● Give positive attention to the child when he is not crying or whining. Say something like the following: "Thank you for using a regular voice. I can understand you better and you're more fun to be with."

● Cut off a whiny voice as soon as it begins by saying, "Please use your regular voice so I can understand you better."

● Tell the child who is crying excessively that he can cry as much as he needs to where his crying won't disturb everyone else. Help him move to an area that is safe, visible to adults, but away from the other children. Tell him, "When you are ready to talk about what is making you cry, come back because I'm very interested in helping you." This will let him know that crying and feelings are okay but that you won't let this behavior disrupt the classroom, worry other children, or become an "attention-getter."

● Talk with parents to determine possible reasons for the behavior. Brainstorm solutions together. Suggest a physical examination from a doctor to rule out any physical problems.

● Ask your supervisor or a respected coworker to observe you with your children to make sure you are not inadvertently supporting and promoting the behavior. Ignoring this behavior can be hard and any attention you are paying to it may be giving the child just what he wants from the behavior. Ask for suggestions for changing the behavior.

• Observe carefully to determine if the behavior happens mostly at particular times during the day, when the child plays with certain other children, or when he is with specific staff members. For example, the child may cry more near lunchtime because of hunger or in the middle of the afternoon because of tiredness. Be flexible and make any necessary changes to meet his needs.

• Help the child find other ways to deal with his intense feelings. While validating the feelings, help him learn, for example, that he can ask for a snack when he is hungry or to rest when he is tired. Follow through consistently on these requests so he will know that they are more effective than whining or crying.

Resources

Eberlein, T. 1997. *Child Magazine's guide to whining: Tactics for taming demanding behavior.* New York: Pocket Books.

Ricker, A., and C. Crowder. 2000. *Whining: Three steps to stopping it before the tears and tantrums start.* New York: Fireside.

Web Sites

Getting Rid of Whining. Parenting Tips and Tools Archive. Parenting Press. January 9, 1999. www.parentingpress.com. Click on Tip Archive, then Guidance and Discipline, then scroll down to article title.

How to Help Your Child Stop Whining by Dr. Scoresby www.practicalparent.org.uk. Enter "whining" in the search box.

No More Whining. Parenting Tips and Tools Archive. Parenting Press. May 29, 1999. www.parentingpress.com. Click on Tip Archive, then Guidance and Discipline, then scroll down to article title.

Whining and Complaining. From a Field Guide to Raising Kids by Shelly Butler and Deb Kratz. Family Fun. family.go.com. Link on Raising Kids, then Children, then Field Guide to Parenting (under Parenting Tools).

9. Hitting and Aggression —

This is probably the greatest single behavior concern of teachers. Realizing that a certain amount of this behavior is normal and to be expected with young children is important. Many children are not fully able to control their strong feelings and they act impulsively. They are also not able to understand the consequences of their actions. At home, or in certain communities, some children are actually encouraged to hit and act aggressively. They see this behavior modeled by adults in their neighborhoods and homes and in the media. However, young children can learn to act differently in different places. In fact, this is a very helpful skill to teach them. They can learn to accept that hitting may be allowed at home but words must be used at school.

These behaviors are seen more often in boys than girls. The reason for this is probably a combination of male hormones, expectations, child-rearing practices (boys are handled and talked to differently from girls, almost from the moment of birth), modeling, and reinforcing environments. Many girls have aggressive tendencies, too, but girls tend to express their aggression verbally. (For aggression more typically found with girls, see "Mean and Cruel" on pp. 148–149.)

Make sure you are seeing the behaviors that are truly aggressive and not meant to be playful or are unintentionally aggressive. For example, many children will try to engage other children in rough play as a way of being friendly or simply because this is the only way they know how to interact with others. (See "Roughhousing," on p. 150, for ways to deal with this behavior.)

Aggressive acts include anything meant to deliberately hurt another, including cruel words, hitting, kicking, or spitting. The essential task is to teach children how they can get their needs met—get the toy they want, show their anger or frustration, respond to meanness from others—through methods other than hitting or being cruel. Teaching these new skills requires you to be vigilant and persistent. You can't let an act of aggression slip by and you need to repeat your lessons over and over. All children need to know that aggression toward others is not acceptable and will not occur in your classroom. Let them know often that, "This is a safe classroom. I won't let you hurt anyone and I won't let anyone hurt you."

A child who continues to be very aggressive, endangering the safety of other children, even after you have tried the ideas in this chapter, needs special support services or will be better served in another program. Somehow the child's needs are not being met and perhaps a program that specializes in children with emotional disabilities would be the best situation for this child. (See the chapter, "Children with Severe Behavior Problems" on p. 133.)

Preventing Problems

● Read the first two chapters of this section carefully for many ideas that will help you prevent aggressive behaviors from happening.

● Teach all children social skills for getting along with others. Do this on an ongoing basis. Do it both when there are conflicts and during small or large group times. There are numerous curricula that you can use if you find them helpful. They are listed in the resources in the chapter, "Preventing Behavior Problems" on p. 126.

● Read books, role-play, and use puppets to teach about solving problems without physical or emotional violence.

● Create a physical and emotional environment in your class that keeps frustrations to a minimum. Have many choices of engaging activities and give children ample time to engage them. Avoid situations where children have to wait, be still, or be quiet for more than a minute or two.

● Anticipate problems. Separate children from sitting next to each other who tend to "set each other off." Watch for conflicts between children and intervene to teach them how to resolve the conflict before it gets to the point where there is hitting or aggression.

● Give children many outlets for big, loud, physical play in acceptable ways. Children will be less likely to channel the need for such play in aggressive ways.

● Provide many opportunities for children to have power and control in acceptable, age-appropriate ways. Give them many choices throughout the day: what books to read, what songs to sing, how much snack to eat, weather to play indoors or out, and so forth. In classrooms where children have many opportunities to be truly powerful by making choices, being leaders, taking responsibility, being treated with respect, and having their feelings supported and their frustrations attended to, the amount of violent play is minimal.

Dealing with Existing Problems

● For a child who continues to hit or be aggressive while being taught appropriate behavior, use "child choice": "You must tell other children what you want. If they won't listen to you, then ask me for help. Now you can choose an activity to do like a puzzle, a book, or a table game. When you think you can play with other children and talk with them about what you want, you can join the other children."

● If a child tends to be victimized by aggressive children more than other children, teach the skills needed to stand up for himself. Give him words to use if necessary and teach him to make his voice sound strong and his face to show anger. Give him several strategies: "You can walk away and play with other children or ask for help from a teacher." Have him practice these skills.

Grabbing Toys

● Use this situation as an opportunity to teach good social skills. Help the child use words to negotiate a turn-taking system, a trade, or some fair method of sharing the toy. Give as much help as necessary, but no more. Make sure that all the children have easy access to a timer or a clock so that they can negotiate a solution on their own.

● Help the child find a good strategy for waiting for a turn. Offer a choice: "Would you like to watch Lynn play with the toy or draw a picture while you are waiting?"

● If, after many attempts to teach better methods, a child continues to grab toys, use "child choice" while continuing to teach correct behaviors. Remember that this child is most likely a little less mature than other children but that she will develop better behavior with patience and kind guidance.

Wrecking Other Children's Projects

A typical aggressive act in an early childhood classroom is when a child knocks down the carefully constructed block structure that other children have spent much time making. Whether this or ripping a drawing or scribbling on another's painting, if it is deliberate, is an act of aggression meant to hurt others. It is also information for you that this child needs your help. In some cases the child is trying to interact with other children and be part of their play, but he doesn't know how. At least, through this aggressive act, he gets their attention. In some cases it is to get revenge on another child (jealousy of a popular child, perhaps), to test your ability to set limits, or to get your attention.

● Just as with all aggressive behaviors, give minimal attention to the behavior itself and help the child to get what he wants or express his feelings in a socially acceptable way. A good consequence for this behavior is to have the child help fix the destroyed object: tape the picture, hang a fresh sheet or paper on the easel, or pick up the blocks.

War, Gun, or Violent Play

Although play in which children act out violent scenes (including superhero play) may not involve direct acts of aggression against other children, many teachers find this kind of play disturbing. It glorifies aggression and often leads to a child getting hurt, even if not intentional. Some teachers limit the play by allowing it only outside. Others are opposed to the play totally and see it as limiting and harmful to children's development.

Young children have a strong need to work on issues related to good and evil (right and wrong) and power and powerlessness. They develop for themselves clear lines of who are "good guys" and who are "bad guys," usually aligning themselves on the side of good. The bad guys must come to a bad end so that everything is right with the world and the children are safe. This type of play is important because it helps young children develop a sense of who they are in the world, how to control their own desires to be "bad." It gives them a chance to grapple with what is acceptable behavior and what is not, and gain enough control to be safe. Because of this, children spend a surprising amount of time involved in this type of play.

The challenge for teachers then becomes how to give children opportunities to play out these themes and concepts while supporting play that is not aggressive or violent.

● Use aggressive play as an opportunity to expand the children's understanding of issues of violence. For example, ask, "What is another way you can protect yourself from the bad guy? How can you use 'brain power' instead of 'muscle power?'"

● Set clear rules, such as the following:

▶ "Use your body and words without hurting others or yourself."

▶ "Remember that anyone can call a time-out, leave the game, or rotate roles at any time."

● Help the children rotate roles so that all children get to be the "bad guy" as well as the "good guy."

● Provide alternative scenarios that do not involve weapons yet give children power. For example, set up firefighting play, emergency rescue, or tracking down a wild animal to give it medicine to get well or to be moved to a safer place. Move the evil or danger away from residing in another person and place it in something else—like fire or a dangerous animal.

● Redirect children into cooperative games that involve working together to complete a task, overcoming an obstacle, or winning against time. (See "Action: Actively Teach and Promote Cooperation," on p. 129, for ways to do this.) Read original fairy tales and other books, and make up stories that deal with issues of power and control through cleverness (brain power) rather than force.

Resources

Boyatzis, C. J. 1997. Of Power Rangers and v-chips. *Young Children* 52 (7): 74–79.

Carlsson-Paige, N., and D. E. Levin. 1987. *The war play dilemma: Balancing needs and values in the early childhood classroom.* New York: Teachers College Press.

———. 1990. *Who's calling the shots? How to respond effectively to children's fascination with war play and war toys.* Philadelphia: New Society.

———. 1995. Viewpoint #4. Can teachers resolve the war-play dilemma? *Young Children* 50 (5): 62–63.

Davis, J., and T. L. Hyland. 1999. *Angry kids, frustrated parents: Practical ways to prevent and reduce aggression in your children.* Boys Town, Nebr.: Boys Town Press.

Feeney, S., B. M. Caldwell, and K. Kipnis. 1988. Ethics case studies: The aggressive child. *Young Children* 43 (2): 48–51.

Kostelnik, M. J., A. P. Whiren, and L. C. Stein. 1986. Living with He-Man: Managing superhero fantasy play. In *Reducing stress in young children's lives,* edited by J. B. McCracken. Washington, D.C.: NAEYC.

Parens, H. 1995. *Aggression in our children: Coping with it constructively.* New York: Jason Aronson.

Schneider, L. B., and M. Torbert. 1992. *Follow me too: A handbook of movement activities for children.* New York: Pearson Learning.

Web Sites

Childhood Aggression: Where Does It Come From? How Can It Be Managed? by Karen DeBord. National Network for Child Care.
www.nncc.org. Click on Articles and Resources, then Child Development, then scroll down to article title under Emotional and Social.

Fighting and Biting. American Academy of Child and Adolescent Psychiatry. Facts for Families #81.
www.aacap.org. Link through Facts for Families and then scroll down to article title.

Hitting in the Classroom. Early Childhood Educator Teacher Tips.
www.edpsych.com/TeCall.html

Redirecting a Child Who Throws Things When Angry. Parenting Tips and Tools Archive. Parenting Press. April 14, 2001.
www.parentingpress.com. Click on Tip Archive, then Guidance and Discipline, then scroll down to article title.

Safe Start: How Early Experiences Can Help Reduce Violence. National Parent Information Network.
www.npin.org. Click on Search, then on the NPIN Virtual Library, then enter "safe start" in the search box.

Safely and Appropriately Expressing Anger. Parenting Tips and Tools Archive. Parenting Press. October 12, 1996.
www.parentingpress.com. Click on Tip Archive, then Feelings, then scroll down to article title.

Superhero Play in the Early Childhood Classroom: Issues in Banning Play from the Classroom by Brenda J. Boyd.

Earlychildood.com.
www.earlychildhood.com/Articles/index.cfm. Click on Antiviolence/Peace Education.

Teach Children to Cope with Frustration. Parenting Tips and Tools Archive. Parenting Press. April 19, 1997.
www.parentingpress.com. Click on Tip Archive, then Feelings, then scroll down to article title.

Teaching Children to Share by Sue Grossman. Earlychildhood.com.
www.earlychildhood.com/Articles/index.cfm. Click on Child Development, then scroll down to article title.

Violence and Aggression in Children and Youth by Mary K. Fitzsimmons. ERIC Digest. 1998.
ericeece.org. Link through Publications, then Digests, then Title, then scroll down to article.

10. Lying

All young children lie occasionally. In most cases they do not see this as doing something wrong or immoral. They believe it is acceptable to lie if the lie prevents them or a friend from being punished. Because young children think very differently than adults, moral lectures will not change the behavior. Instead, adults can avoid putting children in situations that force them to lie in order to save face. Children also lie to build themselves up in the eyes of others. We can also forgive the occasional lie as a typical behavior of young children.

Preventing Problems

● Help children see the difference between reality and fantasy whenever the opportunity arises: "It's fun to play Batman, but is he real?" If necessary, explain that he is a character someone made up and wrote about in books and movies, although it would be exciting if he were real.

● Avoid putting children in the position where they feel like they have to lie to protect themselves from consequences. Say, "Tell me what happened in your argument over the toy" instead of "Did you grab the toy away?" If you help children solve their differences fairly, take a "teaching and problem solving" approach to challenging behaviors and avoid punishments, children will not feel the need to protect themselves from punishment by lying.

● Build self-esteem by making sure children are accepted and appreciated unconditionally for who they are and not only for what they can do or say. Do this by saying many positive things to all children: "Your beautiful smile brightens my day" or "I really enjoy being with you every day" or "I like you, just because you are you." Be physically warm and affectionate. Give children many opportunities to be responsible and expect that they can handle their responsibilities, even if this means offering a little assistance.

● As lying can often be an attention-getting behavior, give all children a great deal of individual attention. Know their strengths and weaknesses well and be responsive to their needs.

Dealing with Existing Problems

Young children will often make up improbable stories and insist that they are true. This is not so much lying as it is fantasizing. Support the child's ability to imagine and the fulfillment he gets through the story: "You tell wonderful stories that are fun to listen to." This gives the child a positive message and at the same time lets him know that you know the story is a fantasy. Avoid asking if the story is true as that only puts the child in a position of having to lie.

Compulsive lying, or lying that happens frequently and consistently, is a sign that the child feels a great deal of shame about himself. He has the need to build himself up and to be seen as always good and right, in order to protect his weak sense of self from further damage. Build this child's self-esteem through a wide variety of methods. Help him to see all that is positive in himself. "You really know how to be a good friend to Amanda. That must make you feel very proud."

● When the child lies directly to you, do not confront him with the lie. If the lie has to do with telling about an untrue incident—claiming to be hit when you know he wasn't—respond by validating the feelings behind the lie: "You feel hurt and feel badly treated." Tell him you appreciate that he came to tell you about the problem and didn't hit back. Then move on to helping solve the problem if there was a conflict, or redirect him to another activity, or just provide comfort. Follow through by helping him figure out what he can do when someone hits him: "You can say that you are angry and you don't like it and you are going to play with someone else. What else can you do?"

● Try to determine if there is a purpose for the lie, such as to get sympathy, attention, or affection. Tell the child how he can achieve his purpose in a better way: "If you need a hug, ask me for one, and I will be very glad to give you one. If I can't because I'm busy, I will give you a hug as soon as I can."

● If the lie has to do with denying wrongdoing ("I didn't take Celia's doll"), say: "I know you're a very good person. Everyone does things he shouldn't sometimes and it's okay. Let's talk with Celia and figure out how to solve the problem." Again, do not confront him with the lie.

● Work with parents to determine the root cause of the problem and discuss approaches for helping the

child. Help the parents to see the importance of being positive with the child as opposed to using punishment. If the lying persists or gets worse in spite of using these strategies, recommend counseling, as a young child who lies compulsively has a quite serious problem with his sense of self.

Resources

Adams, L. K. 1998. *Dealing with lying. The conflict resolution library*. New York: Powerkids Press.

Web Sites

Children and Lying. American Academy of Child and Adolescent Psychiatry. Facts for Families #44. www.aacap.org. Link through Facts for Families and scroll down to article.

Lying. Center for Effective Parenting. www.parenting-ed.org. Click on Search the CEP Web site, then enter "lying" in the search box.

Lying: An Excerpt from the Book *Positive Discipline A–Z*. www.positivediscipline.com. Click on For Parents, then Articles for Parents, then scroll down to article.

Teaching Truthfulness and Honesty—Part I: Preschoolers. Parenting Tips and Tools Archive. Parenting Press. March 1, 1997. www.parentingpress.com. Click on Tip Archive, then Values, then scroll down to article title.

11. Masturbation and Self-Stimulation

It is not unusual to see this behavior with young children. They usually are not masturbating but comforting or stimulating themselves by rubbing their genitals. If a child does this often and overtly, it is a sign of serious emotional problems (see the chapter, "Children with Severe Behavior Problems" on p. 133). For most children it is a sign of boredom or anxiety. They do not realize that it is inappropriate to do in public. Like other behaviors that are socially acceptable in some places but not others, or at certain times but not others (taking off your shoes, scratching yourself, eating with your hands), it is difficult for young children to figure out the social rules and follow them. It is a slow, gradual process of learning, so be patient, understanding, and persistent.

Preventing Problems

● Make sure that your curriculum and activities are individualized and reasonably challenging. Boredom is the most common reason for such behaviors.

● Provide many opportunities for children to express and relieve their anxieties every day through drawing and many open-ended sensory activities such as sand and water play, clay, and playdough.

Dealing with Existing Problems

● Use the behavior as a cue to you that your activity is boring. Stop and change the activity or give the child another choice of an activity that will be more engaging.

● Give the child a stuffed toy animal to hold and stroke, a soft ball, or other object that may satisfy her need for soothing or stimulation.

● At a later point, away from others, talk to her about the behavior. "I know it feels good, but some people are upset when they see other people touching their genitals. You can do this at home, but not at school. Let's think of some things that you can do instead."

- If it is a habit, help her realize when she is doing it by giving her a nonverbal cue. This will signal her to stop and do the more socially acceptable behavior instead.

- Talk to her parents about the possible reasons for the behavior, their view of it, and suggestions for helping their child. Develop a plan together to change the behavior. Tell the parents not to punish the behavior or to be overly concerned.

Resources

Sexuality Information and Education Council of the United States (SIECUS). 1995. *Right from the start: Guidelines for sexuality issues, birth to five years.* New York: SIECUS.

Wilson, P. M. 1991. *When sex is the subject: Attitudes and answers for young children.* Santa Cruz, Calif.: Network Publications.

Web Sites

Masturbation. Center for Effective Parenting. www.parenting-ed.org. Click on Search the CEP Web site, then enter "masturbation" in the search box.

Masturbation in Young Children. Parent Soup. iVillage. www.parentsoup.com. Enter "masturbation" in the search box.

Masturbation: Is This Normal for Preschoolers? Parent Soup. iVillage. www.parentsoup.com. Enter "masturbation" in the search box

Responding to Sexual Play by Christine M. Todd. National Network for Child Care. www.nncc.org. Click on Articles and Resources, then on Guidance and Discipline, then scroll down to article title under Behavior Management.

Sexuality Information and Education Council of the United States www.siecus.org

Young Children and Self-Stimulation. Family Psychologist. Parent Soup. iVillage. www.parentsoup.com. Enter "self-stimulation" in the search box.

12. Mean and Cruel

Mean and cruel behaviors are very disturbing to see. We worry about children who seem to lack a conscience and we wonder if they will grow up to be adults who commit criminal acts without regard to the pain and suffering of others. Children who exhibit mean and cruel behaviors, often and in the extreme, may do so because they have not been securely bonded with a loving adult or because they have seen these behaviors in their homes or neighborhoods.

Teachers can help these children by being empathetic. Let them know that you think they are good people worthy of love, although you do not approve of some of their behaviors. Accept their anger and rage as legitimate feelings to have and then show them better ways of expressing it. "I know you are angry and it is okay to be angry. If you don't like what Sara is doing you can use words or choose someone else to play with." Give them a great deal of positive encouragement and attention when they are acting in acceptable ways or just acting neutral. Children develop consciences as a result of knowing that an adult cares deeply about them. You can provide this for children and make a difference in their lives, even if no other adult can.

Common, less extreme, mean and cruel behaviors are a form of aggression. Mean words may seem less egregious than mean actions, but they need to be taken very seriously and dealt with quickly and consistently, as with any aggressive behavior.

Preventing Problems

- Create a classroom environment that fosters kindness and respect. Establish a classroom rule: "Use your body and words without hurting others or yourself." Remind them of this rule often.

- Assure all children often that you will not let anyone be mean to them and that you will not let them be mean to anyone else.

- Teach the children the correct words to use and the correct actions to take during conflicts, when they are being excluded, when someone hurts them, and other difficult situations. Teach them negotiation and turn-taking skills.

- Provide many outlets for children to express their strong feelings safely. Be available to talk to and write stories with them and give them plenty of time for large-motor play. Provide the children with blank paper and pens with which to draw, sand and water to sift and pour, playdough and clay to mold, hammers and nails to bang, and beanbags to throw at a safe "target." Validate their feelings often: "You really are very angry and that's okay." Help them express their feelings safely and verbally, and then help them deal with the cause of the anger.

● Give children ways to express positive feelings and words about other children. Have them say something good about another child during a small circle or group time. Rotate until all the children have had a turn at both expressing and receiving positive comments about themselves and what they do. Make books throughout the year about each child. Invite every child to draw a picture and write or dictate positive information about the child whose book is being composed. Then put all the papers together to form a book. When a child does something positive for another, such as helping to zip up a coat, make sure the child who received the help expresses appreciation.

Dealing with Existing Problems

Actions

Cruel actions, such as picking on a vulnerable child, hurting small animals, or causing excessive pain to others, are signs of a child who is in a great deal of emotional pain herself. She may have been or is being hurt emotionally and/or physically and is acting out her pain rage. (See "Children with Severe Behavior Problems," on p. 133, and "Parents Who May Be Abusive to Their Children," on pp. 176–179, for ways to deal with this.)

Words

Verbal cruelty is more common with preschoolers, particularly girls. Girls tend to express aggression with words and with indirect actions such as excluding others. This may be because they tend to have more advanced language and social skills than boys. They know that the most hurtful thing to do to another girl is target their aggression in the area of social relations (rather than physical aggression). "You can't come to my birthday party," is much more painful than a punch to most girls. They also see the behaviors modeled by women at home, in their neighborhoods, and in the media. Their behavior is reinforced by their success at hurting others. Seeing sophisticated verbal cruelty in very young children is upsetting but, unfortunately, not uncommon.

The children who do this use a variety of methods, including excluding others, rule making, forming cliques, placing certain children in subservient roles, and making cruel comments directly to others just within hearing range or "behind their backs."

● Intervene when this happens and make children aware of the impact of their behavior. Help them use different words to express their feelings in ways that are not hurtful: "When you told Ana, 'We don't want to play with you, go away,' she felt hurt. Speak only for yourself and use words that don't hurt. Let's find a role Ana can take that will make your play more fun." (See "When You See Bias Happening," on p. 82.)

● Realize that the child who is being cruel may be building herself up by putting down others. Help her see the good in herself that is independent of comparisons to others: "Everyone is special and important. You really enjoy art and are fun to play with." Use many other methods to build her self-esteem. Be physically affectionate and tell her when she is being kind: "You helped Jason tie his shoes. You are a good friend, and you help make this a fun classroom."

● Help the child who is the object of the cruel behavior to stand up for herself by coaching her to say such words as: "I can play where and when I want to." You cannot make children like each other, but you can teach children to respect each other. Be sure that the child who is sometimes cruel knows ways that will help her successfully join in play. (See the first two chapters of this section, for more information.)

Resources

Also see the resources in the chapter, "Cursing, Name-Calling, and Hurtful Language" on p. 140.

Paley, V. G. 1993. *You can't say you can't play.* Cambridge: Harvard University Press.

Web Sites

Bullying. American Academy of Child and Adolescent Psychiatry. Facts for Families #80. www.aacap.org. Link through Facts for Families, and scroll down to the article.

Dealing with Name-Calling. Parenting Tip and Tool of the Week. Parenting Press. January 6, 2001. www.parentingpress.com. Click on Tip Archive, then Problem Solving, then scroll down to article title.

Go Away! You Can't Play! by Eleanor Reynolds. EarlyChildhood.com www.earlychildhood.com/Articles/index.cfm. Click on Discipline, then scroll down to article title.

Helping Your Child Respond to Teasing. Parenting Tip and Tool of the Week. Parenting Press. January 6, 2001. www.parentingpress.com. Click on Tip Archive, then People Skills, then scroll down to article title.

Teasing and Bullying in Day Care or Preschool. Several articles. Day Care. About.com. daycare.about.com. Enter "bullying" in the search box, then scroll down to topic.

13. Roughhousing

Roughhousing is part of childhood. Teachers will never be able to eliminate the need some children have for it. For many children, especially boys, it is a way of expressing affection for another child. The following suggestions will give you ways to allow rough-and-tumble play in the classroom or outdoors, while keeping it to a safe and reasonable level.

Preventing Problems

● Teach children other ways to interact: "Use words. Say to your friend, 'Let's play with the blocks.'" Assist the children in this process until they are able to do it on their own, relying less on roughhousing as their main form of interaction.

● Provide many opportunities for children to make physical contact with each other in a safe way. For example, play movement games and teach simple dances, yoga, or exercises in which children interact physically with partners. Make the rules and directions very clear to avoid anyone getting hurt.

● Give children outlets and plenty of time for loud, big, fast, physical play. This will of course need to happen outdoors or in a gym. Placing the play within a dramatic play scenario—fire fighting, emergency rescue, saving animals, searching for rare jungle species to photograph—helps to keep it from getting "out of hand."

● Before the start of an organized activity, physically separate children who have a hard time keeping their hands off each other. This will reduce the strong temptation to interact.

● Teach children other ways of expressing physical affection for each other, such as hugging, holding hands, and putting arms around each other's shoulders. Suggest to children that they ask before they touch others: "Kim, would you like to hold hands with me?" Follow this suggestion yourself. Remember that some children dislike being touched and all children need to be sensitive to and respect the feelings and

the bodies of others. However, most children enjoy spontaneously receiving and giving physical affection.

● Provide a gym mat where children can roughhouse safely. Establish some ground rules such as the following:

- ▶ "No punching."
- ▶ "When one child says stop the other must do it."
- ▶ "Only stocking or bare feet on the mat."
- ▶ "No other objects can be on the mat"

If children have trouble stopping or if others are waiting to use the mat, limit their time on it. Offer roughhousing on the mat as a free choice activity.

Dealing with Existing Problems

● If children are roughhousing at an inappropriate time, such as during circle time, tell them "Now is a time for listening (or singing, sharing, and so on). During free choice time, you may choose the gym mat." Separate the children from each other. Tell them that if roughhousing happens again, they can choose a quiet activity away from other children (child choice). Follow through if necessary, giving the children the opportunity to return to the group when they are ready to listen without roughhousing.

● Give children who roughhouse during sedentary times something active to do with their hands (hold a book or a stuffed animal), or an adult lap to sit on, the option of holding a friend's hand, or an alternative activity to do.

Resources
Web Sites

Rough and Tumble Play by Elizabeth Byrne Ferm. Chapter 15 of Freedom in Education. www.factoryschool.org/home.html. Click on Publications, then on Elizabeth Ferm: Freedom in Education.

When a Child Plays Rough by Polly Greenberg. Scholastic. teacher.scholastic.com. Click on Search, then enter "when a child plays rough" in the search box. Click on Child Development: Solving Sharing Issues.

14. Running Inside

Young children need to be active, and running is a natural way for them to move. Changing this behavior to assure their safety requires doing many things. You have to eliminate the temptation to run, establish clear expectations, give many reminders, and allow children plenty of time during the day to run outdoors or in a gym.

It is often best to redirect children who are running inside into another, safer activity, rather than trying to get them to walk. For example, a chasing game requires running. It makes no sense to walk and chase someone. By redirecting both children into a different game, preferably something active, the running will stop. Remind them that they can chase each other outside or in the gym during large-motor time.

Preventing Problems

● Establish a class rule: "Only walk inside." Be very consistent about enforcing this rule. Explain that the reason for the rule is to make sure no one falls or runs into another person and gets hurt.

● Remind children before they enter the classroom from outside and before transitions to other activities, to walk in the room.

● Arrange your equipment and furnishings so that there are no long, open corridors that invite running.

● Stop the child who is running and have her practice telling herself to walk. Recognize that the reason for the behavior is usually because the child is excited and wants to get to an activity as soon as possible. Tell her: "It's great that you want to get to the activity quickly, but walking will keep you from getting hurt." Start walking with her to get her going successfully. Show her how to walk quickly without running.

● If logical consequences are needed, have the child walk with a teacher holding her hand. Next time the situation arises, ask the child ahead of time if she would like to walk on her own or have help. The commonly used consequence of making a child go back to where she started and walk rarely works because it is punitive and frustrates the child by forcing her to do the opposite of her intentions (getting there quickly). Teach correct behavior in a helpful, instructive way that helps children get what they want more effectively.

● Pair the child up with another child who is good about walking. Have them be partners when walking somewhere is necessary.

● Remind the child of the reason that walking is important. Through role play, demonstrate in slow motion how a person coming around a corner can have a serious accident with a child who is running because he cannot see the child in time to stop.

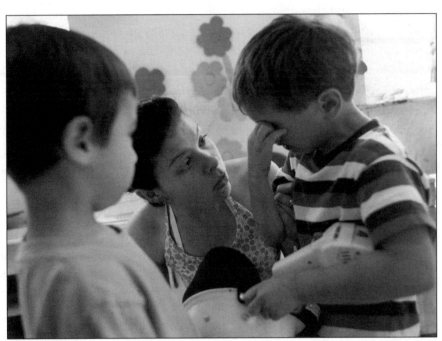

● Reassure the child that when she is outside, she will get to run all she wants.

● Let children know, when they are walking, that you recognize the appropriate behavior: "Thank you for walking in the room. You know how to keep yourself and others safe."

Resources
Web Sites
Setting Limits: When a Child Runs Wild by Polly Greenberg. Scholastic.
teacher.scholastic.com. Click on Search, then enter "setting limits" in the search box, then click on article title.

15. Shy and Withdrawn ———

This personality or temperament characteristic can stay with people throughout their lives, even though many shy people express a lot of pain and unhappiness about the condition. Few shy children or adults are happy about their condition. Shy children can grow up to be adults who are very social, but they usually have to really push themselves to change, and often still do not feel comfortable. The causes can be numerous, but shy children tend to have shy parents, and many shy children have low self-esteem. They feel that they will be laughed at or not accepted by others if they assert themselves or that they are not as worthy as other children. You may not be able to make the shyness go away, but you can make shy children feel more comfortable, more sure of themselves, and more able to connect with other children and adults. At the extreme, shyness can be a very debilitating condition, "social phobia," which requires intensive help from a mental health professional. (See the chapter "Children with Severe Behavior Problems" on p. 133).

Preventing Problems

● Make all children feel loved, desirable, and respected.

● Rotate assignments and classroom jobs and provide opportunities for the children to make choices and be leaders in a way that is optimal for each child. A shy child may blossom when given formal opportunities to be a leader (for example, the opportunity to choose children to leave the circle time area by the colors of their clothes). Give the child many opportunities to make decisions that impact others and be a leader.

● Provide a wide variety of challenging activities that involve different numbers of children. See that some activities are only for one (a puzzle), some for two (a board game), some for three (a lotto game), and so on.

● Accept and appreciate every child's feelings, ideas, and statements, even if these are just attempts at vocalizing.

● Do most of your group activities in very small groups because shy children tend to be less shy around fewer children.

● Give some one-on-one attention to each child at some point during the day.

Dealing with Existing Problems

● Accept a reasonable level of shyness as a normal individual difference. Intervene only if shyness causes the child to have problems making friends, playing, and being involved in activities that he really wants to be involved in.

● Don't push the shy child. Respect his need to stay back and move slowly. Continue to offer opportunities and suggestions for participation, however. Be patient, be positive, and be persistent. Expect changes to come gradually.

● Learn as much as you can about the shy child. Do a home visit so that you can see if the child is shy at home. Most shy children are quite normal, even boisterous, at home. The shyness is still something to be concerned about and deal with, but less so if the child acts normal at home. Find out the child's interests, strengths, family, pets, and neighborhood friends. Use this information to connect with the child during class time and to help him connect with other children through similar interests.

● Start a game or activity together with the child. In a while, invite one or two other children to join. When he is actively engaged with the other children, quietly move away.

● Set up a game that involves only two children. Encourage another, less shy child to ask the shy child to join him in that game.

● Actively teach the child specific social skills and ways to enter play with other children. (See the first two chapters of this section for ideas.) The fear of involving himself in play with others may come from failed attempts to do so. Help him say the words and do the actions needed to join others. Gradually do less for the child as he develops the skills.

● Incorporate the child into play activities without making him change his behavior. For example, if you have involved a group of children in acting out "The Three Little Pigs," acknowledge the shy child's important role as a watcher and listener: "Thank you for being an attentive audience member. Plays aren't much fun without an audience." As the child feels more comfortable, incorporate him even more in the activity by having him take the role of a house or a guard. (This requires little movement or talking.) Again show appreciation for his important role.

Continue to encourage him to take more and more of an active part (Chenfeld 1989).

● Give positive feedback to the shy child whenever he involves himself with others: "It's nice to hear you talk and laugh. It must feel good to have fun and enjoy playing with others."

● Give the shy child several options for participating. For example, if he refuses to join a movement game ask him if he would like to lead the game or keep track of who had a turn. Provide other options such as being the "audience" or having the last turn (there is security in first seeing how everyone else participates).

● Limit the amount of time the child spends in a private, quiet area in the room. Tell him that other children want opportunities for quiet also and that it is important to do a variety of activities.

● For a child who uses a very quiet voice, stop him quickly and encourage him by saying, "I love hearing your big five-year-old voice (or four-year-old voice). It's beautiful to listen to!" Avoid saying, "Don't use that quiet voice" or "Speak up, we can't hear you" as this further embarrasses the child.

● Suggest to the child's parents that they arrange to have him spend time with another child outside of school. This can often cement friendships that provide more play opportunities back at school.

● Encourage the shy child to bring items from home, as "transitional objects," to make the connection between home and class or as a way to help him form friendships. (Put some limits on the use of these toys as discussed in "Toys from Home," p. 55.)

Resources

Chenfeld, M. B. 1989. From catatonic to hyperactive: Randy snapped today. *Young Children* 44 (4): 25–27.

Honig, A. S. 1987. Research in review: The shy child. *Young Children* 42 (4): 54–64.

Morris, J. C. 1994. Introverts. *Young Children* 49 (2): 32–33.

Swallow, W. K. 2000. *The shy child: Helping children triumph over shyness.* New York: Warner Books.

Trawick-Smith, J. 1988. "Let's say you're the baby, OK": Play leadership and following behavior of young children. *Young Children* 43 (5): 51–59.

Zimbardo, P. G. 1990. *Shyness: What it is, what to do about it.* Cambridge, Mass.: Perseus Press.

Zimbardo, P. G., and S. L. Radl. 1999. *The shy child. Overcoming and preventing shyness from infancy to adulthood.* Palo Alto, Calif.: Malor Books.

Children's Books

Bechtold, L. 1999. *Buster: The very shy dog.* New York: Houghton Mifflin.

Crary, E. 1996. *I'm scared.* Seattle: Parenting Press.

———. 1996. *I want to play.* Seattle: Parenting Press.

Hood, S. 2000. *Tyler is shy.* Pleasantville, N.Y.: Reader's Digest Children's Publishing.

Johnston, M. 1997. *Let's talk about being shy.* New York: Powerkids Press.

Wells, R. 1992. *Shy Charles.* New York: Puffin.

Web Sites

The Shy Child by Marion C. Hyson and Karen Van Trieste. ERIC Digest. 1987. ericeece.org. Link on Publications then Digests, then Title, then scroll down to the article.

Keys to Living with the Quiet, Easily Discouraged Child. Parenting Press's Tip and Tool of the Week. December 13, 1997. www.parentingpress.com. Click on Tip Archive, then on Temperament, then scroll down to article title.

Living with the Sensitive, Cautious Child. Parenting Press's Tip and Tool of the Week. September 5, 1998. www.parentingpress.com. Click on Tip Archive, then on Temperament, then scroll down to article title

Understanding the Child Who Is Slow-to-Approach. Parenting Press's Tip and Tool of the Week. March 23, 2002. www.parentingpress.com. Click on Tip Archive, then on Temperament, then scroll down to article title.

Work with Your Child's Shyness, Not Against It. Parenting Press's Tip and Tool of the Week. November 2, 1996. www.parentingpress.com. Click on Tip Archive, then on Feelings, then scroll down to article title.

16. Silliness ─────────────

This common behavior in preschool children, especially four-year-olds, can become a problem if it happens too often or at inappropriate times. A main reason for this behavior is to get the attention and the admiration of other children and adults. A child who feels unloved can successfully make herself feel better this way. (This is also known as the "class clown syndrome.") Another common reason for silliness is boredom. Children who feel unchallenged or not engaged by activities you have developed may act silly as a way to relieve the stress of boredom. A child who is silly a great deal of the time may be using the behavior to avoid dealing with some important issues in her life. When you try to have a serious discussion, the pain she may have to face during that discussion is too great. Acting silly is her way of escaping this pain.

Preventing Problems

● Give many opportunities for children to be silly and even encourage silliness at times that are appropriate, such as free choice and outside. When the children are silly, let them know that this is a good time to be silly because it doesn't disturb others or make talking about important things hard.

● Set rules for activities that require earnest behavior:

  ▶ "Listen while someone else is talking."

  ▶ "Be serious during important talks."

● Don't require that everyone participate, as some children will find serious discussions too challenging, but do require that everyone listen and show respect.

● Give children many opportunities to express their innermost feelings safely and confidentially.

● Give a great deal of individual attention and affection to all children. Give many choices and other actions that help build self-esteem.

● Make sure your curriculum and activities are engaging and challenging. Provide extra challenges to children who are advanced or gifted.

Dealing with Existing Problems

● Stop the child as soon as she starts silly, inappropriate behavior by saying: "Now it is important to be serious. In ten minutes when we're outside, you can be as silly as you want. I'm very interested in what you have to say if you would like to talk seriously." Tell the child that if this silly behavior happens again, she will have to choose an activity away from the group (child choice). Follow through if the behavior does happen again, and tell her she can join the group when she feels able to be serious.

● Give minimal attention to the silly behavior. Redirect the child into an engaging activity.

● Meet with parents to determine the root cause of the problem—the pain that the child is avoiding. Help in any way possible to ease the child's problems. If necessary, make a referral to a social service agency, mental health specialist, or provide a list of community resources.

● Try to spend one-on-one time with the child away from other children. Note that if she is not near her peers, she might be willing to talk seriously. Use books, puppets, and made-up stories to help bring out her inner feelings. Give her opportunities to draw pictures that do not have to be shown to anyone else.

● If several children start acting silly during a planned activity (such as circle time, or while listening to a story), take it as a signal that the activity is boring. Stop the activity and do a movement activity or song, or move on to your next planned activity.

Resources
Children's Books

Curtis, J. L. 1998. *Today I feel silly: And other moods that make my day.* New York: HarperCollins.

Leonard, M. 1997. *Silly (How I feel).* San Diego: Smart Kids.

17. Spitting

This behavior is usually the result of anger and frustration, but can also be an aggressive act. (See the chapter, "Hitting and Aggression" on pp. 143–146.) The child also may have learned that it will get adults very upset and so has a big impact or payoff and therefore is a good "attention-getter."

Preventing Problems

● Let children know that it is okay to be angry and that they can express it with words or safe actions that will not hurt themselves or others.

● Give children many safe outlets to express strong emotions through drawing, pounding on a mat or pillow, hammering nails, crying while being held, and more.

● Read to them and role-play in ways that show children acting to prevent themselves from getting in frustrating or infuriating situations and that show them expressing their anger appropriately, if they do.

● Do all you can to keep frustrations and stress to a minimum. Have a challenging but warm and supportive curriculum and environment, keep sedentary activities short, allow much time for active and interactive play, allow for safe risk taking, and more.

Dealing with Existing Problems

● Don't overreact. Say calmly, "I know you are angry. Let me help you find words or safe actions instead to solve the problem. Spitting hurts and is not safe."

● Soothe the child who has been spit at.

● Have the child help clean up the spit.

● A bit later talk to the child. "Spitting is not okay. It can make another sick. This is a safe classroom and I won't let you hurt anyone or let anyone hurt you. Let's think of what you can do the next time you are angry." Alternatives can include using angry words or going to an adult for help.

● Determine what situations lead to spitting and help the child avoid getting into them. It may mean choosing to play with certain children rather than others or choosing a less complex toy or game. It may mean learning negotiation or turn-taking skills.

Resources
Children's Books

Crary, E. 1992. *I'm frustrated.* Seattle: Parenting Press.
———. 1992. *I'm mad.* Seattle: Parenting Press.
———. 1996. *I'm furious.* Seattle: Parenting Press.

Web Sites

Spitting and Hitting by Jan Faull. FamilyFun. family.go.com. Enter "spitting" in the search box.

18. Stealing

Unless a child is being encouraged to steal by an adult, which is very unusual, most children who steal do so because they feel deprived. They feel they are missing something that other children have. Because they cannot get affection and attention, they obtain material objects for themselves as a substitute. This is, of course, not satisfying because it does not solve the real problem, so they do it again and again. Adults do this too, by buying themselves presents or eating sweets when they feel unhappy or unloved.

A younger child may pocket small toys and not realize or understand that this action is stealing. Explain that school toys must stay at school so that all children can play with them. Remind the child that the toys will be there to play with when he returns to school.

Preventing Problems

● Build your children's self-esteem. Make this an important part of your curriculum.

● Maintain good parent communication so you know what problems a child might be facing. You can then be helpful, empathetic, and supportive to that child.

● Have a class lending library for children to borrow an inexpensive book or toy. Have a checkout system to track who borrowed what. Set clear rules about how long something can be borrowed and that it must return in good condition. The currently borrowed item must be returned before checking out another item.

Dealing with Existing Problems

● If you're not sure that a child actually is stealing, ask him to empty his pockets at the end of the day. Do this when no other children are around. If nothing was taken, explain your reasons for asking him and apologize.

● If you catch a child stealing, support his needs and feelings: "You really like that toy and would like to have it. I wish I could give it you, but other children want to play with it. It will be here for you to play with tomorrow. Let's make a list for using it tomorrow and put your name first." Calmly ask him to put the object back. Do not shame him.

● Give a child who is stealing positive verbal feedback hourly or daily (depending on how often he steals) when he does not steal. Tell him: "Thank you for leaving things here at school so that you can play with them tomorrow. I know how much fun it would be to have these toys at home, so you have great self-control when you leave them." Give the child a hug so he will know that acting appropriately will get him positive attention and affection.

● Meet with the child's parents to coordinate strategies to deal with the problem. Make them aware of the importance of being empathetic and positive and not punishing the behavior. Ask them if they are aware of any possible causes for the behavior. Help them develop ways to build their child's self-esteem.

● Give the child many opportunities to be a leader and helper in the classroom. This will make him feel important.

● If the other children are aware of the stealing, talk to them about being friendly and about helping that child. Act positive yourself to provide a model for the children.

● Ask another teacher or supervisor to observe your classroom to determine if any pattern to the behavior is apparent or if you may be unintentionally contributing to the behavior.

● If the problem persists, team with the child's parents to get help from a mental health specialist.

Resources

National Association for the Education of Young Children (NAEYC). 1997. Using NAEYC's Code of Ethics. Mary and the missing bracelet. *Young Children* 52 (3): 66–67.

Web Sites

Can a Five-Year-Old Be a Thief? by Jan Faull. FamilyFun. family.go.com. Enter "stealing" in the search box.

Children Who Steal. American Academy of Child and Adolescent Psychiatry. Facts for Families #12. www.aacap.org. Link through Facts for Families, and scroll down to the article.

Stealing. Center for Effective Parenting (also in Spanish). www.parenting-ed.org. Click on Search CEP Web site, then enter "stealing" in the search box.

19. Tattling

This is usually an attention-getting behavior and also serves to boost the ego of the child who tattles by casting others in a bad light.

Preventing Problems

● Give a great deal of positive, individual attention to all children as often as possible. Give extra attention to children who are more emotionally fragile.

● Give children practice saying positive things about other children. Have them say something good about another child during a small circle or group time. Rotate until everyone has had a turn at both expressing and receiving a positive statement.

● Make books throughout the year about each child. Invite every child to draw a picture and write or dictate positive information about the child whose book is being compiled. Then put all the papers together to form a book.

● When a child does something positive for another, such as helping to zip up a coat, make sure the child who received the help expresses appreciation.

● During a small group or circle time, talk with the children about tattling. Help them understand what is wrong with the behavior and what they can do instead. (See below for some ideas.) Role-play alternatives to tattling so they can practice the skills.

Dealing with Existing Problems

● Give minimal attention to the tattling but do not stop it or cut it off. (There is no way to know if the child might be giving you some important information about other children.) When she is finished talking and you know that she truly is tattling and not telling something you need to act on, then you can work to minimize the tattling.

- Thank the child who tattles: "I'm glad you care and are concerned about your friends."

- Tell the child to talk about the behavior to the child on whom she is tattling, not to you.

- Put the problem back on the child by asking her what she would like to do about her concern.

- Ask her to tell you about the positive behaviors of other children: "I'd love to hear about the good things Madison does."

- Encourage the child when she is talking to you without tattling: "I enjoy talking with you when it is not about other children."

Resources
Children's Books
Hammerseng, K. M. 1996. *Telling isn't tattling*. Seattle: Parenting Press.

Web Sites
Discouraging Tattling. Parenting Press's Tip and Tool of the Week. June 22, 2002. www.parentingpress.com. Click on Tip Archive, then Guidance and Discipline, then scroll down to article title.

Responding to Tattling. Parenting Press's Tip and Tool of the Week. June 28, 1997. www.parentingpress.com. Click on Tip Archive, then Guidance and Discipline, then scroll down to article title.

Teaching the Difference between Telling and Tattling. Parenting Press's Tip and Tool of the Week. March 1996. www.parentingpress.com. Click on Tip Archive, then Guidance and Discipline, then scroll down to article title.

20. Temper Tantrums ———

This behavior is fairly common in toddlers, but if seen in children older than three-and-a-half, it is a cause for concern. Toddlers throw tantrums because they do not have the language to express strong needs, or the emotional maturity to deal with them. All their frustrations in understanding and coping with the world of "giants" build up to the point where they explode. Preschool children, however, usually can express their needs with words, can think abstractly enough to get their needs met with other people, and have more self-control and emotional maturity.

The preschool child who does have temper tantrums and who is not developmentally or language delayed may be under great stress, has great anger, and could possibly benefit from professional counseling or other assistance. The causes of emotional stress can be numerous—expectations from parents or others that are too high or too low, abuse or neglect, or fighting and tension in the family.

Other possible causes of tantrums include having a medical problem that causes pain, having been overly indulged, lacking social skills, or having been (unintentionally) rewarded for such behaviors: they worked and got the child what he wanted.

Preventing Problems
- Provide many outlets for children to express their emotions and feelings in acceptable ways.

- Reduce frustrations by offering children many choices of a wide variety of hands-on, self-directed activities for most of their time at school. Make sure your activities are not too challenging or too easy for children. Have reasonable expectations of the abilities of your children. Do not make them sit and listen for more than a few minutes at a time. (See "The Daily Schedule: An Active and Purposeful Program" on pp. 7–8, for more information on the appropriate length of time for various activities.)

- Observe carefully. As soon as you see children get frustrated, step in to help them solve their problems, if necessary. Do and say only as much as you need to so that they can gain the skills to be self-sufficient.

Dealing with Existing Problems
- Give minimum attention to the temper tantrum, except to ensure the safety of the child and others. Remember that the goal of the behavior is for the child to get what he wants or to let off steam. In either case, giving any attention (negative or positive) to the behavior will result in an increase in the number of tantrums because you will be helping the child meet his goal.

- If the tantrum is causing a disruption, move the child quickly to a safe area away from other children. Tell him calmly, "It's okay to be frustrated and angry, but it's not okay to disturb others. When you're ready to be calm, you may join us."

- Watch the child carefully to observe when the tantrums occur most frequently or what tends to set them off. Make adjustments in your schedule or environment to help the child. If an interaction with one other particular child triggers the tantrum, separate the children after a few minutes of play to ease the tension. Help both children interact with each other differently and more amiably. Help them engage in cooperative games or activities.

- Invite a respected peer or your supervisor to observe in your classroom. She can help you see if you may be inadvertently contributing to the behavior or give you ideas for changing the behavior.

- Meet with the child's parents to discuss possible causes of the problem. Brainstorm possible solutions together. Recommend counseling or the help of a social service agency if the above strategies do not significantly decrease the tantrums.

Fits of Anger

A child who is out of control may hurt himself or another child. If you cannot reason with the child, lead him to a safe place, within your sight, such as to a gym mat, to vent his feelings. Tell him that when he feels calm, he can join the group or choose a quiet activity to do on his own. If he may hurt himself, stay close by him (or have an assistant stay by him). If he is not too resistant to your touch, hold him and assure him that you will not let him hurt himself.

- Help the child find ways to calm himself down. He can generate his own ideas and/or you can suggest that he listen to music, look at a book, sing, talk, draw, or play with sand, water, or clay.

- When the child is calm, help him determine how he could deal with the problem that made him so angry. Help him practice the words and actions he can take to get his needs met. For example, he can tell the child who has just knocked over his block structure to help him build it back up again or to put the blocks away. He can also ask an adult to assist him in dealing with the other child.

Resources

Laforge, A. E. 1996. *Tantrums: Secrets to calming the storm*. New York: Pocket Books.

National Association for the Education of Young Children. 1988. Ideas that work with young children. Discipline: Are tantrums normal? *Young Children* 43 (6): 35–40.

Ricker, A., and C. Crowder. 2000. *Whining: Three steps to stopping it before the tears and tantrums start*. New York: Fireside.

Children's Books

Blumenthal, D. 1999. *The chocolate-covered-cookie tantrum*. New York: Clarion Books.

Crary, E. 1996. *I want it*. Seattle: Parenting Press.

Web Sites

Ideas for Dealing with Temper Tantrums. Parenting Press's Tip and Tool of the Week. October 25, 1997. www.parentingpress.com. Click on Tip Archive, then Guidance and Discipline, then scroll down to article title.

Taming Temper Tantrums by Lesia Oesterreich. National Network for Child Care. www.nncc.org. Click on Articles and Resources, then on Child Development, then scroll down to article title under Social/Emotional.

Temper Tantrums. Various articles. FamilyFun. www.family.go.com. Enter "temper tantrums" in the search box.

Temper Tantrums: What Causes Them and How Can You Respond? by Dawn Ramsburg. National Parent Information Network. www.npin.org. Click on Search, then on The NPIN Web site, then enter "temper tantrums" in the search box.

21. Thumb-Sucking

For children under four years old, thumb-sucking is not a problem and should be ignored. Some doctors and dentists consider it a concern at four years of age and older because the risk of dental problems increases.

If a child who sucks her thumb has many other emotional problems, ignore the thumb-sucking and concentrate on getting her help. Thumb-sucking may be an important comfort for that child. Take no action on thumb-sucking without consulting the parents. They

may want you to ignore the behavior, or they may have some good ideas about how to deal with it.

Preventing Problems

- If the thumb-sucking is a new behavior or has recently returned, meet with the parents to determine if there are any new changes at home that might be causing stress. If the stressful situation will be temporary, ignore the problem for now.

- If not a new behavior, it is likely to be a habit, making it an unconscious behavior and difficult to change.

- Often children will stop sucking their thumbs at around four years of age because other children will poke fun at the habit. This can be an effective way of ending the habit, but the child will need your support to help keep up her self-esteem and to find alternative ways to deal with her stress.

Dealing with Existing Problems

- Redirect the child when she sucks her thumb into something equally comforting. Suggest holding and stroking a stuffed animal or lying on a soft pillow and looking at a book.

- Remember that comforting habits are challenging to break. When she has not sucked her thumb for a time, tell her often, but privately: "You really must be proud of yourself."

- Be aware that even a child who is ready and wanting to stop thumb-sucking will most likely need some help. Because habits become unconscious behaviors, the child will sometimes not realize that she is sucking her thumb. Use a mutually agreed upon visual cue to remind the child that she is sucking her thumb. For example, scratch your head or pull your ear. Be discrete so as not to cause embarrassment.

Resources
Children's Books

Dionne, W. 2001. *Little thumb*. Gretna, La.: Pelican Publishing.

Heitler, S. M. 1996. *David decides about thumb-sucking: A story for children, a guide for parents*. Denver: Reading Matters.

Web Sites

Coping with Stress by Lilian Katz. National Parent Information Network.
www.npin.org. Click on Search, then on The NPIN Virtual Library, then enter "coping with stress" in the search box.

Thumb Sucking. Various articles. FamilyFun. family.go.com. Enter "thumb sucking" in the search box.

Thumb Sucking. drgreene.com. www.drgreene.com. Enter "thumb sucking" in the search box.

Thumb Sucking, Pacifier Use May Damage Children's Teeth. American Dental Association. December 2001. www.ada.org. Enter "thumb sucking" in search box.

Thumb Sucking—Stop It Early. KidSource Online. www.kidsource.com. Click on the pull-down menu, Explore the Site, then click on Search, then enter "thumb sucking" in the search box.

22. Too Loud

A healthy, happy classroom full of active learning is one that has a fairly constant, medium noise level. Expect your class to sound that way. Don't be jealous of the ultra-quiet class next door. Important learning about social skills, language development, self-concept, or a variety of other skills probably is not developing there. Young children cannot get their learning needs met without actively talking and doing. In your classroom, focus on dealing only with talking that is overly loud or strident. A child who seems to always have a loud voice, may have a hearing problem. Refer him for hearing testing and request that a physician check his ears.

Preventing Problems

- Establish a classroom rule: "Use quiet voices inside." Enforce it consistently. Explain the reason for the rule: "A quiet room will keep us all from getting a headache and we will be able to hear each other. Using a quiet voice will also keep you from getting a sore throat."

- Remind the children of the rule before entering the classroom from outside or before they begin a free choice activity.

- Use a calm, quiet voice yourself. Children will raise their voices to match your noise level. Give children plenty of opportunities to talk and to be loud when such behavior is appropriate—outside, in the gym, or when singing an energetic song.

Dealing with Existing Problems

- Tell all the children to remind other children of the classroom rule about quiet voices when they hear someone being loud.

- Ask the child who is being too loud to tell you the rule about quiet voices. Remind him that he will get a chance to be as loud as he wants to be when you go outside: "You have a big strong voice; use it when you get outside."

- For the child who continues to be loud after numerous reminders, use "child choice." Invite him to pick a quiet, solitary activity and return to the group when he feels ready to use a quieter voice.

- If possible, allow the child to go outside and shout for a few minutes. Make sure he is supervised by an adult.

- Remind the child of the quiet rule just before coming in from outside or before free choice. Tell the child individually.

- Thank the child when he uses his voice correctly: "Thank you for speaking quietly. I can easily hear what other children are saying."

23. Won't Listen, Defiance, and Power Struggles

There are a variety of reasons for these behaviors: children who seem to ignore you, do not follow through on rules or directions, or overtly defy what you tell them ("No, I won't do it and you can't make me!"). Be careful to distinguish between not listening because of not being able to focus or remember and not listening deliberately or being defiant. Although all children act this way on occasion, mostly to test your willingness and ability to set and keep limits, some children do these often to assert their needs for power and control.

Children engage adults in power struggles because they are very effective—from the child's perspective! Most adults feel that they have to assert their authority in these situations, which escalates the problem and gives children what they want: attention, power, and control. Children have no legal or ethical restraints on their behavior, as do adults, so the child can always take the power struggle to a "greater" level than the adult and win.

Preventing Problems

- Review the ideas in the first two chapters of this section. For children with intense needs you will have to use many effective prevention strategies.

- Most young children listen better when told something individually rather than as part of a group. Your undivided attention directed at a child tells her clearly that the information is meant for her; it makes the child feel important and helps her to attend. When individual attention is not possible, meet in very small groups with some individual follow-up.

- When talking with children, remove distractions, such as extraneous noises and enticing toys.

Resources
Web Sites

Managing Loud Voices in Inappropriate Places. Parenting Press's Tip and Tool of the Week. June 16, 2001. www.parentingpress.com. Click on Tip Archive, then Guidance and Discipline, then scroll down to article title.

- If possible, back up your verbal information with something visual and with physical action. Most people (children especially) are visual learners but everybody learns best by actually doing or practicing the skill. For example, if you want your children to wash their hands properly, tell them how to do it while showing them. Then have them practice. As a reminder, post pictures above the sink showing proper hand washing.

- Ask the children to repeat back to you, individually, the information they received. Expressing it verbally helps to set it in their minds.

- Use a great deal of variety in your voice. Change the pitch (high and low), speed, and volume often. When you need to make an important point use a slightly louder and faster voice, or a lower and slower voice, than you normally use.

Dealing with Existing Problems
Won't Listen, but Not Defiant

See the chapter, "Active and Distracted" on pp. 135–137 for more ideas.

- If a child doesn't listen, but appears not to be deliberate or defiant, have her hearing tested, as a physical problem may be the cause.

- Some children can't listen because they are overwhelmed by their feelings and emotions. They have too much anxiety. Be patient, nurturing, and supportive. With support and love, in time her anxiety will ease and it will be easier for her to pay attention.

- Experiment with a variety of methods to get the child to attend. Different children have different learning styles. Some children may be able to listen at any time, while others may only be able to focus their attention in certain circumstances.

- Ask the child to look at you before you talk, unless the child's culture or family practices deem this disrespectful to adults.

- Give the child a specific visual cue along with your words. For example, if you want the child to remember not to touch other children, fold your hands together when you tell her each time. Have her do this too. Eventually you can just give the visual cue, and she will recognize it.

- Because some children listen better when touching something or using their hands, teach the child some words in American Sign Language. Or, give the child a stuffed animal or other item to hold when she has to listen.

- Allow the child to lie down or change her position to be more comfortable. This can greatly improve listening skills for some children.

- Try using a slightly louder voice, a quieter voice, or a slower voice to get the child's attention.

- Make physical contact with the child (a hand lightly on the shoulder) when talking to her.

Defiance and Power Struggles

- Be aware of what behaviors directed at you make you most upset or "push your buttons." Then you can remind yourself that you will likely overreact to such behaviors. For some teachers it is a direct, in-your-face "no." For others it is whining, cursing, shouting, or grabbing.

- Although some children learn quickly and well how to "push your buttons," it is important to stay calm. This is difficult because it is likely that your first impulse is to react strongly. Upsetting you and rattling your composure often is the goal of the behavior, as the child then is in control of you.

- Do not ignore the behavior, as that can send a message that the behavior is okay.

- Respond to the defiant statement, "No, you can't make me" by saying calmly and empathetically, "I know you don't want to and I see that you are upset. Yes, I can't make you (clean up, sit down, or whatever), but tell me how I can help you so it's not so hard." Avoid explaining reasons why she should do this, as it is not the issue at this point. If the child still refuses, tell her that you will wait until she is ready. "Until then you can choose to draw a picture or do a puzzle (or some other choice that is acceptable to you and

may help calm her down). When you are ready to do what you need to, then do so." After some time, if she is calmer but has not done the task voluntarily, ask her if she would like your help or if she would like to do it on her own. You can also use the strategy below.

- If possible, remove yourself from the interaction temporarily: walk away or go into another room. Do this only if the child's health and safety is not compromised. This will give you time to calm yourself down, the child to calm down, and stop the power struggle before it starts. Tell the child (as calmly as you can), "I will talk to you later when you can be more respectful (or more calm)." After a time, talk to the child and tell him that you will not respond to such behaviors. If she is angry or needs something, she will have to use respectful words or actions. Give her some words or actions she can use (tapping your arm rather than hitting or grabbing) and have her practice them. Then respond calmly to her needs or concerns.

- The next time she attempts to engage you in a power struggle, stop her quickly and say calmly, "Remember to be respectful if you want me to respond."

- Have her practice better ways of getting your attention or responding to you when she does not want to do something during small group or free choice times, not during an incident or when she is upset.

Resources

Barkley, R. A., and C. M. Benton. 1998. *Your defiant child.* New York: Guilford Press.

Riley, D. A. 2002. *The defiant child: A parent's guide to oppositional defiant disorder.* Cutton, Calif.: Taylor Publishing.

Taylor, J. F. 2001. *From defiance to cooperation: Real solutions for transforming the angry, defiant, discouraged child.* Roseville, Calif.: Prima Publishing.

Web Sites

Eighteen Ways to Avoid Power Struggles by Jane Nelson. Positive Discipline. www.positivediscipline.com. Click on For Parents, then on Articles for Parents, then scroll down to article title.

Responding to Backtalk. Parenting Press's Tip and Tool of the Week. April 15, 2000. www.parentingpress.com. Click on Tip Archive, then Guidance and Discipline, then scroll down to article.

Power Struggles. Numerous articles. Parenting Press's Tip and Tool of the Week www.parentingpress.com. Click on Tip Archive, then Power Struggles, then scroll down to article

When "No" Is Your Child's Favorite Word. Parenting Press's Tip and Tool of the Week. November 3, 2001. www.parentingpress.com. Click on Tip Archive, then Guidance and Discipline, then scroll down to article.

Part VI

Working with Parents and Families

1. The Challenge of Connecting with All Parents: Creating Partnerships

The terms "parents" and "families" in this section of the book refer to any primary caretakers of a child in your class, including grandparents, foster parents, aunts, older siblings, or others.

Although some parents will present a variety of challenges to you, most parents are appreciative and look to you for support and advice. Parents are under great pressure. Most parents of young children are not young themselves, or are early in their careers and not earning as much as they need. This is a particularly difficult time and America is a particularly difficult place to raise a family. Almost all other industrialized countries have child and family policies that are more supportive and generous—paid parental leave, more paid vacation time, and subsidized early childhood programs for all children. Like early childhood teachers, parents are underpaid, underappreciated, and overworked! (See The War Against Parents, by Hewlitt and West in resources at the end of this chapter)

While we all are working to change this situation, the best strategy for coping is to create mutual empathy and to partner with parents for the benefit of the child. This is a very different relationship than customer/client, amateur/professional, or needy one/helper. It is an equal relationship where both you and the parents have important contributions to make. You both have expertise in certain, and usually different, areas. By working together, you both are better off, both your jobs are easier, and the child is the big winner.

You can do many things to establish and maintain a partnership with families. Don't leave it to chance or just let it happen; that will result in partnerships with only the few families with whom you have an affinity. Deliberate actions on your part will help establish partnerships with many more of your families.

What You Bring to the Partnership

▶ Distance and perspective that comes from less intense emotional involvement with the child than the parents have.

▶ An understanding of the child as compared to other children and what is "typical" behavior for the child's age.

▶ Experience working with many different children and families, and expertise in certain areas.

▶ Knowledge of good resources: people, agencies, print and online materials (see resources at the end of the chapter).

▶ Information categorized by subject (files of articles, book lists, Web sites).

▶ Ideas and a variety of strategies for helping with problems.

▶ An empathetic ear.

What Parents Bring to the Partnership

▶ Expertise about their child.

▶ Knowledge and experience in many areas.

▶ Information about their child in the context of the home, family, and neighborhood—many children act very differently at home than at school.

▶ A stronger emotional connection to their child and greater concern.

▶ Advocacy for getting the best for their child.

Attitude Is Number One

Your attitude gets expressed in every interaction with families—often nonverbally and unintentionally. When you meet with families sitting next to each other or across a table, it sends a "partnership" message. When you sit behind a desk or on an adult chair and they sit on a small chair, it sends a very different message.

Approach All Interactions with a "Partnership" Attitude

● Don't assume. Instead, ask for information or make tentative statements. "What have you already tried to solve the problem?" "Am I correct in thinking that your wife is Jason's stepmom?"

● Offer yourself as a resource and support, rather than an expert. "Is there anything I can do to help?"

● Offer expertise, if you have it, only when asked for. If neither you nor the parents have the needed information, say, "Let's find some resources to get more information."

- Approach all issues from a "strength" perspective. Assume that families are doing the best they can. Find the strengths and positive aspects of your families. In conflicts with families, usually each of you has the same goals but different methods. Focus on the goals.

- Make sure all written materials reflect a partnership approach. The "voice" used in written materials, including policies and procedures, should be supportive and express concern for the well-being of the child and family. That is, after all, the reason for policies and procedures.

- Start off right. Do a home visit, if the family feels comfortable, or meet early in the relationship. Use most of your time in those first interactions to establish a trusting relationship.

- Keep the "program requirements" information to a minimum. Ask such questions as

  ▶ What do I need to know about your child to be a very good teacher for her?

  ▶ What are her strengths and interests or favorite activities?

  ▶ What are your goals for her this year?

  ▶ What three adjectives describe her best?

  ▶ How does she deal with stress?

- Make your approach and expectations clear ahead of time, especially for potentially controversial issues like celebrating holidays, teaching academics, dealing with swearing, and other challenging behaviors.

Parents Who Are "Different"

If the primary caretakers are not the child's biological father and mother, they will have particular needs to which you will want to be sensitive so that they feel included and respected. So much of our interactions with parents and resources developed for parents assume that they are the biological parents. The same is true for parents with other "differences," such as single parents, adoptive parents, stepparents, parents of biracial children, immigrant parents with little or no English, ethnically diverse parents, gay or lesbian parents, and more. This is not to imply that these families are "needy" or not healthy and happy. It is just important to have a heightened awareness and some skills so that you can be responsive and sensitive in your interactions with them. This will go a long way toward developing positive relations, which is necessary to successfully share the task of helping that child grow.

- Use the ideas and resources in previous chapters to respond to the needs of the children from families who are "different." It is important that the children know that their unique families are seen, validated, and important. This helps counteract the many places and times when they feel that their particular family is invisible or diminished. It also provides tremendous support for the parents.

- Try to talk with someone from the same "community" who can give you insight into the issues, values, views, and strengths of your "different" family. Ask what terms you should use to describe the family that are supportive and not demeaning—how do they like to refer to themselves or have others refer to them?

- At your initial meeting, ask, "What can I do to make sure your family and your child feel fully included and valued?"

- Provide translations of materials in the families' languages and arrange for interpreters when meeting. If there are no funds for this, often the family has a relative or friend they can use for this purpose.

- Talk about your approach to discussing and including all families throughout your curriculum and ask for suggestions.

Parents with Special Needs

You will occasionally work with parents who may have a disability, such as a developmental delay, hearing or visual impairment, physical disability, or mental health problems. These present particular challenges, especially if the disability seems to get in the way of the child's healthy development (mostly true where parents have an emotional or cognitive disability). In most cases, the parents will have a "case worker" and other support people, such as relatives. Meet with this person or persons to get information about the family and learn strategies for being helpful. Make sure you can access and get permission to call on any key health professionals who work with the family during the year as questions and issues arise.

- Meet with the parents early, often, and regularly to stay on top of issues. Ask open-ended questions to determine how to best support them and their child.

- If there is a problem or concern, go directly to the parents about it first. Use your knowledge of them to approach the issue in a supportive way that the parents will understand. Go to their support persons next, if the problem does not seem to get resolved.

● Find out as much as you can about the particular disability and how it is manifested in adults and these adults in particular. You may be able to find information about the typical needs of children of parents with that particular disability. Health providers are a good source for this.

● Individualize your interactions with the child. Get to know the child well and do not make assumptions. Different children will respond differently to similar circumstances and have different needs. In one case, developmentally delayed parents had a child who was gifted. She needed help with some very basic hygiene skills, but also needed to be intellectually challenged.

● If you have serious concerns about the welfare of the child, discuss the issue with their support persons. Also, see the chapter "Parents Who May Be Abusive to Their Children" on p. 176 if you suspect abuse or neglect.

Resources

Boutte, G. S., D. L. Keepler, V. S. Tyler, and B. Z. Terry. 1992. Effective techniques for involving "difficult" parents. *Young Children* 47 (3): 19–22.

Diffily, D., and K. Morrison, eds. 1996. *Family-friendly communications for early childhood programs*. Washington, D.C.: NAEYC.

Farber, B., ed. 1997. *The parents' and teachers' guide to helping young children learn: Creative ideas from thirty-five respected experts*. Cutchogue, N.Y.: Preschool Publications.

Hewitt, D. 1997. *So this is normal too? Teachers and parents working out developmental issues in young children*. St. Paul: Redleaf Press.

Hewlett, S. A., and C. West. 1999. *The war against parents*. New York: Mariner Books.

Koch, P., and M. McDonough. 1999. Improving parent-teacher conferences through collaborative conversations. *Young Children* 54 (2): 11–15

Lally, J. R., C. Lerner, and E. Lurie-Hurvitz. 2001. National survey reveals gaps in the public's and parents' knowledge about early childhood development. *Young Children* 56 (2): 49–53.

MacDonald, S. 2000. *Idea bags: Activities to promote the school-to-home connection*. Torrance, Calif.: Frank Schaffer Publications.

———. 2002. *Idea bags for the kitchen: Activities to promote the school-to-home connection*. New York: Fearon/Janus/Quercus.

Rockwell, R. E., M. K. Hawley, and L. C. Andre. 1996. *Parents and teachers as partners: A guide for early childhood educators*. San Diego: Singular Publishing.

Walker-Dalhouse, D., and A. D. Dalhouse. 2001. Parent-school relations: Communicating more effectively with African American parents. *Young Children* 56 (4): 75–80.

Parent Education Programs (some are also for teachers)

Active Parenting Today
810-B Franklin Court, Marietta, GA 30067
www.activeparenting.com

The Incredible Years. Teachers, Parents, and Children Training Series.
1411 8th Avenue West, Seattle, WA 98119
www.incredibleyears.com

Parent Effectiveness Training (PET)
531 Stevens Avenue West, Solana Beach, CA 92075
www.thomasgordon.com

Parenting Works! Raising Preschool Children
SI Video, P. O. Box 968, Englewood, FL 34295
www.sivideo.com/parenting

Positive Parenting
University of Minnesota Extension Service
240 Coffey Hall, 1420 Eckles Avenue, St. Paul, MN 55108
www.extension.umn.edu. Click on Family, then on Positive Parenting.

Project SUCCEED (Supporting and Understanding Challenging Children's Emotional and Educational Development)
Portland State University, Regional Research Institute, P. O. Box 751, Portland, OR 97207
www.rri.pdx.edu

Videos

High/Scope Press
600 North River Street
Ypsilanti, MI 48198-2898
www.highscope.org
Involving Families in Active Learning Settings, 23 min.

Educational Productions
9000 SW Gemini Drive
Beaverton, OR 97008
www.edpro.com
The Parent Education Collection. Five 30-min. videos.

Web Sites

Children of Alcoholics. American Academy of Child and Adolescent Psychiatry. Facts for Families #17. www.aacap.org. Link through Facts for Families, then scroll down to article title.

Children of Parents with Mental Illness. American Academy of Child and Adolescent Psychiatry. Facts for Families #39. www.aacap.org. Link through Facts for Families, then scroll down to article title.

Communicating with Parents. Many articles. National Network for Child Care. www.nncc.org. Click on Articles and Resources, then on Child Care Family Relationships, then on Building Positive Relationships.

Teacher-Parent Relations. Various articles. Earlychildhood.com. www.earlychildhood.com/Articles/index.cfm. Click on Family Support.

Comprehensive Sites—Access to Information Targeted to Parents on Many Topics

American Academy of Child and Adolescent Pyschiatry. See especially Facts for Families link. www.aacap.org

Center for Effective Parenting. See especially Parenting Handouts link. www.parenting-ed.org

FamilyFun. See especially Raising Kids link. www.family.go.com

KinderStart search engine. See especially Child Development link. www.kinderstart.com

National Parent Information Network. See especially Virtual Library, then Full Text Resources. www.npin.org

Parenting Press. See especially Tip Archive link. www.parentingpress.com

Parent Soup. Scroll down to topics or use the search box. www.parentsoup.com

Online Parenting Courses

Eight Weeks to a Well-Behaved Child: Putting Discipline Skills to Work. Effective Parenting Strategies with James Windell. www.jameswindell.com

A Certificate for Parenting. Canadian Society for the Prevention of Cruelty to Children. parenting.telecampus.com

Practical Parenting Plus. Practical Parent. www.practicalparent.org.uk. Scroll down to Online Parenting Course.

Principles of Parenting. The Alabama Cooperative Extension Service, Auburn University. www.humsci.auburn.edu/parent

2. Parents Who Want You to Teach Reading

All parents want their children to excel and be successful. For some, this desire means reading before first grade. However, knowing how to read does not necessarily mean a child is interested in or enjoys reading. Children who learn to read early are not always better or more avid readers than other children when they are older. Pushing children to read before they are ready may make them feel negative about books and reading. It promotes reading as a skill to perform, rather than as a process to enjoy. However, for young children who are ready and interested in learning to read, it is important to help them do so. For most children, creating a program that promotes a love of books, helping them understand the purpose of written language and promoting oral language development, is the best way to teach young children to "read."

Preventing Problems

- Assure parents that reading is being taught. Young children in your class are learning to read by

  ‣ Being exposed to good literature and a great deal of print and books.

  ‣ Having many opportunities to write and being challenged to write better.

  ‣ Being encouraged to recognize and write their own names and those of the other children.

  ‣ Dictating stories that are written down by adults and then read to them or by them.

  ‣ Seeing the pictures they draw labeled.

  ‣ Becoming good at rhyming.

  ‣ Hearing and using new words.

- Explain that this is teaching reading to preschoolers in an appropriate way. It is not just prereading or reading readiness. Develop a written statement about this issue to give to parents who are looking at your program or who are new to the program. Make this part of a parent handbook (either for your class or for the whole program). Post the statement in the class-room. Ask new parents what their opinions are on teaching reading to determine if your philosophy and their's mesh.

- Save examples of children's work, such as stories they have dictated to you, signs they have made, their attempts at writing, pictures they have made that are labeled, and similar items, to show to parents as examples of reading and writing development in your class.

Develop a Sensible Plan for Teaching Reading and Writing

Use all or some of the following ideas and information to develop an approach to reading and writing development for your preschoolers. Explain your approach to parents.

Read Aloud Often

- Reading stories that children enjoy is one of the best ways to ensure that they will become readers in the future. Do this often (at least once a day in half-day programs and twice in full-day programs) and let parents know you are doing it.

- Select books carefully. Choose those that will hold the children's interest and will not be too difficult to follow. Use original versions of classic children's literature and avoid watered-down updates. If the children start to get restless, stop reading. Continue the book at a later time or choose a more interesting book to read. Read with enthusiasm and expression in your voice.

- Read aloud to individual or small groups of children at various times of the day, including free choice.

Silent Reading

- Set aside a short time when everyone, including the adults, is quietly looking at or reading books. Afterward, meet in small groups and have each child who wishes tell everyone his favorite part or picture. This develops a respect for the process of reading, that it is usually a quiet/private activity, and a sense that books are enjoyable. Post information about this part of the day on your schedule so that parents are aware that it takes place.

Avoid Worksheets

Children who learn reading and writing skills from workbooks do not become better readers than children who learn those skills from hearing stories,

dictating stories, doing art, writing stories, having fun browsing through books, singing and rhyming, and seeing print and hearing it read in many different places and forms. Examples of print in various forms include signs and labels in the room and outside on the street, names in cubbies and on charts, simple graphs, and classroom shelves labeled with pictures and writing. Remember that worksheets force children to be too passive and to learn rote skills. As you know, children learn more when they actively participate in the real activity and handle actual books and reading materials. Make parents aware of this.

Individualize

Most children are interested and ready to read between six and seven years of age. The children in your class who are younger than this and yet are ready and interested in reading will have many opportunities to do so through the methods discussed in this chapter. Provide additional assistance to them, however, and give them as much help as they need to read a bit better than they could on their own. Start with words that are emotionally important to them: mommy and daddy; family, friends, and pets' names; and favorite toys or animals. Make simple books together. Provide some enjoyable, easy-to-read books such as those by Dr. Seuss. For many children, *Hop on Pop* or *Green Eggs and Ham* are the first books they read independently.

- For all children, give individualized assistance in the area of language and vocabulary development, writing letters or simple words, reading simple words ("stop" on a stop sign, "push" on a door), decoding symbols (number symbols, graphic symbols like those found on road signs and bathroom doors), rhyming and breaking down words into their sound parts through songs, poems, and finger plays. Give various kinds of help so that you stretch children's abilities slightly and do not give too much, or too little help.

Promote Language Development

Good language skills and a good vocabulary are closely tied to developing good reading and writing skills. Show parents that you demonstrate good speaking skills, encourage children to use language as much and as well as they are able, and expose them to many new words and phrases.

- Establish a sharing time when children who wish to can formally speak to the rest of the children, who in turn respond by asking questions and sharing insights.

- Use mealtimes as a time for children to use language to get food passed, milk poured, and so on.

- Teach many songs and read stories that contain new words. Explain the meaning of the words to the children.

- Set up board games and dramatic play areas where the children will want to talk to each other in order to work out roles, ideas, and rules.

- Recite finger plays and poems and sing songs that involve rhyming. Leave off words on occasion so children can "catch" the rhyme and say it on their own.

Create a "Literate" Classroom

- Having a print-rich classroom will make it obvious to parents when they look around your room that learning to read is encouraged and highly valued. Create this kind of classroom by including the following:

  ▶ Signs that have pictures and words on them.

  ▶ A daily sign-in sheet for children to write their names when they arrive.

  ▶ Turn-taking sheets, where children sign up to use a popular toy or area of the room, then cross off their names and call the next child on the sheet when they are done.

  ▶ Displays of children's writing on the walls and bulletin boards.

  ▶ A cozy book corner with soft pillows and many books displayed attractively.

  ▶ Marking pens and blank sheets of paper available in the block area, dramatic play area, and art area.

  ▶ Alphabet games, letter puzzles, magnetic letters, sandpaper letters, cookie cutter letters, and so on available on open shelves.

  ▶ Labels on items in the room, such as the word *window* printed on a strip of paper and taped to the window.

  ▶ Children's names written and posted for jobs to do, on birthday charts, to identify cubbies, and many other ways.

  ▶ A dramatic play area set up as an office, hospital, post office, library, or similar place so children can emulate the reading and writing that adults do in those places.

  ▶ Shelves and toy containers labeled with pictures, symbols, and/or words that children match when putting things away.

  ▶ Sets of "key words"—words that have emotional importance to children, such as mommy, daddy, friends' names, names of favorite toys, things that are scary—that children who are starting to sight-read have in their vocabulary.

Be Aware of Potential Problems

The best predictor in young children of being a good reader in later childhood is having good language skills. So children with poor language skills (making many grammatical errors, using only a few words in a sentence, very limited vocabulary) are a cause for concern. Use a simple screening tool for language as discussed in the chapter "Suspected Disabilities" on p. 67. Make a referral to a speech and language specialist for testing and evaluation. Catching the problem early can be very helpful in preventing reading problems.

Resources

Ashton-Warner, S. 1986. *Teacher.* New York: Touchstone Books.

Burns, M. S., P. Griffin, and C. Snow, eds. 1999. *Starting out right: A guide to promoting children's reading success.* Washington, D.C.: National Academy Press.

Davidson, J. I. 1996. *Emergent literacy and dramatic play in early education.* Albany, N.Y.: Delmar Publishers.

Fox, M. 2001. *Reading magic: Why reading aloud to our children will change their lives forever.* New York: Harvest Books.

Greenberg, P. 1990. Ideas that work with young children. Why not academic preschool? Part 1. *Young Children* 45 (2): 70–80.

———. 1992. Autocracy or democracy in the classroom? Why not academic preschool? Part 2. *Young Children* 47 (3): 54–64.

Neuman, S., C. Copple, and S. Bredekamp. 1999. *Learning to read and write: Developmentally appropriate practices for young children.* Washington, D.C.: NAEYC.

Owocki, G. 1999. *Literacy through play.* Portsmouth, N.H.: Heinemann.

———. 2001. *Make way for literacy: Teaching the way young children learn.* Washington, D.C.: NAEYC and Portsmouth, N.H.: Heinemann.

Roskos, K., and J. F. Christie. 2002. Knowing in the doin': Observing literacy learning in play. *Young Children* 57 (2): 46–54.

Schickedanz, J. A. 1999. *Much more than the ABCs: The early stages of reading and writing.* Washington, D.C.: NAEYC.

Videos

Educational Productions
9000 SW Gemini Drive
Beaverton, OR 97008
www.edpro.com
Bigger Than Books: Promoting Literacy by Reading Aloud, two videos, 30 min. each

Washington Research Institute
150 Nickerson Street, Suite 305
Seattle, Washington 98109
www.wri-edu.org
Language Is the Key (available in five languages), two videos,
20 min. each

Web Sites

Critical Issue: Addressing the Literacy Needs of Emergent and Early Readers. North Central Regional Educational Laboratory. www.ncrel.org/sdrs. Click on Literacy, then scroll down to article title.

Early Literacy. Various articles. Earlychildood.com www.earlychildhood.com/Articles/index.cfm. Click on Early Literacy.

Early Literacy. Numerous resources from The Knowledge Loom. knowledgeloom.org/literacy/index.jsp

Learning to Read and Write. Joint position statement of NAEYC and International Reading Association. www.naeyc.org. Click on Resources, then Position Statements, then scroll down to and click on Improving practices with young children, then scroll down to article.

Literacy. Many articles specific to young children. Early Childhood Educators' and Family Web Page. users.stargate.net/~cokids. Click on Teacher Pages, then scroll down and click on Literacy.

3. Complaining Parents————

Most parents are very reasonable and simply want the best for their children. Provide an easy, comfortable way for them to give you feedback. Don't ignore legitimate complaints. Take their input seriously and act on requests whenever feasible. When parents see that you are responsive you will win their favor and support.

Some parents, however, make unreasonable requests or complain very often. The suggestions in this chapter will help you minimize complaining behaviors from parents and give you constructive ways to deal with unreasonable complainers.

Preventing Problems

● Meet with parents before or soon after the child enters your class. At this meeting, make your goals, philosophy, and expectations clear to avoid misconceptions.

● Let parents know that they are welcome in your classroom to observe and participate at any time.

● Give parents a parent handbook about your center, school, or classroom. If your program does not have a handbook, volunteer to be on a committee to develop one. Write one for your classroom because they are a must for good parent relations.

● Ask for input from the parents about what they would like their child to gain.

● Ask parents to help in the classroom if possible or to help in another way (go on a field trip, make a pillow for the book area, and so on).

● Welcome parents to be involved with your class in any way or on any level with which they feel comfortable.

● Provide information about your goals, philosophy, and expectations to all new parents. Provide this through written materials (in the parents' native language) and verbally (to reinforce the written information and to help parents who are uncomfortable with reading).

● Before presenting information to your children that may cause some parents concern (sex education, sex-abuse prevention strategies, antiracism education, and so on), send written information home about what you will be doing and arrange a meeting with all interested parents to discuss the issue.

● Tell parents often about the great things their children say and do. Write these comments down for them. Send notes home often to let parents know the wonderful things you and the children are doing.

● Schedule regular parent meetings (perhaps one every other month) with the parents of the children in your class to allow parents to speak their minds, express concerns, and ask questions. Whenever you meet with a group of parents, arrange the chairs in a circle. When you meet with individual parents, sit near them rather than across a desk. This sets the stage for working together as partners, not adversaries.

● Communicate with parents and encourage parents to communicate with you as much as possible. Use bulletin boards, letters home, forms for parents to return, a notebook that children can carry between school and home daily (this makes children feel grown up too), informal chats, meetings, conferences, and so on.

● Ask to visit the children in your class and their parents at their homes. At least once during the year invite all the families to your home (perhaps for a backyard barbecue) or on a field trip. Or, if you prefer, invite the families to your home one at a time.

Dealing with Existing Problems

Chronic Complainer

● Act quickly, as unresolved concerns make matters worse and an unhappy parent may be talking with other parents.

● Assume that there is a misunderstanding or miscommunication. Take a positive, problem-solving approach.

● Set up a meeting with the complaining parent, yourself, and your supervisor to get at the root cause of her unhappiness. It may have to do with the rates, a recent loss of income, marriage problems, guilt about not being home with her child, or some other cause over which you have little control. Remember that a sympathetic ear may be a big help. Ask for the parents' advice about how you can assist them in solving the problem.

Behind Your Back

A parent, or a few parents, may be unhappy about the program, a policy, the food, or another concern but not let you or the director know. Instead, they will "network" with other parents to get support for their cause. In time everyone's anger will build up and suddenly, one day, you may feel as if you are being confronted by an angry mob. Worst of all, you will not even realize that there is a problem. Parents do this because they want their perceptions verified and because there is safety in numbers.

● Don't try to deal with the problem without preparation and help from your supervisor, supportive parents, and other staff. Arrange for a meeting where all the people involved can get together. Invite to the meeting a neutral third party, such as a supportive parent or a sympathetic board member.

The Angry Parent

● When confronted with an irate parent, regardless of the cause, just listen at first. Don't defend yourself, even if the parent is clearly misguided or misinformed. Remember that challenging the person only fuels the fire of her anger. Listen intently and sympathetically and use active listening techniques such as

reflection ("What happened is really upsetting," "That really is a serious problem") and clarification ("What I hear you saying is that . . ." "Tell me more about exactly what happened next"). This should diffuse much of the anger.

● Apologize. Even if the problem was clearly not your fault, you can apologize for the anguish that the misunderstanding caused the parent. In many cases, this is all the parent is looking for.

● Tell the parent that you will do what you can to ease her concern. If you need more information or advice about the problem, tell her what you will do and when you will get back to her. Waiting a day or two will often put the problem in its correct perspective, even if the parent felt that the end of the world had come at the time. Remember that some form of compensation can help a great deal: "I wish I could replace the lost jacket. I can't, but I can offer you one of the jackets from our extra clothes box. I'm sorry I can't do better."

● When the immediate anger has cooled, you may be able to offer an explanation or rationale—your side of the story. Be aware, however, that some people are not interested in, nor are they able to, reason. If this is the case, empathize with their concern and say what you have done to make sure the problem will not happen again. Leave the situation at that.

Complaints about Your Curriculum or Style

This problem typically happens over clashes in values. You believe, for example, that children have the right to know the facts (appropriate to their age level) about sexual orientation or death. However, some parents believe that young children should not hear this information or that it should come only from parents. These parents may get very emotional and let you know clearly of their concerns.

● Meet with the parents to give them a forum for their concerns. Let them know that arguing with you in your classroom during class time is not acceptable. Invite all interested parents. Make sure that some are there who support your approach. Discuss your perspective calmly using documented principles of early childhood development or recommendations from experts. Invite a local child development expert to the meeting. Acknowledge the validity of the parents' concerns and feelings. In *Anti-Bias Curriculum* (1989), Louise Derman-Sparks recommends the following options:

▶ Request that the parents allow their child to participate in the activities and meet again to discuss the results.

▶ Continue discussions and meetings while the activities are carried out.

▶ If possible and if acceptable to you, come to some compromises, such as dropping one or two activities or modifying your approach slightly. But don't abandon your values or curriculum or style.

A Last Resort

The director or the parent may ultimately decide that the parent might be happier in another program or school. This is a difficult decision, but it may be a necessary one if the parent's expectations or wishes cannot be realistically met. Remember that your program cannot meet every family's needs.

Resources

Bernstein, A. J. 2000. *Emotional vampires: Dealing with people who drain you dry.* New York: McGraw-Hill.

Bernstein, A. J., and S. C. Rozen. 1996. *Dinosaur brains: Dealing with all those impossible people at work.* New York: Ballantine Books.

Bramson, R. M. 1988. *Coping with difficult people.* New York: Dell Books.

Derman-Sparks, L. 1989. *Anti-bias curriculum: Tools for empowering young children.* Washington, D.C.: NAEYC.

Fisher, R., and W. Ury. 1991. *Getting to yes: Negotiating agreement without giving in.* New York: Penguin.

Galinsky, E. 1988. Parents and teacher-caregivers: Sources of tension, sources of support. *Young Children* 43 (3): 4–12.

Greenberg, P. 1989. Parents as partners in young children's development and education: A new American fad? Why does it matter? *Young Children* 44 (4):61–74.

Myers, P., and D. Nance. 1994. *The upset book: A guide for dealing with upset people.* Notre Dame, Ind.: Academic Publications.

Web Sites

Tips on How to Deal with Difficult People. British Broadcasting Corporation.
www.bbc.co.uk. Enter "difficult people" in the search box.

Dealing with Difficult People. Various articles. Bascal and Associates.
www.work911.com. Click on Articles by Robert Bascal, then scroll down to Communication and Conflict Related.

Dealing with Difficult People. Concern—Employee Assistance Program.
www.concern-eap.com. Click on FYI Library, then scroll down to article title.

4. Parents Who Are in a Hurry

Parenting today is very hard. Many parents are single or are struggling financially. Even well-off parents with spouses have difficult lives trying to balance work and family obligations. Most parents feel they have put in forty-eight hours at the end of each day. Be understanding of their situations and why they are always in a hurry.

Some parents hurry out the door for helpful reasons. They know that their child will continue to cry or act out until they leave. Because they do not want to prolong the problem, they leave quickly out of consideration for you and the class. Some parents want to spend as little time as possible in your class because they find it stressful.

Preventing Problems

● Say a kind word to parents when they pick up their child at the end of a hard day. Avoid talking about their child's problem behaviors or other concerns at this time. Doing that more formally at a less stressful time is a wiser option. Use the phone for busy working parents.

● Choose your words carefully. When a parent picks up a child who is being fussy at the end of the day and you say, "I didn't have any trouble with him today," the parent may interpret that as meaning, "I can handle your child better than you." Instead of this, say, "Many children are fussy at the end of the day. What can I do to help?" (Galinsky 1988).

● Offer a cup of coffee, tea, or juice to parents when they arrive to pick up their child. Set up an area in your room or, if your room is not large enough, somewhere nearby where parents can sit for a minute and relax. Provide comfortable seating, something to drink, and some helpful parenting books or articles. By doing this you give parents the clear message that their presence is welcomed.

● Provide many convenient ways for parents to communicate with you. Give them your home phone number, because busy parents often have to take care of things after working hours. However, put clear limits on when the parent can call you, such as, only between 7:30 and 9:00 P.M.

• Set up the situation so parents have to spend only a little time at the beginning and at the end of the day dealing with any additional stress. Make signing children in and out easy and convenient for parents and organize the children's cubbies so that they are easy to find and get to. Make sure children have gathered their belongings, art work, and messages together and placed them in their cubbies before parents arrive. Have children wash their faces and hands before the end of the day. Most parents associate this with being well cared for. Your thoughtfulness will also save parents time and stress if they need to go to the store or to a doctor's office directly from school.

Dealing with Existing Problems

• Tell the parent about the importance of staying for a few relaxed minutes when leaving or picking up his child. Explain that this helps the child move between school and home. Parents will have to build the time into their schedule by leaving home or work a few minutes earlier.

• Suggest a specific activity that the parent and child can do together each day at "pick-up time." The ritual nature of it helps establish a routine. It should be reasonably short but not something that is hurried. It should have a clear end to it, so the child will know it is time to go when the activity is over. For example, they can read a favorite story together, do a puzzle, or listen to a song.

• Ask the parent who hurries to find a few minutes to talk to you so you can help him think of ways to save time and reduce stress. This will give you information about the reason for the hurrying and insights into how to help. It will also make you very appreciated by most parents.

• Help the parent by brainstorming solutions together for easing the rush and stress. Set a plan of action to implement the one or two best solutions. Meet again to evaluate the results; to revise the plan, if it is not working; or to tackle a new problem if it is. Be assured that the best plans involve you, the parent, and the child in making some changes or adjustments.

Resources

Galinsky, E. 1988. Parents and teacher-caregivers: Sources of tension, sources of support. *Young Children* 43 (3): 4–12.

Greenberg, P. 1989. Parents as partners in young children's development and education: A new American fad? Why does it matter? *Young Children* 44 (4): 61–74.

Hewitt, D. 1997. *So this is normal too? Teachers and parents working out developmental issues in young children.* St. Paul: Redleaf Press.

Hewlett, S., and C. West. 1999. *The war against parents.* New York: Mariner Books.

Rockwell, R. E., M. K. Hawley, and L. C. Andre. 1996. *Parents and teachers as partners: A guide for early childhood educators.* San Diego: Singular Publishing.

5. Parents Who Linger

Another result of stress in the lives of parents may be their need for support wherever they can find it. Many early childhood teachers are experts at giving support and parents take more then full advantage of it. This may mean that you have parents who demand your time and attention when you need to focus on the children or get home to your own family.

Another reason parents may linger is because they have trouble separating from their children. They feel guilty or remorseful about leaving them. The stress facing them at work or at home may be a further inducement not to leave too fast. They may also find the classroom to be a comfortable, enjoyable place—a pleasant break from the office or home.

Preventing Problems

• Have a written statement in your parent handbook with guidelines for leave-taking at the start of the day. In the statement, recommend that parents stay for no more than ten minutes at the start and at the end of the day, unless they are actively participating in the morning's activities. If they need to talk to teachers for longer than that, encourage them to make an appointment.

• Describe a helpful procedure for bringing and picking up children. (See "Dealing with Existing Problems," below, for an example.) Have a message pad posted by the door. This will allow parents to leave you notes without disturbing your work with the children.

Dealing with Existing Problems

- Tell the parent: "I don't want to interfere, and I enjoy your company. I'm concerned, however, that the mornings might be stressful for Anna. She never knows how long it will be before you will leave. I have some ideas for helping, if you would like to hear them, and you probably have some too." Discuss solutions together. Tell the parent that she might consider the following solution: "Tell your child that you will read one book to her and then will be leaving. When it is finished, you will give one kiss, say goodbye once, and then leave promptly." If reading a book is disruptive of the morning's activity, you can suggest another activity or that she can tell her child she will leave at the end of one of your activities.

- If the problem happens at the end of the day, try the following ideas:

  - Tell the parent you would love to chat longer but must attend to the children and be ready to leave by a specified time. Set a time to meet with the parent when the appointment would be more convenient for you.

  - Tell the parent you will call her later that evening.

  - Have the parent write you a note.

  - Ask the parent to help you close up and leave.

- Involve the parent who lingers in an activity that is helpful to you (preparing some art materials, cleaning, or giving one-on-one assistance to certain children). Ask her to tell you exactly how long she will be staying. Make sure she is familiar with your policies and procedures. Request a regular schedule from her if she will be involved in the classroom. Remind her that consistency and routines are vital to feelings of security in young children.

- Some parents may want to get too involved, interfering in your plans and your approach to teaching and caring. Be aware that they may be doing their children a disservice by not allowing them the space to become independent. Set clear limits about what the parent can and cannot do. Assign her some tasks that will keep her involved with many different children and some that do not involve children at all.

6. Telling Parents about the Difficult Behavior of Their Children

Many teachers dread having to confront a parent with information about their child's behavior. They worry that the parent may become upset, defensive, blame the teacher, or perhaps react too negatively toward their child. However, it is worse not to keep parents informed about their children. This chapter explains ways to talk to parents that minimize strong negative reactions.

If you work in a full-day program, be sure to avoid the all-too-typical routine of informing a parent at 5:45 P.M. how "awful" her child has been during the day. At this time everyone is short-tempered, tired, hungry, irrational. There is no time or space to deal with the concerns properly. Use the following suggestions as a guide to alternatives.

Preventing Problems

- Throughout the year, share a great deal of positive information about their children with parents. Do this daily if possible. Win the trust of parents through helpful, positive, and supportive communications. Show empathy and understanding, and be responsive to their concerns. If you do this, the parents will treat your concerns seriously and respectfully.

- On an ongoing basis, inform parents about how their children are doing. Meet with them when you first see signs of a problem. Don't spring any big surprises. Teachers often avoid doing this because it is difficult, stressful, and many times they can remedy the problem themselves or the child adjusts or matures. However, you must inform parents early, in case the problem does not improve or gets worse. They also may be able to give you vital insights into the concern or know of simple solutions. This can save you weeks of stress. When you meet early on, share your ideas for dealing with the problem, ask for advice, and present a positive outlook for solving it.

- Don't talk to parents about problems when you are in a hurry or will have distractions. Set up a time when you will both have ample time to fully work through the concern. Meet in a place that is relaxing as there will naturally be stress. Arrange the seating so that you are near to each other, or directly across from each other at the same table. This gives the message that you are working together on a problem. Set a specific starting and ending time.

• When you set up a meeting to talk with parents about a concern, tell them the concern specifically and briefly: "I've noticed that Mark is hitting other children. Let's set up a time to talk about helping him." Avoid saying anything such as, "We need to talk about your child." This phrase causes great anxiety and stress for parents.

Dealing with Existing Problems

• Set an agenda with parents before you start, such as the following:

  ▶ You share facts and observations.

  ▶ Parents share their thoughts and concerns and possible reasons for the behavior.

  ▶ You share any additional insight and your current strategies for dealing with the problem at school.

  ▶ Together, you and the parents brainstorm solutions and strategies for school and home.

  ▶ You and the parents develop a plan of action for the best solutions.

  ▶ Set a date to meet again to evaluate the effectiveness of the plan.

• Start the conference by talking about the child's strengths and good points. End the conference on a positive note by reaffirming those strengths.

• When sharing your concern, present objective information. "Mark hit a child at 9:00 A.M. when he wanted the toy the child was playing with. After I talked with Mark about other ways to get a turn, he hit the child again at 9:10. At 9:45, he hit a child on the playground who accidentally bumped into him. At 10:30 he punched the child sitting next to him at snack. I did not see a reason for this."

• Consider parents to be the experts on their children. Take their suggestions seriously and listen to their ideas.

• Follow your agenda and end on time. Note that if the conference lasts too long, parents will be reluctant to meet again. Keep written notes of what you have agreed to do.

• If parents refuse to meet with you, write to them about your concerns and keep a copy of your letter. Some people take written remarks more seriously.

You will also have a record that you made the parents aware of your concerns.

Resources

Bjorklund, G., and C. Burger, 1987. Making conferences work. for parents, teachers, and children. *Young Children* 42 (2): 26–31.

Daniel, J. 1995. New beginnings: Transitions for difficult children. *Young Children* 50 (3): 17–23.

Heath, H. 1994. Dealing with difficult behaviors—Teachers plan with parents. *Young Children* 49 (5): 20–24.

Morgan, E. L. 1989. Talking with parents when concerns come up. *Young Children* 44 (2): 52–56.

Murphy, D. M. 1997. Parent and teacher plan for the child. *Young Children* 52 (4): 32–37.

National Association for the Education of Young Children (NAEYC). 1995. What would you do if discussing a child's behavior resulted in the parent beating him? *Young Children* 50 (5): 50–51.

Stone, J. G. 1987. *Teacher-Parent relationships*. Washington, D.C.: NAEYC.

Resources for Parents About Children's Challenging Behaviors

Brazelton, T. B., and J. D. Sparrow. 2001. *Touchpoints three to six: Your child's emotional and behavioral development*. Chicago: Perseus Books.

Crary, E. 1993. *Without spanking or spoiling: A practical approach to toddler and preschool guidance*. Seattle: Parenting Press.

———. 1994. *Love and limits: Guidance tools for creative parenting*. Seattle: Parenting Press.

Forehand, R., and N. Long. 1996. *Parenting the strong-willed child*. Chicago: Contemporary Books.

Kurcinka, M. S. 1992. *Raising your spirited child: A guide for parents whose child is more intense, sensitive, perceptive, persistent, and energetic*. New York: Harper Perennial.

Nelson, J., R. Duffy, and C. Erwin. 1998. *Positive discipline for preschoolers: For their early year—Raising children who are responsible, respectful, and resourceful*. Rev. 2d. ed. Roseville, Calif.: Prima Publishing.

Parent's Magazine. 2001. *It worked for me! From thumb sucking to schoolyard fights, parents reveal their secrets to solving everyday problems of raising kids*. New York: Griffin Trade Paperback.

Ricker, A., and C. Crowder. 1998. *Backtalk: Four steps to ending rude behavior in your kids*. New York: Fireside.

Tobia, C. U. 1999. *You can't make me: But I can be persuaded*. New York: Waterbrook Press.

Web Sites

See the parenting Web sites listed at the end of the first chapter in this section on p. 166 for many tips targeted to parents on managing children's behavior.

Breaking Bad News to Parents by Susan Miller. Earlychildhood.com. www.earlychildhood.com/Articles/index.cfm. Click on Family Support, then scroll down to article title.

Building Parent-Teacher Partnerships by the National Association for the Education of Young Children (NAEYC). Earlychildhood.com. www.earlychildhood.com/Articles/index.cfm. Click on Family Support, then scroll down to article title.

Does Parent Involvement Make Your Job Easier or More Challenging? by Michele Beery. Earlychildhood.com. www.earlychildhood.com/Articles/index.cfm. Click on Family Support, then scroll down to article title.

A Hands-On Approach to Nurturing the Parent Partnership by Edna Wallace. Earlychildhood.com. www.earlychildhood.com/Articles/index.cfm. Click on Family Support, then scroll down to article title.

Parent Teacher Conferences by Evelyn Petersen. Earlychildhood.com. www.earlychildhood.com/Articles/index.cfm. Click on Family Support, then scroll down to article title.

The Problem-Solving Parent: Why Won't They Do That at Home? by Eleanor Reynolds. Earlychildhood.com. www.earlychildhood.com/Articles/index.cfm. Click on Family Support, then scroll down to article title.

7. Parents Who Are Late

This is a very common and persistent concern for many teachers. Waiting for a parent, not knowing when she might finally show up, is annoying. The child almost always feels worried, hurt, and abandoned. This chapter includes ideas to greatly reduce the problem.

Preventing Problems

● State in your parent handbook your policy on lateness and why parents need to bring in and pick up their children on time. Discuss your need to have time with your own family, to which they can relate.

● Post a large sign in a conspicuous place stating the opening and closing hours and thanking parents for picking up their children on time. In smaller letters, remind them of the consequences of being late.

● Discuss with your supervisor the need to levy fines or raise them for late pick-ups. Be aware that for some parents a few extra dollars for being late is worth the cost. However, programs that charge two dollars for every minute a parent is late, usually have few problems with lateness. Even free, government-funded programs can charge child care fees after their regular hours. Remember that, without adequate consequences, the problem is not likely to go away. Late fees should go directly to the person who is providing the service and the income is taxable. Reduce late fees slightly the first few times parents call to say they will be late due to unavoidable circumstances.

● Thank parents who are always on time. Follow up your verbal thanks with a letter or a certificate of appreciation.

Dealing with Existing Problems

● Meet with parents who are late to pick up their children. Discuss together ways to solve the problem. Let them know how much their tardiness disrupts your life and the extent of the problem it causes you. Take time to let them know that lateness is a problem of great concern to you. Often, this will turn things around.

● Meet with your supervisor and discuss your concerns. Make sure she clearly understands the depth of your unhappiness about staying late. Come prepared with several solutions in mind, including raising fees for being late as discussed above.

● Request to have your shift changed, if possible, so that you are not on the final shift.

- Request that your supervisor or another person stay late with any children who have not been picked up on time or that the task is rotated between different staff people. Because maintaining positive relations with parents is so important, you should not have to be the only one to confront late parents.

- For parents who are chronically late in picking up their children, ask that your supervisor put a number limit on how many more times they can be late and still be served by the program. You should not have to tolerate the intrusion into your life caused by chronically late parents. Do this, however, only as a last resort, because this family may be among the most needy in your program for stable, quality education and care for their children. At the time of enrollment tell all parents of this potential consequence for lateness. Put it in writing.

- If the problem is that the parents bring their children in late, meet with them to discuss the impact this has on their children. Tell them what the children miss, how the adjustment to the day is more difficult, and how it may reduce the formation of friendships. Offer your help in devising solutions to the problem.

Resources

Web Sites

When Parents Are Late by Christine M. Todd. National Network for Child Care. www.nncc.org. Click on Articles and Resources, then Child Care Family Relationships, then scroll down to the article title.

8. Parents Who May Be Abusive to Their Children

Each state has laws on reporting child abuse. Know the law for your state. Contact the agency in your state that deals with child abuse (often called Child Protective Services, Children's Services Division, Bureau of Family Services, or a similar name), and they will tell you the laws and mail you written information about the laws.

In almost all states, you, as a teacher, must report any suspected child abuse. Not doing so is illegal. In turn, you are usually protected from any accusations of wrong doing if you are mistaken.

If You're Not Sure

Children get many cuts and bruises, so deciding if abuse is happening can be difficult. However, be confident that making a mistake and overreporting abuse is better than taking a chance on missing abuse. At the very least, keep a detailed written record of the cuts and bruises as described below under "Write Down the Things You Notice." Note that many cuts, bruises, or burns over a period of time can be evidence of abuse or neglect.

Reporting abuse can be very positive and something to feel good about, as you may be the person who starts the process that will help a family change for the better.

Suspected Physical Abuse

- Report the following signs if you observe any of them:

The child has . . .
- Visible bruises or injuries in places unlikely to be hurt from a fall (the eye, buttocks, genitals, neck, torso, thigh, backs of legs, and arms)
- Bruises in a pattern (belt marks, handprints)
- Frequent burns or burns in unusual places or shapes (cigarette, iron)
- Bite marks
- Numerous bruises in various stages of healing

The child or parent has . . .
- An explanation that seems unlikely to have caused that injury

---

The child offers . . .
- A statement freely given that the injury was the result of being hurt or neglected by a parent, adult, or older child

---

Suspected Neglect

- Report severe neglect because it can be just as disastrous as physical abuse to a child.

> **Indicators of neglect are seen in a child who is often and consistently**
>
> - Hungry
> - Tired and listless
> - Dressed inappropriately for the weather
> - Smelling bad
> - Wearing very dirty clothes
> - Needing medical attention that does not get taken care of
> - Failing to grow and gain weight
> - Left alone at home or in the care of a sibling under twelve years old

Suspected Emotional Abuse

Emotional abuse can be very devastating to a child and can result in negative and antisocial behaviors that last a lifetime. Some states are able to handle reports of emotional abuse and have procedures and trained staff to investigate. Other states focus more on abuse where there is physical evidence, particularly if protective service funds are in short supply.

> **An emotionally abused child is one who is often and consistently**
>
> - Picked on
> - Singled out for punishment arbitrarily
> - Belittled and berated
> - Rejected
> - Cursed at
> - Punished cruelly, such as being locked in a closet
> - Psychologically tortured (in extreme cases)

A number of these behaviors, seen often and over a long period of time (several months), is evidence of emotional abuse.

> **The symptoms seen in the classroom behavior of an emotionally abused child include the child who excessively and regularly**
>
> - Displays extremes of emotions (overly happy, depressed, shy) that are often expressed at inappropriate times or in odd ways, such as laughing when hurt
> - Physically hurts herself
> - Isolates herself from others
> - Displays strange or intense habits such as hair pulling, rocking, or head banging
> - Destroys property or sets fires
> - Displays extreme fears or unusual fears
> - Is cruel to other children or animals
> - Is obsessed with minute details
> - Steals
> - Lies
> - Bites (four years old and older)

Suspected Sexual Abuse

Preschool teachers have a vital role in stopping sexual abuse because approximately one-third of sexually abused children are five years old or younger (Ray-Keil 1988). Teach children, in a concrete and nonthreatening way, about how to avoid sexual abuse and about the importance of getting help. Many good books and curricula are available to help you do this and some are listed at the end of this chapter. Also see the chapter, "The Sexually Precocious Child" on p. 95.

> **Sexual abuse may be occurring if a child**
>
> - Experiences difficulty in sitting or walking due to soreness in the genital or anal area
> - Has stained or bloody underwear
> - Experiences pain or itching in the genital area
> - Displays sexually provocative behavior and adult-like knowledge of sexuality
> - Displays extreme fear of men or precocious seductiveness toward men
> - Draws pictures that depict adults with erect penises or other sexual scenes

Write Down the Things You Notice

• Write down the nature of a bruise, where it is on the body, and the time and date you noticed it. Include any comments made by the child and/or parent. If you suspect neglect, sexual abuse, or emotional abuse, write down any signs, symptoms, and comments.

• Keep your report in a safe place. This is important because several days may pass before a caseworker investigates. Also, one incident may not be considered a cause for concern by the caseworker, but a number of incidents over time may build a case for possible abuse. In many states, a written report of abuse is required.

• Let your supervisor know and let her follow up, make phone calls, and take responsibility. If she refuses, it is your legal (as well as moral) duty to do the reporting yourself. Remember that not doing so may put a child in grave danger.

Never Discuss Your Suspicions with Parents

Because you care about your families, you may feel like asking the parents about the bruises or even informing them first that you will have to report the abuse. Be aware that this is not a good idea. Abusive parents may take their child and leave. You will probably not be able to find them, nor will the caseworker. The parents also may be able to talk you out of reporting, which you may later regret. Your first responsibility is to protect the child.

Warning parents about your suspicions and offering your help will most likely not change long-established patterns of behavior—unless you can offer a comprehensive counseling service with staff trained in abuse and neglect. Abusive parents often do not start to get help until they are involved in the legal system.

If a Parent Asks for Your Help

If a parent is afraid she will be abusive or wants help with an abuse problem, refer her to your local Parents Anonymous organization if there is one. Suggest a counseling agency, social service agency, or the state child abuse agency as alternative choices. Keep the telephone numbers of Parents Anonymous and the other agencies handy in case such a request comes up. You may want to offer to be present when the parent makes the call to be supportive. Remember that admitting a weakness and beginning to change is a big, scary step for anyone.

Resources

Caughey, C. 1991. Becoming the child's ally—Observations in a classroom for children who have been abused. *Young Children* 46 (4): 22–28.

Furman, E. 1987. More protections, fewer directions: Some experiences with helping children prevent sexual abuse. *Young Children* 42 (5): 5–7.

Good, L. A. 1996. When a child has been sexually abused: Several resources for parents and early childhood professionals. *Young Children* 51 (5): 84–85.

Jordan, N. H. 1993. Sexual abuse prevention programs in early childhood education: A caveat. *Young Children* 48 (6): 76–79.

Kehoe, P. 1988. *Helping abused children.* Seattle: Parenting Press.

Lowenthal, B. 2001. *Abuse and neglect: The educator's guide to the identification and prevention of child abuse.* Baltimore: Paul H. Brookes.

Meddin, B. J., and A. L. Rosen. 1986. Child abuse and neglect: Prevention and reporting. *Young Children* 41 (4): 26–30.

National Association for the Education of Young Children (NAEYC). 1998. What would you do? Real-life ethical problems early childhood professionals face. How do you know if you should suspect child abuse? *Young Children* 53 (4): 52–54.

Nunelley, J., and T. Fields. 1999. Anger, dismay, guilt, anxiety—The reality and roles in reporting child abuse. *Young Children* 54 (5): 74–79

Ray-Keil, A. 1988. Prevention for preschoolers: Good, bad, or confusing? *Prevention Notes.* Seattle: Committee for Children.

Tower, C. C. 2001. *When children are abused: An educator's guide to intervention.* New York: Allyn & Bacon.

Support Groups

Parents Anonymous
(909) 621-6184 or find a local support group through the Web site.
www.parentsanonymous.org

Abuse Prevention Curricula

Child Safety—Curricula for Children. Review of various curricula. National Center for Resource Family Support. Casey Family Programs.
www.casey.org/cnc. Click on Publications, then scroll down to article title.

The Safe Child Program
Coalition for Children, P. O. Box 6304, Denver, CO 80206
www.safechild.org

Red Flag, Green Flag: The ABCs of Personal Safety
Red Flag Green Flag Resources, P. O. Box 2984, Fargo, ND 58108-2984
www.redflaggreenflag.com

Talking about Touching
Committee for Children, 568 First Avenue South, Suite 600, Seattle, WA 98104
www.cfchildren.org

Videos

Committee for Children
568 First Avenue South
Suite 600
Seattle, WA 98104
www.cfchildren.org
What Do I Say Now? How to Help Protect Your Child from Sexual Abuse

Web Sites

Child Abuse.org
www.childabuse.org

Child Safety—Curricula for Children. Review of various curricula. National Center for Resource Family Support. Casey Family Programs.
www.casey.org/cnc. Click on Publications, then scroll down to article title.

Child Sexual Abuse. American Academy of Child and Adolescent Psychiatry. Facts for Families #9.
www.aacap.org. Link through Facts for Families and then scroll down to the article.

Child Sexual Abuse: Intervention and Treatment Issues by Kathleen Coulborn Faller. National Clearinghouse on Child Abuse and Neglect Information. 1993.
www.calib.com/nccanch. Scroll down to search box on side bar, enter "child sexual abuse."

Child Sexual Abuse: What It Is and How to Prevent It. ERIC Digest. 1990.
ericeece.org. Click on Publications on the side bar, then on Digests, then on Title, and scroll down to the article.

National Clearinghouse on Child Abuse and Neglect Information. Includes states' statutes.
www.calib.com/nccanch

Parents Anonymous
www.parentsanonymous.org

The Prevention of Child Abuse in Early Childhood Programs and the Responsibilities of Early Childhood Professionals to Prevent Child Abuse. NAEYC Position Statement. 1997.
www.naeyc.org. Click on NAEYC Resources, then Position Statements, then Improving Practices with Young Children, then scroll down to article title.

Prevent Child Abuse America
www.preventchildabuse.org

Responding to Sexual Abuse. American Academy of Child and Adolescent Psychiatry. Facts for Families #28.
www.aacap.org. Link through Facts for Families and then scroll down to the article.

The Role of Educators in the Prevention and Treatment of Child Abuse and Neglect by Cynthia Crosson Tower. National Clearinghouse on Child Abuse and Neglect. 1992.
www.calib.com/nccanch. Scroll down to search box on side bar, enter "role of educators."

Safeguarding Our Children—United Mothers. Various articles, resources, and information.
www.soc-um.org. Link on the Education tab in the side bar.

When a Child or Youth Is Sexually Abused: A Guide for Youth, Parents, and Caregivers. Central Agencies (of Toronto) Sexual Abuse Treatment Program.
www.casat.on.ca. Click on Handbook on the side bar.

Part VII

Working with Other Staff

1. Difficult Bosses

2. Problems Working with Assistants or Volunteers

3. Concerns about Coworkers

1. Difficult Bosses

Fortunately, there are more supportive and reasonable bosses in the early childhood field than there are difficult bosses. Perhaps this is because most people drawn to the field are nurturing, caring people. However, like any profession, there are a great number of supervisors who do not manage other adults well.

Many supervisors in our field have proven their worth as teachers and moved up into supervisory positions with little knowledge or training in personnel management. Like the staff they supervise, they typically are overworked, underpaid, and stretched to capacity. They may really desire to be more flexible or responsive with their staff, but the leaky roof just has to take priority over a teacher's concern about a child.

This does not mean that you should just accept a poor relationship between you and your boss or accept difficult working conditions. There are many things you can do, as suggested in this chapter.

Preventing Problems

● Know the management style you work under best. You may prefer to be basically left alone and given a great deal of autonomy, or you may prefer to get more direction and support from a supervisor.

● During your initial interview when applying for a new position, ask your potential supervisor questions that will reveal her style of managing. If her style is very different from what you prefer, determine if you can accept the discrepancy before taking the position.

● In the interview, ask your supervisor about her short-term and long-term goals for the organization. This will help you determine how well your goals fit with hers. Make sure your teaching style and your values will be accepted and supported by your boss before accepting the position.

● During your first weeks on the job, discretely ask your new coworkers about the strengths, weaknesses, and idiosyncrasies of your boss. Use that information to stay on the good side of your boss.

● Make your supervisor aware of the wonderful things you are doing in your classroom. Give her samples of your children's art work for her office. Offer her some of the good food your children make in a cooking project. If you do special projects for holidays, ask one of the children to volunteer to make something for your supervisor. Most children enjoy this and especially enjoy presenting it to her.

● Remember that bosses need strokes as much as anyone. When your boss does something you appreciate, let her know. Praise her good qualities to others.

● Request regular individual meetings with her to discuss concerns and problems before they become crises. If there are no problems to discuss use the time to get and give positive feedback.

Dealing with Existing Problems

● Talk to your coworkers who seem to get along well with your boss to determine how they do this. You are sure to get some good ideas. Whenever you have a complaint or concern, request to meet with your supervisor at a time that will be good for both of you. Ask for undivided attention and request that phone calls be held. Come into the meeting with at least two reasonable ideas for solving the concern.

● Do not circumvent your boss and go to her supervisor or to the board of directors unless this is absolutely necessary; for example, if she violates personnel policies or does something illegal. They are not likely to be sympathetic or take your side over your boss's. It is likely to make matters worse for you. If you must talk to her supervisors, be absolutely certain that any allegations you make are correct, and offer proof.

● Accept the fact that you probably will not change your boss, so work on ways that you can change your own behavior or your reactions. For example, if your boss demands more paperwork than you think is necessary and discussions with your boss have not solved the problem, find ways to do the work quickly and efficiently. Don't waste time and energy complaining or being angry about the foibles of your boss.

When You Have a New Boss

● If there is a change in supervisors, ask to meet individually with the new supervisor to discuss how you can best work together. At this time, clarify your approach to teaching young children and determine her expectations and goals.

● Invite your new boss to spend time in your classroom—before she has a chance to request it. Ask for her input and feedback about a specific concern you have.

- Have your children make a gift and provide a welcoming party (perhaps during a snack time). Have the children give her a tour of the room and talk about their favorite activities. Sing a favorite song or two for her.

The Dictatorial Boss

- A boss who is overly controlling, demanding, and unapproachable is probably insecure about the organization and her ability to manage it. She may also believe that this management style will get the best performance out of people. Get to know her on a personal level and offer empathy, understanding, and help. If you do this, she will most likely feel more positive toward you and treat you more kindly.

- Know your legal rights as an employee. However, even when legal rights being violated is not an issue, but being treated ethically and humanely is, speak up for yourself without being angry or defensive. A dictatorial boss will come to expect compliant and weak behavior from you after a while. When you change your behavior patterns and take control of the interactions between you and your boss, she will also change her behaviors. Seek nurturance and support from friends or coworkers and stop expecting it from your supervisor.

The Incompetent Boss

- Your boss may seem incompetent because she has more to do than she can possibly handle. Offer to take responsibility for a task that you would like to do and that will give you some additional job experience. For example, volunteer to organize "Week of the Young Child" events, find a trainer for the music workshop, or take responsibility for keeping up the parent bulletin board.

- Your boss may be incompetent because she is not capable of handling the job responsibilities or because she is preoccupied with personal problems, or both. Offer your support and assistance, but take on no more than you can handle. Remember that you may help just by being a good listener. If your boss is new, but smart, she may become competent with some more experience. If she seems to be steadily improving, give her time and be helpful and supportive.

- Decide if you can still do your job well and your school or center can provide quality services to children and families under an incompetent boss. If not,

consider finding another position or, if many things about your program are good, try the ideas below.

- Discretely keep a written, dated log of specific, observable behaviors that show your supervisor's inability to do her job as it affects you. For example, you might note the following: "6/24—Did not show up for staff meeting. Later, at 2:00 P.M., she said that she forgot." Enlist other coworkers who are concerned to also keep a log. Write at home and keep your log there. If her supervisor or board decides to ask for her resignation, your log will be an important document to support that request. You can also choose to take your log to your supervisor's manager or to the board but be prepared for the possible consequence that you will be fired. If several other staff members join you in the process, your concerns may be taken more seriously and your chance of being fired will decrease.

If All Else Fails

- If you have given a great deal of time and effort to getting along with your boss but still find the situation difficult, make a decision to stay or to leave. If you choose to stay, accept the limitations of your boss and find a way to be at peace with your life at work. If your choice is to leave, determine what other employment options you have and begin to discretely seek those out. Remember that you have a right to work in an environment that helps you to be effective in your job. You and the children you teach deserve the best.

Resources

Andre, R., and P. D. Ward. 2000. *The 59-second employee: How to stay one second ahead of your one minute manager.* Campbell, Calif.: iUniverse.com.

Bernstein, A. J., and S. C. Rozen. 1996. *Dinosaur brains: Dealing with all those impossible people at work.* New York: Ballantine Books.

DuBrin, A. J. 1990. *Winning office politics.* New York: Prentice Hall.

National Association for the Education of Young Children (NAEYC). 1994. Using NAEYC's code of ethics: A tool for real life. What would you do if you were Charlene Popper? *Young Children* 49 (6): 50–51

Schonberg, A. R. 1998. *169 ways to score points with your boss.* New York: Contemporary Books.

Web Sites

Dealing with Difficult Bosses. Blue Cross. Blue Print for Health. blueprint.bluecrossmn.com. Enter "difficult bosses" in the search box.

Dealing with Difficult Bosses. Leadership Guide Magazine. leadershipdevelopment.com. Click on Magazine, then on Online Library, then enter "bosses" in the search box.

Human Resources. Various articles. About.com humanresources.about.com. See particularly, Work Relationships and Management sections.

Smart Ways to Work. Many articles on various topics by Odette Pollar. www.smartwaystowork.com. Click on Columns.

Working Effectively with Insecure Bosses. Leadership Guide Magazine. leadershipdevelopment.com. Click on Magazine, then on Online Library, then enter "insecure bosses" in the search box.

Work Relationships. Various articles. Work Relationships. www.workrelationships.com. Click on Articles.

2. Problems Working with Assistants or Volunteers

To successfully manage other people, you must keep in mind their level of knowledge and skill, and you must accept your responsibility to the people you manage. Managing people is a difficult task requiring great effort and time and skills in a variety of areas: counseling, organizing, communicating, and more. The suggestions in this chapter will help you give the people you manage the knowledge, tools, and support to perform well.

Preventing Problems

• Give a thorough orientation to any new people who will be working with you. The time this takes will be worthwhile because ultimately you will have to deal with fewer problems, misunderstandings, or conflicts.

• During the orientation, review your approaches to and reasons for the way you teach, discipline, set your daily schedule, store materials and supplies, work with parents, handle transitions, and deal with crises. Clarify roles and tasks by specifying who will do what and when. Make your expectations and personal priorities known: "Coming on time or a few minutes early is very important to me. Mornings are hectic and there is so much to be done."

• Have some written backup to your orientation. In addition to a staff handbook that outlines general policies and procedures in your program and the job description for the new employee or volunteer, provide written information specific to your class and your procedures.

• Give the new employee a copy of the form that will be used to evaluate her job performance. Make sure that the form is specific and detailed and that it includes such items as the following:

talking positively with children, smiling at children, doing tasks willingly as assigned, coming to work regularly, coming to work on time, maintaining confidentiality, being friendly to parents, learning more about child development, and so on.

• Request from your supervisor that you be involved in hiring or placing new staff or volunteers. You should be the supervisor of any employees who work under you. This means doing their performance evaluations, recommending or not recommending an end to probation, and being able to terminate them—with final approval of your supervisor. If you do not have these rights but do have the responsibility of making sure your assistant does a good job, you are in an untenable situation. If you have neither the rights nor the responsibility, you will find that working well with your assistant, especially if you have concerns, will be difficult and you will waste time. If there are problems, you will have to continually go to her actual supervisor with your concerns. Talk to your supervisor about restructuring lines of command so that you can have both the rights and the responsibility. Help her to see how this chain of command will benefit her by reducing her workload and stress.

• Avoid establishing close personal friendships with any person you supervise. Also avoid having a friend hired as your assistant. If there is a work-related problem, friendship makes dealing effectively with the situation difficult.

• Meet regularly and individually with the people you work with. Use the time to discuss problems, successes, or ideas.

• Read books and magazines, attend workshops, and talk to experienced people about good supervisory skills. Most teachers have no training in this area, yet being an effective supervisor can be a big factor in job satisfaction.

- Set up a meeting with her at a time when you both can be relaxed, not have interruptions, and are not rushed for time. Say, "I'm frustrated about not getting the help I need, especially in the morning. Let's set up a time to discuss ways to help with my problem." This is an example of an "I-message." It focuses on how the behavior impacts you rather than on what is wrong with the other person. Because she will not feel threatened or accused, the "I-message" promotes dialogue and two-way communication.

- Start and end the meeting with positive statements about what the assistant or volunteer does well.

- Be positive with the people who work with you. Thank them often for what they do. Keep a stack of attractive thank-you cards to use. Remember that a written appreciation, which can be kept and looked at over and over again, has a more lasting impact than a verbal thank you. Ask your staff what you can do differently to make their jobs easier or more pleasant.

Dealing with Existing Problems

Whether the problem you have with your assistant or volunteer is that she is inefficient and lazy, interferes with what you do, acts inappropriately with the children, doesn't do the tasks assigned to her, or anything else, the best approach to dealing with the problem is basically the same. Write down your concerns and be very specific and clear. Sometimes, it can be hard for you to tell if the concern is a matter of a difference in style or if the problem is real and significant. Discuss your concerns and share your notes with several other trusted people who can be objective and are not directly involved with the person—such as a supervisor, other teacher, or consultant—to help you make the determination.

If there is a serious violation that endangers the safety or well-being of the children or other staff, dismiss her immediately. Your personnel policies and staff handbook should specify this. For less serious problems, carefully follow the procedures that are in place in your program for disciplining staff, assuming there are some. If they seem to be inadequate or unfair—or if there are none—use the following procedure:

- Meet together and brainstorm solutions to the problem. Be creative and don't lock yourself into a solution. Continue to use "I-messages." Remember, trying to change the behavior directly rarely works. The best ideas usually involve a structural change or the addition of a resource; perhaps some training, adjustments in the environment, changes in assigned tasks or schedules, clarification of roles, or helpful reminders. Make a plan of action for one or two of the best solutions. Write down who will do what and when. Set another time to meet to evaluate how well the plan worked.

- Give her a great deal of feedback during the time that the plan is in effect. Tell her specifically what she is doing well and what she is not doing well. Bring in someone from outside the classroom who does not supervise her, such as another teacher, consultant, or board member to help her.

- If the problem is not fixed after two meetings and several weeks, write down exactly what she does wrong. Keep these careful, objective notes over a period of time. After meeting with your supervisor to discuss your plan, review the notes with her and place her on probation for two weeks. Tell her that she will be dismissed if the situation does not improve. Ask her what supports she needs to improve. Follow through on the consequences, if necessary. Don't accept a little improvement. Remember that you and the children need and deserve to be with people who will do things well.

- If the situation does improve, let her know clearly that you appreciate her efforts. Tell her specifically how what she does helps you, and put your comments in writing: "Thank you for coming on time and doing your tasks. Mornings are now easy. Everyone is more relaxed and the rest of the day seems to go better too." Let her know that you expect things to stay this way. Move on to dealing with other problems, if there are any.

- Continue to give feedback often, both informally and formally. Stay on top of concerns and deal with them early and quickly.

Resources

Albright, M., and C. Carr. 1998. *101 biggest mistakes managers make and how to avoid them*. New York: Prentice Hall.

Caruso, J. J., and M. T. Fawcett. 1999. *Supervision in early childhood education: A developmental perspective*. New York: Teachers College Press.

Child Care Information Exchange. Exchange, P. O. Box 3249, Redmond, WA 98073. This magazine, published six times a year, is aimed at child care directors but contains excellent information for teachers who supervise others. www.ccie.com.

Culkin, M. L. 2000. *Managing quality in young children's programs: The leader's role*. New York: Teachers College Press.

Fournies, F. F. 1999. *Why employees don't do what they're supposed to and what to do about it*. New York: McGraw-Hill Trade.

Straub, J. T. 1999. *The rookie manager: A guide for surviving your first year in management*. New York: AMACOM.

Web Sites

Dealing with Difficult Employees. The Complete Idiot's Guides. www.idiotsguides.com. Click on Tips on Topics and then scroll down to article title under Workplace.

Human Resources. Various articles. About.com humanresources.about.com. See particularly Work Relationships and Management sections.

Smart Ways to Work. Many articles on various topics by Odette Pollar. www.smartwaystowork.com. Click on Columns.

Work Relationships. Various articles. Work Relationships. www.workrelationships.com. Click on Articles.

3. Concerns about Coworkers

You may have coworkers who make your job difficult or who lower the quality of your school or program because of their poor teaching skills. This puts you in a very tough spot because they typically are your peers and you don't supervise them. But you have a right and a moral duty to express your concerns, as long as you do it tactfully. Antagonizing your coworkers will only be counterproductive. As most people do the best they can with what they know, correcting the problems often means getting more information to your coworkers. This chapter will offer you ways to do this without making your coworkers feel defensive.

Preventing Problems

- Establish positive relations with your coworkers. Treat them with respect. Be helpful to them by sharing your materials and ideas without acting superior. Ask for their assistance and ideas without demeaning yourself. Set up a system where each person on staff does a training session for other staff in an area in which she feels particularly strong.

- When returning from a conference, share what you have learned with other staff members and ask them to share what they have learned. Help organize and participate in staff meetings, training sessions, and social events with other staff members.

- Promote a staff retreat where there is a relaxing atmosphere and ample time to solve problems, learn new skills, clarify and agree on a philosophy and program objectives, set exciting goals, eat good food, and have fun. Create a study group to read and discuss new ideas and solutions to shared problems.

- Actively work toward continual improvement of communications and relations between you and your coworkers.

- Invite consultants to do team-building workshops with staff.

- Think of new and better ways to communicate— e-mail, mailboxes, active listening skills, a memo system, a phone tree, a sharing time before each staff meeting.

- Work with your supervisor on developing personnel policies and staff evaluations that include such personal capacities as the following: being friendly with other staff, supporting the growth of other staff, working as a team, sharing resources, and so on. This makes it clear that getting along with coworkers is a vital part of the job.

Dealing with Existing Problems

Common complaints and concerns teachers have about their coworkers are that they are lazy, incompetent, untrained, too strict, divisive, arrogant, competitive, uncooperative, devious, or can't control their children. Note that these complaints fall into three catagories: problems that affect you directly, problems that affect the program, and problems that reveal differences in teaching styles.

Problems with Coworkers that Affect You Directly

● Coworkers who horde supplies or belittle you in front of others create problems that directly affect you, your ability to do your job, and your happiness with your work. When this happens, confront the person directly. Although this is difficult, avoiding this step may create more problems in the end. Say, "I would like to meet with you. I feel hurt by remarks you made, and I would like your help in solving my problem." Stating your feelings in this way is called using "I-messages."

● Meet at a time and place conducive to relaxation, privacy, and no interruptions. Sit side by side, not across from each other. Continue to use "I-messages." Explain how her actions made you feel and ask what her intention was. Be very objective: "I felt put down when you said, 'That's not a good idea.' Did I hear you wrong or am I misunderstanding you?" After her response, specifically ask for what you want and state the consequences: "I want you to make supportive statements or say nothing about me in front of other staff. If you put me down again, I will make a formal complaint to our supervisor."

● If you get a denial, no cooperation, or no improvement in behaviors, follow through on your stated consequence. Keep written records documenting objectively what the person did and when. Talk with other staff members to determine if they have similar concerns. If so, ask them to keep written records too. Complaints from several people to a supervisor carry much more weight than from one.

● Use all legal and appropriate channels to stop the problem. Keep written documentation of all your meetings and the responses you received. If your supervisor clearly intends to do nothing about the

concern, go to her superiors (board of directors, for example) and/or to a lawyer, if appropriate. A lawyer can help you determine if your rights are being violated because of sexual harassment, racial bias, or other reasons. Be prepared for almost certain negative consequences from your supervisor and others if you do this.

● If all else fails, decide whether you can live with this troublesome coworker or not. Either find ways to be happy in your job or start looking for a better situation.

Problems with Coworkers that Affect the Program

Certain concerns you have about others may involve how they interact with other staff, children, or parents. These concerns do not affect you directly. However, you feel compelled to do something, because you care about your coworkers, children, families, and the reputation of your program.

● Offer your assistance in a supportive way: "I noticed you had some difficulty with the children in the gym. I used to have the same problem. Would you like some ideas that might help?"

● If the concerns continue, meet with your supervisor and ask her to observe. Make no accusations and do not try to get the other person in trouble. State objective facts about what you saw and why you are concerned: "Two children in Helen's class were sword fighting outside this morning with pointy sticks. She told them to stop, but when they continued, she took no further action. I was very concerned for their safety, so I gave them some foam swords to use instead. It was difficult for my class to wait in the hallway while I did that. I think it might be helpful to Helen if you gave her some pointers."

● If the supervisor does not act to improve the situation, take notes of what you observe and bring them to her supervisor or to appropriate authorities if there are direct health, safety, or well-being concerns. Get additional written evidence of problems from other concerned staff members.

Differences in Teaching Styles and Other Problems

You may have a very different approach toward teaching young children than other staff in your program. Perhaps other teachers use direct teaching methods, worksheets, few choices for children, harsh discipline, rewards and punishment, or long periods of teaching the whole group at once.

- Suggest to your supervisor that the program develop and adopt a unifed philosophy on teaching young children and some guidelines for carrying out that philosophy. Recommend that a group of teachers work together with your supervisor to develop the philosophy and guidelines that will be approved by the whole staff. Volunteer to be a part of the group. Suggest that the program examine the National Association for the Education of Young Children (NAEYC) guidelines for developmentally appropriate practices (Bredekamp and Copple 1997) as one source for developing the philosophy. Suggest that the program pursue NAEYC accreditation (NAEYC 1998). This process includes a self-examination of the program's quality—at the classroom level and beyond—based on a set of high standards.

- If other concerns you have do not threaten the health, safety, or well-being of the children, then you may have to either accept your coworkers or find work in a program that has a greater emphasis on quality.

- Remember that disparities between teachers in their abilities, energy levels, and motivations will exist in almost all programs. You can reduce these disparities by being helpful and supportive to others and by creating excitement and enthusiasm through the suggestions in Preventing Problems in this chapter.

Resources

Bolton, R. 1996. *People styles at work: Making bad relationships good and good relationships better.* New York: AMACOM

Bredekamp, S., and C. Copple., eds. 1997. *Developmentally appropriate practice in early childhood programs.* Rev. ed. Washington, D.C.: NAEYC.

Brinkman, R. 1996. *Dealing with people you can't stand.* New York: McGraw-Hill

Jorde-Bloom, P. 1997. *A great place to work: Improving conditions for staff in young children's programs.* Rev. ed. Washington, D.C.: NAEYC.

National Association for the Education of Young Children (NAEYC). 1994. Using NAEYC's Code of Ethics: A tool for real life. *Young Children* 50 (1): 62–63.

———. 1998. *Accreditation criteria and procedures of the National Association for the Education of Young Children.* Washington, D.C.: NAEYC. www.naeyc.org/accreditation.

———. 1998. Using NAEYC's Code of Ethics: My colleague doesn't understand how to teach reading. *Young Children* 53 (1): 64–67.

Web Sites

Dealing with Difficult Coworkers. Nursing Network. www.nursingnetwork.com/diffwork.htm

Human Resources. Various articles. See particularly, Work Relationships and Management sections. About.com humanresources.about.com

Motivating Coworkers. Nursing Network. www.nursingnetwork.com/motivate.htm

Smart Ways to Work. Many articles on various topics by Odette Pollar. www.smartwaystowork.com. Click on Columns.

Work Relationships. Various articles. WorkRelationships. www.workrelationships.com. Click on Articles.

Part VIII

Your Own Needs

1. Not Enough Time

2. Burned Out/Stressed Out

3. Underpaid

4. In over Your Head

1. Not Enough Time

Although this is a particularly difficult problem for people who work in full-day programs, almost everyone working in early childhood classrooms feels short of time. Often, this is because of a lack of funds to pay people adequately for the time they need to plan and organize. In spite of this, there are likely some things you can do to organize your time better.

Preventing Problems

● Take the time to make time. Read up on and use tried-and-true time-management strategies (see resources at the end of this chapter).

● Keep yourself well organized. One of the biggest time-wasters is the time spent looking for the things you need. Get the tools you need to keep organized: file cabinets, shelf space, labels, and so on.

● Use a calendar planner to keep track of appointments and tasks. Always keep it with you, but if not practical, keep a small pad and a pen with you so you can jot down notes to yourself. Copy them into your planner as soon as possible. Don't rely on your memory.

● Make a list of tasks you need to get done each day. Prioritize them so that you make sure the important ones get done.

● Think "long term" and "big picture." Decide on one or two personal and professional goals that you can achieve in a year and one or two that are five to ten years down the road. Break these long-term goals into smaller steps to help you get there and so they do not feel overwhelming. It is easy to let daily, mundane tasks and crises eat up all your time. Make sure you allow time to work regularly on your long-term goals.

Dealing with Existing Problems

Short on Planning Time

● If you never have enough time, you may not be asking for the time you need to plan and get organized. In order to improve your situation, assert your needs to your family, coworkers, or supervisor. Remember that planning and organizing are essential to doing your job well and staying in control. It will ultimately save time.

● Plan classroom activities at least two weeks in advance to allow time to gather supplies, arrange field trips, and so on.

● Use an effective planning tool to reduce the time and effort needed for planning. Trying to work with a generic form may result in inadequate planning. Find or develop a lesson plan form that works for you. The form should reflect your classroom schedule, priorities, and goals.

Time Seems to Slip Away

● To manage your time well, set personal goals for yourself and for your teaching. If you set a goal of obtaining a college degree, the time you spend working toward that goal will be time well spent. Goals for your teaching might include encouraging the children to be more independent or involving them more actively in music activities. Not having goals will make you feel frustrated—as if time is slipping away from you.

● Choose one realistic goal to work toward and achieve it. You will feel successful and in control.

● Track children's progress toward the goals you and their families have set for them. Use a systematic format for recording progress (see the chapter "Assessment and Accountability," on pp. 44–47). Doing ongoing assessments of children will allow you to regularly see the positive impact you are making on their development.

● Mark and celebrate successes and milestones—the end of a complex project or unit, the anniversary of your start in teaching, the completion of a restructured playground, and so on.

Too Many Committees and Meetings

● Early childhood teachers often try to be all things to all people. For your own mental health, limit your activities and commitments to what you can realistically handle and to only those which are very important to you. Learn to say no.

Rushed and Hassled

● If possible, go to work about an hour early to organize yourself and the day's activities and to do some planning. Most people work better and are more efficient in the morning. Feeling ready and prepared when children start arriving makes the whole day go well. Note that once you are involved with the children, getting any time for yourself is difficult.

Procrastinating

● Break down large tasks into small steps and accomplish them one day at a time. For example, to make more games for your classroom can be a big, time-consuming job, but if you plan to make one game a week, the task will be manageable. Design the game one day, make the board the next day, make the pieces and directions another day, and laminate the game on another. In a month, you will have four new games.

Too Much to Do

● Delegate some tasks and responsibilities to coworkers, assistants, or supervisors. For example, if you are a lead teacher and have an assistant, she may enjoy the challenge of planning and carrying out all music activities, especially if she has some talent in that area. You will be doing her a favor, while reducing your workload.

● Be careful not to delegate all the things you dislike doing. If you dislike them, your assistant probably will too. Negotiate task assignments to make sure that you both have enjoyable tasks that are opportunities for growth.

Resources

Emmit, R. 2000. *The procrastinator's handbook: Mastering the art of doing it now.* New York: Walker & Co.

Gore, M. C., and J. F. Dowd. 1999. *Taming the time stealers: Tricks of the trade from organized teachers.* Thousand Oaks, Calif.: Corwin Press.

Morgenstern, J. 2000. *Time management from the inside out: The foolproof system for taking control of your schedule and your life.* New York: Henry Holt.

Strohmer, J. C., and C. Carhart. 1997. *Time saving tips for teachers.* Thousand Oaks, Calif.: Corwin Press.

Web Sites

It's About Time by Kathy Prochaska-Cue. University of Nebraska Extension Service.
www.ianr.unl.edu. Click on Search, then enter "time management" in the search engine, then scroll down to article title.

Organizing Tips. Many short articles.
www.organizetips.com

Time Management. Various articles. Stress Management at About.com.
stress.about.com. Scroll down to and click on Time Management on the side bar.

Time Management: Manage Yourself, Not Your Time. Total Success.
www.tsuccess.dircon.co.uk. Scroll down and click on Time Management, then scroll down and click on Click here for even more tips on time management strategies.

Time Management Techniques. Total Success.
www.tsuccess.dircon.co.uk. Scroll down and click on Time Management, then scroll down and click on Click here for more tips on time management strategies.

Tips for Getting Organized. A variety of articles. Stress Management at About.com.
stress.about.com. Scroll down to and click on Organizing Tips on the side bar.

Thirteen Timely Tips for More Effective Time Management by Kathy Prochaska-Cue. University of Nebraska Extension Service.
www.ianr.unl.edu. Click on Search, then enter "time management" in the search engine, then scroll down to article title.

2. Burned Out/Stressed Out

The entire field of education is underfunded, but in early childhood education, the problem is severe. Ironically, young children need the most funding, because smaller class sizes and more teachers per pupil are required, but they receive the least. About one-third of preschool teachers leave their jobs each year. Teachers of young children everywhere feel overworked and underpaid, so your burned-out feeling is no surprise. Long hours, tremendous responsibilities, and the high level of skill needed to do the work combined with low salaries, little respect from society for the work, and small budgets for supplies almost guarantees burnout. Feeling a sense of "lack of control" tends to be a bigger factor in contributing to burnout than too much work,

for most people. See below for ways to gain more control over your situation.

Preventing Problems

Get Involved

● Get involved politically to advocate for more funds from your agency, local government, or the federal government to help reduce your feeling of hopelessness. You will be actively doing something about the problem. This is also a good way to meet people with whom you will have much in common. Political work can be stressful too, however, and may contribute to burnout, if you take on more than you have time for or if you hope to accomplish more than is realistic.

Find a Support Group

● Being involved in associations that sponsor workshops, conferences, and networking meetings can help by giving you support for your feelings and frustrations. Be assured that many teachers share common concerns and have similar problems. Much can be gained by sharing them and discussing solutions that have worked. Your involvement in promoting professionalism through these associations can bring a great deal of satisfaction. (To locate your nearest chapter of the National Association for the Education of Young Children, check their Web site: www.naeyc.org.)

• Find a like-minded colleague in a program that serves children who are different than the children you serve (perhaps ethnically different or rural if you are urban). Partner together for the children to visit each other's classrooms, communicate with each other, and to share ideas and interests.

Learn Something/Teach Something

• Attend workshops and classes to give you fresh new ideas, as well as to validate your current abilities. Visit teachers in other programs to learn new ideas and to connect with peers. Request time to do this from your supervisor as part of your training. The expense to your program of paying a substitute for the day is well worth the return in increased quality.

• Offer to give a class or workshop to fellow staff members, at a conference or through a local college. You probably have a particular area of expertise or a special skill that others will love to learn. If you do not, cultivate an area of expertise that is particularly interesting to you. For example, become the local expert on creative dramatics or the use of computers with young children by reading all you can about it, talking to experts, attending classes, and trying out many ideas with your class. (For more information about early childhood education associations and advocacy groups, read the chapter, "Being an Advocate for Families, Children, the Profession, and Yourself" on pp. 203–208.)

Let Your Environment Nurture You

• Set up a classroom that reflects your taste and aesthetic values—one that is fun to be in, is pleasant to look at, and has warm and soothing colors. This will be a classroom you will want to return to every day. It is worth the extra time and effort to carefully set up your classroom and to make periodic changes, which make you feel comfortable being there.

• Provide yourself with a space that you can call your own even if it is just a shelf. This is your private area. You can set it up as you like and it can contain your important materials and books. (One teacher keeps a jar of hot peppers in her area as a daily treat in the afternoons.) A small file cabinet, just for your own use, which contains activity ideas, notes, and articles from magazines, will make your job easier.

• Keep one comfortable adult-size chair in the room. Constant sitting on small, hard children's chairs causes stress. Although being on the same level with the children is important, an occasional stint on your chair, if only during naptime or to read to a child, will be good for your health.

Take a Break

• Get out of the classroom and take small breaks and a full lunch break every day. Take a brisk walk, jog, exercise, go window-shopping, or read a good novel. Give yourself a mental vacation and get a change of scenery in the middle of each day. Remember that this is vital to maintaining good mental health and preventing burnout.

Take Care of Your Health

• Start an exercise group with your coworkers. Eat healthy foods and sleep as much as you need. Stay home when you are sick. If your energy level is good, you will be better able to meet the challenges of the day.

• A hurt or aching back is an occupational hazard for teachers of young children. Working with a bad back will increase your stress tremendously. Avoid back problems by doing the following:

▶ When standing for long periods, bend your knees slightly, keep your legs apart (directly under the shoulders), have one foot slightly in front of the other, and distribute your weight evenly over both legs.

▶ When sitting for long periods, put your feet on a low box so that your knees are slightly higher than your hips. To avoid leaning forward in your chair or sitting on the edge, push the chair close to the table or desk.

▶ Reach up to get something from a high place by standing on a step designed for that purpose. Don't stand on your toes. Keep your knees bent slightly to avoid losing your balance.

▶ When standing at a sink to wash your hands, bend your knees and rest them against the cabinet below the sink. If the space below the sink is open, put a low box there and put one foot up while washing.

▶ Push, rather than pull, heavy items.

▶ When lifting a child, get down in a squat position with the knee of one leg on the floor, and put your other leg forward, bent at the knee with the foot flat on the floor. Lift with your legs and keep the child close to your body. Or, bend your knees so that you are in a slight squat position and have the child jump up into your arms (from a standing, not running, position) when you both count to three.

Don't Work Alone

Do you have an assistant? In programs for young children there should be at least two capable adults in every classroom at all times. Guiding children, maintaining order, and individualizing are almost impossible with only one adult, but of most importance are safety concerns. If there is an emergency to take care of, someone needs to be with the hurt child while another person is in charge of the rest of the children. Tracking down a supervisor or another adult at this time may leave children unsupervised.

● Working with other adults also helps keep you from burning out. You will have someone with whom to discuss ideas and problems. If at all possible, avoid working in programs where there is only one person in a classroom for children under six years of age. If avoiding this situation is not possible, work on ways of getting an assistant. Consider the following ideas: parent volunteers, college or high-school students (service learning programs, student teachers), and community volunteers—AmeriCorps, Senior Corps, and local chapters of service clubs and social organizations (Lions, Kiwanis, Rotary, and so forth). Or, assist the program director to restructure the budget to include another position.

Get Control

The lack of control over numerous aspects of your job can be a huge source of stress. All adults need to feel that they can try out their ideas, take chances, learn from mistakes, and make changes. Programs using preplanned curricula with daily activities spelled out take that sense of control away from the teacher. This is also true where teachers have to accept whatever materials and equipment are supplied to them.

● If you are in a situation where either of these is true, work cooperatively with the powers that be to get some changes made. Request a small monthly budget with which you can purchase supplies. This is a reasonable request and might be a place to start to gain more control. This is important because a flexible, responsive curriculum that has relevance to your particular group of children is a vital part of a quality preschool. If two children in your class have mothers who are about to give birth, you need to be able to do a unit on babies. Your supervisor should be able to see this as an issue of improving the quality of the program. If she cannot or if she does not have control over the decision, consider implementing your ideas anyway. Many teachers finish the required curriculum quickly and minimally and then use the extra time to implement their own activities. If you cannot impact this issue, consider taking your skills and talents to a program that gives more control to teachers.

Limit Yourself

● Know your own limitations. Early childhood teachers are generally very giving, caring, generous people, but sometimes they have trouble saying no. Involving yourself in the role of therapist for a troubled family or spending your hours after work helping a family in need find resources are noble things to do, but not required. You can easily burn out by taking on more than you can cope with or have skills for. You will then be less able to be a good teacher. Being a good teacher is the first obligation to yourself, your children, and their families.

● Remember that overinvolving yourself in the lives of your families and children may not ultimately be helpful to them because they can develop a dependency on you and never learn to solve problems for themselves. Be a resource and support for solutions, not the solution itself.

Set Goals

● Everyone needs to feel like she is going somewhere, heading in a direction. Set goals as a way to achieve that feeling. You will be much less likely to burn out. You may want to be a head teacher, education coordinator, director, owner, teacher of older children, a consultant, a senator, or a better teacher. Whatever the goal, have one. Then write down the steps needed to achieve it (get an advanced degree, read one professional book each month, and so on), and begin working toward it. Every day do something that will bring you closer to your goal, even if all you have time for is reading one page of a book.

Experiment

● View yourself as a "researcher." Take some risks by trying out new and different ideas with your class. Evaluate the results and discuss them with coworkers to determine what worked, what can be improved, or what needs to be scrapped completely. For example, try a completely new curriculum approach, change your schedule, create an "automobile service station" dramatic play area, or create a theme around TV—visit a TV studio, teach critical viewing skills, create and videotape a TV show in the classroom.

Have Fun

● Making your job more fun may be the single most important thing you can do to prevent burnout. Some of the many ways you can do this include the following:

▶ Have regular parties with other staff.

▶ Use humor (not sarcasm) with your children.

▶ Share the funny things your children say and do with parents and other staff.

▶ Sing funny songs.

▶ Get silly. Paint your face and the kids' (use a cold cream base and add coloring), have a pajama party, make footprint pictures, fingerpaint a huge mural, have a fancy dress-up day and set up an "expensive restaurant" dramatic play, or have a backward day when you reverse your schedule and routines.

● There isn't a better job in the world for having a fabulously, fun time than teaching young children. Just think, you could be working in an office all day!

Resources

Arden, J. B. 2002. *Surviving job stress: How to overcome workday pressures.* Franklin Lakes, N.J.: Career Press.

Bellm, D., and P. Haack. 2001. *Working for quality child care.* Washington, D.C.: Center for the Child Care Workforce.

Greathouse, B., J. E. Moyer, and E. Rhodes-Offutt. 1992. Suggestions from the sunbelt: Increasing K–3 teachers' joy in teaching. *Young Children* 47 (3): 44–46.

Gruenberg, A. 1998. Creative stress management: Put your own oxygen mask on first. *Young Children* 53 (1): 38–42.

Jorde-Bloom, P. 1994. *Avoiding burnout: Strategies for managing time, space, and people in early childhood education.* Beltsville, Md.: Gryphon House.

Maloney, M. S. 1999. My hair turns gray, but . . . *Young Children* 54 (4): 31.

Potter, B. A. 1998. *Overcoming job burnout: How to renew enthusiasm for work.* Berkeley, Calif.: Ronin Publishing.

Web Sites

Battling Burnout. Early Childhood Educator. www.edpsych.com. Click on Teachers, then scroll down to article title.

Staff "Burnout" in Child Care Settings—ERIC Document. www.teach-nology.com. Link through Literature in Education then Early Childhood.

Stress Management. About.com. stress.about.com

Working with Young Children. Early Childhood Educators' and Family Web Corner. users.stargate.net/~cokids. Click on Teacher Pages, then on scroll down to Working with Young Children.

Volunteer Organizations

Corporation for National Service—Includes AmeriCorps, Senior Corps, and Service Learning. www.nationalservice.org

Kiwanis International www.kiwanis.org

Lions Clubs International www.lionsclubs.org

Rotary International www.rotary.org

SERVEnet. Web site for service and volunteering. www.servenet.org

3. Underpaid

As described in the chapter "Burned Out/Stressed Out," being underpaid is a chronic condition of working in the field of early childhood education. Early childhood teachers are one of the lowest paid of all classes of workers.

Accept the fact that wages are low, have been low for many years, and will most likely continue to be low. This does not mean that you should be apathetic. Without many people becoming actively involved in lobbying for better wages, conditions will definitely never improve. This does mean coming to terms with living on less, for now, and finding satisfaction from the work you do. This is important for your own mental health. (For more information about ways to be involved in improving salaries, see "Burned Out/ Stressed Out" on pp. 190–193, and "Being an Advocate for Families, Children, the Profession, and Yourself" on pp. 203–208.)

Preventing Problems

● Know what you are worth in the early childhood job market based on your years of experience, expertise, education, and so on.

● Before you take any job, find out as much as you can about the organization. Know what the salary range is and how it is determined so you can know if you are getting a reasonable offer. Also find out about wages in similar programs in the same community.

● Do not accept the position unless you are sure you can live with the salary. Do not necessarily believe promises of future increases or at least do not count on them.

Dealing with Existing Problems

● Make a list of the positive things about your job. Include the things that most satisfy you. The list might include the following:

　▶ I learn a lot about myself from the children.

　▶ I get joy from seeing happy children.

　▶ I know the children love, trust, and respect me.

　▶ I get strokes from satisfied parents.

　▶ I am doing a great service to society by keeping children safe and happy and by helping them learn and grow.

　▶ I am helping secure a bright future for society by helping to bring up well-adjusted children.

　▶ I am good at what I do.

　▶ I have fun at my job.

　▶ I have the respect of my boss, coworkers, and parents.

● Keep the list where you can read it every morning or when you are feeling depressed about your low wages.

● Many early childhood educators need to cut expenses by sharing housing, clipping coupons, using public transportation or carpooling, shopping for sales, and frequenting discount stores, flea markets, and garage sales.

● Perhaps there are other sources of income you can find to supplement your current income without burning yourself out. Writing or consulting about what you know, starting a small business out of your home, or obtaining a part-time sales job are some possibilities.

Better Paying Jobs in Early Childhood Education

● If staying in the field and earning more money are both important to you, set some career goals for yourself.

● Opening your own program may be a goal for you. The experience and expertise you gain as a teacher will be a great asset as an owner. Although few people make very much money as child care/nursery school owners, the potential is there. You often need to own several sites (expanding after you have been successful) before you can earn substantially more than working for someone else. However, running your own business based on your own ideas, values, and methods can be tremendously rewarding.

● There are some well-paying jobs in the field, but they often require a master's degree or more, specialized training, and years of experience. These include the following: early childhood education instructor, trainer, consultant, writer, editor, publisher, center director, education coordinator, program administrator, researcher, state certifier of child care centers, and manufacturer or seller of supplies and equipment. There may be a job here that you aspire to, although even these jobs usually do not pay as well as similar jobs in other fields.

● Early childhood teaching also can lead you into higher paying jobs in closely related fields, although some specialized training will most likely be necessary. Teaching in early childhood education requires a wide variety of skills, and these provide good training for related careers. These include the following: social worker, business owner, principal, human resource specialist, family life instructor, parenting instructor, recreation director, extension agent, journalist, politician, therapist (also psychologist and counselor), children's book writer (also editor and publisher), community education director, child development specialist, health educator, public relations director, pediatric nurse, and pediatrician.

Grants

You may want to get involved in helping your program write grant proposals. Many programs have been able to increase salaries and expand job opportunities by obtaining grants for setting up new programs or for expanding existing programs. Obtain grants from the federal government, your state or local government, foundations, businesses, and agencies.

- Start with an idea or project that you have passion for and meets a great need, as it will require a great deal of work and time to refine your idea, to find and apply for funding, and to get it going.

- Develop projects with other organizations in your community, such as mental health programs, parent education agencies, child nutrition programs, or programs for children with disabilities. Agencies that give grants usually prefer projects in which two or more agencies collaborate to help children and families. When you collaborate, more expertise is available, services are consolidated, and dollars can be stretched.

Resources

Bellm, D., and P. Haack. 2001. *Working for quality child care.* Washington, D.C.: Center for the Child Care Workforce.

Modigliani, K. 1988. Twelve reasons for the low wages in child care. *Young Children* 43 (3): 14–15.

National Association for the Education of Young Children (NAEYC). 1998. Quality, compensation, and affordability. *Young Children* 53 (5): 42–43.

Ramekin, C. 1996. Food for thought: The cold reality of worthy wages: We limited size to protect quality and staff well-being. *Young Children* 51 (6) 28–29.

Whitebook, M., and A. Eichenberg. 2002. Finding a better way: Defining policies to improve child care workforce compensation. *Young Children* 57 (3): 66–72.

Whitebook, M., and D. Bellm. 1998. *Taking on turnover: An action guide for child care center teachers and directors.* Washington, D.C.: NAEYC.

Web Sites

Advocacy. Various resources. Early Childhood Educators' and Family Web Corner.
users.stargate.net/~cokids. Click on Teacher Pages, then on Advocacy.

Center for the Child Care Workforce. Many resources including current data on child care compensation.
www.ccw.org

Child Care Workforce Salaries. National Child Care Information Center.
www.nccic.org. Click on Frequently Requested Information, then scroll down to Child Care Workforce section and click on article title.

Child Care Compensation: What Does It Mean for Parents? National Parent Information Network.
www.npin.org. Click on Parent News, then on 2000, then on March–April 2000, then scroll down to article title.

Compensation Guidelines for Early Childhood Professionals. NAEYC Position Statement. 1993.
www.naeyc.org. Click on Resources, then Position Statements, Improving Early Childhood Professional Development and Professionalism, then scroll down to article title.

Earning Respect for Teachers: Re$pect. Early Childhood Educator.
www.edpsych.com. Click on Teachers, then scroll down to article title.

Foundation for Child Development. Includes a number of publications on this topic.
www.ffcd.org. Click on Publications, then scroll down to pertinent articles.

Quality, Compensation, and Affordability in Early Childhood Programs. NAEYC Position Statement. 1995.
www.naeyc.org. Click on Resources, then Position Statements, Improving Early Childhood Professional Development and Professionalism, then scroll down to article title.

4. In over Your Head ———

If you work with young children and have less experience or training than you need to do the job well, you are not alone. Many people started out that way and learned on the job. Experienced teachers often look back on their first year or two on the job and wonder how they and the children ever survived. Many teachers have found the same problem happening when they switch positions to work with a different group of families or in a different setting (such as moving from a half-day toddler program for children of middle-class families to a full-day four-year-old program for low-income families), even with many years of experience. Do not let your fear of being "in over your head" stop you from working with a different group of children or in a different setting. New challenges can be very rewarding and rejuvenating.

Dealing with Existing Problems

Don't muddle through by pretending that you know what you are doing. Accept that you will make mistakes. People who know their limitations and actively work at overcoming them get far more respect and are "cut more slack" than people who make similar mistakes but act like they are skilled.

● Ask for help from coworkers who are competent. They will most likely be flattered by your request and be glad to offer suggestions and direct assistance. Other teachers in your own program are apt to know practical ways of dealing with problems specific to your situation.

● Ask for more training from your supervisor. She will probably be very willing to help you. Supervisors

sometimes put training needs on the bottom of their priority list (coping with numerous crises comes first) but are responsive when asked directly.

● Read books and magazine/journal articles. Specialty publishers, libraries, and bookstores are carrying more and better books about early childhood education. (See "Being an Advocate for Families, Children, the Profession, and Yourself," on pp. 203–208, for a list of magazines and journals.)

● Delegate some of your work to other coworkers or supervisors. Ask others to take on some tasks that are particularly difficult for you while you learn ways to do them better. (This will free up some time and energy to train yourself on other aspects of your job.)

● Develop a network of support people who can help you solve problems and who can answer questions. Include among these people local health professionals, early childhood education instructors, trainers, consultants, and experienced teachers. Although most of these people charge for their services, they often are willing to help occasionally for a short time at no charge or for a small favor in return from you.

● Have confidence in your ability to learn and to improve. Take the pressure off by giving yourself two years to gain the skills and knowledge you need to be a good teacher by attending classes, workshops, reading, asking people with expertise, and so on.

Resources

Working with Young Children. Early Childhood Educators' and Family Web Corner.
users.stargate.net/~cokids. Click on Teacher Pages, then on scroll down to Working with Young Children.

Part IX

Promoting Yourself as a Professional

1. Protecting Yourself from Being Accused of Abuse

2. Making Tough Ethical Decisions

3. Being an Advocate for Families, Children, the Profession, and Yourself

1. Protecting Yourself from Being Accused of Abuse ——

In spite of the fact that quality early childhood programs are a major force for the prevention of abuse and neglect, teachers of young children have to deal with this concern. The reality is that abuse of young children is too prevalent, that it does happen in early childhood programs (very rarely), and that the concern of parents and professionals about this issue will always be there.

The good news is that the concern is not as out of proportion as it was in the early to mid eighties and that you can do many things to reduce the concern. Male teachers need to be particularly vigilant about doing these things, as they are more likely to be accused of abuse.

Be Proactive

"The best defense is a good offense." This may be an old sports cliche but it is very helpful for this situation. You can take the offensive on the issue of abuse by letting families know how you are protecting the safety of their children and helping their children to protect themselves.

● Ask your supervisor about the procedures used, the role of the program, and the insurance coverage available if a staff person is accused of abuse. Find out the procedures that the program would use if a parent made an accusation of abuse by a teacher. If the policies seem unfair or inadequate to protect you or other staff if falsely accused of abuse, work with your coworkers to have the policies changed.

● Consider obtaining your own personal insurance policy. Contact your insurance agent, independent broker, or the National Association for the Education of Young Children (NAEYC), 800-424-2460, about such policies.

● Inform parents verbally and in writing about your policies and procedures to prevent abuse in your program and classroom.

● Inform parents about the facts: A child is less likely to be abused in an early childhood program than in her own home. The number of teachers who are abusive is extremely small (Finkelhor 1988). In fact, quality early child programs are considered a major force for the prevention of abuse and neglect.

● Tell parents about your professional background, including work history and education. Request that your supervisor inform parents that criminal background checks and references are thoroughly checked on any staff member who is hired.

● Teach children to protect themselves from being abused. Do this by reading books, using curriculums designed for that purpose, using puppets, and doing role plays. (See the resource list in "Parents Who May Be Abusive to Their Children" on pp. 178–179.) Let parents know that you are doing this as well as how and when you are doing it. Hold a meeting beforehand for any interested parents to discuss all the issues surrounding abuse prevention for children.

● Post the phone number of local help numbers, such as children's services and Parents Anonymous, in a prominent place.

● Make sure that all parents know they are welcome to visit or participate in your classroom at any time. Explain that calling ahead is appreciated but not necessary. This open-door policy assures parents that no harm can be done to their children behind their backs.

● Educate yourself about the signs and symptoms of abuse. Report abuse right away. There have been a number of cases where a teacher has been blamed for the abuse of a child that was done by someone else.

● Make an official accident report of any injury a child has to the genital or anal area. This is important because bruises caused by injuries at school can be misconstrued as abuse.

● Insist on having another person working with you at all times. Insist that your volunteer or assistant teacher never works alone with the group of children. Join with another teacher if you find yourself alone with only a few children (typically at the beginning or end of the day). At naptime, avoid being alone if at all possible or at least keep yourself visible to other staff. This will protect you and other staff from false accusations of abuse, as there will always be a witness, and will prevent anyone who works with you from committing an abusive act.

● As the majority of abusive incidents in child care programs happen in the toileting area (Finkelhor 1988), make sure that this area is open and visible, that it cannot be locked, that adults do not go in there if it is not necessary, and that children stay out of adult bathrooms.

• Do not take children away from the school or center setting unless for a prearranged, approved field trip with permission from each parent. Do not take a child to an isolated, private area of the building.

• Work hard toward positive, open, clear, and trusting communications with all your parents.

If You Are Falsely Accused

For those who are falsely accused of abuse, the situation is highly traumatic, emotionally wrenching, and impacts the rest of their lives. Many of them have left teaching and feel very bitter. Because the experience is so awful, implementing the prevention strategies discussed above is extremely important.

If you are accused of child abuse, your actions will be greatly limited by what you are told to do by state authorities and your supervisor. During an investigation, you may be asked to take a leave with pay, be given office work, or have restrictions placed on you while at work. You can't be fired or forced to take an unpaid leave unless you are actually convicted of a crime or a supervisor or credible person witnessed the abuse.

• Get a lawyer. You will need one in almost all cases. Some programs have insurance to help you pay for this, but many do not.

• Avoid discussing the situation with anyone or gathering evidence in your defense without the advise of a lawyer experienced in these matters. If you go about

defending yourself in the wrong way, you could hurt your case.

• Demand the confidentiality from staff and supervisors to which you are entitled. Gossip will make matters worse. Keep yourself private. Do not talk to the press, police, or parents directly. Do not attempt to publicly defend yourself. Discuss the situation only with those in authority who are experienced and knowledgeable about these matters (state children's protective service) or to people who can be helpful and supportive.

• Seek the advice and support of someone who has been through a similar situation. Deal with the isolation by seeking support from friends, relatives, and a professional counselor experienced with abuse cases. If other parents call you to give you support, suggest that they form a support group with other parents and start a legal defense fund.

• Ask for clarification of policies and procedures and know your rights every step of the way. Your lawyer or state agency doing the investigation will be able to tell what those rights are. Find out exactly what you are being accused of, by whom, and based on what evidence.

• Write down, while still fresh in your memory, exactly what you were doing and who was there during the time that you are accused of abuse. Also write down everything you can remember about your interactions with the parents and the child and their interactions with each other.

• Avoid taking out any resentments you have against your supervisor, board of directors, or coworkers. Don't quit your job or burn any bridges. Be assured that the best way to heal from this is to stay around long enough to get your reputation back.

• Once you are cleared, ask for the support you need from your supervisors and coworkers to begin the healing process. You and your supervisor should meet with all the parents to explain what happened, to answer questions, to ease anxiety, and to discuss what will be said to the children.

• Speak to the police and state authorities after you have been cleared to find out any missing information you were not allowed to know during the investigation.

Resources

Finkelhor, D., L. M. Williams, and N. Burns. 1988. *Nursery crimes: Sexual abuse in day care*. Newbury Park, Calif.: Sage Publications.

Mikkelsen, E. D. 1997. Responding to allegations of sexual abuse in child care and early childhood education programs. *Young Children* 52 (3): 47–51.

Web Sites

Child Abuse. Numerous articles. National Network for Child Care. www.nncc.org. Click on Articles and Resources, then on "Child Abuse."

Creating Safety Zones for Child Care Providers by Jackie Reilly and Sally Martin. National Network for Child Care. www.nncc.org. Click on "Information Station," then on Abuse and Neglect, then scroll down to article title.

Developing Child Abuse and Neglect Policies by Thomas Buch. University of Connecticut Cooperative Extension Service. www.canr.uconn.edu/ces. Click on Cooperative Extension's National Network for Child Care, then on About Newsletters, then on Family Child Care Connections, then on May–March 1999, then scroll down to article title.

Caregivers of Young Children: Preventing and Responding to Child Maltreatment by Derry Koralek. National Clearinghouse on Child Abuse and Neglect Information. 1992. www.calib.com/nccanch. Click on Publications, then on The User Manual Series, then scroll down to article title.

Prevention of Child Abuse in Early Childhood Programs and the Responsibilities of Early Childhood Professionals to Prevent Child Abuse. NAEYC Position Statement. 1996. www.naeyc.org. Click on Publications, then Position Statements, then NAEYC position statements related to improving program practices with children, then scroll down to the article title.

The Role of Child Day Care in Strengthening and Supporting Vulnerable and At-Risk Families and Children by Bruce Hershfield. Child Welfare League of America. www.cwla.org. Click on Programs, then on Child Day Care, then scroll down to article.

2. Making Tough Ethical Decisions

A major hallmark of a professional is the ability to confront an ethical dilemma and make a good decision about what to do based on a sound code of ethics. The National Association for the Education of Young Children has developed such a code (Feeney and Kipnis 1989).

Early childhood teachers face tough ethical decisions almost daily. Some examples are the following: Should you force a child to stay on her cot during naptime even though she is clearly not tired? If so, for how long? Should you physically restrain a child who is hurting another child, and if so how much force can you use? Do you follow a father's wish that his child not take a nap because she doesn't fall asleep at home until 11:00 P.M., even though she is very tired at naptime? Should you follow a mother's request that the child's father not pick up the child, because he has been abusive, until she can get a restraining order? Should you follow a father's request that his child not be seen by his estranged wife because she has threatened to kidnap the child? Should you allow a child to use a bathroom inside the building alone or should you accompany her, leaving the children who are playing outside by themselves? Do you report your own program to state authorities if the supervisor tells you to do something that violates licensing laws?

Dealing with Ethical Dilemmas

The following recommendations are for your consideration when dealing with ethical dilemmas. They are meant as helpful guidelines. Ultimately you have to do what you believe is right after you have carefully thought through the issues and potential consequences.

● Remember that your children's health, safety, and well-being are your main priorities. Choose a child's well-being over the wishes of a parent or a supervisor or the smooth running of your classroom. Above all, do no harm to the child.

● Carefully determine the best way to put children first without hurting yourself. Note that licensing standards are established to protect the health and well-being of children and therefore any violation has to be reported. You can do this, however, without giving your name, so your supervisor cannot retaliate. Your own health, well-being, and job security are important considerations in making an ethical decision. Anything that jeopardizes these is not a good choice. Not only will you suffer but your children will be harmed because you will be less effective in your job.

- Work out a compromise or alternative solution whenever possible, if it will not harm the child. Note that a third or fourth option often can be found, although these typically involve more work. For example, if a parent asks you to keep her child awake during naptime, discuss the possibility of allowing the child to sleep for half of the naptime while the parent enforces a regular, reasonable bedtime at home. Gradually increase the amount of time the child naps while the parent gradually makes the bedtime earlier. If this kind of compromise cannot be worked out, the bottom line is that you cannot keep the child awake because this is harmful to her. When refusing, explain clearly and graciously to parents your reasons, based on your professional knowledge.

- Follow the letter of the law, unless the child will be harmed by it. Recall that people with high ethical standards, many of whom have come to be our heros (Gandhi, Martin Luther King Jr.), sometimes have had to break unjust laws because they believed the laws themselves hurt people. If possible, however, do not let yourself be put in this position, especially when acting on behalf of your organization or your school. If a parent cannot legally ask you to stop her spouse from picking up his child, then you should not keep the spouse from the child. Instead, ask the parent to keep the child home until a restraining order is obtained or agree that you will call her if the spouse shows up, although you will not stop the spouse. Do not allow yourself to be put into a lose-lose dilemma of breaking the law or harming the child. No one has the right to force that on you.

- Choose the course that will cause the least harm to the fewest numbers of children. One solution to the dilemma of the child who has to use the bathroom is to gather all the children together and go inside with all of them for a few minutes. Several children probably need to use the bathroom, anyway. Although this is harmful to the children who are outside because it shortens their gross-motor time and disrupts their play, it is less harmful than the potential dangers of leaving any young child unsupervised.

- Before making a decision, gather as much information as you can about a situation. Often a solution is easy to see once you obtain a key piece of information.

- Continue to monitor the results of your decision. Many times situations change or new information is obtained. Few decisions are irreversible. A sign of a person with high ethics is someone who can change her mind, or even a passionately held belief, when faced with new evidence.

- Work on developing policies and procedures that will help eliminate, or at least minimize, ethical dilemmas. Being alone with a group of children will put you in dilemmas over and over again. Work with your supervisor on solving the problem. Perhaps an inexpensive intercom, two-way radio, or cell phone can be purchased. (See "Don't Work Alone" on p. 192 for more ideas.)

- When making an ethical decision be careful not to impose your own values or biases on others. Carefully consider the family's beliefs and values before making your decision, but do not let their values be the only criteria. There are cases in every state of families whose beliefs preclude giving medical services to their children yet the state may intervene if the child is in danger.

- Remember that every decision has repercussions. What seems like a good choice now may not ultimately be good for a family. For example, you may decide to help a family out of an immediate crisis, but the long-term result may be that they become dependent on you to bail them out of other crises. In this case, assist the family in finding ways to help themselves.

- Read the various ethical case studies listed in the resources below. If you have not already encountered some, you surely will in the future. Learning about possible solutions and thinking through the dilemmas will help you tremendously when you actually have to face them.

Resources

Brophy-Herb, H. E., M. J. Kostelnik, and L. C. Stein. 2001. A developmental approach to teaching about ethics using the NAEYC Code of Ethical Conduct. *Young Children* 56 (1): 80–84.

Feeney, S., and N. K. Freeman. 1999. *Ethics and the early childhood educator: Using the NAEYC code.* Washington, D.C.: NAEYC.

Feeney, S., B. M. Caldwell, and K. Kipnis. 1988. Ethics case study: The aggressive child. *Young Children* 43 (2): 48–51.

Feeney, S., and K. Kipnis. 1989. Code of Ethical Conduct and statement of commitment. *Young Children* 45 (1) : 24–29.

Feeney, S., L. Katz, and K. Kipnis. 1987. Ethics case studies: The working mother. *Young Children* 43 (1):16–19.

Feeney, S., S. S. Riley, and K. Kipnis. 1988. Ethics case studies: The divorced parents. *Young Children* 43 (3): 48–51.

Freeman, N. K. 1997. Using NAEYC's Code of Ethics. Mama and Daddy taught me right from wrong—Isn't that enough? *Young Children* 52 (6): 64–67.

Hanson, 2001. *The moral heart of teaching: Toward a teacher's creed.* New York: Teachers College Press.

Nash, R. 2002. *Real world ethics. Frameworks for educators and human service professionals.* 2d ed. New York: Teachers College Press.

National Association for the Education of Young Children (NAEYC). 1994. Using NAEYC's Code of Ethics: A tool for real life. *Young Children* 49 (6): 50–51.

———. 1995. How many ways can you think of to use NAEYC's Code of Ethics? *Young Children* 51 (1): 42–43.

———. 1995. What should you do if you don't like a child in your care? *Young Children* 50 (4): 72–73.

———. 1995. What would you do if discussing a child's behavior resulted in the parent beating him? *Young Children* 50 (5): 50–51.

———. 1996. Using NAEYC's Code of Ethics. When a staff member violates ethical principles, what should a parent do? *Young Children* 52 (1): 66–67.

———. 1996. Using NAEYC's Code of Ethics. Why don't you teach the basics? *Young Children* 51 (5): 48–49.

———. 1997. Using NAEYC's Code of Ethics. Mary and the missing bracelet. *Young Children* 52 (3): 66–67.

———. 1997. Using NAEYC's Code of Ethics. Who is the biter? *Young Children* 52 (2): 54–55.

———. 1998. Using NAEYC's Code of Ethics. My colleague doesn't understand how to teach reading. *Young Children* 53 (1): 64–67

———. 1998. Using NAEYC's Code of Ethics. What happens when school/parent relationships aren't good? *Young Children* 53 (6): 75

———. 1999. Using NAEYC's Code of Ethics to negotiate professional problems: How do we balance cultural diversity and our own cultural values? *Young Children* 54 (5): 44–46.

———. 1999. Using NAEYC's Code of Ethics to negotiate professional problems: What should a teacher do when a parent defines academically rigorous education differently than she does? *Young Children* 54 (6): 56–57.

Rand, M. 2000. *Giving it some thought: Cases for early childhood practice.* Washington, D.C.: NAEYC.

Web Sites

Code of Ethical Conduct and Statement of Commitment. NAEYC Position Statement. www.naeyc.org. Click on Resources, then on Position Statements then scroll down to and click on Improving early childhood professional development and professional development, then scroll down to article title.

Code of Ethics of the Education Profession. National Education Association. www.nea.org/code.html

Developing a Code of Ethics for the Early Childhood Education by Kenneth Kipness and Stephanie Feeney. Ethical and Policy Issues Perspectives on the Professions. Fall 1999. Illinois Institute of Technology. Center for the Study of Ethics in the Professions. www.iit.edu/departments/csep. Click on Perspectives on the Professions under publications, then on Writing a Code of Ethics, then on article title.

Ohio Association for the Education of Young Children Code of Ethics www.oaeyc.org/ethics.html

3. Being an Advocate for Families, Children, the Profession, and Yourself

The results of conducting yourself and promoting yourself as a professional will not only benefit the families and children you serve, but ultimately yourself. Without a public perception of early childhood teachers as professionals, better salaries and benefits, more respect, better working conditions, and more funds to help parents pay for services may not happen. Professionalism is mostly based on public perception and public perception can be swayed. You, as an individual, can have a great impact on helping families and promoting the cause of quality care and education for young children. Everything you do really does make a difference.

Building a Professional Image

● Dress appropriately but well. Wearing a business suit to work with young children makes no sense, but wearing neat, clean, fashionable (but conservative) and comfortable clothes does. Keep a change of clothes and a bottle of stain remover with you. Wear shoes with rubber soles for comfort and for running with children, but do not wear torn, dirty sneakers. Keep a good pair of shoes on hand for meetings or for parent conferences.

● Join professional groups, clubs, political groups, and civic organizations. These should not only include those within the profession but groups such as Kiwanis, American Association of University Women, Junior League, Red Cross, Lions, National Association of Jewish Women, Democratic or Republican Club, National Organization for Women, and so on. Many of these groups consider issues related to educating and caring for young children an important part of their work. They will benefit from your expertise and you will benefit by being recognized as an active, interested community member.

● Educate yourself about current political issues related to the field. Get involved in helping to pass beneficial state and federal legislation. Do not feel that you have to be an expert or a great public speaker or that you have to invest a huge amount of time. There is a great deal of work to do and any help, from stuffing envelopes to gathering signatures on a petition, would be a great contribution.

● Know what the opposition is and why it is there. Many people would like to keep early childhood teachers from becoming more professional because they are worried that the cost of care would increase. Others believe that it threatens the "sanctity" of motherhood. Work together with parents to fight for more state and federal funds and business contributions to help them pay for the more expensive care their children deserve and the better salary you deserve.

● Know the results of a few key research studies that support the work that you do. For example, the Perry Preschool Study showed that for every dollar invested in a good preschool program for children from low-income families, four to six dollars were returned to society later in reduced costs for less crime, unemployment, welfare, and special education services (Schweinhart, Barnes, and Weikart 1993). Another study found that good, quality child care and preschool is beneficial to children's development (Cost, Quality, and Outcomes Study Team 1995). Other studies show that giving children choices and helping them learn through play benefits them more (even academically) than direct, teacher-controlled teaching methods (Stipek, Feiler, Daniels, and Milburn 1995; Marcon 1992; Epstein, Schweinhart, and McAdoo 1996).

● Learn what constitutes good management practices for people who operate or supervise early childhood programs. (This book contains many ideas.) Offer suggestions to your supervisor or work with other staff to lobby for improvements. Be assured that this will make life easier for you, allow you to be a more effective teacher, and provide a higher quality program to children and families.

● Refer to yourself as a child development specialist, an educator, a teacher, or a teacher-caregiver. (Unfortunately, teacher has a more professional connotation than caregiver or provider.) Correct anyone who uses terms such as "baby-sitter."

● Follow a set of principles of what constitutes the best practices in early childhood education. Be able to articulate those principles clearly and explain how you put them into practice. See the initial section of this book on pp. 1–4 for ideas.

● Follow a code of ethics as described in the previous chapter.

● Learn the jargon used in the field. For good or bad, all professional groups have their own jargon. Help parents and new colleagues interpret the jargon. (See the "Glossary of Common Terms and Jargon," pp. 209–213.)

● Be helpful to others in the field. Be a mentor to a new teacher, offer to help a coworker solve a problem, share favorite songs of your children.

● Build bridges between yourself and colleagues who work in other types of programs (Montessori, public school, private child care, Head Start, and so on). Focus on all the things you have in common rather than on the few differences between your programs.

● Ask for the tools you need to help you do your job effectively and efficiently and the training you need including a two-way radio or cell phone, a computer with Internet access, a mentor, and courses or workshops. If necessary, help find grants or help raise money to pay for them.

Your Own Professional Development

● Continue your own education by working toward a higher degree or credential, taking classes, workshops, reading, and attending conferences. Subscribe to or use library copies of magazines and journals in the field to keep current.

● Use the Internet. It's literally an entire library of information at your fingertips. Although it can be frustrating to use it at times, knowing a few tips will minimize this problem and save you time.

● If you have trouble finding an article, try entering the entire name of the article within quotation marks in Google.com or another general search engine.

● If you enter a Web site address in the address bar and you get an error message, try using the root address (this is the part that begins with "http://" and ends with ".com" or ".org" or ".net"). This will usually bring you to the main page of the Web site. If there is a search box on this main page enter in the name of the article or resource you are looking for. If not, try to find it through logical links such as "Publications" or "For Teachers."

● You can open more than one Web browser (MS Explorer or Netscape are the most common) window at a time. While you are waiting for a page to "load," you can click on your browser icon again and start searching for something else. Be aware, however, that if your computer does not have a good deal of memory, opening too many browser windows may cause it to freeze.

Comprehensive Web Sites

The following is a list of Web sites specifically for early childhood teachers. They have many full-text articles on a variety of subjects. Some are easy to navigate with effective search engines within the site. Others are more complicated and the articles are difficult to find. Some have annoying flashing graphics or many advertisements. I eliminated the most egregious ones, but there are still some on this list that are quite annoying; however, the rich resources on the site make them worth using nonetheless. The comprehensive Web sites for parents listed on p. 166 also have useful information for teachers. The sites are listed in order of most comprehensive or useful to least, based on this author's experience with them. However, they are all very good.

Earlychildhood.com
www.earlychildhood.com. The Reading Center brings you to hundreds of articles.

National Network for Child Care
www.nncc.org. Try out the Articles and Resources tab.

Early Childhood Educators' and Families Web Corner
users.stargate.net/~cokids

Early Childhood Education On Line
www.ume.maine.edu/ECEOL-L/website.html

What You Need to Know about Daycare/Preschool. About.com.
daycare.about.com

Education World—Early Childhood Community
www.education-world.com/early_childhood

Early Childhood Educator
www.edpsych.com

Child Care Online. Resource Center.
childcare.net/library.shtml

Facts in Action. Associated Early Care and Education.
www.factsinaction.org

ERIC/EECE. Clearinghouse on Elementary and Early Childhood Education.
ericeece.org

Early Childhood Education E-Newsletter. The Northwest Regional Educational Laboratory. See current and archived newsletters.
www.nwrel.org/cfc

National Child Care Information Center. The Frequently Requested Information link leads you to many helpful articles.
www.nccic.org

KinderStart search engine. The Child Development link gives you access to many excellent resources.
www.kinderstart.com

Child Care Source
www.childcaresource.org/ages.htm

The Chalkboard
patricia_f.tripod.com

Preschool by Stormie
www.preschoolbystormie.com

Perpetual Preschool. It has a very good internal search engine.
www.perpetualpreschool.com

Peggy's Early Childhood Care and Education Resources
home.sprintmail.com/~peggyriehl

Teach-nology. Link on Teachers then scroll down to Early Childhood Education.
www.teach-nology.com

BANANASinc.org
www.bananasinc.org/freePubs.php

Action Alliance for Children. Click on Resources.
www.4children.org

The Whole Child. Three sections: ABCs of Child Development, For Early Childhood Education Providers, and For Parents.
www.pbs.org/wholechild

Early Childhood Education Web Guide
www.ecewebguide.com

Helping Children with Books. Eugene, Oregon Public Library. A bibliography of children's picture books categorized by subjects such as death, new baby, anger, adoption, divorce, separation, illnesses, and many more.
www.ci.eugene.or.us/Library/staffref/therapy.htm

Professional Organizations and Agencies

Accreditation—See *National Academy of Early Childhood Programs.*

American Educational Research Association (AERA)—Advances educational research and its practical application. www.aera.net

Association for Childhood Education International (ACEI)—Promotes and supports in the global community the optimal education and development of children. www.udel.edu/bateman/acei

Association for Supervision and Curriculum Development (ASCD)—International, nonprofit, nonpartisan association of professional educators whose jobs cross all grade levels and subject areas. www.ascd.org

Black Child Development Institute—See *National Black Child Development Institute.*

Center Accreditation Program—See *National Academy of Early Childhood Programs.*

Center for the Child Care Workforce—Advocates for better wages, and the rights and needs of early childhood workers. www.ccw.org

Child Care Action Campaign—Works for quality and affordable child care for all families. www.childcareaction.org

Child Care Law Center—Uses legal tools to foster the development of quality, affordable child care. www.childcarelaw.org

Child Development Associate (CDA)—See *Council for Professional Recognition.*

Child Welfare League of America (CWLA)—Develops and promotes policies and programs to protect America's children and strengthen America's families. www.cwla.org

Children's Defense Fund (CDF)—The organization that coined the term "Leave No Child Behind." It works to ensure every child a Healthy Start, a Head Start, a Fair Start, a Safe Start, and a Moral Start in life and successful passage to adulthood with the help of caring families and communities. www.childrensdefense.org

Council for Exceptional Children (CEC)—See *Division for Early Childhood (DEC).*

Council for Professional Recognition—Administers the Child Development Associate credential (CDA), a national certificate certifying basic competence in working with young children. Houses Reggio Children/USA and other programs. www.cdacouncil.org

Division for Early Childhood (DEC)—Advocates for individuals who work with or on behalf of children with special needs, birth through age eight, and their families. www.dec-sped.org

ERIC/EECE (Educational Resources Information Center/Elementary and Early Childhood Education)—Clearinghouse for information on development, education, and the care of children birth through early adolescence. ericeece.org

Families and Work Institute—Center for research that provides data to inform decision making on the changing workplace, changing family, and changing community. www.familiesandwork.org

High/Scope Educational Research Foundation—A research, development, training, and public advocacy organization with a mission to improve the life chances of children and youth by promoting high-quality educational programs. www.highscope.org

I Am Your Child Campaign and Foundation—Seeks to raise public awareness about early childhood development and to try to influence public policy makers to increase spending on early childhood programs. www.iamyourchild.org

National Academy of Early Childhood Programs—Administers NAEYC's national, voluntary, professionally sponsored accreditation system to help raise the quality of all types of preschools, kindergartens, child care centers, and school-age child care programs.

National Association of Child Care Resource and Referral Agencies—Provides vision, leadership, and support to community child care resource and referral and to promote national policies and partnerships committed to the development and learning of all children www.naccrra.org

National Association for Family Child Care (NAFCC)—Dedicated to promoting quality child care by strengthening the profession of family child care. www.nafcc.org

National Association for the Education of Young Children (NAEYC)—The leading professional membership organization and largest single organization in the field. www.naeyc.org

National Black Child Development Institute (NBCDI)—Initiates positive change for the health, welfare, and educational needs of all African American children. www.nbcdi.org

National Center for Children in Poverty—Identifies and promotes strategies that prevent child poverty in the United States and that improve the lives of low-income children and families. www.nccp.org

National Center for Clinical Infant Programs—See *Zero to Three.*

National Coalition for Campus Children's Centers—Supports research and activities affecting college and university early childhood education and service settings, family and work issues, and the field of early childhood education in general. www.campuschildren.org

National Even Start Association—Provides a national voice and vision for Even Start Family Literacy Programs. www.evenstart.org

National Head Start Association (NHSA)—Provides a national forum for the continued enhancement of Head Start services for poor children ages birth through five, and their families. www.nhsa.org

Society for Research in Child Development—Promotes multidisciplinary research in the field of human development, to foster the exchange of information among scientists and other professionals of various disciplines and to encourage applications of research findings. www.srcd.org

U.S. National Committee of the World Organization for Early Childhood Education (OMEP)—Strives to use every possible means to promote the optimum conditions for the well-being of all children and their development and happiness within their families, institutions, and society.

Zero to Three: National Center for Infants, Toddlers, and Families—Works to strengthen and support families, practitioners, and communities to promote the healthy development of babies and toddlers. www.zerotothree.org

Governmental Agencies

Administration on Children, Youth, and Families (ACYF)—The federal agency that administers Head Start and other federal programs. www.acf.dhhs.gov/programs/acyf

Child Care Bureau, Administration for Children and Families (ACF), Department of Health and Human Services (DHHS)—Dedicated to enhancing the quality, affordability, and availability of child care for all families. The Child Care Bureau administers federal funds to states, territories, and tribes to assist low-income families in accessing quality child care for children when the parents work or participate in education or training. www.acf.dhhs.gov/programs/ccb

Even Start Family Literacy Program, Office of Elementary and Secondary Education (OESE), U.S. Department of Education—Even Start's premise is that combining adult literacy (adult basic education or instruction for English language learners), parenting education, early childhood education, and interactive parent and child literacy activities into a unified family literacy program offers promise for helping to break the intergenerational cycle of poverty and low literacy in the nation. www.ed.gov/offices/OESE/CEP/evenstprogresp.html

Head Start Bureau, Administration for Children and Families (ACF), Department of Health and Human Services (DHHS)—Head Start and Early Head Start are comprehensive child development programs which serve children from birth to age five, pregnant women, and their families. They are child-focused programs and have the overall goal of increasing the school readiness of young children in low-income families. www2.acf.dhhs.gov/programs/hsb

National Center for Early Development and Learning (NCEDL)—A national early childhood research project supported by the U.S. Dept. of Education's Office of Educational Research and Improvement (OERI) and operated by the FPG Child Development Center, UNC-Chapel Hill in collaboration with the University of Virginia, and UCLA. Focuses on enhancing the cognitive, social, and emotional development of children from birth through age eight. www.fpg.unc.edu/~ncedl

National Child Care Information Center, Child Care Bureau, Administration for Children and Families (ACF), Department of Health and Human Services (DHHS)—A national resource that links information and people to complement, enhance, and promote the child care delivery system, working to ensure that all children and families have access to high-quality comprehensive services. www.nccic.org

National Institute on Early Child Development and Education (NIECDE), Office of Educational Research and Improvement (OERI), U.S. Department of Education—Sponsors comprehensive and challenging research in order to help ensure that America's young children are successful in school and beyond—and to enhance their quality of life and that of their families. www.ed.gov/offices/OERI/ECI

Magazines and Journals

The Web sites give you access to more information about the journals. The full texts are not available online, although a few of the journals offer the full text of some selected articles.

The American Journal of Orthopsychiatry www.amerortho.org/ajo.htm

Child Care Information Exchange www.ccie.com

Child Development. Journal of the Society for Research in Child Development. www.srcd.org/cd.html

Child Study Journal www.buffalostate.edu/~edf/csj.htm

Child Welfare. Journal of the Child Welfare League of America. www.cwla.org

Childhood Education. Journal of the Association for Childhood Education International. www.udel.edu/bateman/acei/cehp.htm

Developmental Psychology. Journal of the American Psychological Association.
www.apa.org/journals/dev.html

Early Childhood News
www.earlychildhoodnews.com

Early Childhood Research Quarterly.
www.udel.edu/ecrq

Early Childhood Today
teacher.scholastic.com/products/ect

Educational Leadership. Journal of the Association for Supervision and Curriculum Development.
www.ascd.org/frameedlead.html

Exchange—See *Child Care Information Exchange*.

The Future of Children. Publication of the David and Lucille Packard Foundation.
www.futureofchildren.org

Journal of Child and Youth Care
www.uofcpress.com/UCP/JCYC.html

Journal of Early Intervention. Council for Exceptional Children, Division for Early Childhood.
www.fpg.unc.edu/~jei/

Merrill-Palmer Quarterly. Journal of Developmental Psychology, Wayne State University.
muse.jhu.edu/journals/mpq

Topics in Early Childhood Special Education
www.proedinc.com/tec.html

Young Children. Journal of the National Association for the Education of Young Children.
www.naeyc.org

Young Exceptional Children. Journal of the Division for Early Childhood of the Council for Exceptional Children.
www.dec-sped.org/YEC

Online Journals

The full texts of the articles in these journals are available online

Child Care Bulletin. Child Care Bureau.
nccic.org/ccbullet.html

Contemporary Issues in Early Childhood. Free to individuals.
www.traingle.co.uk/CIEC

Early Childhood Research and Practice. Sponsored by ERIC/EECE.
ecrp.uiuc.edu

Early Developments
www.fpg.unc.edu/~ncedl. Click on "Publications," then scroll down and click on "Early Developments."

ERIC/EECE Newsletter
ericeece.org/pubs/eece-nl.html

Teachers College Record
www.tcrecord.org

Glossary of Common Terms and Jargon

Accommodation: Term used by Jean Piaget to describe how children learn by altering old concepts to include new information. For example, a child alters his idea of "dog" to include small, short-haired creatures after seeing a Chihuahua for the first time. This is the second part of the *adaptation* process. *Assimilation* is the first part.

Accreditation: Certification by a legitimate organization (NAEYC, state Departments of Education, and so on) of having met a set of standards. It can be for a program or an individual and can range from meeting minimal to very high standards.

Action Research: Research that is done by teachers in classrooms. The teacher identifies a question he wants to know the answer to or problem to solve and carries out activities in the classroom to find the answer. For example, the teacher may try several different schedules over a period of time to determine which seems to best meet the needs of the children and make the class run smoothest.

Active Listening: A variety of techniques to be able to listen well, elicit information from others, and communicate effectively. Includes using "I-messages," restating what the person says, making eye contact, and asking clarifying questions.

ADA: See *Americans with Disabilities Act.*

Adaptation: Term used by Jean Piaget to describe how children learn by *assimilating* new information and *accommodating* their previous knowledge to incorporate this new information.

ADD: See *Attention Deficit Disorder.*

ADHD: Attention Deficit Hyperactivity Disorder.

Affect: The emotional part of a person, including values, feelings, interests, and motivations.

Affective Development: See *Affect.*

Americans with Disabilities Act (ADA): Federal legislation passed in 1990. It gives civil rights protections to individuals with disabilities similar to those provided to individuals on the basis of race, color, sex, national origin, age, and religion. It guarantees equal opportunity for individuals with disabilities in public accommodations, employment, transportation, state and local government services, and telecommunications.

Areas of Development: Typically includes social, emotional, cognitive, self-help, language, and small-motor and large-motor skills. Can also include dispositions, creativity, motivation, behaviors, play abilities, and more.

Assessment: A tool or system for determining a child's skills, abilities, or knowledge. Assessments can range from very formal (psychometric, standardized tests like the Wechsler Intelligence Scale for Children) to very informal (checklists of children's development). Screening tests, developmental assessments, readiness tests, and diagnostic tests are all types of assessment used for different purposes.

Assimilation: Term used by Jean Piaget to describe how children learn by taking in new information and sensations. For example, a child sees a Chihuahua and hears an adult say "doggie." This is the first part of the *adaptation process. Accommodation* is the second part.

Associative Play: Children playing together but in an unorganized way, without a central purpose.

At-Risk: A term used to describe a child with a number of risk factors for whom there is concern that he might not develop well or do well in school.

Attention Deficit Disorder (ADD): The inability of a child to concentrate or pay attention to something so that the child's behavior causes problems in learning or getting along with others. It must happen consistently and in all situations to be labeled ADD.

Authoring Software (or Tools): Computer software that enables one to develop a Web site or a complex document that can include text, photos, video, animation, and sound. It allows teachers to develop electronic spaces for children or to document class events or student work electronically.

Behavior Modification: Changing a person's behavior through rewards, punishment, or some system of reinforcement.

Behaviorism: Branch of psychology that ascribes the cause of all human behavior to how other people and the environment reinforce it or do not reinforce it.

Benchmarks: Expectations of what children should be able to do or know at a given age or grade level. It is usually used in relation to standards and testing. A benchmark is set for a particular standard and then the child is tested on his ability to meet that benchmark. For example, a benchmark in the area of literacy might be that a child can recognize his name when written in large block letters by four years old.

CDA: See *Child Development Associate.*

CDF: See *Children's Defense Fund.*

Child Development Associate: A national certificate certifying basic competence in working with young children. Administered by the Council for Early Childhood Professional Recognition.

Children's Defense Fund: Organization that educates and lobbies for better lives for children and families.

Classification: Grouping items by like characteristics. For example, sorting all red objects into a box.

Cognition: The process of thinking or coming to an understanding of something.

Cognitive Development: See *Cognition.*

Communicative Competence: The ability to make one's message clearly known to others by any means (words, sign language, writing, and so on).

Compensatory Preschool Programs: Programs such as Head Start and Title I that are designed to help children from low-income families compensate for some experiences and skills they may have missed due to lack of resources.

Computer Literacy: The ability to use computers and a variety of common software with a good degree of skill and accuracy for one's developmental level.

Conflict Resolution: A set of skills for solving a conflict effectively and peacefully. It usually involves brainstorming solutions, discussing possible consequences of the solutions, negotiating a compromise, and deciding on and taking a course of action.

Conservation: The principle that amounts of things stay the same even when they are moved or reshaped. Most preschool age children cannot conserve. They believe, for example, that after a liquid is poured from a short, wide glass into a tall, thin glass, the latter contains more liquid than the original container did.

Constructive Play: Play in which the child builds or creates something.

Constructivism: Term used by Jean Piaget to describe the process by which children learn. They construct their own knowledge of the world and how it works by interacting with real things and people. For example, a child invents or constructs for himself the idea of "half" by dividing up his playdough in equal amounts to give some to his friend.

Cooperative Play: Children playing together with a common purpose.

Criterion-Referenced Assessments: Tests whose scores are based on comparing a child's performance to certain, explicit criteria. This contrasts with *norm-referenced* assessments where the score is based on a comparison to other children.

Cultural Competence: The ability to understand, work effectively, and be responsive to a variety of cultures. It involves a set of skills that includes empathy, flexibility, listening carefully, asking appropriate questions, reading body language, getting information from a variety of sources, and more.

DAP: See *Developmentally Appropriate Practice.*

Developmental Delay: Any handicap or disability that results in the child's skills and learning ability maturing more slowly than his peers.

Developmental Milestones: Major points in a child's life by which his growth is measured. Examples include sitting up, crawling, walking, first word, first primary tooth, first primary tooth falling out, and so on.

Developmental Psychology or Developmental Education: The branch of psychology or education that ascribes human behavior to the interaction between the growth/maturing process and the environment.

Developmentally Appropriate Practice: Guidelines by which teachers do activities, interact, and create environments that meet the needs of young children according to their age level and their individual strengths, weaknesses, and interests. These guidelines are described in the following

publication: *Developmentally Appropriate Practice in Early Childhood Programs Serving Children from Birth through Age Eight* Revised Edition, edited by S. Brekekamp and C. Copple. Washington, D.C.: NAEYC, 1997.

Dramatic Play: Situations in which children interact while taking on roles. Some examples are children playing a family on a camping trip, firefighters putting a house fire out, or superheroes fighting "bad guys."

ECE: Early Childhood Education.

Egocentricism: Term used by Jean Piaget to describe the inability of young children to see the world through another's eyes, and the belief that events and actions are caused by or directed at them.

ELL: English language learners.

Emergent Skills: Abilities that are in the process of developing in children. Emergent literacy refers to a child's early attempts to write and read.

Empathy: The ability to understand and relate to how another person feels or thinks.

Empowerment: To give someone the ability to have control over a situation, themselves, or their lives. Children are empowered when they are given choices and encouraged to make meaningful decisions.

ESL: English as a second language. Also see *ELL* and *LEP.*

Evaluation: Usually refers to a process for determining the effectiveness of a program. Sometimes called "Program Evaluation."

Expressive Language: The ability to use words or sounds to communicate.

Eye-Hand Coordination: The ability to use the hand and the eye together to complete a task, such as putting a peg in a hole or hammering a nail.

Family-Centered Practices: Ways of working with families that respects them as individuals and considers their needs, unique qualities, and strengths. Any assistance or intervention provided is based on that knowledge of families.

Fine Motor: See *Small Motor.*

Free Choice: The part of the program day when the children choose from a wide variety of activities and materials and make decisions about how to participate and for how long.

Functional Play: Repetitive, practice play in which the child performs the same action over and over.

Goals: Statements of what adults hope to help children gain, accomplish, or achieve. For a very shy, withdrawn child, an example of a long-term goal (one year or more) might be the following: "The child will play cooperatively with other children." An example of a short-term goal (a few months or less) would be "The child will engage in associative play with one other child." The length of a goal depends on a child's ability level. Goal statements are typically followed by objectives.

Gross Motor: See *Large Motor*.

Guidance: Helping children to develop self-control and self-efficacy.

Hot-Housing: Pushing children to grow and learn faster than is appropriate for their ages or abilities.

Hyperactive: Behavior characterized by a very high activity level and the inability to remain still for even a short period of time. This behavior occurs consistently over time and in all situations.

I-Messages: Communicating by starting a sentence with "I." This tells how the speaker is feeling or thinking, as opposed to beginning with "you," which tends to interrogate, accuse, or blame.

IEP: See *Individualized Educational Plan*.

IFSP: See *Individualized Family Services Plan*.

Inclusion: Involving children with differences—usually disabilities—fully in the activities and social fabric of a typical classroom.

Individualized Educational Plan: Required by law for all children receiving special services, this plan details the child's current abilities, sets educational goals and objectives, lists the services the child will receive, and tells where the child will spend his time. A team of people including the teacher, specialists, and the parents develop the plan. Parents must approve and sign the plan before it can be implemented. It must be reviewed and updated periodically.

Individualized Family Services Plan: Required by PL 99-457 for children from birth to age three with special needs, this plan is similar to an individualized educational plan, but it also includes supporting the needs of the family to aid the child.

Individualizing: Meeting the needs of each child by altering activities, interactions, the schedule, and the environment to optimize each child's learning and well-being.

Instrumental Aggression: An aggressive act done in order to get something that the child wants. It is the most common type of aggression.

Integration: Serving typical and disabled children in the same classroom and ensuring the full participation of children with handicaps in all activities.

Interactionalism: Vygotsky's theory that development happens and is only understood within interactions among people. Intelligence, in this theory, is not a fixed concept but will vary based on the people involved. The same person can be very intelligent in his community but not in a school setting, for example.

Intersubjectivity: Vygotsky's concept describing when there is clear and correct mutual understanding of the communication between people. The implication for teachers is that too often teachers assume that child understands what she means when that is not the case. Intersubjectivity must be achieved for true teaching and learning to take place.

Kinesthetic: Sensation or learning achieved through touching, feeling, or moving any part of the body. Petting real animals, feeling three-dimensional figures of animals, or moving the way various animals move are kinesthetic ways to become familiar with animals.

Lanham Act: Federal funding of child care during World War II. Produced widespread, quality, affordable, or free child care but ended when the war ended in 1945.

Large Motor: Skills related to using the head, arms, legs, and feet. Running and climbing are large-motor skills. Also called *Gross Motor*.

LEP: Limited English proficient.

Literacy: The ability to read and write text or interact with books with a good degree of facility and accuracy for one's developmental level. It is emergent in young children but must be taught explicitly to be developed. Also see *Numeracy, Computer Literacy*, and *Media Literacy*.

Logical Consequences: Using the typical result of a problem behavior as a way to help the child see the concern about the behavior and prevent it from happening again. The logical consequence of misusing a toy, assuming that the child has been taught and reminded how to use it properly, is not to have access to that toy for a period of time. It needs to be used in conjunction with teaching the appropriate behavior, redirection, and other strategies to be effective.

Looping: The teacher stays with the same group of children for multiple years.

Mainstreaming: Process of integrating children with disabilities into classrooms that mostly contain typical children, either part or full time.

Manipulatives: Toys or activities that involve using the hand and the eye to work them. Legos and Tinkertoys are manipulatives.

Media Literacy: The ability to critically view TV, film, video games, advertisements, and other media, in order to understand any attempts at manipulation, its purposes, strengths and weakness, and discern fact from fiction for one's developmental level. It is emergent in young children, but needs to be taught explicitly to be developed.

Meta-Cognition: The ability to think about how one is thinking. Even young children can begin to develop such self-awareness.

Modalities: Various senses by which children learn. These include visual, auditory, tactile, olfactory (smell), and taste. Most children learn best by using several modalities.

Modeling: Demonstrating a behavior or action by showing how it is done. Adults who use polite words model good manners for children.

Multiple Intelligences: A theory developed by Howard Gardner that describes different people as having different types of intelligences, many of which are not valued in schools. This can put some children at a disadvantage in school, although they may have great strengths and abilities. A child with great interpersonal intelligence may get in trouble for talking too much if there are not enough opportunities to interact.

Norm-Referenced Assessments: Tests whose scores are based on a comparison to a representative group. For example, a child who scores low on a screening test for language does not speak as well as most other children his age.

Numeracy: The ability to use numbers and math to solve daily problems with a good degree of facility and accuracy for one's developmental level. It is akin to literacy, but relates to numbers rather than text. It is emergent in young children but needs to be taught explicitly to be developed.

Object Constancy: The principle that objects stay the same even when they are moved, turned, or felt rather than seen.

Object Permanence: The principle that objects still exist even when hidden from view.

Objectives: Statements of what children will do to meet a goal. Usually they are specific, measurable, observable, and follow a sequence. Objectives for the goal, "The child will engage in associative play with another child," may be the following: (1) the child will play near another child for ten minutes each day; (2) the child will play with the same materials and near another child for ten minutes each day; and (3) the child will play with the same materials and with another child for five minutes each day. Objectives are typically followed by teaching strategies for implementing the objectives.

Onsets and Rimes: Onsets are the initial sounds in words and rimes are the ending sounds. Teaching about "word families" employs onsets and rimes. In the word *hat*, "h" is the onset and "at" is the rime. The word *bat* has a different onset but the same rime.

Outcomes: Expected results from an action, activity, or program. Outcomes for children from attending preschool might include the ability to get along with a wide variety of people, a love of books and learning, curiosity, the ability to negotiate and solve conflicts peacefully, and the ability to get his needs met appropriately.

Parallel Play: Children playing alongside each other, usually with the same materials, but playing independently.

Phonemes (Phonemic Awareness): The sounds of a language. Phonemic awareness refers to the ability to hear and say the separate sounds in words. It is considered by many to be an important precursor skill to reading.

Piaget, Jean: Swiss developmental psychologist who developed the constructivist theory of how intelligence develops in children. Most of his research was done by observing his own children.

Portfolio Assessment: The use of a set of tangible examples of a child's work or behavior to evaluate his skills, knowledge, and abilities. For example, a collection of a child's self-portraits done over the course of the school year to show growth and progress in motor and eye-hand coordination, sophistication of observation and detail, and self-concept.

Preoperational: Term used by Jean Piaget to describe the ages from about two-and-a-half to eight. Children in this stage think concretely, are egocentric, and learn by actively interacting with real things.

Pro-Social Behavior or Skills: The ability to interact with others in positive, pleasing ways; the ability to make and maintain friendships.

Projects (Project Approach): Long-term, large-scale efforts through which a wide variety of subject matter and teaching and learning are integrated. Projects usually involve children working together cooperatively and results in a finished product such as a report, display, collection, book, video, and so forth.

Punishment: A negative consequence for a negative behavior, such as sitting in a time-out chair for hitting another child.

Receptive Language: The ability to understand what is said by another person.

Red-Shirting: Starting a child in school at an older age than he is eligible to start at, so that he will experience academic success.

Redirection: Helping a child to do a more acceptable activity to one that is causing a problem, but that will meet the same need.

Reggio Emilia: A town in north-central Italy known for its uniquely high-quality early childhood programs. Part of the approach of these programs involves helping children express themselves using a wide variety of art materials at a very high level of skill and creativity.

Reinforcement: Providing verbal or tangible rewards or punishment to increase a behavior.

Representational Art: Art that attempts to represent actual objects. Children's drawings of themselves, families, and houses are representational art, as opposed to drawings of shapes, squiggles, or designs.

Representational Play: See *Symbolic Play*.

Resiliency: A term used to describe certain children who have the ability to do well and have a healthy sense of self in spite of great obstacles and risk factors such as poverty, violence in their community, and so on. Factors that increase and support resiliency include a supportive relative or teacher, a safe place to go in the community, and access to resources such as books.

Risk Factors: Negative or harmful events or circumstances that put children "at-risk" for poor development or outcomes, or not doing well in school. These typically include developmental problems, low birth weight, single parent families, poverty, violence in the home or community, substance abuse in the home, homelessness, schools with few resources, and so on.

Scaffolding: Based on Vygotsky's theories, it is a process of helping a child move up to his next level of development or learning by providing materials and assistance. Then when the child is fully capable on his own, helping to move him to the next level, and so on.

Schema: A set of pieces of knowledge or skills that becomes automatic. People have schemas for everything from how to tie their shoes to how other people should behave. Set schemas help keep the world clear and organized; however, schemas for the same activities can vary greatly among people. Children are in the process of developing new schemas rapidly.

Screening: Determining (usually with a test) a child's general areas of strength and weakness. Typically a child who is weak in one or more areas of development is referred for further testing.

Self-Concept: The sense of who one is and how a person sees himself. This includes a person's view of his own roles (sibling, son, friend), abilities, interests, values, beliefs, and more. Children with good self-concepts have a realistic sense of their own strengths and weaknesses. They feel comfortable with who they are and with what they like and dislike.

Self-Efficacy: The ability to have a positive impact on one's environment and to get one's needs met intentionally. That is to have a goal, create and carryout a plan, and achieve one's goal in a positive way.

Self-Esteem: The feelings of one's worthiness. It is one part of self-concept. Children with good self-esteem generally feel competent, worthwhile, able, confident, and positive about themselves.

Self-Help Skills: The ability to take care of one's own basic needs such as toileting, dressing, washing, and eating.

Sensorimotor Stage: Term used by Jean Piaget to describe the first stage of life. It is characterized by learning through all the senses without language. For example, infants typically put things in their mouths to learn through taste what the object is.

Sensory Integration: The ability to fully integrate a number of related bodily feelings and skills such as balancing, knowing where you are in space, feeling one's weight in specific places, and so on. Most people have these abilities naturally, but a few do not to varying degrees.

Sensory Integration Dysfunction: The lack of ability to fully integrate a number of related bodily feelings and skills such as balancing, knowing where you are in space, feeling one's weight in specific places, and so on. Children with this disability have a hard time focusing, behaving appropriately, and performing simple motor tasks. There are specific strategies that physical and occupational therapists use to help children overcome the problems or compensate for them.

Seriation: Ordering items based on their size, weight, thickness, quantity, or similar quality.

Small Motor: The ability to use the hands and fingers, and to manipulate objects. Stringing beads is a small-motor task.

Social-Cultural Development: Vygotsky's theory: All development can only be viewed and understood within particular social and cultural contexts. Knowledge and intelligence is always culturally based. The long history associated with any society or culture has a great bearing on individual development.

Social Skills: The ability or lack of ability to interact, form, and maintain relationships with others.

Spatial Relations: The sense of how things relate to each other in terms of their position in space. For example: *on, below, above, behind, to the left,* and so on.

Standards: Agreed upon expectations for what constitutes high-level, challenging teaching and learning in the content areas (reading, writing, math, and so on). A math standard for a young child might be the ability to use numbers to solve simple everyday problems, such as determining how many cups are needed so that everyone at the table has one.

Strengths-Based: An approach to working with children and families that builds on what they can do well to help them do better.

Symbolic Play: Play in which the child substitutes pretend items for the real thing, such as using a block to represent a glass of milk.

Tactile: The sense of touch.

Temporal Relations: The sense of how things relate in time, such as knowing that a past event happened yesterday, last week, last month, or last year.

Transitional Objects: Items such as blankets and stuffed animals that help children make the transition from the security of home to another place.

Transitioning: Helping a child make a positive move from preschool to kindergarten or from any grade to the next.

Transitions: This term has two common meanings. One meaning refers to the change from one activity to another in the classroom. The second meaning refers to the change from one school or grade to another.

Trilemma of Child Care: Refers to the three issues of quality, affordability, and accessibility and how they interact with each other. Increasing or improving one, often decreases the others.

Verbal Skills: The ability to speak and to be understood.

Vygotsky, Lev S.: Russian developmental psychologist who espoused a social-cultural theory of human development. He believed that the development of all higher mental functioning starts in interactions between a child (interpersonal) and an adult—or more capable child—and then becomes internalized (intrapersonal).

Zone of Proximal Development: Vygotsky's idea of the area between what a child can do on his own and what he can do with assistance from someone more capable. The implication of this for schools is that teachers should target their assistance within that zone.

Other Resources from Redleaf Press

So This Is Normal Too? Teachers and Parents Working Out Developmental Issues in Young Children
by Deborah Hewitt
Makes the challenging behaviors of children a vehicle for cooperation among adults and stepping-stones to learning for children.

The Optimistic Classroom: Creative Ways to Give Children Hope
by Deborah Hewitt and Sandra Heidemann
Over seventy activities will develop ten strengths that allow children to meet and cope with the challenges they face.

Transition Magician: Strategies for Guiding Young Children in Early Childhood Programs
by Nola Larson, Mary Henthorne, and Barbara Plum
Offers over 200 original learning activities that will help teachers smoothly weave everyday activities together.

Transition Magician 2: More Strategies for Guiding Young Children in Early Childhood Programs
by Mary Henthorne, Nola Larson, and Ruth Chvojicek
More than 200 original learning activities and more than fifty props and games; includes adaptations for toddlers and for children with special needs.

Transition Magician for Families: Helping Parents and Children with Everyday Routines
by Ruth Chvojicek, Mary Henthorne, and Nola Larson
Dozens of activity ideas for caregivers to share with families to simplify the everyday transitions outside of child care.

That's Not Fair! A Teacher's Guide to Activism with Young Children
by Ann Pelo and Fran Davidson
Real-life stories of activist children, combined with teachers' experiences and reflections, create a complete guide to childhood activism.

What the Kids Said Today: Using Classroom Conversations to Become a Better Teacher
by Daniel Gartrell
Contains 145 stories that explore how teachers can use conversations with children to build skills such as acceptance, cooperation, creative and peaceful problem solving, and appropriate emotional expression.

800-423-8309
www.redleafpress.org